Righteousness, Holines... Full Salvation Throu... of the Lord Jesus Christ

MW00880144

This Is the Printed Version of the E-Book

Published by Karl Kemp Teaching Ministries
karlkempteachingministries.com

Copyright © 2014 by Karl Kemp

This e-book (this is the printed edition of the e-book), which quotes extensively from my paperback book, *Holiness and Victory Over Sin*, serves as a good introduction for the paperback book, which is available at amazon.com

This e-book, which deals to a large extent with the interpretation of passages of the Bible (especially the New Testament) that deal with the super-important topic of righteousness, holiness, and victory over sin is packed with good news, very good news! The New Testament clearly, and consistently, teaches that God calls, and enables, us to walk with the victory over sin, by grace through faith. No true Christian wants to sin! God hates sin and He paid an infinite price in the Sacrifice of His Son to set us free from spiritual death and bondage to sin.

We will never walk in the righteousness and holiness of God with the victory over sin BY FAITH until we are convinced in our hearts that God has called us to such a walk and has provided the grace for us to do what He has called us to do. The New Testament makes it quite clear that the victory over sin is far from being automatic, or always easy. We have powerful enemies against us: the world, the flesh (the old man who wants to continue to sin), and the devil and his hosts, but the saving grace of God in Christ is far more powerful for those who appropriate His grace by faith (a faith that is based on God and His Word). The saving grace of God in Christ includes all the work of the Holy Spirit, the infinite Spirit of God, who dwells in all true Christians.

We don't want to repeat the error of the people of Israel at Kadesh (Numbers chapters 13, 14), where they believed in their hearts (and spoke and acted accordingly) that they could not do what God had called them to do. Of course God did not expect them to defeat the Canaanites by their strength; he did, however, expect them to trust Him and walk by faith.

We must make living in the righteousness and holiness with the victory over sin a top priority. WE MUST AIM AT THAT TARGET! WE CERTAINLY WON'T HIT THE TARGET IF WE ARE NOT AIMING AT IT! God knows our hearts! Also, it is good to know that He has promised to forgive us IF we should sin, when we repent.

The twenty-eight articles in this e-book were taken, with some modifications (including adding bold, underlining, italics and some other improvements) from the written text behind my twenty-eight half-hour radio broadcasts titled "Holiness and Victory Over Sin." (You can hear some of these broadcasts or purchase CDs of the broadcasts on my internet site: karlkempteachingministries.com.)

These articles cover this super-important topic rather thoroughly, and they serve as a good introduction for my paperback book, *Holiness and Victory Over Sin: Full Salvation Through the Atoning Death of the Lord Jesus Christ*. I quote extensively from the book in these articles. If you like this e-book, you will also like the paperback book, which is available at amazon.com and on my website. The paperback book contains a large amount of information that is not included in this e-book, and the e-book contains quite a bit of information that is not included in the paperback book.

I highly recommend reading the e-book first. Like I said, it serves as a good introduction for the paperback book, and it is easier to read. I always quote from the *New American Standard Bible* (NASB), 1995 edition, unless I mention otherwise, but some quotations in this e-book were taken from the 1977 edition, which was used in my paperback book. Based on what I have observed, the differences between the 1977 edition and the 1995 edition are typically minor and do not change the meaning of the verse.

Contents, Including the Primary Content of these Twenty-Eight Articles:

Article # 22. Finish Ephesians 4:17-32; start study on three Hebrew nouns for sin, iniquity, transgression, guilt of sin, and PENALTY for sin (including the major penalties of spiritual death and bondage to sin) that will help us understand Christ's all-important atoning death and new-covenant salvation (discuss Genesis 4:8-13). (page 214)

Article #23. Continue study on three Hebrew nouns; includes a study on Leviticus 16:20-22 (includes "Azazel"); start a study on Isaiah 53:4-6, 11. (page 224)

Article #24. Finish study on three Hebrew nouns and the study on Isaiah 53:4-6, 11 (for one thing, the Righteous One makes Righteous the many); start "Hebrews 10:8-18 with Special Emphasis on the Meaning of *Aphesis* as it Is Used in Hebrews 10:18." (page 234)

Article # 25. Finish the study on Hebrews 10:8-18; we also discuss Hebrews 8:6-13; 10:26-31; 11:39, 40; 12:23 in this article; start a study on the topic of holiness (holy, saint, make holy, sanctify, sanctification) through the atoning death of the Lord Jesus Christ that is based on the last chapter of my book, *Holiness and Victory Over Sin: Full Salvation Through the Atoning Death of the Lord Jesus Christ*; all the emphasis in this study is on the ideal state of Christians actually being set apart from sin and living for God in an abiding state of holiness. (page 244)

Article #26. We discuss 1 Corinthians 1:1, 2; 6:8-11; 2 Corinthians 11:2-4; and Ephesians 5:22-33 on the topic of holiness. (page 255)

Article #27. We discuss Romans 1:7; 6:19, 22; 12:1-3; 1 Corinthians 1:1, 2; 2 Corinthians 6:14-7:1; 1 Thessalonians 3:6-13; 4:1-8; 5:23; 2 Thessalonians 2:13; and 1 Timothy 1:21 on the topic of holiness. (page 265)

Article #28. We discuss Ephesians 5:3-8; Colossians 1:21-23; Hebrews 12:14; 1 Peter 1:13-19; and Revelation 22:12-15 on the topic of holiness. (page 275)

Abbreviations and Other Such Information

cf. compare

e.g. for example
f., ff. following verse or verses

I typically quote the primary Scripture passages we are discussing in bold throughout this e-book.

I frequently make comments in the middle of quotations in brackets [ ] or [[ ]] to make them more obvious.

Acknowledgements

Greg Holtzmann produced the cover for this book (the e-book and the printed version of the e-book). Norma Wagner proofread the manuscript, which enabled me to remove quite a few typos. I want to thank all of the students I have had dealing with the topic of righteousness, holiness, and victory over sin for the past more than forty-five years. They encouraged me and many of them helped support my ministry, which enabled me to have the time and resources to do the things I have done.

Lastly, I would like to acknowledge my infinite debt to God (God the Father, God the Son, and God the Holy Spirit). Apart from the Father's saving grace in Christ Jesus and all the work of the Holy Spirit, I would still be lost and spiraling downward. I readily acknowledge that my Christian life and ministry is totally dependent on the sufficient grace of God in Christ Jesus, which includes all the work of the Holy Spirit. The triune God must receive all the glory forever! He is the ultimate source for truth, righteousness, holiness, victory over sin, life, peace, order, and everything else that is good!

May God's will be fully accomplished in the hearts and lives of His people through this e-book! In Jesus' name!

Holiness and Victory Over Sin #1

Since this is the first article, I'll give a little background information. I received BS and MS degrees in engineering from St. Louis University, and I worked throughout the 60s on various space projects. Much of that was very interesting. Very often we were doing things for the first time.

In 1964 the best thing that ever happened to me happened. I became a born-again Christian. Thanks be to God! My life began to change, greatly. For the first time in my life I had peace with God. I had an assurance of salvation, and I have had that assurance ever since. Again, thanks be to God! One of the first things I noticed after I became a born-again Christian was that my cussing stopped. I had tried to quit cussing for at least ten years with no success. I would embarrass myself quite often. But God just took it away, with no effort on my part, and there were other things like that. He did some spectacular things, convincing me that the Bible is true and that new-covenant salvation is real.

But there was one area, at least one area, where temptation increased, and the spiritual warfare was intense. What was I going to do? As I began to cry out to God for help, I got highly motivated to study what the Bible had to say about holiness and victory over sin. God began to open up Romans chapter 6 to me, which is a powerful passage on righteousness, holiness, and victory over sin. (We will go through that chapter verse-by-verse, starting in article #4, and we will look at many similar passages.) I began to see that God was clearly saying that we are called and enabled to walk in holiness with the victory over sin. That was good news to me, very good news. I didn't get condemned by the fact that I wasn't fully walking in that victory yet, but I rejoiced in that I could see that the victory was available.

I could also see that the victory over sin wouldn't be easy. The world, the flesh, and the devil and his multitudinous hosts are engaged in intense warfare against us, and I began to see that most Christians wouldn't be much help. Most of the Christians I knew were trying to talk me out of the idea that we can have the victory over sin in this life. And I was receiving the same message from most of the Christian literature I was reading. I don't mean that they were saying that sin is OK, but they made it quite clear that they didn't think it was possible for Christians to stop sinning while living in this world.

In the fall of 1969 I quit my job as an engineer. I thought it might be temporary, but I never got back to engineering. I liked it (in fact, for a long time it was one of my primary gods), but I found Someone and something that was much better. Of course we have to do what God calls us to do. For one thing, I wanted to go to seminary. I wanted to learn everything I could possibly learn that would help me understand the Bible. It is super-important for us to rightly divide God's Word, to understand it, and to live it. One thing I really wanted to learn was New Testament Greek. I have found Greek to be very helpful. I took all the Greek they offered at seminary, and I studied quite a bit more on my own, and I have taught quite a few classes in New Testament Greek. I also wanted to learn Old Testament Hebrew, and I have found that to be quite helpful too. However, the most important thing I learned as a young Christian is that we are totally dependent on the Holy Spirit to be able to rightly divide, to understand, and to live God's Word.

I am interested in every detail that will help me understand the Bible. We can't understand a verse of the Bible until we understand the meaning of the words in the verse. I'm willing to spend ten hours, twenty hours, even a hundred hours to find out what one key word means. I have spent over a hundred hours studying a few key words like righteousness, holiness, and faith.

I finally graduated from Covenant Seminary in St. Louis with an MA degree in Biblical Studies in 1972. Since then I have been prayerfully studying and teaching classes in churches, Bible colleges, home Bible studies, etc. My primary topic has always been holiness and victory over sin, but I have also spent a lot of time on topics like faith, grace, and the end times. Most of my study and teaching has involved going through passages of the Bible, or books of the Bible, verse-by-verse. Each verse must be understood in its context.

The last twenty years I have been doing a lot of writing. I wrote two books, *The Mid-Week Rapture: A Verse-by-Verse Study of Key Prophetic Passages* and *Holiness and Victory Over Sin:* [This is a good sub-title] *Full Salvation Through the Atoning Death of the Lord Jesus Christ.* "Full salvation" very much includes righteousness, holiness, and victory over sin. The Lord Jesus Christ didn't die just so we could be forgiven and have right standing with God, as important as that is. It is equally true that His atoning death dethroned sin, Satan, and spiritual death and enables us to be born again and to walk in the righteousness and holiness of God. For example, 1 Peter 2:24 says, "He bore our sins in His body on the cross that we might die to sin and live to righteousness; for by His wounds you were healed." As I mentioned, I will always quote from the *New American Standard Bible* unless I mention otherwise.

I have also written quite a few articles and papers. The primary emphasis has been on holiness and victory over sin, but quite a few papers deal with the end times. One paper is titled *Once Saved, Always Saved?* Another is titled *A Paper on Faith*, and another *The Christian, the Law, and Legalism*. Many of the papers are over 100 pages. I recommend you take a look at them. Most of my papers are posted on karlkempteachingministries.com (Google to Karl Kemp Teaching).

Now I'm going to turn to the Preface of my book, *Holiness and Victory Over Sin*, and read four paragraphs. I'll be reading from the book quite a bit in these radio broadcasts (articles). For one thing, I would like to get you motivated to get a copy of this book AND TO STUDY IT. The book is not light reading, but the topic is extremely important, and I believe the book is quite accurate. The primary goal for this book and for these radio broadcasts (articles) is that we rightly divide God's Word and understand the gospel of new-covenant salvation, and then live it, by grace, through faith (faith in God and His Word). The book gets into a lot of details, but details are necessary, important, and good if they help us understand the Bible.

The first paragraph I'm going to read from the Preface is under the heading, Need for revival [reformation]? Quite often when I read from my book, I will make additional comments and sometimes I will modify what is written in the book for these articles. More and more I hear Christians speak of the need for revival. There is a growing awareness that all is not well with the Christian church of our day. (I wrote this book about fifteen years ago. Some things are better now than they were fifteen years ago, but I believe that most things have gotten worse.) I certainly agree that we have a great need for revival, but I'm interested in a revival/reformation that is solidly based on the Bible and puts the emphasis on such things as truth, grace, holiness, righteousness, humility, and true Christian love. (There is a counterfeit love that's big in our day.) The studies contained in this book show something of the foundation needed for a true, Bible-centered revival/reformation.

Now I'll turn to another heading in the Preface, The major theme of these studies. The major theme that permeates these studies is the fact that the

9

Lord Jesus Christ has dethroned sin, Satan, and spiritual death through His atoning death and it is mandatory, therefore, for Christians to make it a top priority item to walk in righteousness and holiness through faith. This is not a burden; this is a great privilege! We don't want legalism and striving in the flesh, and we certainly don't need more condemnation. What we need is the transformation to the righteousness and holiness of God that only the Holy Spirit can produce and maintain. We need to humble ourselves before God and cry out to Him to forgive and sanctify His people.

I trust that most sincere Christians know that sin is our greatest enemy and want the full victory over sin. Admittedly, many, or most, Christians don't believe that victory over sin is possible during this present life, but they at least agree that we must wage warfare against sin with the highest priority. (((This double parenthesis continues for two paragraphs.] I feel a need to modify the second half of that last sentence, where I said, "they at least agree that we must wage warfare against sin with the highest priority." I wish it were true that all, or most, evangelical Christians agree that we must wage warfare against sin with the highest priority, but I'm sorry to say it isn't true, far from it, and it is getting worse all the time in some circles. I'm talking about evangelical Christians waging warfare against the sin of evangelical Christians, especially our own sins, not about waging warfare against the sin of the world. Some are ignoring sin more than they are waging warfare against sin. For one thing, we don't want to offend anyone. We had better get more concerned with offending God.

One thing is for sure, we will not hit the target of walking in the righteousness and holiness of God with the victory over all sin if we are not even aiming at the target. Something is seriously wrong when Christians are not making it top priority to walk with the victory over sin by grace through faith. I'm totally convinced from the New Testament that God has called us to such a walk. This is good news! Very good news! What God calls us to do, He enables us to do. No true Christian likes feeling guilty. No true Christian wants to continue sinning. No true Christian wants to commit one act of sin. We will spend a lot of time discussing these super-important things in these articles.))

Holiness, which includes victory over sin, like forgiveness, must be received from God by grace through faith. But we cannot have a solid faith to receive and walk in holiness unless we are convinced that this is part of the gospel (according to the New Testament). A primary goal for these studies is to show that the gospel does indeed call Christians to walk in holiness with the victory over sin.

There is very little said in this book about Christian growth. Clearly, Christian growth is necessary and important, but the emphasis of these studies is on the need to get rid of anything and everything that God considers sinful in the heart and life of each Christian now. Everything that is truly sinful should be dealt with now. Christian growth will take place as it should if we take care of the basics. The basics include the following: #1 laying a solid foundation of repentance and faith in God and in the truth of the gospel; #2 establishing and maintaining a proper relationship with God (for example, make Him and His will top priority, walk by the Spirit [not the flesh], and spend adequate time in worship, Bible study, and prayer); #3 establishing and maintaining a proper relationship with the people of God (for example, become part of a God-centered, Bible-centered church); and #4 continuing to walk in the light that we have now, as we continue to learn more of God's Word and of His will for our lives.

For our first Bible passage to study let's turn to GALATIANS 5:16-25, which is a very important passage. I'll read from the NASB, 1977 edition, which was the edition I used in my book. Today we won't get beyond the first verse, verse 16, which is a very important verse on the topic of holiness and victory over sin. The apostle Paul was writing here to the Galatian Christians. He was the one who had shared the gospel with them. I'll start to read Galatians 5:16, **But I say, walk by the Spirit** [It is very important to see that this is the Holy Spirit. "Walk by the Spirit," or we could translate "walk after the Spirit" or "walk in the Spirit." We can't walk by the Spirit until we are born again and indwelled by the Spirit of God. Paul was writing to born-again Christians. How do we walk by the Spirit? First and foremost, we walk by faith, faith in God and faith in what the Word of God teaches about new-covenant salvation in the Lord Jesus Christ.] **and you will not carry out the desire of the flesh.**

If we walk by the Spirit all the time, we will not carry out **the desire of the flesh.** What is the desire of the flesh? The desire of the flesh is to sin. Later in this chapter, in verses 19-21, Paul lists some of the works of the flesh. The desire of the flesh is to do the works of the flesh. The works of the flesh equals all sin. I'll read Galatians 5:19-21. "Now the deeds [I like the translation "works" better.] are evident, which are: immorality, impurity, sensuality, idolatry, sorcery, enmities, strife, jealousy, outbursts of anger, disputes, dissensions, factions, envying, drunkenness, carousing, and things like these, of which I forewarn you just as I have forewarned you that those who practice such things shall not inherit the kingdom of God." Not inherit the kingdom of God? We had better listen then; we don't want to miss the kingdom of God.

One important thing to notice here is that many of these sins have little or nothing to do with the physical body. For example, idolatry, sorcery, and envying. The **flesh**, as Paul uses this word in Gal. 5:16 ("you will not carry out the [sinful] desire of the flesh") and in Gal. 5:17, 19 and many other verses, equals the old man. The flesh equals the old man. The old man is everything we were before we became born-again Christians. It is man in spiritual death; it is man without the Spirit of God; it is man in bondage to sin. The flesh is not at all limited to the physical body (as many Christians think it is). We will talk more about the meaning of the word flesh as we continue.

The desire of the flesh is to sin, as the works of the flesh demonstrate. **Walk by the Spirit and you** [most certainly] **will not carry out the** [sinful] **desire of the flesh** [of the old man]. I would translate **you** [most certainly] **will not.** The Greek supports this translation in that the Greek has an intensive negative here. It has the words *ou* and *me*. The apostle is saying, walk by the Spirit all the time, and you won't be sinning. That sounds good doesn't it? Forgiven, but also so transformed by the saving grace of God in Christ that we stop sinning. That's a big part of what the good news of new-covenant salvation is all about!

Walk by the Spirit and you [most certainly] **will not carry out the** [sinful] **desire of the flesh** [of the old man]. In other words the sin problem will really be solved; we won't just be forgiven; we will stop sinning and live in the righteousness and holiness of God. And this full salvation comes 100 percent by the grace of God, and He gets all the glory.

Our holiness and victory over sin doesn't come automatically, because our walking in faith and by the Holy Spirit all the time is not automatic. First we have to know and understand the gospel, and then we must live

12

the gospel on a continuous basis by grace through faith. **Walk by the Spirit and you** [most certainly] **will not carry out the** [sinful] **desire of the flesh** [of the old man]. Did the apostle Paul consider this to be the impossible dream, that we could walk by the Spirit all the time and not sin? Emphatically not! God calls us to walk by the Spirit all the time, and no one can stop us from walking by the Spirit all the time. Now I didn't say it was always easy. There is intense warfare against us by the world, the flesh (the flesh is the old man that wants to live and manifest itself in sin), and the devil and his hosts. But God's grace is sufficient for those who appropriate it by faith, on a continuous basis, in accordance with His Word. We must know and understand the gospel, and we must walk by faith on a continuous basis.

One of the main problems we have in the body of Christ is that the gospel is often presented in a very shallow and unacceptable way, and Christians have often been taught that they cannot have the victory over sin in this life. Many sincere, solid Christian leaders are convinced that the New Testament teaches that we cannot have the victory over sin in this life. Well, for a start, the apostle Paul certainly exhorted Christians to always walk by the Holy Spirit so that they would not sin in Gal. 5:16. We'll be talking more about these super-important things as we continue. Everything I am sharing with you is good news, very good news!

Now I am going to turn to page 196 of my book and read part of what I said under Gal. 5:16, and I will be making some additional comments too. Galatians 5:16 (in its setting with Gal. 5:13-25) is one of the most important verses in the New Testament which shows that Christians can (and should) always walk in holiness with the victory over sin. I could have said "which shows that Christians can (and should and must) always walk in holiness with the victory over sin." God never said that sin is a legitimate option for Christians. We should not make room for sin in our hearts and lives. God hates sin!

I didn't say we couldn't be forgiven, but we're not supposed to be sinning, "He bore our sins in His body on the cross that we might die to sin and live to righteousness; for by His wounds you were healed" (1 Peter 2:24). That's good news, isn't it? Even if a Christian is not fully walking with the victory over sin, it is good news to learn that the victory is available. We don't have to continue living in sin. When we find out who Jesus is (God the Son) and the infinite price that was paid to redeem us from the kingdom of sin, it would be surprising, even shocking, if we could not have the victory over sin. Jesus didn't do all that He did just so we could be forgiven, as important as that is; He came to set us free from our former evil taskmaster of sin. Again, God hates sin! If it really is sin, it is against God, and it is a serious matter; for one thing, sin always messes things up and destroys divine order.

(I'll skip the next three paragraphs. We'll pick up the information contained in these paragraphs later.) "The desire of the flesh" (Gal. 5:16) is to do the "deeds [works] of the flesh." For Christians to not carry out the desire of the flesh (as they walk by the Spirit, the Holy Spirit) is for them to live above sin. A partial list of "the works of the flesh" is included in Gal. 5:19-21. We already read those verses. "The works of the flesh" as these words are used in Gal. 5:19-21 embrace all sin. Such things as sinful attitudes and motives are included in what the apostle means by "the works of the flesh." Note that he listed jealousy, envy, etc. Those sins are not associated with the physical body, and it is very important to know that sin is of the heart. In Mark chapter 7 Jesus taught us that sin is of the heart. The sin problem is not situated in the physical body. If it was centered in the body, it would be very easy for God to solve the sin problem. He could just kill all the bad bodies and take all the good spirits to heaven. But it's not like that; sin is of the heart/inner man. The root sins of pride and unbelief, for example, are sins of the heart.

In summary, the apostle Paul exhorts Christians to walk by the Spirit on a continuous basis so that they will not carry out the sinful desire of the flesh, so that the flesh will not be able to manifest itself in sinful works. It is very important to see that the flesh here equals the old man. The emphasis is not on the physical body, but the physical body is included. Those who walk by (or we could translate "after" or "in") the Spirit on a continuous basis will walk above sin, by grace. I am not speaking of self-righteousness or self-holiness, this is God's saving grace in Christ, and we appropriate this grace by faith. If I understand the apostle Paul (and I'm quite sure that I do), he did not at all consider it an unattainable ideal for Christians to continuously walk by the Holy Spirit. However, as Gal. 5:17, for example, shows, the apostle did not teach that a continuous walk by (after/in) the Spirit is automatic, or that it would always be easy. There is intense warfare taking place. The flesh/old man has not been annihilated yet, and Satan works in the realm of the flesh/old man. The old man can still live, and will still live to the extent we allow it.

It is all too obvious that Christians can sin. We will, in fact, sin to the extent that we do not walk by the Holy Spirit, by faith, on a continuous basis. We cannot walk by the Spirit apart from the knowledge of the Word of God (especially the gospel) because our faith must be based on the Word of God. And we must rightly divide God's Word and understand it or we cannot fully cooperate with God's saving grace through faith.

Now I'll quote the *Amplified Bible* on Gal. 5:16 (Quite often the *Amplified Bible* is helpful, and it is helpful here): "But I say, walk and live habitually in the (Holy) Spirit – responsive to and controlled and guided by the Spirit; then you will certainly not gratify the cravings and desires of the flesh – of human nature without God."

Now we come to the heading, The Meaning of "The Flesh" As These Words Are Used in Galatians 5:13-25. I have several paragraphs here. It is common for the apostle Paul (and others) to use the words "the flesh" to speak of fallen man (man in spiritual death, man separated from the Spirit of life). The NIV has "the sinful nature" instead of "the flesh" throughout Gal. 5:13-25. The *Amplified Bible* at Gal. 5:16 defines the flesh as "human nature without God." Often, as here, there is a contrast between "the Spirit" (the Holy Spirit) and "the flesh" and I list quite a few verses. We'll look at some of these verses:

First we'll look at John 6:63. Jesus said, "It is the Spirit [the Holy Spirit] who gives life [No matter what man does, he cannot generate the life of God; life must come from Him, and we're talking especially about spiritual life, which includes the power for man to be righteous and holy.], the flesh profits nothing; the words that I have spoken to you are spirit [Spirit] and are life."

Now I'll turn to Romans 7:5, 6, two very important verses. "For while we were in the flesh [[The apostle Paul was speaking here of Christians from a Jewish background (Gentiles were not under the Mosaic Law, but all mankind was "in the flesh" apart from new-covenant salvation; we were spiritually dead; we were slaves of sin, as Paul showed for example in Romans chapters 1-6); we had a total need to be born again by the Holy

15

Spirit.]], the sinful passions which were *aroused* by the Law [[The apostle was speaking of the Mosaic Law, which was the foundation for the old covenant. The Law could not solve the spiritual death and bondage to sin problem. In fact, as Paul frequently mentions, the Law intensifies the sin problem. Here he speaks of "the sinful passions which were *aroused* by the Law."]], were at work in the members of our body to bear fruit for death." We (the Christians from a Jewish background) were bearing sinful fruit. When they were in the flesh and under the Law (before they were born again), they did not have the power to fully keep the Law. Therefore they could not be saved by the Law. God always planned to save all believers through the Lord Jesus Christ, the Lamb of God. As I mentioned, the Law intensified the sin problem rather than solve the sin problem. The Law could not save us from spiritual death and bondage to sin. We will be speaking much more about these important things as we continue with these studies on holiness and victory over sin.

I'll read Romans 7:5 again and then we'll go to verse 6, "For while we were in the flesh, the sinful passions which were *aroused* by the Law, were at work in the members of our body to bear fruit for death. (6) But now we have been released from the Law [That is, the Christians from a Jewish background have now been released from the Mosaic Law and the old covenant.], having died to that by which we were bound [They were bound to the Mosaic Law, which could not save them (or us); but, more importantly, we were all slaves of sin in the kingdom of sin, spiritual death, and darkness], so that we serve in newness of the Spirit and not in oldness of the letter [the letter of the Mosaic Law]." The newness of the Holy Spirit, who is given to us in new-covenant salvation, makes all the difference. He gives us life (the very life of God), which enables us to live in the righteousness and holiness of God. Once we are born again, we are in the Holy Spirit, not in the flesh, and we are enabled (and required, and privileged) to walk by the Spirit (on a continuous basis). Again, this is very good news!

It's time to stop. We'll come back to this study in the next article. God bless you!

Holiness and Victory Over Sin # 2

Holy Father we humble our hearts before you. We admit that we are totally dependent on your grace. We want to rightly divide your Word; we want to understand it; we want to live it. We want to be fully ready for the return of the Lord Jesus Christ and to stand before you. We pray in His mighty name. Amen.

I consider it a great privilege to be able to study these things and to share them with you. I consider these things to be infinitely important. We are talking about the heart of the message of the gospel of new-covenant salvation in the Lord Jesus Christ. Man has one primary problem, the sin problem, and Jesus Christ is the only answer, and He is the full answer. I realize that many Christians are doing a lot of sinning, but it is not OK. To be living in sin is a dangerous place to be. The good news is that we are called to stop sinning, and God's grace is sufficient, even if it's not always easy. This is good news, isn't it?

The first passage we began to look at last week was Galatians 5:16-25. We didn't finish our discussion of the first verse, verse 16, which is a super-important verse. I'm trying to be thorough and to explain the details that will enable us to understand this verse. First I'll read Galatians 5:16. I'll read it from my book, which uses the *New American Standard Bible* (NASB), 1977 edition. I'll read the verse and make a few comments. Then we'll go back to where we stopped last time. Frequently I'll make comments in the middle of quotations using brackets [ ] or [[ ]] to make the brackets more obvious. **But I say** [the apostle Paul writes to the Galatian Christians] **walk by the Spirit** [the Holy Spirit]**, and you will not carry out the desire of the flesh.** As I mentioned last time, I would translate, **But I say, walk by the Spirit and you** [most certainly] **will not carry out the** [sinful] **desire of the flesh** [of the old man]**.**

The desire of the flesh is to sin. Walk by the Spirit on a continuous basis, and you most certainly will not carry out the sinful desire of the flesh. In other words, you will not sin. The desire of the flesh is to do the sinful works of the flesh, which equals all sin, and not just sins especially associated with the physical body. For example, in Gal. 5:19-21 the apostle lists many works of the flesh, and he includes idolatry and sorcery, which are clearly sins of the heart/inner man. Walk by the Holy Spirit all the time (by faith) and you will be walking above sin. Now doesn't that sound good? And who gets the glory. Our holiness, which includes our victory over sin, comes 100 percent by the grace of God in Christ, and He gets all the glory, as it must be.

Now a walk by the Spirit is not automatic. A walk in faith is not automatic. We must understand God's Word, commit ourselves to it in faith, and live it by God's sufficient grace. The victory is far from being automatic. We could be born again, but still quite fleshly and worldly. The New Testament demonstrates this point, but it also makes it clear that this is a dangerous place to be. The only secure place to be is in the center of God's will, walking by His Spirit, walking in His righteousness, walking in faith based on what His Word says. Walk by (or after, or in) the Spirit, and you most certainly will not carry out the sinful desire of the flesh. Galatians 5:16 is one of the most important verses in the New Testament which shows that we can, and should, have the victory over all sin.

Part of God's definition of what it means to be a Christian is to walk by the Holy Spirit all the time. This is not an optional matter. When we become Christians, we sign a contract (so to speak) agreeing to the terms of God's new covenant, which includes the requirement to walk by the Spirit all the time. But this is a great privilege! This is a great blessing! This isn't bondage! This is liberty! And God wants to transform us, not to condemn us. Praise God! When we truly repent, He is quick to forgive, but we need to make it top priority to walk in His righteousness and holiness, with the victory over all sin. We need to be aiming at that target, not making any room for sin in our hearts and lives.

Now I'm going to turn back to where we stopped last time, on page 197 of my book, *Holiness and Victory Over Sin: Full Salvation Through the Atoning Death of the Lord Jesus Christ*. First I'll reread a few sentences. We are under the heading <u>The Meaning of "The Flesh" as These Words Are Used in Galatians 5:13-25.</u> It is common for the apostle Paul (and others in the New Testament) to use the words "the flesh" to speak of fallen man (man in spiritual death, man separated from the Spirit of life, the Holy Spirit). "The flesh" is not at all limited to the physical body. (The NIV has "the sinful nature" instead of "the flesh" throughout Gal. 5:13-25. The Amplified Bible at Gal. 5:16 defines the flesh as "human nature without God.") Often, as here, there is a contrast between "the Spirit" (the Holy Spirit) and "the flesh." The contrast that Paul is concerned with here, and often, is not the contrast between our spirit and our body (as some

Christians think), but the contrast between the Holy Spirit and man in the flesh.

Last week we looked at two of the cross-references I listed here. We looked at John 6:63 and Rom. 7:5, 6. The next passage I listed is Rom. 8:1-14, and I listed some other verses too. We will just take the time to look at Rom. 8:3, 4 here. Later we will go through Rom. 8:1-14 verse-by-verse. These verses are extremely important. I'm turning to Romans 8:3, 4; I'm using the NASB, 1995 edition here. "For what the Law could not do [[Paul was speaking of the Mosaic Law. What was it that the Mosaic Law could not do? It was from God and it was good, but it wasn't designed to dethrone spiritual death and sin and to give people the new birth and victory over sin.]], weak as it was through the flesh [[The Law could not solve the sin problem for man in the flesh, for man in spiritual death, for man without the Spirit of God, because man in the flesh doesn't have the power to fully keep God's Law. Rather than solve the sin problem, the Law intensified the sin problem in some ways.]], God did [How did He do it?]: sending His own Son in the likeness of sinful flesh and as an offering for sin, He condemned sin in the flesh. [[Sin, which used to reign over us, has been condemned and dethroned through the atoning death of the Lamb of God. Sin will still reign over us to the extent we allow it, but sin has no legal right to reign over us now, and as we walk by the Holy Spirit on a continuous basis, according to the terms of the new covenant, we will walk in the righteousness and holiness of God with the victory over all sin.]], (4) so that the requirement of the Law might be fulfilled in us, who do not walk according to the flesh, but according to the Spirit." This is the bottom line of Christianity, so that the requirement of the Law might be fulfilled in us. Instead of breaking God's Law and sinning, now we keep the requirement of His Law in our daily lives as we walk by the Spirit of God, who enables us to walk in the righteousness and holiness of God, with the victory over sin. We are not required to keep the ceremonial law of the Old Testament, but we are required to keep God's moral law in our daily lives. God hates sin, and His moral laws cannot change. Sin goes against God and His divine order. God hates sin! I'll read Romans 8:4 again: "So that the requirement of the Law might be fulfilled in us, who do not walk according to the flesh, but according to the Spirit [the Holy Spirit]." We fulfill the requirement of God's Law as we walk by the Holy Spirit through faith, having been born again and raised above the realm of the flesh/the old man.

Now I'll turn back to page 197 of my book and go on to the next paragraph. For a Christian to walk according to the flesh is to walk according to the old man, but this ought not (need not) be [[(This double bracket goes on for four paragraphs.) And I listed several verses here. We'll stop to look at a few of them. These verses are quite important. First we'll look at Rom. 6:6, but before I turn there I'll read that last sentence again. "For a Christian to walk according to the flesh is to walk according to the old man, but this ought not (need not) be." Romans 6:6 says, "knowing this, that our old self [I would translate "our old man"] was crucified with Him, in order that our body of sin might be done away with [In other words, after we become born-again Christians, we should no longer have a body associated with sin; it should be a body associated with righteousness], so that we would no longer be slaves to sin."

That sounds good, doesn't it? It is good news, very good news! Throughout Romans chapter 6 the apostle Paul repeatedly says that we used to be slaves of sin, but now (through new-covenant salvation, in union with the Lord Jesus Christ) we are slaves of God and of His righteousness. The saving grace of God in Christ enables us to stop sinning. This is a great privilege! We are united with the Lord Jesus Christ in His death, His burial, His resurrection, and in His present life. I'll read Romans 6:6 one more time, "knowing this, that our old man was crucified with Him, that our body of sin might be done away with, so that we would no longer be slaves to sin." We will go through all of Romans chapter 6, verse-by-verse, when we finish Gal. 5:16-25.

Now we'll look at another verse which demonstrates that born-again Christians are no longer to walk according to the flesh and do the sinful works of the flesh. Let's look at Ephesians 4:22, "that, in reference to your former manner of life [your life before you became born-again Christians], you lay aside the old man [and then Paul continues, but these are the primary words we need for our present discussion]." For Christians to lay aside (or put off) the old man once-for-all, and completely, is the same thing as crucifying the old man, which is spoken of in Rom. 6:6, which we just read and in Gal 5:24, for example. As we walk by the Holy Spirit by faith, in accordance with the terms of the new covenant, the old man/the flesh, will not be able to manifest itself in sin.

We'll look at one more verse here, Col. 3:9, which is similar to Eph. 4:22. Colossians 3:9 says, "Do not lie to one another, since you laid aside the old man with its evil practices." Do not lie to one another, or do any other sin, since you laid aside (or, put off) the old man once-for-all, and completely, when you became born-again Christians. In the ideal case we would never sin again after we become born-again Christians. The apostle Paul and other writers of the New Testament repeatedly speak of this glorious ideal. God hates sin, and no true Christians want to sin, so this is very good news. But the New Testament also makes it quite clear that there is intense warfare against us from the world, the flesh/the old man, and the devil and his hosts, and that a victorious walk by faith and by the Holy Spirit is far from being automatic, or always easy.

Now I'll continue to read from page 197 of my book, *Holiness and Victory Over Sin: Full Salvation Through the Atoning Death of the Lord Jesus Christ*.]] The Christian is to be dead to the old man; he has crucified the flesh (the old man who wants to keep on living in sin) with its passions and desires. Where did I get that? From Gal. 5:24, which we haven't read yet. I'll read Galatians 5:24. "Now those who belong to Christ Jesus have crucified the flesh with its passions and desires." In the ideal case we would crucify the flesh when we become born-again Christians, and we would never sin again. But that doesn't mean that we won't be tempted, or have wrong desires, or that we cannot sin.

The world, the flesh (the old man who wants to continue to live in sin) and the devil and his hosts are waging intense warfare against us. In Gal. 5:17 the apostle makes it clear that born-again Christians can have wrong desires, even strong wrong desires, but that isn't sin. Wrong thoughts and wrong desires are not sin if we resist them by the Holy Spirit. The Holy Spirit will always give us the power to resist wrong thoughts and desires as we walk after the Spirit on a continuous basis by faith (faith in God and His word, knowing that His Word teaches that victory over sin has been provided in new-covenant salvation).

Christians are to be dead to the flesh/the old man; they have, as Gal. 5:24 says, "crucified the flesh with its passions and desires." The flesh and the old man are equivalent in meaning in verses like Gal. 5:16 and 24. We can speak of the old man being crucified with Christ (see Rom. 6:6, which we read above; also see Gal. 2:20; that is the verse where the apostle Paul said "I have been crucified with Christ....") We can speak of the old man being crucified with Christ, and we can speak of crucifying the flesh. To crucify the flesh and to crucify the old man means the same thing. The only way we can do this is by grace through faith, in accordance with the gospel. The old man, however, will still live and manifest itself in sin to the extent that Christians do not walk by the Spirit on a continuous basis, appropriating God's grace by faith. Only the Holy Spirit has the power to keep the old man/the flesh from manifesting itself in sin.

These things we are talking about are extremely important. A primary reason why the flesh is such a formidable opponent for Christians is that Satan and his horde of demon spirits are very active in the realm of the flesh. Satan is the god of this world (see John 12:31; 16:11; Eph. 2:1; 2 Cor. 4:4). Fallen man could undoubtedly sin in all the ways listed in Gal. 5:19-21, where the apostle gives a partial listing of the sinful works of the flesh, without the involvement of demon spirits, but demon spirits work in each of these areas, greatly intensifying the sin problem. This reality makes it all the more necessary for Christians to walk by the Holy Spirit on a continuous basis and to not give the devil any place. Ephesians 4:27 says, "and do not give the devil an opportunity [a place]." As the margin of the *New American Standard Bible* shows, a more literal translation would be "place" instead of "opportunity." Don't give the devil any place in you!

Paul wrote these words of Eph. 4:27 in a context of exhorting Christians to walk in righteousness and holiness, having laid aside all sin. In Romans 13:14 the apostle Paul says, "But put on the Lord Jesus Christ, and make no provision for the flesh in regard to its lusts." Make no provision for the flesh. Don't leave any room for the old man (including the work of demon spirits) to have any place in you. The flesh/the old man hasn't been annihilated yet, and it still wants to manifest itself in sin. The world, the flesh/old man, and the devil and his hosts are against us, but the saving grace of God in Christ is much greater than our opponents.

Let's go on to Galatians 5:17. First I'll read the verse and make some comments; then I'll read part of what I said under Gal. 5:17 in my book. **For the flesh sets its desire against the Spirit** [the Holy Spirit; it's very important to see that the apostle is speaking of the Holy Spirit here]**, and the Spirit against the flesh** [The Holy Spirit is always for the righteousness and holiness of God. The flesh/the old man is always for sin.]**; for the flesh sets its desire against the Spirit, and the Spirit against the flesh; for these are in opposition to one another** [The verb used here for being in opposition to one another can be used of two armies being arrayed against one another], **so that you may not do the things that you please.**

Now it is an amazing thing to me, a sad thing, that many Christians (something like one-half of evangelical Christians) think that the apostle Paul was saying in this verse (Gal. 5:17) that we can never quit sinning in this life. I'm totally convinced that they are totally wrong in that interpretation. For one thing, that interpretation contradicts what the apostle Paul just said in Gal. 5:16, not to mention what he said many other places. All of us have the all-too-real potential to misunderstand God's Word. But how sad it is when we think God sent the apostle Paul to teach us that we cannot have the victory over sin in this life. The devil won a mighty victory with that interpretation. Our faith must be based on the Word of God, and we certainly cannot adequately wage warfare against sin if we believe the New Testament teaches that the victory is unattainable. It's no wonder we have problems with sin in the body of Christ.

I'll read Galatians 5:17 again, **For the flesh sets its desire against the Spirit, and the Spirit against the flesh; for these are in opposition to one another, so that you may not do the things that you please.** The apostle speaks of warfare between the Spirit and the flesh in this verse, but he certainly doesn't think in terms of the Holy Spirit losing any battles to the flesh. The Spirit of God is well able to win every battle against the world, the flesh/the old man, and the devil and his hosts, and we will always win the battle against sin if we always walk by the Holy Spirit through faith, which we are called, and enabled, to do. Remember what the apostle just said in Gal. 5:16, "But I say, walk by the Spirit and you [most certainly] will not carry out the [sinful] desire of the flesh [of the old man]."

Let's discuss the meaning of the last words of verse 17, **so that you may not do the things that you please.** "The things that you please" speaks of the sinful things Christians may be tempted to do. Paul had just spoken of the fact that Christians can have sinful desires with his words at the end of verse 16, where he spoke of the sinful "desire of the flesh/the old man." But Paul made it very clear in verse 16 that new-covenant salvation gives Christians the victory over sin. He showed that Christians are called, and enabled, to always walk by the Holy Spirit, so that they will not carry out the sinful desire of the flesh/the old man. At the end of verse 17, the apostle tells us that we must not yield to the sinful desires of the flesh/the old man that we may have on occasion, since we are engaged in intense warfare with the world, the flesh/old man, and the devil.

The Holy Spirit always makes the victory over sin available, and we appropriate that victory by walking in faith and by the Holy Spirit. Let me repeat an important point, "the things that you please" at the end of verse 17 means the same thing as "the desire of the flesh" at the end of verse 16. The desire of the flesh/the old man is to sin, but the Holy Spirit is always against sin, and He doesn't lose battles to the world, the flesh/old man, or the devil, or anybody else. If we walk by the Spirit by faith (which we are called, and enabled, to do), we will never sin. Now isn't that good news? God hates sin, and He paid an infinite price to set us free from sin and give us the victory over sin.

Now let's consider the wrong interpretation of this verse. They typically assume that verse 17 means something like the following: Intense warfare against us is taking place, with the result that, even though we are born-again Christians and want to do what is right and to not sin, we are not always able to do the good that we want to do. We will necessarily lose quite a few battles and sin. This verse is frequently used by many Christians to try to prove that Christians cannot stop sinning in this life. (Martin Luther and John Calvin, for example, who were both very influential, interpreted Gal. 5:17 that way in their commentaries on Galatians.) I am thankful that I can say with great assurance that they are misunderstanding what the apostle Paul said in Gal. 5:17. As I mentioned, that view contradicts what the apostle just said in verse 16, Walk by the Spirit and you most certainly will not carry out the sinful desire of the flesh (of the old man).

Galatians 5:17 is quite important in that it shows that the victory over sin is not always easy and it certainly is not automatic. And it is important for us to know that sincere dedicated born-again Christians can have wrong thoughts and wrong desires, even strong wrong desires. These things, though undesirable, are not sin if we resist them by the Holy Spirit. Many Christians have gotten discouraged when they found themselves having wrong thoughts and desires, and the devil has convinced some Christians that they must not be true Christians, and he has convinced other Christians that they might as well go ahead and sin since they are already in sin through their wrong thoughts and desires.

I'll read Galatians 5:16, 17 one more time; then I'll read part of what I said on verse 17 in my book. **But I say, walk by the Spirit and you** [most certainly] **will not carry out the** [sinful] **desire of the flesh** [of the old man]. **(17) For the flesh sets its desire against the Spirit, and the Spirit against the flesh, for these are in opposition to one another, so that you may not do the things** [that is, so that you may not do the sinful things] **that you please.** I'm going to turn to page 198 of my book and read just about all that I said under Gal. 5:17. This is so important, and it is so controversial. As I mentioned, many Christians disagree with what I am saying here. I am not attacking those Christians. Many of them are sincere, solid Christians, but I believe they are making a serious mistake here. You need to decide. Does Gal. 5:17 really teach that we cannot have the victory over sin in this life? This is a question of key importance!

First I discussed the meaning of the word **For** at the beginning of verse 17. I said, This conjunction ties verse 17 to verse 16. In verse 17 the apostle expands on the absolute necessity for Christians to walk by the Spirit. To the extent we do not walk by the Spirit, sin (the desire of the flesh of Gal. 5:16) will be the inevitable result. In other words, we will yield to the sinful desire of the flesh, and we will sin; we will do sinful works of the flesh.

We'll discuss the words **the flesh sets its desire against the Spirit.** The *Amplified Bible* has "For the desires of the flesh are opposed to the Holy Spirit." The NIV has, "For the sinful nature desires what is contrary to the Spirit [the Holy Spirit]." The Greek noun *epithumia*, which is the noun translated **desire** in Gal. 5:16, was derived from the verb *epithumeo*, which is translated **sets its desire** in Gal. 5:17. As I mentioned under Gal. 5:16, **the desire of the flesh** embraces all sin. All sin is against the Holy Spirit. He is called the Holy Spirit for a reason, and we could also call Him the Righteous Spirit.

We'll discuss the words **and the Spirit against the flesh** of Gal. 5:17. The Holy Spirit is, of course, against all the sinful desires of the flesh. All those who walk by (or, after/in) the Holy Spirit will walk in victory over sin. Is the Holy Spirit able to keep us in the righteousness and holiness of God with the victory over all sin? Is God's saving, sanctifying grace sufficient to enable us to do God's will? There is no doubt about these things, but we must do our part, and faith is our part. We must appropriate God's grace and walk by the Spirit all the time, by faith, in accordance with the gospel. If we don't understand these things and are wavering in faith, wondering whether we can stop sinning, or not, we cannot stop sinning. We need all the grace that God has made available, and to the extent we are wavering in faith, we will be defeated by the world, the flesh, and the devil.

We'll discuss the words **for these are in opposition to one another** of Gal. 5:17. Like two armies, the Spirit and the flesh are arrayed against one another. However, the Spirit of God and the flesh (even when Satan and his evil angels and demons are included as part of the flesh) are not equally powerful contestants. The Spirit of God is well able to overpower the flesh in every encounter. Christians will, therefore, always walk with the victory over sin when they walk by the Spirit. And as I have tried to emphasize, nothing can keep us from always walking by the Holy Spirit through faith. It is the will of God for us to always walk by the Spirit, and we can always walk by the Spirit. This is good news! This is a great privilege! I didn't say, however, that it would always be easy, or fun. Warfare is not easy, or fun, but it comes with the salvation package we signed up for.

We'll discuss the words **so that you may not do the things that you please** of Gal. 5:17. I'm sorry to say that many Christians have understood these words to teach that Christians cannot have the victory over sin during this present life. They understand the apostle to say something like the following: "so that you may not [always] do the [righteous] things that you want to do." In other words, the flesh (the old man) is certain to win some battles. In the light of Gal. 5:16 (also see Gal. 5:24, where the apostle Paul speaks of the fact that Christians have crucified the flesh with its passions and desires), I'm surprised by this interpretation. In Gal. 5:16 the apostle has just exhorted his readers to always walk by the Spirit so that they will not carry out the sinful desire of the flesh, so that they will not do the sinful works of the flesh; so that they will not sin.

The apostle did not write Gal. 5:17 to deny that Christians can always walk in victory over sin. He wrote this verse to emphasize the need for Christians to always walk by the Holy Spirit (which includes walking in line with God's Word, by faith), since the flesh is an active and formidable

26

opponent. I'm quite sure that the apostle's words mean something like the following: Although you as a sincere Christian may, at times, have desires (even strong desires) to sin (because the flesh has not been annihilated yet), you may not (must not) do the sinful things that you (as far as the flesh/the old man is concerned) may want to do (namely the sinful works of the flesh); the Holy Spirit will always enable you to have victory as you walk by Him (which you are called to do as Christians). "The [sinful] desire of the flesh" of Gal. 5:16 is the equivalent of "the sinful things that you please" of Gal. 5:17. I should mention that sinful desires, though very undesirable, are not in themselves sin or defeat. It's time to stop. We'll come back to Gal. 5:16-25 in the next article. God bless you!

Holiness and Victory Over Sin #3

Holy Father, we humble ourselves before you. We want to rightly divide your Word. We want to understand your Word. We want to live in line with your Word, by your sufficient grace. We want to be fully ready for the return of the Lord Jesus Christ, so He can say to us words like, "Well done good and faithful servant." We don't want to hear words like, "Depart from Me, I never knew you, you who practice lawlessness, you workers of iniquity" that Jesus warned about in Matthew chapter 7. We pray in Jesus' mighty name! Amen!

In the past two articles we have been looking at Gal. 5:16-25; we rather thoroughly discussed verses 16, 17. We'll come back to those verses in a few minutes, but I want to do one thing first. I'm going to turn to my book, *Holiness and Victory Over Sin*, which has a good sub-title, *Full Salvation Through the Atoning Death of the Lord Jesus Christ*. "Full salvation" includes righteousness and holiness and the full victory over sin. On page 194 of the book, I have a heading, <u>A Discussion of the Three Most Important Passages Often Used to Try to Prove that Christians Cannot Walk in Victory over Sin During this Present Age</u>. To me it's a very sad thing that we have lists like this, lists to try to prove that we cannot have the victory over sin.

I'll read what I said here. My studies indicate that the three most important such passages are Rom. 7:14-25; Gal. 5:17; and 1 John 1:8. At the top of these lists they typically have Romans chapter 7 and 1 John 1:8. From my point of view, much damage has been done to the Body of Christ through a serious misunderstanding of these passages. To give you an idea how widespread this problem is, about half misunderstand Romans chapter 7; about half misunderstand Gal. 5:17; and some 80-90 percent misunderstand 1 John 1:8.

I don't believe any of these passages suggest that Christians cannot walk in total victory over sin. In fact, each of these passages is set in a context that clearly teaches victory over sin. I believe the New Testament consistently teaches that Christians can, and should, live above sin (without sin). This is the Christian ideal. The call, and enablement, to walk in victory over sin is a big part of what salvation in Christ is all about. Let me add, if you understand what I am saying, this is very good news! God didn't say these things to bring condemnation; He wants to bring transformation.

Salvation, including salvation from the authority and power of sin, comes by grace through faith. We cannot walk in victory over sin apart from faith for that victory, and since our faith is based on the Word of God – our faith must be based on God and His Word – we cannot have faith for victory over sin if we believe that some passages teach that such a victory is unattainable. All the many passages that clearly teach victory over sin (Romans chapter 6, for example) cannot be taken at face value; they must be substantially qualified by those who don't believe such a victory is possible. Victory over sin is often put off until after the resurrection.

It is very important for us to rightly divide the Word of God on this topic, and on every topic, but this is one of the most important topics by far. There are powerful enemies arrayed against us that want to keep us in sin: the world, the flesh (the old man that still wants to live in sin), and the devil and his hosts. We will never defeat the enemy on a consistent basis apart from the sufficient grace of God appropriated by faith.

Let's turn back to Galatians 5:16-25. Galatians 5:16 is a super-important verse that is full of good news. The apostle Paul was writing this epistle to born-again Galatian Christians (and really to all of us too). I'll start to read verse 16. (I'll read from the *New American Standard Bible*, NASB, 1995 edition. I frequently make comments in the middle of quotations using brackets [ ] or [[ ]].) **But I say, walk by the Spirit** [[the Holy Spirit; or we could translate, walk in the Spirit, or walk after the Spirit. But wait a minute, can we always walk by the Spirit? I'm sure Paul would say, "Emphatically, yes!" Who can stop us from walking by God's Holy Spirit all the time? In fact, when we become Christians we sign a contract, so to speak, and we must accept the terms of God's covenant, the new covenant. We can't change the terms of the covenant; we have to submit to His terms. Those terms include a requirement to be faithful to God and His Word by His grace; to walk by His Spirit all the time; and to die to the old man and live in the righteousness and holiness of God.]], **and you** [most certainly] **will not carry out the desire** [the sinful desire] **of the flesh** [of the old man]. **The desire of the flesh** is to do the sinful works of the flesh (see Gal. 5:19-21); **the desire of the flesh** is to sin. As we have discussed, the flesh equals the old man; and the only way we can keep the old man from manifesting itself in sin is for us to always walk by God's Spirit through faith, a faith that is based on God's Word. **But I say, walk by the Spirit, and you** [most certainly] **will not carry out the desire** [the sinful desire] **of the flesh** [of the old man].

Now Galatians 5:17; here the apostle shows why it is totally necessary for us to always walk by the Holy Spirit. If we don't walk by the Spirit, we will sin. The old man hasn't been annihilated yet, and it still wants to sin. As we have discussed, the old man is man in spiritual death, man without the Holy Spirit, and man without the Holy Spirit doesn't have the power to stop sinning. Through the new covenant in the blood of Christ, we are forgiven, and we receive the Spirit of God, who enables us to walk in the righteousness and holiness of God, but a walk by the Spirit doesn't happen automatically when we are born again; we must cooperate with the Spirit of God through faith on a continuous basis. Forgiveness of sin and victory over sin both come by grace through faith.

Galatians 5:17. **For the flesh sets its desire against the Spirit, and the Spirit against the flesh** [The Holy Spirit is for righteousness and holiness; the flesh is for sin.]; **for these are in opposition to one another** [The Holy Spirit and the flesh are arrayed against one another like two armies; but the good news is that the one army is much greater than the other army. The Holy Spirit never loses, and we won't lose either if we walk by the Spirit. We can always do God's will by His sufficient grace.], **so that you may not do the things that you please.** Paul means so that we may not do the sinful things that we (so far as the old man is concerned) may want to do. Since the old man has not been annihilated, we may have wrong desires (or wrong thoughts) at times. Paul concluded verse 16 with the words, "you [most certainly] will not carry out the desire [the sinful desire] of the flesh [of the old man]."

The "desire of the flesh" (Gal. 5:16) is to sin. Here at the end of verse 17 Paul says, **so that you may not do the things** [the sinful things] **that you please**; so that you may not yield to the sinful "desire of the flesh." Yes, we may have wrong desires (or wrong thoughts) at times, but if we walk by the Spirit all the time, we will not sin. It may not always be easy, and the victory certainly isn't automatic, but we are called, and enabled, to walk in victory over all sin, by God's sufficient grace through faith. We must have a solid assurance that God has given us the authority and power to walk in His righteousness and holiness, with the victory over sin. If we don't believe (have faith) we can stop sinning, we can't.

For the flesh sets its desire against the Spirit, and the Spirit against the flesh; for these are in opposition to one another, so that you may not do the things [the sinful things] **that you please** [that you may want to do]. God hates sin, and He has paid an infinite price to set us free from spiritual death and bondage to sin.

As I mentioned, many Christians (about half) believe verse 17 teaches that we cannot have the victory over sin in this life. Typically they are saying that verse 17 teaches that we are not always able to do the good that we want to do. However, I am sure that the apostle was not making room for sin in verse 17. He was acknowledging that we must wage warfare against sin by the Holy Spirit, but he was not suggesting that we will sin. He has already told us in verse 16 that we will not sin if we always walk by the Holy Spirit, which we are called, and enabled, to do. **But I say, walk by the Spirit, and you** [most certainly] **will not carry out the desire** [the sinful desire] **of the flesh** [of the old man]. This is good news, very good news, but we must be convinced this is what God says. WE MUST BE CONVINCED IN OUR HEARTS THAT THIS IS WHAT GOD SAYS!

Galatians 5:18. **But if you are led by the Spirit, you are not under the Law.** Being led by the Spirit here is the equivalent of walking by (or, after) the Spirit in verse 16. How often should we be led by the Spirit? We are required to be led by the Spirit all the time. And if we are led by the Spirit all the time, we never will sin. The Holy Spirit leads to holiness; the

Righteous Spirit leads to righteousness. He never leads to sin. Victory over sin is what we want, isn't it?

But if you are led by the Spirit, you are not under the Law. Are Christians required to keep God's Law? In some ways we are not under the Mosaic Law, and we are not required to keep the ceremonial laws of the Old Testament, but we are required to keep God's moral law by His grace. God's moral law cannot change. His moral law derives from who He is; His moral law gives His definition of righteousness and of sin. It is essential for Christians to know that the New Testament teaches that we must keep God's moral law, by His saving grace in Christ Jesus. See my paper titled, *The Christian, the Law, and Legalism* on my internet site. (Google to Karl Kemp teaching.)

We have already briefly discussed Rom. 8:3, 4 in these broadcasts. Romans 8:4 shows that we Christians are enabled to keep the requirement of the Law in our daily lives, as we walk by the Holy Spirit. The apostle says the same thing in Rom. 2:26-29 and in 1 Cor. 7:19, for example. I'll read Romans 8:4, "so that the requirement of the Law might be fulfilled in us, who do not walk according to the flesh but according to the Spirit [the Holy Spirit]." The requirement of the Law is fulfilled in us as we walk by the Spirit in the righteousness and holiness of God. To the extent we do not walk by the Holy Spirit, we will sin. Some of the Corinthians Christians, for example, were quite fleshy, and we read of a lot of sin in Paul's epistles to the Corinthians, but the apostle was continually exhorting them, warning them that they must repent and begin to live as Christians are enabled, and required, to live. I'll also read 1 Corinthians 7:19, where the apostle Paul said, "Circumcision is nothing, and uncircumcision is nothing, but what matters is the keeping of the commandments of God."

Why did Paul say "you are not under the Law" in Galatians 5:18? When we understand the background for this epistle to the Galatian Christians, these words are easy to understand. Throughout this epistle, Paul refutes the false gospel of the Judaizers. He repeatedly warns the Gentile Christians at Galatia that they must reject the false gospel of the Judaizers. The apostle had shared the gospel with these Gentiles, and many of them had become solid born-again Christians, but he had learned that some of them were now seriously listening to the false gospel of the Judaizers, who were telling these Gentile Christians that they must submit to the ceremonial works of the Mosaic Law and be circumcised, etc.

In Gal. 5:2-4, for example, the apostle strongly warned the Galatian Christians that they must not accept the false gospel of the Judaizers. I'll read Galatians 5:2-4, "Behold I, Paul, say to you that if you receive circumcision, Christ will be of no benefit to you. (3) And I testify again to every man who receives circumcision, that he is under obligation to keep the whole Law. (4) You have been severed from Christ, you who are seeking to be justified by law; you have fallen from grace." To be severed from Christ and to fall from grace is to lose your salvation. (See my paper titled, *Once Saved, Always Saved?* on my internet site. I really tried to give the balanced truth on that controversial topic. We desperately need the balanced truth of what the Bible teaches.)

The apostle Paul would not tolerate anyone trying to change the gospel that came from heaven. I'll read Galatians 1:6-9, 11, 12. "I am amazed that you are so quickly deserting Him [God the Father] who called you by the grace of Christ, for a different gospel; (7) which is really not another [because it is a false gospel]; only there are some who are disturbing you and want to distort the gospel of Christ. (8) But even if we, or an angel from heaven, should preach to you a gospel contrary to what we have preached to you, he is to be accursed! (9) As we have said before, so I say again now, if any man is preaching to you a gospel contrary to what we have preached to you, he is to be accursed! ... (11) For I would have you know, brethren, that the gospel which was preached by me is not according to man. (12) For I neither received it from man, nor was I taught it, but I received it through a revelation of Jesus Christ."

I'll read Galatians 5:18 one more time, **But if you are led by the Spirit, you are not under the Law.** Being led by the Holy Spirit (as we must be), we keep the righteousness of God's moral law, but we are saved by the grace of God in Christ, not by the Law, and we are not required to keep the ceremonial works of the Mosaic Law. The Judaizers were wrong!

Galatians 5:19-21. These verses strongly confirm that Christians are required to always walk by the Holy Spirit and not do the sinful works of the flesh (of the old man that wants to live in sin), which equals not sinning at all. This is good news! What God calls us to do, He enables us to do. **Now the deeds [or, works] of the flesh are evident, which are:**

immorality, impurity, sensuality, (20) idolatry, sorcery, enmities, strife, jealousy, outbursts of anger, disputes, dissensions, factions, (21) envying, drunkenness, carousing, and things like these, of which I forewarn you, just as I have forewarned you, that those who practice such things will not inherit the kingdom of God. To not inherit the kingdom of God is to miss heaven. The New Testament makes it very clear that Christians must make it top priority to repent, as required, and to always walk by the Holy Spirit in the righteousness and holiness of God – by grace through faith. True Christians do not want to continue in sin; they want to avoid all sin.

Let's go on to Galatians 5:22, 23. After giving a long list of works of the flesh in verses 19-21, Paul now lists some of the good fruit the Holy Spirit produces in Christians, as we walk by (and after) the Holy Spirit by faith. **But the fruit of the Spirit is love, joy, peace, patience, kindness, goodness, faithfulness, (23) gentleness, self-control, against such things there is no law.** As we walk by the Holy Spirit, we keep the requirements of God's moral law, in His truth, righteousness, and holiness.

I'll read Galatians 5:24, which is a very important verse. **Now those who belong to Christ Jesus** [In other words, those who are true Christians] **have crucified the flesh with its passions and desires.** For us to crucify the flesh (by the grace of God in Christ) is the same thing as our crucifying the old man. The old man cannot manifest itself in sin if it has been crucified. In the ideal case, we would crucify the old man when we become Christians, and we would never sin again. That sounds good doesn't it? But we must understand that the old man isn't annihilated during this age; it will still live and manifest itself in sin to the extent we do not walk by faith on a continuous basis in the righteousness and holiness of God by the Holy Spirit. **Now those who belong to Christ Jesus have crucified the flesh with its passions and desires.** I'll read Galatians 5:16 again, "But I say, walk by the Spirit, and you [most certainly] will not carry out the desire [the sinful desire] of the flesh [of the old man]."

Romans chapter 6 is a very important cross-reference that speaks of crucifying the old man. We will discuss Romans chapter 6 in some detail when we finish Galatians chapter 5. I'll read several key verses from Romans chapter 6 and make a few comments. I'll read from the New King James Version. I'll read Romans 6:1, 2, "What shall we say then? Shall we continue in sin so that grace may abound? (2) Certainly not! How shall we who died to sin live any longer in it?" In the ideal case, the old man would be crucified and we would be dead to sin from the time we become Christians. I'll read Romans 6:6, 7, where Paul speaks of the old man being crucified, "knowing this, that our old man was crucified with Him [with Christ], that the body of sin might be done away with, that we should no longer be slaves of sin. (7) For he who has died has been freed from sin."

And I'll read Romans 6:11-14, "Likewise you also, reckon yourselves to be dead indeed to sin, but alive to God in Christ Jesus our Lord. [[We reckon ourselves to be dead indeed to sin and alive to God in Christ Jesus by faith, based on the gospel of new-covenant salvation. The gospel calls us, and enables us, to be dead to sin and alive to God and His righteousness and holiness.]] (12) Therefore do not let sin reign in your mortal body, that you should obey its lusts. [Christians may have sinful, lustful desires at times, but if we walk after the Holy Spirit (by faith), we most certainly will not carry out the sinful desire of the flesh/old man (see Gal. 5:16).] And do not present your members as instruments of unrighteousness to sin, but present yourselves to God as being alive from the dead, and your members as instruments of righteousness to God. (14) For sin shall not have dominion over you, for you are not under law but under grace." The Mosaic Law (or any other law) could not set us free from spiritual death and bondage to sin, but new-covenant salvation has the authority and power to set us free. The apostle Paul emphasizes this fact in Galatians chapter 5; Romans chapter 6; and in many other passages. And we find this same good news throughout the rest of the New Testament.

This good news is so important I'll take the time to read two more passages from Paul's epistle to the Romans. First I'll read Romans 8:12-14. The apostle Paul makes it very clear in these verses that Christians are totally obligated to always walk by the Spirit and keep the old man from manifesting itself in sin. This "obligation" is a great blessing, not a burden. I'll read from the NASB, 1995 edition. "So then brethren, we are under obligation, not to the flesh, to live according to the flesh—(13) for if you are living according to the flesh, you must die [In other words, if Christians give themselves over to live for sin, instead of living for God and His truth, righteousness, and holiness, they forfeit His life and go back into spiritual death.]; but if by the Spirit you are putting to death the deeds [or, works] of the body you will live. [For Christians to put to death the sinful works of the body by the Holy Spirit means that they walk by the Holy Spirit on a continuous basis and do not let the old man manifest itself in sinful works (in sin).] (14) For all who are being led by the Spirit of God, these are the sons of God." To be led by the Spirit is the same thing as walking by the Spirit. We are led by the Righteous, Holy Spirit to walk in the righteousness and holiness of God, with the victory over all sin. In the ideal case we will walk with the victory over all sin. Paul says here that it is only those who are being led by the Spirit of God that are the true sons of God.

I'll also read Romans 13:13, 14, "Let us behave properly as in the day, not in carousing and drunkenness, not in sexual promiscuity and sensuality, not in strife and jealousy. (14) But put on the Lord Jesus Christ, and make no provision for the flesh in regard to its lusts."

Let's go on to Galatians 5:25. **If we live by the Spirit, let us also walk by** [or, follow] **the Spirit.** The words **if we live by the Spirit** mean if we have been born again by the Holy Spirit (the Spirit of life). The new birth by the Holy Spirit was not available under the old covenant. The Mosaic Law could not impart life (see Gal. 3:21, for example), but all true Christians have life by the indwelling Spirit of life (see Rom. 8:2, 9, for example).

Let's discuss the words **let us also walk by the Spirit** at the end of verse 25. The NASB has a note in the margin showing that the Greek verb used here can also be translated "let us follow the Spirit." I believe follow the Spirit is the right idea here. The Greek verb used here (*stoicheo*) is different than the verb translated "walk" in Gal. 5:16. The BAGD Greek Lexicon gives "follow the Spirit" as the meaning here. We are called to follow the Spirit on a continuous basis. As we have discussed, if we follow the Spirit (which equals being led by the Spirit and walking by the Spirit) we will not sin. The Spirit of God always leads us to (and enables us to) walk in the truth, righteousness, and holiness of God.

God hates sin, and He paid an infinite price in the sacrifice of His Son to set us free from spiritual death, sin, and Satan. If we have life by the Spirit, we must be consistent and follow after the Spirit. As I mentioned, when we become Christians we sign a contract, so to speak, agreeing to always put God and His righteousness first, and to always walk by His

Holy Spirit. This is a big part of what Christianity is all about. Praise God for such a salvation! And God has provided forgiveness for Christians who fall into sin when they repent. Forgiveness comes by God's grace through the atoning death of the Lord Jesus Christ, even as the enablement to walk with victory over sin comes by God's grace through His atoning death. Praise God for the atoning death of the Lamb of God!

That completes our discussion of Galatians 5:16-25. Now I'll read GALATIANS 6:7-9 and make a few comments, **Do not be deceived, God is not mocked; for whatever a man sows, this he will also reap. (8) For the one who sows to his own flesh** [to the old man that wants to live in sin] **will from the flesh reap corruption, but the one who sows to the Spirit** [the Holy Spirit] **will from the Spirit reap eternal life. (9) Let us not lose heart in doing good, for in due time we will reap if we do not grow weary.** We will reap eternal life in God's eternal kingdom that is filled with His glory if we stay faithful to Him by His grace and walk by His Spirit. Those who live a life of sin in the flesh will reap eternal death, the second death.

Now I'm going to turn back to the Preface of my book, *Holiness and Victory Over Sin,* and read what I said under the heading, Dealing with guilt feelings and bondages. I realize that many Christians are burdened with guilt feelings. (I know I have had them, and I didn't like them at all.) We are not solving the problem by trying to get rid of the guilt feelings through minimizing God's call to righteousness and holiness. (And I might add, we are not solving the problem by putting all the emphasis on forgiveness and legal, positional righteousness, which is so common in our day. And we are not solving the problem by putting all the emphasis on God's love, while ignoring the fact that the Bible, very much including the New Testament, speaks of His wrath against sin as much as it speaks of His love.) God's answer (the only satisfactory answer) is to drive out the sin by the power of the atoning blood of the Lord Jesus Christ. Even if this is not always an easy path to follow, it is the only right path, and we must choose this narrow path (see Matt. 7:13-27, for example). Where sin is the problem, we must repent and deal with the sin. Where condemnation and guilt feelings are caused by false accusations of the devil, we must resist the lies of the devil through faith in God and His Word. We must believe that when we repent the sins we have confessed are forgiven through the blood of the Lord Jesus Christ (see 1 John 2:1, 2 for example).

I realize that many Christians have bondages in many areas. We are not solving the sin problem by accepting such bondages as just the way it is. Even if it is not always easy, we must press on to drive out all bondages by the Spirit of God through faith, to the glory of God. God hates sin, and He has paid an infinite price in the sacrifice of His Son to give us the victory over sin – by grace through faith, in accordance with the gospel. This is good news!

In the next article, we will begin a verse-by-verse study of Romans chapter 6. As I have mentioned, this chapter is very special to me. This is the first passage that God used to show me that Christians are called, and enabled, to have the victory over all sin in, and through, the Lord Jesus Christ. God bless you!

Holiness and Victory Over Sin #4

Holy Father, we humble our hearts before you; we want to rightly divide your Word; we want to know the balanced truth of what your Word teaches about the gospel. We want to understand it; we want to live it, for your glory, for our good, and for the good of the people we can be a blessing to. In Jesus' mighty name! Amen!

Before we turn to Romans chapter 6, I'll read a few paragraphs from the Preface of my book under the heading Whatever happened to the New Testament call for repentance? Repentance includes turning from sin and darkness to God and His light, and His light includes His truth, His righteousness, and His holiness. It seems that we never hear the word *repentance* in many Christian circles of our day. The New Testament makes repentance an important part of conversion (see, for example, Matt. 4:17; Mark 1:14, 15; 6:12; Luke 13:1-5; 24:47; Acts 2:38; 17:30, 31 26:20). Equally important, the New Testament calls for Christians in sin to repent (see, for example, 2 Cor. 7:8-13; 12:19-21; Rev. 2:4, 5, 14-16, 20-24; 3:2-5, 15-20). The verses I just cited from the book of Revelation strike me as being especially relevant and awesome. The Lord Jesus Christ Himself was speaking to seven literal churches that existed at that time (about AD 95), but what He said to those churches is directly applicable to any church (or any Christian) that is in the same situation.

One of the most startling things about the messages to the seven churches is the frequent and powerful call to repent, or else. The Lord Jesus Christ warned the Christians at Ephesus that if they didn't repent, they would find themselves no longer belonging to His church; the fact that they still had a lampstand confirmed that they still belonged to His church (see Rev. 2:4, 5; 1:20). If we no longer belong to His church, we are not headed for heaven.

He warned the majority of the Christians at Sardis that if they didn't repent, He would come upon them in judgment as a thief (as a thief in the night; see Rev. 3:1-4), and He warned that He would erase their names from the book of life (see Rev. 3:5). If He erased their names from the book of life, they would not be headed for heaven. The fact that their names had been in the book of life from the foundation of the world confirms that they were true Christians (see Rev. 13:8; 17:8, for example). Furthermore, the majority would not have had garments to soil if they had not become born-again Christians (see Rev. 3:4, 5 with Rev. 19:8, 14). In Rev. 3:4 Jesus told the few at Sardis who had not soiled their garments that they would walk with Him in white. As Rev. 19:8 shows, the white garments very much includes "the righteous acts [and lifestyle] of the saints." Jesus was calling those who needed to repent to repent and get their garments white through the saving, sanctifying grace of God in Christ. Since many Christians insist that the Christians who needed to repent at Sardis had never become born-again Christians, I'll point out that what Jesus said in Rev. 3:2 also confirms that the Christians who needed to repent had become true Christians. Jesus exhorted them to "wake up and strengthen the things that remain, which were about to die." These words show that they still had some remnants of true Christianity, but they must repent with a top priority. See my paper *Once Saved, Always Saved?* on my internet site.

Lastly, I'll mention that Jesus exhorted the self-satisfied Christians at Laodicea to repent before He spit them out of His mouth (see Rev. 3:15-20). Many have pointed out that there is all-too-much similarity between the ancient church at Laodicea and much of the church of our day.

Some suggest that God doesn't take the sins of Christians seriously. I have even heard Christians say that God doesn't see our sins because He looks at us through the atoning blood of Jesus Christ. I believe it is true that He doesn't see our past (forgiven) sins; but if we are living in sin, He sees it, and it is a serious matter that needs to be dealt with in a high priority manner. The messages to the seven churches are sufficient to show that God does take our sins seriously. They also show that repentance is more than asking for forgiveness. One last comment here, repentance is something we do; it is not something God does; we repent in response to His Word and His grace, and by His grace; but repentance is something we must do.

Now I'll turn to page 96 of my book, *Holiness and Victory Over Sin,* and read part of the introduction to ROMANS CHAPTER 6; then we'll start a verse-by-verse study of this super-important chapter. Romans chapter 6 is one of the most important chapters in the New Testament which shows that Christians can and should walk in victory over sin through the Lord Jesus Christ. But there is much about victory over sin in Romans chapters 1-5 and in other chapters of Romans, especially chapter 8, and throughout the rest of the New Testament.

Before we became Christians, sin was our master. We were slaves of sin (see, for example, Rom. 6:6, 17, 19, 20, and 22). But now, as Rom. 6:18 says, "and having been freed from sin, you became slaves of righteousness." Sin and spiritual death have been dethroned by the saving grace of God in Christ Jesus (see Rom. 5:21; 6:14). We are no longer slaves of sin (see, for example, Rom. 6:6, 11, 12, 14, 17, 18, 19, and 22). We are slaves of God and of His righteousness (see Rom. 6:13, 18, 19, and 22).

To be a slave of righteousness means to live in righteousness (see 1 John 2:29; 3:7). I'll quote 1 John 3:7, where the apostle John said, "Little children, make sure no one deceives you [There were deceivers in John's day, and there are many deceivers around today.]; the one who practices righteousness [or, the one who is doing righteousness] is righteous, just as He [God] is righteous." If we want to be righteous, we have to live in God's righteousness by His grace. It's not a matter of just being forgiven, or having a declared righteousness, we must have an imparted righteousness; we must live in God's righteousness. But this is good news, very good news! This is about 90 percent of what Christianity is all about.

The grace of God through the powerful shed blood of the Lord Jesus Christ sets us free from sin and enables us to live for God in His righteousness and holiness. John said here that we are to be righteous just as God is righteous. That certainly includes the victory over all sin. It may not always be easy, but we must aim at the target of walking in God's righteousness with the victory over all sin. Something is seriously wrong when Christians are not even trying to stop sinning, because they think they cannot stop sinning. As we have discussed, many Christians believe the Bible teaches that we cannot stop sinning this side of glory. Some Christians are convinced that they must fulfill their daily quota of sin.

I'm turning to Romans chapter 6. What a privilege to be able to study this chapter. Romans 6:1. **What shall we say then? Are we to continue in sin so that grace may increase** [or, **may abound**]? Romans 3:8 will help us understand this verse. Some people misunderstood the apostle Paul, and many totally rejected the gospel he proclaimed. He put the emphasis on grace and on faith, not on the Law and works of the Law. Some thought, for one thing, that he was saying that Christians do not have to keep God's Law. But we do have to keep God's Law. Christians are not required to keep the ceremonial law of the Old Testament, but as we have discussed, we are enabled, and required, to keep His moral law. Through new-covenant salvation in union with the Lord Jesus Christ, we are set free from bondage to sin and enabled to keep God's moral law in our daily lives. This is good news, very good news! (See Jer. 31:33; Ezek. 36:25-27; Rom. 8:4; 1 Cor. 7:19, for example.) God's moral law defines righteousness and sin and shows what He requires of us.

I'll read Romans 3:8. "And why not say (as we are slanderously reported and as some claim that we say), 'Let us do evil that good may come?' Their condemnation is just." Paul hated being charged with teaching "Let us do evil that good may come." Anyone who thought Paul was minimizing the need for Christians to live in the righteousness of God by His grace didn't understand what he was teaching. It is true that Paul strongly emphasized grace, but that grace includes sanctifying grace that enables Christians to live in the righteousness and holiness of God. The apostle Paul went out of his way in the epistle to the Romans to emphasize that God's grace enables (and requires) us to keep the requirements of His moral law and to live in His righteousness.

I'll read Romans 6:1 again, **What shall we say then? Are we to continue in sin so that grace may increase** [or, **may abound**]**?** Look what Paul says in the next verse, Romans 6:2, **How shall we who died to sin still live in it?** According to the gospel Paul preached (which he received from the resurrected Christ), Christians have died to sin; so how can we continue in sin so that grace may abound? According to the gospel Paul preached, we Christians are to be dead to spiritual death and to sin; and Satan and his demons have no more authority over us. **How shall we who died to sin still live in it?**

I'll read 1 Peter 2:24, "and He Himself bore our sins [with the guilt and the penalties, including the major penalties of spiritual death and bondage to sin] in His body on the cross, SO THAT WE MIGHT DIE TO SIN AND LIVE TO RIGHTEOUSNESS [my emphasis]; for by His wounds you were healed." We frequently find this same message throughout the New Testament. I'll read Romans 6:6, "knowing this, THAT OUR OLD MAN WAS CRUCIFIED WITH HIM, IN ORDER THAT OUR BODY OF SIN MIGHT BE DONE AWAY WITH, SO THAT WE WOULD NO LONGER BE SLAVES TO SIN [my emphasis]." If our old man has been crucified with Christ, we are dead to sin. We die to sin when we are crucified with Christ (when we become Christians), and in the ideal case we would never sin again. That sounds good doesn't it?

And I'll read Romans 6:11. "Even so CONSIDER [or, RECKON] YOURSELVES TO BE DEAD TO SIN, BUT ALIVE TO GOD IN CHRIST JESUS [my emphasis]." The fact that we are to consider, or reckon, ourselves to be dead to sin demonstrates that this death to sin is not automatic when we become Christians. We must continually cooperate with God's saving grace by faith (a faith that is based on God and His gospel). Or to put it in different words, we must continually walk by the Spirit, so that we will not carry out the sinful desire of the flesh (of the old man that still wants to live in sin); in other words, so that we will not sin – we will be dead to sin (see Gal. 5:16).

41

Romans 6:3. **Or do you not know that all of us who have been baptized into Christ Jesus have been baptized into His death?** When we become Christians, we are baptized into the death of the Lord Jesus Christ. He, the Lamb of God, died in our place, bearing our sins with the guilt and the penalties (including the major penalties of spiritual death and bondage to sin). When we become Christians, we die with Him to the old man. In the ideal case, the old man would never manifest itself in sin again. The Holy Spirit enables us to keep the old man from manifesting itself in sin, as we walk by the Spirit through faith.

Or do you not know that all of us who have been baptized into Christ Jesus have been baptized into His death? He died in our place. We have every right to appropriate His death as our death. We become united with the Lord Jesus Christ when we become Christians. We die with Him; we are buried with Him; we are raised with Him; and we are united with Him from then on (by faith and by the Holy Spirit). The life of God is imparted to us in Christ, and the righteousness and holiness of God are imparted to us. Again, I am not saying that victory over sin is automatic, or that it is always easy. The world, the flesh, and the devil are against us, but God's grace is sufficient, and no one can keep us from doing God's will.

Romans 6:4. **Therefore we have been buried with Him through baptism into death** [death to the old man] [[This double bracket continues for five paragraphs. I'll read what the apostle Paul said in the first part of Colossians 2:12, "having been buried with Him in baptism." The old man is buried with Christ when we become Christians. (At least in the ideal case the old man is buried with Christ when we become born-again Christians.) We desperately need the balanced truth of what the New Testament teaches about water baptism. I'll read Romans 6:3 and the first part of Romans 6:4 again, **Or do you not know that all of us who have been baptized into Christ Jesus have been baptized into His death. Therefore we have been buried with Him through baptism into death....**

I believe it is clear that there is some reference to water baptism here, but as I mentioned, we need the balanced truth of what the New Testament teaches regarding water baptism. The apostle Paul certainly isn't saying that water baptism is the one thing that gives us spiritual life and makes us righteous and holy. As a matter of fact, if the Christian basics aren't right, water baptism is nothing more than another dead ritual. What are the basics that are more important than water baptism? And by the way, water baptism is quite important, according to the New Testament.

Here are the things that are more important than water baptism, without which water baptism is another dead ritual: We must hear the truth of the gospel. We must understand the truth of the gospel; at least we must understand the foundational truths of the gospel. Our faith must be based on God and His Word. If we don't understand the foundational truths of Christianity, we cannot commit ourselves to God and His gospel, and we cannot cooperate with His Word. We must know, for example, what God has done for us in the sacrifice of His Son, and we must know what He requires of us. We must hear the gospel; we must understand the gospel; we must commit ourselves to God and the gospel in faith, and it must be an abiding commitment; furthermore, we must have all the work of the Holy Spirit as He draws, convicts, reveals, teaches, imparts life, transforms, leads us to a life of righteousness and holiness, etc.

Now if the basics are right, water baptism is quite significant. Water baptism is the appropriate biblical occasion for us to complete (by faith) the transactions of being forgiven and washing away our past sins (see Acts 2:38; 22:16); of our becoming united with the Lord Jesus Christ (see Rom. 6:3; Gal. 3:27); and of our old man dying with Him and being buried with Him (see Rom. 6:3, 4; Col. 2:11, 12). I am not saying (nor do I believe) that we cannot be saved apart from water baptism, or that we cannot die to the old man apart from water baptism.

It seems clear to me that many have been saved apart from water baptism and that many have died to the old man apart from water baptism. The Salvation Army, for example, doesn't practice water baptism, but I am confident that many of them are genuine Christians. Anyway, I believe it is clear in the New Testament that we should be baptized in water. Just because God has been generous with us and blessed us in spite of our deviations from the balanced truth of what His Word teaches, doesn't mean that it is OK, or that it doesn't make any difference. The more we do things God's way, the more He will be glorified; the more we Christians can be united in the balanced truth of what the Bible teaches; and the more He can bless us and use us.]], **so that as Christ was raised from the dead through the glory of the Father, so we too might walk in newness of life.** As I mentioned, we

43

are united with Christ in His death, in His burial, in His resurrection, and in His present life. As born again Christians, we are enabled to walk in "newness of life," manifesting the very righteousness and holiness of God. We are no longer spiritually dead slaves of sin; we are born-again children of God, indwelled by the Spirit of life, the Spirit of righteousness and holiness.

Romans 6:5. **For if we have become united with *Him* in the likeness of His death, certainly we shall also be *in the likeness* of His resurrection.** We don't just die with Christ, we are raised with Him, and we are literally united with Him as born-again Christians by the Holy Spirit. In a very real sense, we are new creations (see 2 Cor. 5:17, for example). We have already been resurrected spiritually, and we will be resurrected bodily and glorified at the end of this age. After we are glorified, we will not have to wage warfare against the world, the flesh, and the devil, but during this present age the warfare can be intense. The old man still wants to live and manifest itself in sin, and the world (whose god is the devil) and the demons substantially intensify the sin problem.

The Bible makes it clear that Christians can sin, but it also shows that God's grace is sufficient to keep us from sinning. If we walk by faith (based on what the New Testament teaches) and by the Holy Spirit, which we are called and enabled to do, we will walk above sin. That sounds good doesn't it?

Romans 6:6 (another glorious verse). **knowing this, that out old self** [or, better yet, **our old man**] **was crucified with *Him*, in order that our body of sin might be done away with, so that we would no longer be slaves to sin.** By God's definition, our old man is supposed to be crucified and dead from the time we become Christians. Like Paul said in verse 2 (we died to sin); like he said in verse 3 (we have been baptized into His death); like he said in verse 4 (we have been buried with Him through baptism into death); and like he said in verse 5 (if we have become united with Him in the likeness of His death). If our old man is really crucified, it will not be able to manifest itself in sin. The indwelling Spirit of God will always enable us to walk in the righteousness of God as we walk by the Spirit through faith, in accordance with the gospel of new-covenant salvation.

I'll read Romans 6:6 again. **knowing this, that our old man was crucified with _Him_, in order that our body of sin might be done away with** [From the time we become Christians, we should no longer have a body of sin; our body is to be consecrated to God and His righteousness.]**, so that we would no longer be slaves to sin.** Several places in this chapter the apostle mentions that we used to be slaves of sin, but now we are called, enabled, and required to be faithful slaves of God and of His righteousness. I'll read Romans 6:18 and the first part of 6:22, and there are quite a few similar verses in this chapter, "and having been freed from sin, you became slaves of righteousness" and "But now having been freed from sin and enslaved to God...."

Now I'm going to turn to page 97 of my book (_Holiness and Victory Over Sin_) and read part of what I said under these verses. I'll also add to what I said there. This will involve some repetition, but repetition is good if it helps us understand these super-important truths and to get them solidly planted in our hearts. First I'll read what I said under verses 1, 2. Christians are not to continue in sin (by sinning) that grace might increase (or, abound). The grace of God is a sanctifying grace (see Rom. 3:24; 5:21; 6:14; and Eph. 2:8-10). I'll read Romans 6:14 and make a few brief comments: "For sin shall not be master over you [or, have dominion over you], for you are not under law but under grace [the powerful, saving, sanctifying grace of God in Christ]." One point that the apostle makes here is that if all we had was the Mosaic Law (and the old covenant established on that Law), then sin would still have dominion over us. But the saving grace of God in Christ dethrones sin, spiritual death, and Satan. "For sin shall not be master over you [or, have dominion over you], for you are not under law but under grace." "What the [Mosaic] Law could not do, weak as it was through the flesh, God did, sending His own Son in the likeness of sinful flesh and as an offering for sin, He condemned sin in the flesh, so that the requirement of the Law might be fulfilled in us, who do not walk according to the flesh but according to the Spirit [the Holy Spirit]" (Romans 8:3, 4).

We are forgiven by God's grace, and we are sanctified and made righteous by His grace. The fact that we are saved by grace means that every aspect of our salvation is a gift, totally unearned. We didn't earn forgiveness, and we didn't earn the gift of the Holy Spirit to bring us life and make us righteous and holy. God gets all of the glory for our righteousness and holiness. It is His righteousness and holiness imparted to us through His Son and by His Spirit.

By God's definition Christians are to die to sin at the time of conversion. This is the ideal. The apostle discusses this death to sin on through Rom. 6:11, then in the rest of the chapter he speaks of freedom from slavery to sin and slavery to God's righteousness.

Now I'll read part of what I said regarding the words, "our old man was crucified with *Him*" of Romans 6:6. First I said, "compare Gal. 2:20; 6:14, 15." I'll read those verses and make a few comments. In Galatians 2:20 the apostle Paul said, "I have been crucified with Christ; and it is no longer I who live, but Christ lives in me; and the *life* which I now live in the flesh I live by faith in the Son of God, who loved me and gave Himself up for me." When Paul spoke of the life which he now lived in the flesh, he meant the life he was living in his physical body. He certainly did not mean that he walked in the flesh. He walked in and by the Holy Spirit. As Paul said in Gal. 2:20, he (his old man) had been crucified with Christ. And I'll read what the apostle said in Galatians 6:14, 15, "But may it never be that I would boast, except in the cross of our Lord Jesus Christ, through which the world has been crucified to me, and I to the world. For neither is circumcision anything, nor uncircumcision, but a new creation." We are new creations in Christ (2 Cor. 5:17).

Now I'll continue to read what I said regarding the words **our old man was crucified with Him** of Romans 6:6. To the extent that the old man ((the old man is fallen man, man in Adam, man in spiritual death, man in the flesh, man in bondage to sin. I had an endnote here, which I'll read; "endnote" means that the note is at the end of the chapter; it's on page 131. The expression "old man" is also used in Eph. 4:22 and Col. 3:9. Both of these verses, in their contexts, confirm that the old man is not just automatically crucified, or set aside, but that this is the ideal for Christians, a very real, very attainable ideal. Now back to page 97.)) To the extent that the old man has been crucified with Christ on an experiential level, we will walk in righteousness with victory over sin. For the old man to be crucified is part of God's definition of what it means to be a Christian. This is the Christian ideal, and we must not say that it is an unattainable ideal. God's transforming, sanctifying grace is sufficient, but we must appropriate and cooperate with His grace by faith.

These things are far from being automatic. Christians can sin, and we will sin to the extent the old man has not been crucified with Christ; to the extent we do not walk in "newness of life" (see Rom. 6:4); to the extent we do not walk by the Holy Spirit (see Rom. 8:12-14; Gal. 5:13-25). Galatians 5:16-25, which we have discussed already, makes it clear that the old man is not just automatically crucified; I'll read Galatians 5:24, "Now those who belong to Christ Jesus have crucified the flesh with its passions and desires." We must walk by faith on a continuous basis and appropriate God's sanctifying grace, which includes walking by and after the Holy Spirit on a continuous basis, or the old man will still live and manifest itself in sin. And before we can walk by faith with the victory over sin, we must be convinced from the Scriptures that God has truly called us to such a walk and has provided sufficient grace.

Now I'll read what I said under the words **that our body of sin might be done away with, that we should no longer be slaves of sin** of Romans 6:6. To the extent that the old man truly has been crucified with Christ, we won't have a "body of sin"; that is, our body will no longer be used in the service of sin; it will be a body of righteousness (see Rom. 6:12, 13, 19; 8:12, 13). I'll read those verses. First I'll read Romans 6:12, 13, and 19, "Therefore, do not let sin reign in your mortal body so that you obey its lusts, (13) and do not go on presenting the members of your body to sin as instruments of unrighteousness; but present yourselves to God as those alive from the dead, and your members as instruments of righteousness to God. [And I'll read the second sentence of verse 19.] For just as you presented your members as slaves to impurity and to lawlessness, resulting in further lawlessness, so now present your members as slaves to righteousness, resulting in sanctification [or, better yet, resulting in holiness (an abiding state of holiness)]."

And I'll read Romans 8:12, 13, "So then brethren, we are under obligation, not to the flesh, to live according to the flesh—(13) for if you are living according to the flesh, you must die; but if by the Spirit [the Holy Spirit] you are putting to death the deeds [or, works] of the body, you will live." On the "body of sin," also see Rom. 7:5, 23-25; Gal. 5:19-21, 24; Col. 2:11-13; 3:5-9.

We'll come back to Romans chapter 6 in the next article.

Holiness and Victory Over Sin #5

Holy Father, we humble our hearts before you. We ask you to open the eyes of our hearts, so we can understand the gospel, what you have given us in the Lord Jesus Christ and what you require of us. Thank you! We pray in Jesus' mighty, holy name! Amen!

Let's turn back to Romans chapter 6. In the last article we discussed the first six verses of Romans chapter 6 in some detail. Those verses are extremely important. Romans 6:1. **What shall we say then? Are we to continue in sin so that grace may increase** [or, **abound**]? Paul strongly emphasized God's grace (which means that our salvation is a gift; it is totally unearned), but it is a sanctifying grace, a grace that sets us free from spiritual death and bondage to sin, and it enables us to live in the righteousness and holiness of God. Holiness and victory over sin come by God's grace, even as forgiveness comes by His grace.

The apostle answers the question of verse 1 (**Are we to continue in sin that grace may abound?**) with an emphatic negative in **Romans 6:2**. He says, **May it never be! How shall we who died to sin still live in it?** We died to sin through becoming united with the Lord Jesus Christ in His atoning death and resurrection when we became Christians. We died with Him, and the old man was buried with Him. In the ideal case, we would never sin again after we become Christians.

I'll read Romans 6:3 and the first part of 6:4, where Paul continues with this theme, **Or do you not know that all of us who have been baptized into Christ Jesus have been baptized into His death? (4) Therefore we have been buried with Him through baptism into death....** I'll also read the first part of Romans 6:5 and 6:6, 7, where the apostle continues with this theme of our being dead to sin. **For if we have become united with Him in the likeness of His death.... (6) knowing this, that our old self [our old man] was crucified with *Him*, in order that our body of sin might be done away with, so that we would no longer be slaves to sin; (7) for he who has died is freed from sin.** Paul makes it very clear throughout Romans chapter 6 (and other places) that we used to be slaves of sin, but now we are enabled, and required, to be slaves of God and of His righteousness. As I mentioned, in the ideal case we would never sin again after we become Christians. That sounds like very good news to me! That's what we want, isn't it?

We died to sin and were buried with Christ when we became Christians. But we also are united with Him in His resurrection, and we are united with Him in His present life. The apostle Paul speaks of our being resurrected with Christ and of our being united with Him from then on in the second half of verse 4 and in verse 5. I'll read Romans 6:4, 5, **Therefore we have been buried with Him through baptism into death, so that as Christ was raised from the dead through the glory of the Father, so we too might walk in newness of life. (5) For if we have become united with *Him* in the likeness of His death, certainly we shall also be *in the likeness* of His resurrection.**

Now we'll discuss Romans 6:7. **for he who has died is freed from sin.** It is very clear in context what the apostle means by the words **he who has died.** In verses 2, 3, 4, 5, 6, and on into verses 8-11, Paul speaks of our having died with Christ and being dead to sin and to the old man. **He who has died** [through becoming united with the Lord Jesus Christ in His atoning death] **is freed from sin.** As we have discussed, in the ideal case we would never serve our old master of sin again, by sinning. WE MUST AIM AT THAT TARGET!

I'm going to say quite a bit more about this verse. There is another very important detail that we should discuss. The Greek verb that is translated **is freed** here would normally be translated "is justified," or, "has been justified." The translation "is freed" communicates well, but I prefer the translation "is justified" (or, "has been justified"), because this translation will help us understand the meaning of the super-important verb "justify" (and the meaning of the noun "justification"). The context here in Romans chapter 6 demonstrates that the verb justify includes our being set free from slavery (or, bondage) to sin. And it is clear that we must be set free from spiritual death and be born again in order to be set free from bondage to sin. IT IS VERY IMPORTANT FOR US TO KNOW THAT THE VERB "JUSTIFY" IS FREQUENTLY USED IN THE NEW TESTAMENT IN A MUCH FULLER SENSE THAN JUST BEING FORGIVEN AND DECLARED RIGHTEOUS. This verse (and other verses) demonstrates that our being justified includes our being set free from spiritual death and bondage to sin.

The verb justify (and the noun justification) strongly lends itself to include our being set free from spiritual death and bondage to sin, and our being made righteous and holy, when it is used of new-covenant salvation in the blood of Christ and by the Holy Spirit. When we (as individuals) become Christians, we come before God the Judge in a very real sense. Having repented and submitted to Him and the gospel of the new covenant in faith, He says to us, "I declare you righteous." God the Judge says, "I forgive you and I declare you righteous." That's good for a start, but we cannot stop there (like many Christians do).

It must be understood that when God declares us righteous, He is at the same time declaring that spiritual death, sin, and Satan and his demons have lost the authority and power they had over us. Now, since spiritual death has been dethroned, we are born again. And since sin and Satan have lost their authority over us, we begin to live in the righteousness and holiness of God. It is easy to see why the verb justify, when it is used in this full-orbed new-covenant salvation context, includes a lot more than forgiveness and a legal declaration of righteousness. Romans 6:7, and other verses, demonstrate that the verb justify frequently includes our being set free from sin. Sin, our former master, is now under our feet through salvation in the Lord Jesus Christ.

We'll be talking further about this super-important, much fuller meaning of the verb justify and the noun justification as we continue with these studies. The longest chapter in my book, *Holiness and Victory Over Sin: Full Salvation Through the Atoning Death of the Lord Jesus Christ*, deals with the meaning of the words justify and justification. I trust you can see that we are talking about the heart of the gospel. This is extremely important!

Now let's look at this same glorious reality from a somewhat different point of view, but with the same end result. Let's consider the atoning, sacrificial death of the Lord Jesus Christ, the infinitely worthy Lamb of God. He bore our sins in His body on the cross with the guilt and the penalties. He didn't just bear our sins with the guilt, so we could be forgiven and declared righteous in some isolated legal sense. He bore our sins with the guilt and the penalties. In *Holiness and Victory Over Sin* I demonstrate from the meaning of the Hebrew nouns for sin and from passages like Isaiah chapter 53, that the Lamb of God bore our sins with the guilt AND WITH THE PENALTIES. Especially significant is the fact that He bore the PENALTIES of spiritual death and bondage to sin that came upon mankind through our sin, especially the sin of Adam.

The Lamb of God bore the penalties of spiritual death and bondage to sin, so we could get out from under those penalties and be born again and made righteous and holy. God stripped spiritual death, sin, and Satan and his demons of the authority and power they had over us through the atoning death of His Son. Through Christ we get out from under that sinful mess. If we think that the Lamb of God just bore our sins with the guilt, so we could be forgiven and have right standing with God, we have about ten percent of the gospel. We need to appropriate and walk in everything that God has provided for us in the sacrifice of His Son. We need to emphasize – emphasize – righteousness, holiness, and victory over sin through the shed blood of the Lamb of God and in the power of the Holy Spirit.

The more I think about these things, the more I am overwhelmed with the thought that it would literally be shocking if the atoning death of the Lord Jesus Christ didn't give us the full victory over all sin. God hates sin, and He paid an infinite price in the Sacrifice of His Son to set us free from slavery to sin. When we consider who Jesus is and what He has done for us, it would be totally shocking if new-covenant salvation did not include the victory over all sin. Praise God for full salvation in the Lord Jesus Christ! We must focus on the sufficient sanctifying grace of God in Christ, not on the sinfulness of man. We must understand the gospel; we must live the gospel, for the glory of God, and for our sakes. What a blessing! What a privilege!

Let's look at 1 Peter 2:24 one more time. 1 Peter 2:24 contains the same message as Romans chapter 6, "and He Himself bore our sins in His body on the cross [He bore our sins with the guilt and the penalties, including the major penalties of spiritual death and bondage to sin], SO THAT WE MIGHT DIE TO SIN AND LIVE TO RIGHTEOUSNESS [my emphasis]; for by His wounds you were healed." The "wounds" speak of the penalties for our sins that He bore for us that killed Him. The wages of sin is death. These words at the end of 1 Pet. 2:24 are all the more important in that they were borrowed from Isa. 53:5. Isaiah chapter 53 is one of the most important chapters in the Bible dealing with the atoning death of the Lord Jesus Christ. Many of the key verses of Isaiah chapter 53 are discussed in my book *Holiness and Victory Over Sin*.

Now I'm going to turn to page 98 of *Holiness and Victory Over Sin* and read a paragraph that I have under Rom. 6:7. The translation "is freed" is effective here, and it fits the context well (compare, for example, "that we should no longer be slaves to sin" of Rom. 6:6); but more should be said regarding the meaning of the Greek verb *dikaioo*, as it is used here in Rom. 6:7. This Greek verb means more than "freed" in this verse, but it might be difficult to communicate this fact in an English translation. I would rather translate "is justified" or "has been justified," but it would be necessary to explain (in a note) that "justify" is being used here in a very full sense, going far beyond a legal, positional declaration of righteousness.

Christians have been forgiven and declared righteous; they have been set free from spiritual death and born again; and they have been set free from slavery to sin and made righteous. All these things are part of what it means to be justified, using justified in a full sense, and all these things come to believers through the atoning death of the Lord Jesus Christ, by grace (which includes all the work of the Holy Spirit) through faith.

I'm turning back to page 70 of this chapter, and I'll read three paragraphs. First I'll give you the title for this chapter, A Study on the Meaning of Justify/Justification as These Words Are Used in the New Testament. It is common for Christians to define "justify" as "declare righteous" (to forgive the guilt of sin and bring about a right [legal] standing before God). From my point of view, an overuse of this narrow sense of justify has helped perpetuate a very inadequate concept of what Christianity is all about. It is important for Christians to know that they have been forgiven and have a right standing with God. If we stop there, however, or put most of the emphasis there (as it so often happens), we are stopping far short of an adequate understanding of the gospel.

God does not offer justification in the narrow sense of the word in isolation from the new birth and a transformed life. Let me add, there are no smoke and mirrors needed here. God isn't declaring us righteous and leaving us sinners; He is declaring us righteous and making us righteous by grace through faith. We must cooperate (we are obligated to cooperate) with His grace and walk by the Holy Spirit on a continuous basis, by faith.

If we are going to translate the Greek verb *dikaioo* as justify here (and in some other verses), then we must understand that justify is sometimes used in a very full sense that includes the declaration of righteousness, the dethroning of (and the setting free from) sin, Satan, and spiritual death; the impartation of spiritual life, and the making righteous (the impartation of God's righteousness). An understanding of this much fuller sense of justify will help us guard against the all-too-common misunderstanding of the gospel. Justification comes by grace through faith (based on the atoning work of the Lord Jesus Christ). This is true whether justification is understood in a narrow sense or the much fuller sense.

On the basis of the atoning death of the Lord Jesus Christ, God the Father (the ultimate Judge) declares righteous those who submit to the gospel in faith. When God declares us righteous, He is, at the same time, declaring the defeat (and overthrow) of sin, Satan, and spiritual death. These enemies gained their authority over mankind through the sins of mankind, especially through the sin of Adam. Since the Lord Jesus Christ has borne our sins (with the guilt and penalties) in His atoning death, these enemies have lost their authority over those who partake of the benefits of His atoning death by faith. We are set free from sin, Satan, and spiritual death, and we are made alive and made righteous.

Let's go on to Romans 6:8. **Now if we have died with Christ** [As we have discussed, we become united with the Lord Jesus Christ in His death and His burial when we become Christians (see verses 2, 3, 4, 5, 6, and 7).], **we believe that we shall also live with Him.** We are united with the Lord Jesus Christ in His death, in His burial, in His resurrection, and in His present life. We live as born-again Christians, and we are called, and enabled, to walk in the righteousness and holiness of God. What a glorious reality! We are in Christ, and He is in us, and the infinite Spirit of God dwells in us, the Spirit of life, the Spirit of righteousness and holiness.

Romans 6:9. **knowing that Christ, having been raised from the dead, is never to die again; death no longer is master over Him.** We can all readily agree with what the apostle Paul says about the Lord Jesus Christ here, **knowing that Christ, having been raised from the dead, is never to die again, death no longer is master over Him.** It is important to see that the apostle said what he did about the Lord Jesus Christ in

53

this verse and the next verse (verse 10), with a view of applying these glorious truths to us believers in verse 11.

Romans 6:10, 11. **For the death that He died, He died to sin once for all; but the life that He lives, He lives to God. (11) Even so consider [or, reckon] yourselves to be dead to sin, but alive to God in Christ Jesus.** We are called to consider, or reckon, ourselves to be dead to sin (which includes our living with the victory over all sin) and alive to God (living for Him in His righteousness and holiness). What a blessing! But these things don't just happen automatically because we become Christians. We must hear the gospel and understand the gospel in our hearts, and we must appropriate these things on a continuous basis, by grace through faith, in accordance with the gospel of new-covenant salvation. God is glorified when we appropriate His full salvation by faith. On the other hand, He is robbed of glory to the extent we walk in the flesh and sin.

I'll read what I said under Romans 6:11 on page 100 of my book. Romans 6:11 strongly confirms that the apostle has been saying (in Rom. 6:1-10) that Christians are to "be dead to sin, but alive to God in Christ Jesus" from the time of conversion. That is the ideal! This verse also confirms that the apostle did not teach that the victory over sin is automatic. If we don't understand this aspect of gospel truth (our faith must be based on what the Word of God actually says), and if we don't walk by faith, we will still, to some extent, serve the old master of sin, by sinning. We must walk by faith and by the Holy Spirit on a continuous basis.

Remember what the apostle Paul said in Galatians 5:16, "But I say, walk by the Spirit, and you [most certainly] will not carry out the desire of the flesh [the sinful desire of the flesh, of the old man that still wants to sin]." In other words, walk by the Holy Spirit all the time and you won't sin. The apostle never said that it would always be easy; we are still in the flesh in one sense (we will not totally leave the flesh/old man behind until after we are glorified), and we have an enemy and spiritual warfare, whether we like it, or not. The world, the flesh (the old man that wants to live in sin), and the devil and his demons are against us, but they are no match for God and His saving grace in Christ.

Romans 6:12. **Therefore do not let sin reign in your mortal body so that you obey its lusts.** We could yield to sin and obey the lusts of the flesh (of the old man), but that goes against what Christianity is all about. Romans chapter 6 (and many other passages) demonstrates that God has called us, and enabled us, and requires us to be dead to sin and alive to God and His righteousness. Note that Paul spoke of our "mortal" bodies here. As long as we live in these mortal bodies in this world, the all-too-real potential for us to walk in the flesh and to sin still exists, and we will sin if we do not appropriate God's sufficient grace by faith and walk by His Spirit on a continuous basis. (Walking by the Spirit includes walking in line with God's Word.) It will be different after we are glorified.

As we have discussed, it is important to see that our physical bodies are not the primary problem. The sin problem centers in the heart of man, not the physical body (see Mark 7:14-23, for example). Having faith in God, loving Him, and obeying Him are matters of the heart (of the inner man), as are unbelief and disobedience.

Romans 6:13. **and do not go on presenting the members of your body to sin** *as* **instruments of unrighteousness; but present yourselves to God as those alive from the dead, and your members** *as* **instruments of righteousness to God.** In the ideal case we would present ourselves to God once-for-all and completely when we become Christians. That is what we are called to do. We are **alive from the dead** through new-covenant salvation; spiritual death and sin have been dethroned; we have been born again through union with the Lord Jesus Christ and by the indwelling Holy Spirit.

Now we come to Romans 6:14, a verse of key importance. **For sin shall not be master over you** [[or, **have dominion over you.** THE FACT THAT SIN HAS BEEN DETHRONED THROUGH THE ALL-IMPORTANT ATONING DEATH OF THE LORD JESUS CHRIST AND HAS NO MORE LEGAL AUTHORITY OVER US IS THE DOMINANT THEME OF THESE ARTICLES. If we walk by faith and by the Holy Spirit on a continuous basis (which we are called to do), sin will not be able to manifest itself in our lives.]], **for you are not under law, but under grace** [the sufficient saving, sanctifying grace of God in Christ]. One very important point that the apostle makes here is that if all we had was the Mosaic Law and the old covenant, sin would still reign over us. The old covenant was from God, and it was good, but it was not given for the purpose of dethroning spiritual death and sin. The new covenant in the blood of the Lamb of God was required to dethrone spiritual death and sin.

I'll read Galatians 3:21, "Is the Law [the Mosaic Law] then contrary to the promises of God? [Paul is speaking of God's promises of new-covenant salvation in Christ Jesus] May it never be! For if a law had been given which was able to impart life, then righteousness would indeed have been based on law." But the Mosaic Law did not have the authority to overthrow spiritual death (or the bondage to sin that came with spiritual death), and the new birth was not available under the old covenant. Spiritual death and sin were overthrown by the atoning death of the Lord Jesus Christ. The new covenant has the authority to overthrow spiritual death and sin and to enable born-again believers to walk in the very righteousness of God, which is imputed and imparted to them.

I'll read what I said in my book under Romans 6:14, Christians are under grace. In Rom. 5:21 the apostle speaks of grace reigning through righteousness, supplanting the reign of sin. Where the grace of God in Christ is reigning, the righteousness of God is manifested in the hearts of lives of believers. God's grace has dethroned sin, and it makes believers righteous. His sanctifying power comes by grace as much as His forgiveness comes by grace. Everything that we receive is part of God's gift of salvation in Christ Jesus.

If we were under law [the Mosaic Law/the old covenant], we would still be under sin and spiritual death, as shown by Rom. 5:12-21; Romans chapter 7; and Rom. 8:3, for example. Romans chapter 7, which we will discuss verse-by-verse later, expands on the meaning of Rom. 6:14, powerfully demonstrating that the Mosaic Law did not solve the sin problem, but rather intensified the sin problem.

I hope you are hearing this as good news! This is very good news! God is after our transformation to righteousness and holiness; He is not out to condemn us; He is not trying to get rid of us, quite the contrary! He paid an infinite price in the sacrifice of His Son to save us from sin, from spiritual death, and from Satan and his demons. We must never give up and give in to doubt and say I can't do it. (That's what Israel did at Kadesh Barnea, for example; see Numbers chapters 13, 14.) By the sufficient grace of God in Christ we can change. We can change the way we think in our hearts and begin to think in line with God's Word, in faith, by His Spirit. Furthermore, God has promised to forgive us when we repent. God knows if we are making Him and His righteousness top priority in our hearts, which we must do.

Romans 6:15. **What then? Shall we sin because we are not under law but under grace? May it never be** [An emphatic negative]! This is like the question of verse 1, "What shall we say then? Are we to continue in sin that grace may increase [or, abound]?" As I pointed out when we discussed verse 1, Paul was accused of teaching "let us do evil that good may come" (see Rom. 3:8). Paul was always saying that it is grace, not Law; faith, not works; some misunderstood him, and many totally rejected what the apostle taught. The apostle strongly emphasized that it is only through faith in the new-covenant gospel that we can appropriate God's saving, sanctifying grace and live in His righteousness and holiness, keeping His moral law in our daily lives.

Rather than denying or minimizing the need for God's people to live according to His moral law, the apostle Paul was preaching the one message that has the power to dethrone sin, spiritual death, and Satan and to make His people righteous and holy. It is true, however, that the apostle Paul made it clear that Christians are not under the ceremonial laws of the Old Testament. (And it is clear that the old covenant, which was established on the Mosaic Law, has been set aside. But God's moral law has not been set aside, and it could not be set aside. The moral law derives from the very nature of God and gives His definition of what is right and what is wrong.) Things like the need to be circumcised, sacrificial offerings, and dietary laws of the Mosaic Law have been set aside in the new covenant. How could we need sin offerings, for example, after the one Sacrifice of the Lamb of God solved the sin problem forever.

I'm going to read a paragraph from page 101 of my book, The question of verse 15 ("Shall we sin because we are not under law but under grace?") is similar to the question of verse 1. Both questions are answered with an emphatic No! Verses 2-13 went on to show that, by God's definition, Christians are to be dead to sin and cannot continue in sin. In verses 16-23 (and especially in verse 16), the apostle goes on to show that if we present ourselves to sin (to obey sin), we are, by definition, slaves of sin and not slaves of God. In typical Biblical fashion, the apostle doesn't discuss the gray (in between) area of serving God part of the time and serving sin on an occasional basis. Paul consistently taught that we owe everything to God and we owe nothing to our former master of sin. This is good news! What God calls us to do, He enables us to do! No real Christian wants to continue in sin.

We know of course that Christians can sin; the epistles to the Corinthians, for example, demonstrate that point; many of the Corinthian Christians were quite fleshly, and they were born-again Christians, at least many of them were; but Paul made it quite clear that their sin was incompatible with Christianity, and he strongly exhorted them to repent and to submit to the righteousness and holiness of God (by grace through faith).

We will come back to Romans chapter 6 in the next article. Thank you Father for full salvation in the Lord Jesus Christ and by the Holy Spirit. We want to glorify you and be fully ready to stand before you!

Holiness and Victory Over Sin #6

Holy Father we ask you to open the eyes of our hearts. We want to fully understand the gospel and to fully live the gospel by your sufficient grace, for your glory and for our good. In Jesus' mighty name, Amen!

Before we turn back to Romans chapter 6, I would like to ask you a question, a very important question. Are we supposed to fear God? Are we, God's people, supposed to fear Him? Many Christians say we are not supposed to fear God. Let's see what the Bible has to say on this topic. I'll read several verses from the Old Testament and then from the New Testament. The Bible makes it very clear that we are supposed to fear God. In what way are we supposed to fear Him? The dominant idea is that we are supposed to be afraid to sin against Him. God hates sin! God is a good God; He is a loving God and a merciful God, but He also is a Judge, and He has promised that He is going to judge sin.

I'll read some verses, starting with Exodus 20:20 (I'll read from the NASB, 1995 edition. I frequently make comments in the middle of quotations using brackets [ ] or [[ ]].), **Moses said to the people, "Do not be afraid; for God has come in order to test you** [This was at Mt. Sinai, and the people were afraid when God spoke audibly, and other awesome things were happening too. The words that follow in Ex. 20:20 is what we are after.], **and in order that the fear of Him may remain with you, so that you may not sin."** That's clear, isn't it? Deuteronomy 5:29, **O that they had such a heart in them, that they would fear Me and keep all my commandments always, that it may be well with them and with their sons forever!** Deuteronomy 6:2, **so that you and your son and your grandson might fear the LORD** [Yahweh; the four capital letters show that the Hebrew has Yahweh.] **your God, to keep all His statutes and His commandments which I command you, all the days of your life, and that your days may be prolonged.** Proverbs 3:7b, **Fear the LORD and turn away from evil.** Proverbs 8:13, **The fear of the LORD is to hate evil....** Proverbs 16:6b, **And by the fear of the LORD one keeps away from evil.**

Now some verses from the New Testament. Jesus said in Matthew 10:28, **Do not fear those who kill the body but are unable to kill the soul; but rather fear Him who is able to destroy both soul and body in hell** [in Gehenna]. Luke 12:5, **But I will warn you whom to fear; fear the One who, after He has killed, has authority to cast into hell** [again, Gehenna]; **yes, I tell you, fear Him!** In 2 Corinthians 7:1, the apostle Paul said, **Therefore, having these promises, beloved, let us cleanse ourselves from all defilement of flesh and spirit, perfecting holiness in the fear of God.** And I'll quote one last verse, 1 Peter 1:17, **If you address as Father the One who impartially judges according to each one's work, conduct yourselves in fear during the time of your stay on earth.** We must be afraid to sin against God the Judge, the Righteous Judge. That is a good and healthy fear. The Bible talks a lot about God's love, but it talks just as much about His wrath against sin. Let's not try to see how far we can push His love by sinning against Him. Let's make it top priority, and then plus some, to learn His will and to do His will, by His grace, for His glory and for our good.

Let's go back to Romans chapter 6, which is a powerful chapter dealing with righteousness, holiness, and the victory over all sin. We stopped last time after commenting on verse 15. I'll read Romans 6:15 and make a few comments; then we'll go on to verse 16. **What then? Shall we sin because we are not under law but under grace? May it never be!** Anybody who would ask the apostle Paul a question like that, **shall we sin because we are not under law but under grace**, doesn't understand the apostle Paul or his gospel at all. (Paul informs us that he got his gospel from the Lord Jesus Christ.) The bottom line of Paul's gospel was to get us righteous and holy and keeping God's moral law from our hearts, by His saving grace in Christ. Shall we sin? God's grace is a sanctifying grace, and the more grace God has given us the more serious our sin is. **What then? Shall we sin because we are not under law but under grace? May it never be!**

Romans 6:16. **Do you not know that when you present yourselves to someone *as* slaves for obedience, you are slaves of the one whom you obey, either of sin resulting in death, or of obedience resulting in righteousness?** In other words, what kind of a question is that, **shall we sin because we are not under law but under grace?** If Christians present themselves to serve sin, they are turning from God and His righteousness and are turning back into sin and death. The apostle Paul included a strong warning here in verse 16, **when you present yourselves to someone *as* slaves for obedience, you are slaves of the one whom you obey, either of sin resulting in death** [If Christians turn from God and His righteousness and give themselves back to sin, they become unbelievers, and the result will be death, back into spiritual death, and headed for the second death of Revelation chapter 20.], **or of obedience resulting in righteousness.** If we obey God and are faithful to Him by His grace, we can have a clear conscience (which is a very precious thing) and the end result is righteousness, and if we are living in righteousness we are always fully ready to stand before God.

Forgiveness and right standing are an important part of the gospel, but the idea here is that we are righteous because we are obeying God through His saving grace in Christ Jesus. We are living in accordance with His moral law, by His grace, and for His glory. We are truly loving Him and doing things His way from our hearts. This is so important I want to supplement what I just said by reading from my book (*Holiness and Victory Over Sin*) on page 101. This will involve some repetition, but repetition is good if it helps us understand God's Word and helps establish His Word in our hearts and lives. I'm commenting on the words **either of sin resulting in death.** If Christians presented themselves as slaves to sin (to obey sin), the result would be death. They would be turning from God, righteousness, and life and turning to sin and death. The end result would be "eternal death," as Rom. 6:21, for example, shows. Here in Rom. 6:16 death probably includes spiritual death in its present form. In other words, those who turn from God and His life turn back into death. I don't mean to suggest that Christians immediately lose the life of God if they sin, but any sin is clearly a serious step in the wrong direction. Believers can become unbelievers. It's not worth anything to call ourselves believers. If we really have faith, we will make it a top priority to live it. Faith without works is dead. James said it and the apostle Paul would agree. Faith without works is not real faith. It is not saving faith. If we really believe the gospel; if we really have faith in the gospel, then we will make it top priority to live the gospel by God's grace.

Now we'll discuss the words **or of obedience resulting in righteousness** of verse 16. The obedience spoken of is obedience to God, or more specifically (based on Rom. 6:17), obedience to the Word of God, the gospel. When Christians obey God and the gospel (by His grace), the result is righteousness. Such persons are in the kingdom of life, and they are on the straight and narrow pathway that leads to the fullness of eternal life (see Rom. 5:21; 6:22, 23).

Romans 6:17. **But thanks be to God that though you were slaves of sin** [The apostle Paul teaches that we were all slaves of sin before we became Christians, Jews and Gentiles.]**, you became obedient from the heart** [Faith includes obedience. Faith is of the heart. If we really have faith in the gospel, we will obey the gospel.] **to that form of teaching to which you were committed.** Now I'll turn to the book and read what I said on verse 17, starting on page 101. First we'll discuss the words **you became obedient from the heart.** To walk in faith includes being obedient from the heart. Faith is of the heart (see, for example, Rom. 10:9, 10; Mark 11:23; 16:14; Acts 8:37; 16:14; and Heb. 10:22). The Scriptures speak of having faith in the gospel; they also speak of obeying, or not obeying, the gospel (see, for example, Rom. 10:16 KJV; Rom. 2:8; 15:18; 16:26; Acts 6:7; Gal. 5:7; 2 Thess. 1:8 with 2:10-12; and 1 Pet. 4:17). We must have faith in the gospel, and we must obey the gospel. To have faith in the gospel includes obeying the gospel. And if we are obeying the gospel it is by grace through faith.

The main point I want to make here is that faith in the gospel includes obedience to the gospel. I have found that many Christians don't know this. It is not enough to have correct doctrine (as important as that is) or to call ourselves believers and say that we have faith in the gospel; we must make it top priority to live the gospel. If we don't live the gospel, we don't really have faith in the gospel. And if we really have faith, we can live it by the power of the indwelling Holy Spirit. We receive the Holy Spirit through the atoning death of the Lord Jesus Christ. God gets all the glory for every aspect of our salvation. We don't get puffed up. If we really understand righteousness and holiness, we don't get puffed up because we know who is doing it. God paid an infinite price so we could live in His righteousness and holiness.

I'll quote a paragraph from what John MacArthur says under Rom. 6:17, 18 (I'm quoting from his commentary, *Romans 1-8*, published by Moody Press in 1991). "Faith and obedience are inescapably related. There is no saving faith in God apart from obedience to God, and there can be no godly obedience without godly faith. As the beautiful and popular hymn admonishes, 'Trust and obey, there's no other way.' Our Lord 'gave Himself for us,' Paul says, not only to save us from hell and take us to heaven but to 'redeem us from every lawless deed and purify for Himself a people for His own possession, zealous for good deeds.' (Titus 2:14)."

Now we'll briefly discuss the words **to that form of teaching** of Rom. 6:17. That **form of teaching** at least includes the gospel truth that Christians are to be dead to sin and alive to God and righteousness, by the grace of God, through faith.

Now we'll discuss the last words of Romans 6:17, **to which you were committed**. I prefer the translation of the NKJV, "But God be thanked that though you were slaves of sin, yet you obeyed from the heart that form of doctrine to which you were delivered." That form of doctrine to which you were delivered (Greek verb *paradidomi*). This translation, which fits the Greek verb *paradidomi* well, helps communicate the idea that Christians are, by definition, required to be faithful to their new Master. They have been delivered from the old master (sin) to the new Master (God and His righteousness); there is no neutral ground (see Rom. 6:17-23).

To be a slave of God and His righteousness is, in reality, liberty. We really have only two options. We either stay slaves of sin, or accept the new covenant on God's terms and become faithful to it and become slaves of God and His righteousness. There really is no legitimate place in between. If we are going to do it God's way, we must go all the way. We can not take half the gospel or 80 percent or 90 percent of the gospel. God didn't give us that option. And if we go all the way with God, we will be faithful to that form of teaching to which we were delivered over, which puts all the emphasis on living in the righteousness and holiness of God by His saving, sanctifying grace.

Romans 6:18. **and having been freed from sin** [We were slaves of sin, but now we have been set free from sin, as we have seen in many verses of Romans chapter 6. We have been set free from sin through the saving grace of God in Christ. We are united with Him in His death, His burial, His resurrection, and His present life.] **you became slaves of righteousness.** Now that's a good exchange. We were slaves of sin, now we are slaves of righteousness. A slave of righteousness lives in righteousness, doing the will of God, from the heart, by God's grace.

Romans 6:19. **I am speaking in human terms** [In other words, I am giving you this teaching and this exhortation about how you used to be slaves of sin, but now you have been set free, and now you are required and privileged to be slaves of God and His righteousness.] **because of the weakness of your flesh.** [[In your natural selves it is all too easy to sin, even though you are born-again Christians. That's why I am teaching and exhorting you, Paul says. Yes, you could sin, and it's easy to sin, but you must understand the gospel. Now the very Spirit of God dwells in you, and now you are called, enabled, and required to walk in the righteousness and holiness of God, being faithful to the terms of the new covenant.

If we walk by the flesh we will sin. That's why we must always walk by, in, and after the Holy Spirit. Remember Galatians 5:16, "But I say, walk by the Spirit, and you [most certainly] will not carry out the [sinful] desire of the flesh [of the old man]."]] **For just as you presented your members as slaves to impurity and to lawlessness** [back before you became born-again Christians, that is]**, resulting in *further* lawlessness** [The NASB has the word "further" in italics. I would skip that added word. If we are going to add words in italics, I would add words like the following, "resulting in *an abiding state of* lawlessness." Paul tells his readers that they were living in an abiding state of lawlessness in the years before they became born-again Christians.]**, so now present your members as slaves to righteousness.** [You used to be slaves of sin, but now that you are born-again Christians, present yourselves, including your bodies, as slaves to righteousness. Once-for-all, and completely, present yourselves as slaves to God and His righteousness, by His saving grace in Christ, by faith, in accordance with the terms of the new covenant.]**, resulting in**

sanctification. The NASB translates "sanctification" here. I would translate **holiness**, with the KJV, NKJV, and the NIV. And it would be reasonable to add a few words in italics here, **resulting in *an abiding state of* holiness.** You used to be slaves of sin, Paul says, "resulting in *an abiding state of* lawlessness." So, now that you are born-again Christians, present yourselves, including your bodies, as slaves to righteousness, **resulting in *an abiding state of* holiness.** Now you have the requirement, but also the extreme privilege, to live in an abiding state of holiness, set apart from sin for God and His righteousness and holiness.

Romans 6:20. **For when you were slaves of sin, you were free in regard to righteousness.** The other side of this truth is that now that we are born-again Christians, we are to be free in regard to sin. That's not overstated; that's what the apostle is saying throughout Romans chapter 6. This is very good news! This is what all true Christians want! No true Christian wants to sin at all! If we should sin we will be forgiven when we sincerely repent, but that's not the heartbeat of Christianity, sin get forgiven, sin get forgiven, sin get forgiven. The heartbeat of Christianity, like Romans chapter 6 and many other passages show, is that we can, and should, always walk in the righteousness of God by His grace and stop sinning. We must aim at the target of not sinning at all. Sin is not OK.

Romans 6:21. (I'm going to give a more literal translation here for a couple of words, in agreement with the notes in the margin of the NASB.) **Therefore what fruit were you then having from the things of which** [or, concerning which things] **you are now ashamed? For the outcome of those things is death.** The apostle Paul asks his readers to consider the fact that they, like evil trees, had formerly been producing sinful, evil fruit, fruit that would ultimately earn eternal death for them, complete, eternal separation from God and His divine order and goodness.

Romans 6:22. **But now having been freed from sin and enslaved to God** [[That's what new-covenant salvation is all about, being set free from slavery to sin and being enslaved to God and His righteousness. In that we have been set free from our former evil taskmaster of sin, we ought not serve sin anymore. We serve sin by sinning.]], **you have your fruit** [But now the fruit being produced is righteous and good fruit, unlike the fruit spoken of in verse 21.], **resulting in sanctification** [[As in verse 19, I would translate **resulting in holiness** (with the KJV, NKJV, and the NIV), or, better yet, **resulting in *an abiding state of* holiness.** As born-again Christians, we are called, enabled, and required to live in an abiding state of holiness. What a blessing! What a privilege!]], **and the outcome, eternal life.** We will be ready to stand before God at the end of this age, and we will inherit the fullness of eternal life, which includes being glorified and reigning with the Lord Jesus Christ forever. You can't get any better than that! The eternal life here is contrasted with the death, the eternal death, spoken of at the end of verse 21.

Romans 6:23. **For the wages of sin is death** [[For the wages of sin is death (eternal death and separation from God). You serve sin instead of God and righteousness, and when payday comes you will receive death. Sin (and the devil) promises all kinds of good things, but when payday comes, the wages of sin is death. Jesus said the devil is a liar.]], **but the free gift of God is eternal life in Christ Jesus our Lord.** Salvation is a free gift; it comes 100 percent by the grace of God in Christ. We cannot earn the gift, but we are required to appropriate the gift in its fullness by faith. God doesn't give us the option of receiving the grace of His forgiveness and rejecting His sanctifying grace, the grace that will transform us and enable us to walk in His righteousness and holiness, in union with the Lord Jesus Christ.

We are called to walk by faith on a continuous basis (faith in God and faith in His Word, especially the Word of the gospel of new-covenant salvation.), and we are called to walk by the Holy Spirit on a continuous basis. We are literally united with the Lord Jesus Christ, the Lamb of God, in His death, His burial, His resurrection, and His present life. We are called to work out our salvation with fear and trembling (Phil. 2:12) by His enabling grace (Phil. 2:13). God paid an infinite price to provide this salvation to us.

Now we have the great privilege to turn to ROMANS 8:1-17, another super-important passage that is packed with righteousness, holiness, and victory over sin, by grace, through faith, in the power of the Holy Spirit. First I'll read Romans 8:1. **There is therefore now no condemnation to those who are in Christ Jesus.** Why? Now there is no condemnation, because, as the apostle Paul is going to go on to tell us (and he has already told us much about these things earlier in this epistle), we have been saved from sin, Satan, and spiritual death; we have been forgiven,

AND SIN IS UNDER OUR FEET! Now there is nothing to condemn us. I'm going to turn to page 116 of my book, "Holiness and Victory Over Sin," and read much of what I said under Rom. 8:1. Sometimes I skip parts of what is written in the book for these articles and sometimes I add to what is written in the book. Formerly we were all under condemnation. As Rom. 5:12-7:25 (and many other passages) show, this condemnation included spiritual death and bondage to sin; "sin reigned in death" (Rom. 5:21). "Sin reigned in death." What an ugly picture! Ever since the rebellion and fall of Adam and Eve, mankind has been in spiritual death and in bondage to sin. But now there is no condemnation for those who are in Christ Jesus. The sin problem has been solved for believers, and we will be ready to stand before God on the day of judgment (see, for example, Rom. 2:7, 10; 5:9-11, 21; 6:22, 23; and 8:12-17). There certainly is nothing to condemn us now, or in the future, if we are forgiven and living in the righteousness and holiness of God.

As Rom. 8:2-17 show, the emphasis of Rom. 8:1 is on the fact that Christians have been set free from spiritual death and made alive (by the Spirit of life), and they have been set free from sin (their former master) and walk in the righteousness of God (being enabled by the indwelling Spirit of God).

Romans 8:2. **For the law** [or, you could translate **the governing principle.** It is clear that Paul isn't speaking of the Mosaic Law here.] **of the Spirit of life in Christ Jesus has set you free from the law** [or, **governing principle**] **of sin and death.** Before we became Christians, as Paul has made it quite clear, we were spiritually dead and we were slaves of sin. But now, in Christ, we have been set free from spiritual death and are born again, and we have been set free from slavery to sin and have been called, enabled, and required to walk in the righteousness and holiness of God. The Spirit of life, the Righteous, Holy Spirit, now dwells in us, which overthrows the law (or, governing principle) of sin and death and enables us to partake of the very life of God as His born-again children, and enables us to walk in the very righteousness of God, with sin under our feet.

Now I'm going to read part of what I said under Rom. 8:2 in my book, *Holiness and Victory Over Sin.* We are speaking of the heart of God's new covenant plan of salvation. I trust you can see the extreme importance of understanding God's new covenant in our hearts. We must understand God's covenant to adequately walk in line with His covenant. We must understand what He has given us, and we must understand and be committed to live in line with what He requires of us. First I'll read part of what I said under words **the law** [or **governing principle**] **of sin and of death.** Apart from Christ, all people are under the law (or, governing principle) of sin and of death. The apostle has dealt extensively with this truth in Romans chapters 1-7, and he will deal with it further in Rom. 8:3-14.

Now I'll read part of what I said regarding the words, **the law** (or **governing principle**) **of the Spirit of life in Christ Jesus has set you free from the law** (or **governing principle**) **of sin and of death.** Every true Christian is indwelled by the Holy Spirit (see, for example, Rom. 8:9-11). He is the Spirit of life, and His presence cancels spiritual death. His presence overpowers sin and enables Christians to walk in the righteousness and holiness of God, with the victory over all sin (see, for example, Rom. 8:3-14).

I'll comment briefly on verses 3 and 4. We're just about finished with this article, but we will come back to these super-important verses in the next article. **For what the Law could not do, weak as it was through the flesh.** What was it that the Law (the Mosaic Law, which was the foundation for the old covenant) could not do? It could not dethrone spiritual death or sin. It was not given for that purpose. God always planned to save believers through the new covenant. Man in the flesh, man in spiritual death, man without the indwelling Holy Spirit of life does not have the power to fully keep God's Law, so God could not solve the sin problem that way. But Romans 8:3 says, **For what the Law could not do, weak as it was through the flesh, God *did*, sending His own Son in the likeness of sinful flesh and *as an offering* for sin, He condemned sin in the flesh.** Through the atoning death of the Lord Jesus Christ, God dethroned sin, Satan, and spiritual death.

Then in Romans 8:4 the apostle shows that the bottom line of Christianity is that the sin problem really is solved and we are enabled to keep the requirement of God's moral law as we walk by the Holy Spirit. He says, **in order that the requirement of the Law might be fulfilled in us, who do not walk according to the flesh, but according to the Spirit** [the Holy Spirit]. As we walk by the Spirit of God, which we are required to do by covenant, we keep God's moral law and manifest His righteousness in our daily lives. It's time to stop. God bless you!

Holiness and Victory Over Sin #7

Holy Father, we humble our hearts before you. We want to understand your Word. We want to live in the center of your will through new-covenant salvation in the Lord Jesus Christ. We pray in His mighty, holy name! Amen!

We have the great privilege to turn back to Romans chapter 8. Last week we looked at verses 1-4, which are super-important verses, but we didn't finish discussing verses 3, 4. I'll read verses 1, 2 and comment briefly; then we'll go back to verses 3, 4. Romans 8:1, 2. **Therefore there is now no condemnation for those who are in Christ Jesus. (2) For the law [or the governing principle] of the Spirit of life in Christ Jesus has set you free from the law [or the governing principle] of sin and of death.** All true Christians are **in Christ Jesus**, and the **Spirit of life** dwells in us (Rom. 8:9). Having been born again by the Holy Spirit of life, we are no longer under the governing principle of sin and of death. We are no longer spiritually dead and in bondage to sin.

Romans 8:3. **For what the Law could not do** [[The Mosaic Law was the foundation for the old covenant. What was it that the Mosaic Law could not do? It could not set us free from spiritual death and bondage to sin. The Law did not have the authority or power to dethrone spiritual death or the bondage to sin that comes with spiritual death. The Law came from God, and it was good, but it was not given for the purpose of solving the sin problem. In fact, the apostle Paul made it quite clear that the Mosaic Law intensified the sin problem. But that could work for good too. For one thing, the Law has helped many people see that they need the promised new-covenant salvation in the Lord Jesus Christ.]], **weak as it was through the flesh** [Man in the flesh; man in spiritual death; man without the indwelling Holy Spirit of life doesn't have the ability to fully keep God's Law.], **God *did:* ** [How did He do it?], **sending His own Son in the likeness of sinful flesh and *as an offering* for sin** [or **concerning sin**], **He condemned sin in the flesh.** God the Father dethroned spiritual death and sin (and Satan and his demons) through the atoning death of the Lord Jesus Christ.

I'm going to turn to page 117 of my book, *Holiness and Victory Over Sin: Full Salvation Through the Atoning Death of the Lord Jesus Christ*, and read part of what I said under this verse (Rom. 8:3). I take the liberty to modify what I said in the book for these articles. I know that I do some repetition, but I believe this is worthy of repetition. We need to get this! We need to live this, by grace through faith.

For what the Law could not do, weak as it was through the flesh. Apart from Christ, all men are in the flesh (see, for example, Rom. 7:5, 14; 8:5-9; John 3:6); they are not indwelled by the Spirit of life; they are under "the law [or, governing principle] of sin and of death" (Rom. 8:2). As we have discussed, man in the flesh does not have the power to fully keep the Mosaic Law. See Romans chapter 7, for example. In Romans chapter 7 the apostle Paul powerfully demonstrates that we need new-covenant salvation, since the Mosaic Law did not solve the sin problem, but rather intensified the sin problem. You could love the Law; you could memorize the Law, but Romans 7 powerfully demonstrates that man in the flesh cannot fully keep God's Law. We cannot be saved by the Law. We must be saved by the Lord Jesus Christ, including the believers from Old Testament days.

Galatians 3:21 says, "Is the Law [the Mosaic Law] then contrary to the promises of God? May it never be! [[Paul was speaking of "the promises" of new-covenant salvation in Christ Jesus. Of course the Mosaic Law and God's promises of new-covenant salvation were not contrary to one another. They both came from God. The Mosaic Law was a temporary covenant that helped prepare the way for new-covenant salvation. The New Testament makes it quite clear that God always planned to sacrifice His Son to save us, and to overthrow Satan's rebellion.]] For if a law had been given which was able to impart life, then RIGHTEOUSNESS [my emphasis] would indeed have been based on law." It is very important for us to understand that there was no law (including the Mosaic Law) that was able to impart life and overthrow the spiritual death that has been reigning over mankind since the rebellion and fall of Adam and Eve. The atoning death of the Lord Jesus Christ, however, does have the authority and power to overthrow spiritual death and impart spiritual life to all believers. Since the Mosaic Law could not bring life, it could not bring

God's "RIGHTEOUSNESS." The Righteous Holy Spirit of life, however, who comes to dwell in believers through the atoning death of the Lord Jesus Christ, enables us to live in the righteousness of God. God imputes and imparts His righteousness to us through new-covenant salvation.

Romans 8:3 says that **God condemned sin in the flesh** through the Sacrifice of His Son. Sin (which had brought condemnation to mankind and had reigned over mankind since the fall [see Romans 8:1, 2 and Romans chapter 5, for example]) was condemned by God. He condemned sin, and He dethroned the sin (and the spiritual death) that had reigned over mankind, mankind that had been in the flesh since the fall. Romans 8:9, which we will discuss later, confirms that true Christians are not in the flesh, but in the Spirit (the Holy Spirit), and that if the Spirit of God does not dwell in us, we are not true Christians. True Christians are in the (Holy) Spirit, and we are enabled, and required, to walk by the Holy Spirit. We cannot walk by the Spirit until we are born again. As Galatians 5:16 shows, if we walk by the Holy Spirit on a continuous basis, which we are called, and enabled, to do, we will not sin. That sounds good, doesn't it? That is the Christian ideal, and we must aim at that target.

For what the Law could not do, weak as it was through the flesh, God *did:* sending His own Son in the likeness of sinful flesh and *as an offering for sin* [or, concerning sin], He condemned sin in the flesh. (Romans 8:3) God the Father sent His Son (His Son who had always been with Him in glory) into the world (see, for example, John 1:1-18; 3:16, 17. 17:3-5). He became a man, born of the virgin Mary. He came "in the likeness of sinful flesh" (see, for example, Rom. 1:3; Phil. 2:6-8; Heb. 2:14-18). But He was not just a man. He never ceased being the eternal Son of God. He wasn't spiritually dead, and He never sinned. What a worthy Lamb! What a worthy Savior!

He was "the Lamb of God who takes away the sin of the world" (John 1:29). He bore our sin with the guilt (so we could be forgiven) and with the penalties, including the penalties of spiritual death and bondage to sin, so we could get out from under those penalties and live in the righteousness and holiness of God (see, for example, Isaiah chapter 53; Rom. 3:25; 4:25; 5:6-11). In His atoning death, the Lord Jesus Christ condemned and dethroned sin, Satan, and death (see, for example, Rom. 5:14-6:23; John 12:31-33; Col. 2:11-15; Heb. 2:14-18; 7:11-10:30; 1 Pet. 2:24-25).

Romans 8:4. **so that the requirement of the Law might be fulfilled in us, who do not walk according to the flesh but according to the Spirit** [the Holy Spirit]. Since Christians have been set free from the law [or, the governing principle] of sin and of death by the indwelling Spirit of life (see Rom. 8:2), we are enabled to fulfill **the requirement of the Law** [the Mosaic Law] in our daily lives. In other words, we are enabled to live righteous and holy lives, in accordance with the will of God, by the grace of God in Christ Jesus. This is the bottom line emphasis of Christianity. Our living in the righteousness of God is not an optional matter. We are called, enabled, and required to live in the righteousness of God, doing His will from the heart. This is good news!

In some ways Christians are not under the Mosaic Law (see, for example, Rom. 6:14; 7:1-6; Gal. 5:18); however, as we walk **according to the Spirit** (the Holy Spirit)], **the requirement of the Law** is fulfilled in us (see, for example, Jer. 31:31-34 with Heb. 8:8-12; Ezek. 36:25-27; Rom. 2:26-29). Passages like Gal. 5:13-25 and Rom. 8:12-14 make it very clear that Christians do not just automatically walk "according to [or, by] the [Holy] Spirit," but they also show that we are called, enabled, and required to walk by the Spirit all the time, by faith. Both of these passages show that as we walk by the Spirit, we walk in the righteousness of God (keeping the requirements of His moral law) with the victory over all sin. The New Testament makes it clear that Christians are not required to keep the ceremonial laws of the Old Testament, like circumcision (see, for example, Rom. 2:26-29; Gal. 5:1-12; Col. 2:8-23).

Jeremiah 31:31-34; Ezek. 36:25-27; and Rom. 2:26-29 are three important cross-references that speak of new-covenant believers keeping the requirements of God's Law in their daily lives. This is quite important! I'll take the time to read and briefly discuss these passages. I'll read Jeremiah 31:31-34 and make several comments, " 'Behold, days are coming' declares the LORD [Yahweh], 'when I will make a new covenant with the house of Israel and with the house of Judah [Now here's some good news, the New Testament shows that Gentiles are also invited to be saved through the new covenant in the blood of Christ.], (32) not like the covenant which I made with their fathers in the day that I took them by the hand to bring them out of the land of Egypt [in the days of Moses], My covenant which they broke, although I was a husband to them,' declares the LORD. [That was the problem. God gave Israel the old covenant through Moses, but (as the Old Testament shows) they rather consistently broke the covenant and did not fully keep His commandments.] (33) [This verse is of key importance!] 'But this is the covenant which I will make with the house of Israel after those days,' declares the LORD [Yahweh], 'I will put My law within them and on their heart I will write it; and I will be their God, and they shall be My people. [[Instead of handing Israel the Law at Mt. Sinai and telling the people to take the Law into their hearts and to live by its commandments, and then watching them break the commandments generation after generation; in the new covenant God changes our hearts and puts His Law on our hearts, and we end up keeping His Law (His moral law) in our daily lives, by the saving grace of God in Christ, by faith. "I WILL PUT MY LAW WITHIN THEM AND ON THEIR HEART I WILL WRITE IT [my emphasis]; and I will be their God and they shall be My people [My obedient people]."]] (34) They will not teach again, each man his neighbor and each man his brother, saying, "Know the LORD," for they will all know Me, from the least of them to the greatest of them,' declares the LORD, 'for I will forgive their iniquity, and their sin I will remember no more.' " Yes, when God solves the sin problem, which includes forgiving His people and making them righteous and holy through new-covenant salvation, all of His born-again children will know Him. It is significant that the book of Hebrews interprets Jer. 31:31-34 the way I have explained these verses (see Hebrews chapters 8 and 10; I discussed the relevant verses from the book of Hebrews in my book *Holiness and Victory Over Sin*).

Now I'll read Ezekiel 36:25-27 and make several comments. This is another very important prophecy dealing with new-covenant salvation. "Then I will sprinkle clean water on you, and you will be clean; I will cleanse you from all your filthiness and from all your idols. (26) Moreover, I will give you a new heart and put a new spirit within you; and I will remove the heart of stone from your flesh and give you a heart of flesh. (27) [This verse is of key importance for our present purposes. I am showing, for one primary thing, that the Bible teaches that Christians are enabled (and required) to keep God's Law (His moral law) in their daily lives.] I WILL PUT MY SPIRIT WITHIN YOU AND CAUSE YOU TO WALK IN MY STATUTES, AND YOU WILL BE CAREFUL TO OBSERVE MY ORDINANCES [my emphasis]." The indwelling Holy Spirit enables us to walk in the righteousness and holiness of God, doing His will (keeping His commandments) from the heart. We are called, enabled, and required to walk by the Holy Spirit on a continuous basis. The requirement of God's Law is fulfilled in us (as Rom. 8:4 says) as we walk by the Holy Spirit. We receive the Holy Spirit through the atoning death of the Lord Jesus Christ.

God's moral law, which gives His definition of righteousness, cannot change. It comes from His nature, from who He is. God hates sin, and He loves righteousness. He paid an infinite price in the Sacrifice of His Son to save us from spiritual death and bondage to sin. The ceremonial laws of the Old Testament were temporary; they could be set aside, and they have been set aside in the new covenant.

The third cross-reference I mentioned that demonstrates that Christians are called, and enabled, to keep the requirements of God's Law in their daily lives (which means the same thing as walking in His righteousness and holiness) is Romans 2:26-29. This is good news, very good news! No true Christian wants to sin against God. Before I read these verses from Romans chapter 2 and make a few comments, I should mention that in this context the apostle Paul was showing why the sons of Israel (along with the Gentiles) needed new-covenant salvation. His primary point was that no one can fully keep God's Law until they receive the Holy Spirit through new-covenant salvation in the Lord Jesus Christ. In the first three chapters of Romans, the apostle demonstrated that all people (all Jews and all Gentiles) need to be saved through the Lord Jesus Christ, because all are in bondage to sin.

I'll read Romans 3:9, which is an important summarizing verse, "What then? Are we better than they? Not at all for we have already charged that both Jews and Greeks [meaning Gentiles] are all under sin." "We have already charged [meaning earlier in this epistle to the Romans] that both Jews and Greeks are all under sin." All mankind is in spiritual death and under sin; that is why all mankind needs to submit to the Lord Jesus Christ and His salvation. We have to see why we need the Savior before we will submit to Him and His salvation in faith. We must see that sin is the primary problem, and that Jesus Christ is God's only solution to the sin problem, and that the day of judgment is coming.

Romans 2:26. "SO IF THE UNCIRCUMCISED MAN KEEPS THE REQUIREMENTS OF THE LAW [my emphasis], will not his uncircumcision be regarded as circumcision?" Physical circumcision was part of the ceremonial law of the Old Testament. But who is this uncircumcised man who keeps the requirements of the Law? Paul makes it very clear that all people (all Jews and all Gentiles) are under sin. That is, all people apart from those who are united with the Lord Jesus Christ through new-covenant salvation are under sin. Those who have been born again and are living for God, walking in His righteousness and holiness by His grace through faith, are not under sin. That's what new-covenant salvation is all about!

The uncircumcised man who keeps the requirements of the Law in his daily life is a Gentile Christian. Like Jer. 31:33 prophesied, the Law has been written on our hearts. Like Ezek. 36:27 prophesied, God puts His Spirit within us and causes us to walk in His commandments. Like Rom. 8:4 says, "SO THAT THE REQUIREMENT OF THE LAW MIGHT BE FULFILLED IN US [my emphasis], who do not walk according to the flesh but according to the Spirit [the Holy Spirit]." We cannot walk by the Spirit until we have been born again by the Spirit through the Lord Jesus Christ, and we are required to walk by the Spirit on a continuous basis.

I should mention that the apostle spoke of "the uncircumcised man" keeping the requirements of the Law here in verse 26 because he was interacting with the circumcised sons of Israel in this context, trying to help them see that they needed new-covenant salvation too. It would also be true that Christians from a Jewish background are enabled to keep the requirements of the Law in their daily lives.

Romans 2:27. "And he who is physically uncircumcised, if he keeps the law [[The Greek doesn't have a word for "if" here. It would be better to translate, "And he who is physically uncircumcised, KEEPING THE LAW [my emphasis]," or the equivalent. The NIV, for example, has, "The one who is not circumcised physically AND YET OBEYS THE LAW [my emphasis]."]] will he not judge you who though having the letter *of the Law* and circumcision are a transgressor of the Law?" The uncircumcised man who is keeping the requirements of God's moral law, by the saving grace of God in Christ, is the one who will be ready to stand before God on the day of judgment. He will make the circumcised transgressor of the Law look bad by comparison.

Romans 2:28. "For he is not a Jew who is one outwardly, nor is circumcision that which is outward in the flesh." As Paul is going to show

74

in the next verse, if we want to be part of God's true Israel, we must have our hearts circumcised by the Holy Spirit. And as the apostle shows repeatedly throughout his epistles, the only way we can receive the life-giving, sanctifying Spirit of God is through the Lord Jesus Christ and His atoning death.

Romans 2:29, "But he is a Jew who is one inwardly; and circumcision is that which is of the heart, by the Spirit [the Holy Spirit], not by the letter [not by the letter of the Mosaic Law]; and his praise is not from men, but from God." The word "Jew" comes from "Judah" and means "praise." The ones who will be ready to stand before God will be the ones who have been transformed by the saving grace of God in Christ and have lived according to His moral law in His righteousness and holiness.

The Holy Spirit is the only one who can transform a sinner into a saint. Of course, as Jeremiah 31:34, for example, shows, forgiveness is an important part of God's salvation too, but we must put the emphasis on our thinking and living as He requires us to live, by His grace through faith. We must (we have the privilege to) keep the requirement of God's moral Law in our daily lives. I should mention that all the believers from Old Testament days will be saved, but not because they fully kept God's Law. They will be saved through the grace of God in the Lord Jesus Christ.

I'll read another verse from the writings of the apostle Paul that emphasizes our obligation to keep God's moral law, to keep His commandments, 1 Corinthians 7:19, "Circumcision is nothing, and uncircumcision is nothing [As far as the new covenant is concerned, such things are totally irrelevant.], BUT *WHAT MATTERS IS* THE KEEPING OF THE COMMANDMENTS OF GOD [my emphasis]." God hates sin. He paid an infinite price so we could be set free from slavery to sin and live in His righteousness and holiness, keeping His commandments. We must make this top priority. God's grace is sufficient, but it isn't always easy. There is intense warfare engaged against us by the world, the flesh (the old man who wants to continue living in sin), and the devil and his multitudinous hosts, but nothing can keep us from doing God's will.

What God calls us to do; He enables us to do. And when we become Christians, we sign a contract (so to speak) agreeing to put God and His righteousness first place in our hearts and lives, and to walk by faith and walk by His Spirit on a continuous basis. We cannot change the terms of the new covenant. We must submit to the covenant God has given us. And we certainly need to make it a top priority to learn the terms of the new covenant, what He has provided for us, and what He requires of us. This will work for the glory of God and for our good.

I'll read Romans 8:1-4 again, **Therefore there is now no condemnation for those who are in Christ Jesus. (2) For the law [or the governing principle] of the Spirit of life [the Holy Spirit of life] in Christ Jesus has set you free from the law [or the governing principle] of sin and of death. (3) For what the Law could not do, weak as it was through the flesh, God *did:* sending His own Son in the likeness of sinful flesh and *as an offering* for sin [or concerning sin], He condemned sin in the flesh, (4) so that the requirement of the Law might be fulfilled in us, who do not walk according to the flesh but according to the Spirit.**

Many Christians understand verse 4 to only say that the Lord Jesus Christ perfectly fulfilled the Law and that His righteousness is put down to our account in a legal sense. That interpretation falls very far short of what the apostle Paul teaches in Romans chapters 1-8 (including Rom. 2:26-29) and what many other passages throughout the New Testament teach (including 1 Cor. 7:19). So too, it falls very far short of fulfilling what was prophesied in passages like the ones we looked at in the books of Jeremiah and Ezekiel (and there are many more similar prophecies in the Old Testament). The apostle Paul meant that the requirement of the Law is actually fulfilled in Christians as they walk by the Holy Spirit. This is confirmed, for example, by Gal. 5:16-25 and Romans chapter 6, passages we have discussed already, and it is confirmed by the verses that follow in Romans chapter 8, which we will discuss next.

But first I'll read Galatians 5:16, 24, "But I say walk by the Spirit, and you [most certainly] will not carry out the desire of the flesh [the sinful desire of the flesh (of the old man)]." And Galatians 5:24, "Now those who belong to Christ Jesus have crucified the flesh with its passions and desires [with its sinful passions and desires]." It must be understood, of course, that we crucify the flesh through the power of the atoning blood of the Lord Jesus Christ and by the power of the indwelling Holy Spirit (by grace), as we walk by faith and by the Spirit on a continuous basis, all in accordance with the gospel of new-covenant salvation.

76

Romans 8:5. **For those who are according to the flesh** [Who is Paul talking about? All the people who have *not* become born-again Christians. If the Holy Spirit does not dwell in us through the Lord Jesus Christ, we are, by definition, in the flesh (see Rom. 7:5 and 8:9, for example).] **set their minds on the things of the flesh** [[I somewhat prefer the translation **think the ways of the flesh**, instead of "set their minds on the things of the flesh." Thinking the ways of the flesh includes having wrong ideas about God and salvation; wrong attitudes; wrong motives; wrong priorities; and wrong desires. If we are in the flesh, we will think the sinful ways of the flesh, and we will sin. It is important to understand that our most important thinking takes place in our hearts, not in our heads. For us to think right, we need the Word of God and the Spirit of God. He enables us to think in line with God's Word, and He enables us to live right, in the righteousness and holiness of God. For one thing, the Holy Spirit enables us to resist every wrong thought and desire.

If we are going to include the word "mind(s)" in the translation, we must understand that the word "mind" in the Bible is not at all limited to the head. As I mentioned, our primary thinking takes place in our hearts (in our inner man), even as faith is of the heart.]], **but those who are according to the Spirit, the things of the Spirit.** That is, those who are according to the Holy Spirit (which means all born-again Christians) think the ways of the Holy Spirit. As I mentioned, the Holy Spirit enables us to think right (in agreement with God's Word), which includes our having right ideas about God and salvation, right attitudes, right motives, right priorities, and our having the desire to please God in our hearts.

Paul is assuming here that Christians who are indwelled by the Spirit of God will walk by the Spirit of God. However, as we have discussed, a walk by the Spirit does not come automatically. We must walk by, and after, the Spirit by faith on a continuous basis, or the flesh (the old man) will manifest itself in sin. In Rom. 8:12-14 the apostle warns born-again Christians that they are obligated to always walk by the Spirit. In verse 14 he says that it is only those who are being led by the Spirit of God who are true sons of God.

Romans 8:6. **For the mind set on the flesh is death, but the mind set on the Spirit is life and peace.** I somewhat prefer the translation, **For the way of thinking of the flesh is death, but the way of thinking of**

the Spirit is life and peace. The way of thinking of the flesh is death (ultimately the second death, the lake of fire), because the way of thinking of the flesh yields sin, and sin yields death. But the Holy Spirit enables us to think right, and to live in the righteousness and holiness of God, which enables us to maintain a life-flowing relationship with Him and peace (peace with God, peace in the inner man; peace with other Christians; etc.). Those who think right and live right by the saving grace of God in Christ by faith will inherit the fullness of eternal life at the end of this age.

We'll come back to these important verses in the next article. God bless you!

Holiness and Victory Over Sin #8

Holy Father, we humble our hearts before you. We want to understand your plan of salvation. We want to live in line with your plan of salvation, through the infinitely powerful Holy Spirit who dwells within us as born-again Christians. We pray in the mighty, holy name of Jesus. Amen!

We have the great privilege to turn back to Romans chapter 8. These verses are quite important to help us understand righteousness, holiness, and the victory over sin. I know that every sincere born-again Christian wants to live in the will of God, with the victory over all sin. What I am sharing is good news, very good news!

Romans 8:5. **For those who are according to the flesh set their minds on the things of the flesh** [[**Those who are according to the flesh** are the ones who have not been born again through the Lord Jesus Christ. I'll read Romans 8:9, "However, you are not in the flesh but in the Spirit, if indeed the Spirit of God dwells in you. But if anyone does not have the Spirit of Christ [the Holy Spirit], he does not belong to Him." I somewhat prefer the translation, **For those who are according to the flesh think the ways of the flesh.** Thinking the ways of the flesh includes having wrong ideas about God and salvation; wrong attitudes; wrong motives; wrong priorities; and wrong desires. "Those who are according to the flesh think the ways of the flesh," and the end result is sin, and more sin.]], **but those who are according to the Spirit** [the Holy Spirit], **the things of the Spirit** [or, **the ways of the Spirit**]. That is, those who are indwelled by the Holy Spirit are enabled (and required) to think the ways of the Spirit. As we submit to the Word of God and walk by the Spirit of God, we will think right, and we will live in accordance with God's will, in His righteousness and holiness.

It is important for us to understand that our most important thinking takes place in our heart (in the inner man), not in our head. For one thing, *faith is of the heart*. Those who think the ways of the flesh will live in sin, but those who think the ways of the Holy Spirit will live in the righteousness of God. Born-again Christians do not automatically think the ways of the Holy Spirit or walk by the Holy Spirit, but we are enabled, and required, and privileged, to think by the Spirit and walk by the Spirit on a continuous basis by grace through faith.

Romans 8:6. **For the mind set on the flesh is death** [[or **For the way of the thinking of the flesh is death.** The way of thinking of the flesh brings sin, and sin brings death, ultimately the second death, the lake of fire, eternal separation from God and everything that is good.]], **but the mind set on the Spirit** [or **the way of thinking of the Spirit**] **is life and peace.** When we think the ways of the Holy Spirit, which is part of our walking by the Holy Spirit, we walk in the righteousness of God, which enables us to maintain a life-flowing relationship with Him, and ultimately we will inherit the fullness of eternal life and the glory of heaven. It also enables us to have peace with God. As the next verse shows, we certainly cannot have peace with God while we are hostile toward Him and living in rebellion against Him and His moral law, against His divine order.

Romans 8:7. **because the mind set on the flesh** [or **the way of thinking of the flesh**] **is hostile toward God** [Why?]; **for it does not subject itself to the law of God, for it is not even able** *to do so*. Man in the flesh, man in spiritual death is hostile toward God and His laws. As Romans chapter 6, for example, shows, man in the flesh is a slave of sin. We cannot have peace with God while we are rebelling against Him and His divine order. The apostle Paul frequently makes the point that man in the flesh, man in spiritual death, does not have the ability to fully keep God's Law. But Paul also had the good news to proclaim, that God has solved the spiritual death, bondage to sin problem in the Sacrifice of His Son.

Born-again Christians are no longer under the authority of spiritual death, sin, or Satan and his demons. We are forgiven through the atoning death of the Lord Jesus Christ, and we are indwelled by the infinite Spirit of God, who imparts God's life, righteousness, and holiness to us, as we walk by the Spirit through faith. It is very obvious that Christians must not think the ways of the flesh any longer; we are enabled, and required, to think by the Holy Spirit and to live by the Holy Spirit on a continuous basis.

Romans 8:8. **and those who are in the flesh cannot please God.** They cannot please God because they are hostile toward Him, as verse 7 says. They are living in rebellion against Him and His commandments.

Romans 8:9. **However, you are not in the flesh but in the Spirit if indeed the Spirit of God dwells in you** [The apostle Paul is speaking of the Holy Spirit dwelling in Christians from the time they become born-again Christians.]. **But if anyone does not have the Spirit of Christ** [the Holy Spirit], **he does not belong to Him.** That is, he does not belong to the Lord Jesus Christ, and he is not a true Christian. To confirm that the **Spirit of Christ** is the Holy Spirit, see Acts 16:7; Gal. 4:6; Phil. 1:19; and 1 Pet. 1:11.

Romans 8:10. This verse is a little difficult, but the overall meaning is clear enough, and I believe I understand the details too. We'll get into the details here. I'll read the verse before we get into the details of the verse, **If Christ is in you, though the body is dead because of sin, yet the spirit is alive** [or better, **the Spirit is life**] **because of righteousness.** Again, **If Christ is in you** [Many verses show that Christ is in all born-again Christians, and we are in Him (by the Holy Spirit)], **though the body is dead** [[(This double bracket continues for three paragraphs.) It is very clear that the apostle does not mean that our physical body is dead. The bottom line of what Paul means here is that it is still all-too-easy for born-again Christians to walk in the flesh and to sin. It is all-too-easy for born-again Christians to walk after the flesh and do the sinful works of the flesh. But Paul warned Christians that they must not do the sinful works of the flesh in Gal. 5:19-21. And in Rom. 8:13 he warned Christians that they must not do the sinful works of the body, which means the same thing as doing the sinful works of the flesh.

Born-again Christians still have the all-to-real potential to walk by the flesh because our salvation isn't complete yet. And a continuous walk by the Holy Spirit doesn't come automatically when we become born-again Christians. In Rom. 8:23, for example, the apostle speaks of the fact that our bodies haven't been redeemed yet. In other words, we haven't been glorified yet. In Rom. 8:11 Paul speaks of the fact that God will give life to our mortal bodies at the end of this age. Now we have mortal bodies, bodies that will die if the Lord doesn't come first, bodies that haven't been fully redeemed yet; but after we have been glorified, we won't have mortal bodies. After we are glorified, the old man will be annihilated, and we won't have the all-too-real potential to walk after the flesh and to sin. It is important to understand though that the sin problem does not center in the physical body. As Jesus taught us in Mark chapter 7, for example, sin is of the heart. But the body can lend itself to sin, and demons can work through the physical body.

We Christians must understand that the flesh (the old man) still wants to manifest itself in sin, and it has the help of the world and the demons. We must be strongly motivated to always walk by the Holy Spirit by faith, so we won't sin. As I have mentioned, when we become Christians we sign a contract (so to speak), agreeing (for one thing) to always walk by the Holy Spirit. Isn't that what we want? Isn't it good news to know that we can always walk by the Holy Spirit and not sin? The Holy Spirit always enables us to walk in line with the Word of God.]] **because of sin** [[What does Paul mean by the words, "because of sin." He means that mankind died spiritually and is "in the flesh" because of the **sin** of Adam. See Romans chapter 5, where Paul discussed the fact that death (both spiritual death and physical death) and bondage to sin came upon mankind because of the sin of Adam. I'll read a key verse from Romans chapter 5 as we continue to demonstrate this important point. We have been born again, but (as I mentioned) we aren't fully redeemed yet (cf. Eph. 4:30; Rom. 8:23), and we still have the all-too-real potential to walk in the flesh and to sin, even though sinning goes against what Christianity is all about.]], **yet the spirit is alive because of righteousness.** I don't agree with the translation "the spirit is alive." I believe the *King James Version* and the *New King James Version* translate the Greek in the sense intended by the apostle Paul and the One who sent him. They translate **the Spirit is life**, (the capital "S" refers to the Holy Spirit).

81

Now we'll discuss the meaning of the words **yet the Spirit** [the Holy Spirit] **is life because of righteousness.** Earlier in this verse the apostle said, "If Christ is in you, though the body is dead because of sin [because of Adam's sin]," now he says **yet the Spirit is life because of righteousness.** These last words mean that we Christians have the Spirit of life dwelling in us (and power over sin) because of the **righteousness** of the Lord Jesus Christ. HIS RIGHTEOUSNESS IS CONTRASTED WITH THE SIN OF ADAM. His righteousness here refers to His atoning death, where He dethroned spiritual death and sin and earned the right for us to receive the Holy Spirit of life and to walk with the victory over all sin.

I'll read Romans 5:18 where the apostle Paul speaks of the one transgression of Adam that resulted in the spiritual death and bondage to sin of mankind, and of the one act of righteousness of the Lord Jesus Christ (the last Adam) that set us free from spiritual death and bondage to sin, and eventually takes us to eternal glory, to a place very much higher than what Adam had before the fall. "So then as through one transgression there resulted condemnation to all men [a condemnation that included spiritual death and bondage to sin], even so through one act of righteousness there resulted justification of life to all men." We believers have the justification of life. Spiritual death has been dethroned, and we participate in the very life of God as born-again Christians through the Holy Spirit who dwells in us. And the Righteous, Holy Spirit enables us to walk in the very righteousness and holiness of God, with the victory over all sin, even though we still have the all-too-real potential to walk after the flesh (the old man) and to sin.

I'll read Romans 8:10 one more time, **If Christ is in you, though the body is dead because of sin, yet the Spirit is life because of righteousness.** The Spirit is life, but we must walk by the Righteous, Holy Spirit of life on a continuous basis (by faith) to appropriate that life and the righteousness and holiness of God.

Romans 8:11. **But** [or, And] **if the Spirit of Him who raised Jesus from the dead dwells in you** ["Him who raised Jesus from the dead" is God the Father. "The Spirit" is the Holy Spirit.]**, He who raised Christ Jesus from the dead will also give life to your mortal bodies through His Spirit who dwells in you.** God the Father will give life to our mortal bodies when He glorifies us at the end of this age. After we are glorified, we will not have the all-too-real potential to walk by the flesh (the old man) and to sin. When we are glorified we will leave the world, the flesh (the old man), and the devil behind. That sounds good doesn't it? Until then we must make it a top priority to always walk by the Holy Spirit by faith to keep the old man from manifesting itself in sin. Now our bodies are mortal bodies, but they are also temples of the Holy Spirit

I'll read Romans 6:12, which is another verse where the apostle mentioned our mortal body), "Therefore do not let sin reign in your mortal body so that you obey its lusts." I'll also read what the apostle said in Romans 13:14 and then Galatians 5:16, 24, "But put on the Lord Jesus Christ, and make no provision for the flesh in regard to its lusts." Galatians 5:16, "But I say, walk by the Spirit [the Holy Spirit], and you [most certainly] will not carry out the desire [the sinful desire] of the flesh [of the old man that still wants to live in sin]." And Galatians 5:24, "Now those who belong to Christ Jesus have crucified the flesh [the old man] with its passions and desires [with its sinful passions and desires]." Also, in Ephesians 4:22 Paul exhorted his Christian readers to once-for-all and completely lay aside (or put off) the old man, and in Colossians 3:9 he spoke of his readers having laid aside (or put off) the old man with its evil practices.

Let's go on to Romans 8:12-14, which are super-important verses. Here the apostle Paul says that we are totally obligated to always walk by the Holy Spirit and keep the flesh (the old man) from manifesting itself in sin. According to the terms of God's new covenant, we are obligated to always walk by the Holy Spirit and keep the flesh (the old man) from manifesting itself in sin. This isn't an optional matter, but this is good news! What God calls us to do, He enables us to do. God didn't say things like this to condemn us, but to transform us. His saving, sanctifying grace is sufficient, but that doesn't mean that it will always be easy. Anyway, WE MUST AIM AT THIS TARGET! And God provides forgiveness and restoration for Christians who fall into sin when they repent.

Romans 8:12, 13. **So then, brethren** [Paul is speaking to born-again Christians.], **we are under obligation, not to the flesh, to live according to the flesh** [We are under obligation to God and His covenant.]—**(13) for if you are living according to the flesh, you must die** [[(This double bracket goes on for three paragraphs.) To live according to the flesh, as we have seen, means to live in sin. If Christians give themselves back to their old master of sin, to live according to the flesh, they must die. (See Rom. 6:16. for example.) They become unbelievers. How much sin can we get by with and still be classified as believers? I'm sure that the apostle Paul would not like that question, especially if Christians are trying to make room to serve sin part of the time. We are called to always walk by the Holy Spirit and not make any room for sin. That is the Christian ideal, and WE MUST AIM AT THAT TARGET! Any sin, if it really is sin, is too much sin. The New Testament shows that true Christians can sin, but it also makes it clear that any sin is too much sin, and it powerfully warns Christians living in sin with the need to repent with top priority.

When we consider who Jesus is, God the Son, who condescended to become a man (though He was much more than just a man) and who condescended to die for us, bearing our sins with the guilt and the penalties (including the major penalties of spiritual death and bondage to sin), and that He was raised from the dead on the third day and is now seated at the right hand of God the Father, and that God hates sin, it would be totally shocking if God's saving grace in Christ Jesus was not sufficient to overthrow sin and give us the full victory over sin.

If we turn from God and His righteousness and do not walk by His Spirit by faith, we turn back into spiritual death, and we will not have a place in His eternal kingdom.]]; **but if by the Spirit** [the Holy Spirit] **you are putting to death the deeds** [or, **works**] **of the body, you will live.** We will live in the sense that we maintain the spiritual life that we have as born-again Christians, and we will inherit the fullness of eternal life at the end of this age. To put to death the sinful works of the body means to keep the flesh (the old man) from manifesting itself in sin. The sinful "works of the body" here is the same thing as the sinful "works of the flesh" of Galatians 5:19-21, which equals all sin, and not just sins especially associated with the physical body. And the apostle warned his Christian readers in Galatians 5:21 (as he had forewarned them) "that those who practice such things will not inherit the kingdom of God"; they will inherit eternal death.

According to Romans chapter 8; Galatians chapter 5; and many other passages, the only satisfactory option is for us to always walk by the Holy Spirit by faith and not leave any room for sin. That sounds good, doesn't

84

it? That's what every true Christian wants. WE MUST AIM AT THAT TARGET!

We are saved by grace through faith, but we must understand God's Word, and if our faith is real, we will walk by the Holy Spirit in the righteousness and holiness of God on a consistent basis. Faith without works is dead. It isn't saving faith.

Romans 8:14. **For all who are being led by the Spirit of God, these are sons of God.** Those **who are being led by the Spirit of God** in this context are the ones who "by the Spirit are putting to death the [sinful] works of the body" of verse 13. They are the ones who walk by (and after) the Spirit by faith all the time and do not carry out the sinful works of the flesh of Gal. 5:19-21. They are LED BY THE SPIRIT OF GOD to live a life of righteousness and holiness, with the victory over all sin.

For all who are being led by the Spirit of God, these are sons of God. Part of what Paul is saying here is that those who are *not* being led by the Spirit of God to a life of righteousness and holiness are not sons of God. Being led by the Holy Spirit to a life of righteousness and holiness is a big part of what new-covenant salvation is all about.

I consider Romans 8:12-14 to be extremely important, so I'm going to supplement what I said here by reading much of what I said under these verses in my book, *Holiness and Victory Over Sin: Full Salvation Through the Atoning Death of the Lord Jesus Christ.* This will involve some repetition, but repetition is good if it helps us get the Word of God implanted in our hearts and lives.

Romans 8:12. Christians still have the (all too real) potential to live according to the flesh because the flesh has not been annihilated yet (see, for example, Rom. 6:12, 13; 8:10; 13:14; Gal. 5:13-25; 6:8). To live according to the flesh means to live in sin; it means to do the sinful works of the flesh (see Rom. 8:13). Christians are under obligation to God to walk according to the Holy Spirit and be faithful to the terms of the new covenant.

Romans 8:13. "for if you are living according to the flesh, you must die;" Any people (whether they call themselves Christians, or not) who continue to live a life of sin, "according to the flesh," will find that the path

85

ends in eternal death (see, for example, Rom. 6:16, 21, 23; 7:5; 8:6; Rev. 20:6, 12-15). The words "you must die" here are contrasted with the words "you will live" in the second half of the verse.

"but if by the Spirit you are putting to death the deeds [or, works] of the body, you will live." "The works of the body" here are the equivalent of the "works of the flesh" of Gal. 5:19. Both of these expressions embrace all sin, not just sins especially associated with the physical body. (See Gal. 5:19-21.)

For us to put to death the sinful works of the body by the Spirit means that we refrain from sinning, being enabled by the indwelling Spirit of God (see, for example, Rom. 6:12, 13 with all of Romans chapter 6; Rom. 7:6; 8:1-11; Gal. 5:13-25). Galatians 5:16 says the same thing with different words, "But I say, walk by the Spirit, and you [most certainly] will not carry out the desire [the sinful desire] of the flesh [of the old man]." So does Gal. 5:24, "Now those who belong to Christ Jesus have crucified the flesh with its [sinful] passions and desires." (Also see Rom. 13:11-14; Eph. 4:22-24; Col. 2:11-15; 3:1-11.)

It is obvious that Christians do not just automatically walk by the Spirit with the victory over sin; we must cooperate with the Spirit of God through faith, in line with the gospel. Otherwise we will still walk according to the flesh to some extent, and sin will be the inevitable result. The apostle Paul taught that Christians are required to walk by the Spirit all the time; it is not an acceptable option to walk by the flesh part of the time. Also, we must understand the gospel before we can walk in line with the gospel by faith. We must make it a top priority to rightly divide and understand God's Word.

Romans 8:14. In this context, "all who are being led by the Spirit of God" are being led to live in righteousness and holiness, as they put to death the sinful works of the body, of the flesh, of the old man (see verses 12, 13). They are the ones who "[walk] according to the Spirit" and fulfill the requirement of the Law in their daily lives (see Rom. 8:4). The clear implication of Rom. 8:14 is that it is only those "who are being led by the Spirit of God" that are the true "sons of God." In typical fashion, the apostle does not mention the in-between state (the gray area) of those who are led by the Spirit of God to some extent but who also live according to the flesh to some extent. This in-between state is not an acceptable option. The New Testament makes it clear that we should not have any sin, and that if we do, we must repent with a high priority. Living in sin is a totally unacceptable and a dangerous place to live.

God knows our hearts. He knows if we are making Him; His will; and His righteousness and holiness a top priority. He knows if we are making it a top priority to change anything, and everything, that needs to be changed, by His sufficient grace through faith. He is good and merciful; He is not trying to get rid of us, quite the opposite! But we had better take His warnings against sin very seriously.

I'll read Romans 8:15-18 and briefly discuss these verses. I'll read these verses from the NKJV. Romans 8:15, **For you did not receive the spirit of bondage again to fear, but you received the Spirit** [the Holy Spirit] **of adoption by whom we cry out, "Abba, Father."** When we become born-again Christians, we are adopted into the family of God, in union with the Lord Jesus Christ, and the Holy Spirit of God begins to dwell in us. As the next verse shows, the indwelling Spirit bears witness with our spirits that we have become children of God in this very special, glorious sense, and He enables us to cry out, "Abba, Father." "Abba" is an intimate Aramaic word for Father. In truth and with full assurance, we can cry out, "Abba, Father"; God becomes our Father in a very special, glorious sense when we are adopted into His family through union with God the Son in new-covenant salvation. We are born-again children now. We will be born into the fullness of eternal life and glorified at the end of this age.

Romans 8:16-18. **The Spirit Himself bears witness with our spirit that we are children of God** [This inner witness is extremely important, confirming the reality of our salvation.], **(17) and if children, then heirs— heirs of God and joint heirs with Christ** [[We receive the first installment of our inheritance (of our salvation) when we become born-again Christians, but most of the glory is reserved for the future, when we will be glorified and begin to reign with the Lord Jesus Christ. If we stay faithful throughout this age, by the saving grace of God in Christ, we will inherit the fullness of glory when the Lord Jesus Christ returns. The apostle Paul goes on to speak of our need to persevere during this present life, which includes some suffering with, and for, Christ.]], **if indeed we suffer with *Him*, that we may also be glorified together.** [[This present age involves some suffering. Things like resisting

87

temptation, being misunderstood and being persecuted, and being engaged in warfare with the forces of Satan involve suffering with, and for, Christ. However, as the apostle goes on to show in the next verse, the suffering that comes to us through our being faithful to God is extremely small when compared with the never-ending glory reserved for us in the very near future.] **(18) For I consider that the sufferings of this present time are not worthy *to be compared* with the glory which shall be revealed in us.**

We are just about finished with this article, but I'll read three very important verses from the Gospel of John. In John 14:15 Jesus said, "If you love Me, you will keep My commandments." John 14:23, "Jesus answered and said to him, 'If anyone loves Me, he will keep My word [keeping His word includes keeping His commandments]; and My Father will love him, and We will come to him and make Our abode with him.' " In John 15:10 Jesus said, "If you keep My commandments, you will abide in My love; just as I have kept My Father's commandments and abide in His love." God bless you!

Holiness and Victory Over Sin #9

Holy Father, we humble our hearts before you; we want to understand the gospel (the full gospel); we want to live the gospel; for your glory and for our good. In Jesus' name! Amen!

We have the great privilege to turn to ROMANS 1:16, 17. For one thing, there is widespread agreement that these two verses give the theme for the apostle Paul's Epistle to the Romans, which is a very important epistle.

Romans 1:16. **For I am not ashamed of the gospel, for it is the power of God for salvation to everyone who believes, to the Jew first and also to the Greek.** Again, **For I am not ashamed of the gospel** [The Greek word behind the word **gospel** is *euaggelion*; this Greek word is made up of two Greek words; *eu* means good and *aggelion* means message or news; the gospel is "good news" indeed.]**, for it is the power of God for salvation** [[The Greek preposition translated "for" here is *eis*; we will come across this preposition again as we continue. It could be translated "for salvation"; "unto salvation"; "to salvation"; or "resulting in salvation." Salvation from what? Salvation from being in spiritual death and being a slave of sin; and salvation from the wrath of God that will come against those who are committed to sin at the end of this age.]] **to everyone who believes** [[To everyone who believes in God and His Son and His gospel. To believe in God and His Son and His gospel includes a commitment from the heart to live for God and His Son and to live in line with the gospel (by God's enabling grace, which includes His **power**). In English we often use the verb "believe" in a very shallow way, but in the Bible to believe in God and His Son and His gospel includes living for God and His Son and living in line with His gospel, from the heart. If we believe God's Word, we will live God's Word.

There is no difference between believing in God and His Son and His gospel and having faith in God and His Son and His gospel. And faith without works is dead. It isn't real faith. It isn't saving faith. We must submit to God and appropriate His saving grace in Christ Jesus, by faith, on a continuous basis. In the Greek it is easy to see that the verb translated "believe" and the noun translated "faith" are closely related. The Greek verb translated believe is *pisteuo*, and the Greek noun translated faith is *pistis*. The Greek verb was derived from the noun.]], **to the Jew first and also to the Greek.** Greek here means Gentile.

Romans 1:17. (We'll spend a lot of time here; this verse is extremely important, and we need to discuss several important details. I'll quote the entire verse before we get into the details.) **For in it [by it]** *the* **righteousness of God is revealed [manifested] from faith [by faith] to faith; as it is written, "but the righteous man shall live by faith [he who is righteous by faith shall live]."**

For in it [by it] *the* **righteousness of God is revealed [is manifested].** I would translate **For by it** [by the gospel] *the* **righteousness of God is manifested.** We'll spend a lot of time discussing the meaning of these words before we get back to the words that follow in Rom. 1:17. What does it mean that the righteousness of God is manifested by the gospel? Well, briefly for a start, the primary thing that it means for this age is that the righteousness of God is manifested in the hearts and lives of those who submit to the gospel by faith. God imputes (in a legal, positional sense) and imparts (in a transforming sense) His righteousness to believers, just like He said He would do in many Old Testament

89

prophecies. Every Christian should manifest the righteousness of God in everything they say and do. That is the Christian ideal; and what a privilege; what a blessing. We need to always aim at that target instead of making room for sin. God's righteousness is manifested in our hearts and lives as we walk by faith (in accordance with God's Word) and walk by the Holy Spirit on a continuous basis, which we are called to do. Remember Galatians 5:16, "But I say, walk by the Spirit, and you [most certainly] will not carry out the desire [the sinful desire] of the flesh [of the old man]."

For by it [by the gospel] **the righteousness of God is manifested.** This is extremely important. I'm going to turn to quite a few passages in the Old Testament where God prophesied that He was going to manifest His righteousness through new-covenant salvation in the atoning death of His Son, and by His outpoured Spirit, who dwells in all true Christians.

Let's start with Isaiah 32:15, "Until the Spirit [the Holy Spirit] is poured out upon us from on high [[As we have discussed, God's pouring out His Spirit on believers is a big part of what new-covenant salvation is all about. God pours out His Righteous, Holy Spirit of life, and we are born again and are enabled to walk in the very righteousness and holiness of God.]], And the wilderness becomes a fertile field, And the fertile field is considered as a forest. (16) Then JUSTICE WILL DWELL IN THE WILDERNESS AND RIGHTEOUSNESS WILL ABIDE IN THE FERTILE FIELD [my emphasis] [[Where God pours out His Spirit, His righteousness is manifested. During this age God's righteousness is manifested in the hearts and lives of Christians. In His new heaven and new earth, with its new Jerusalem, His righteousness will permeate everything in full measure.]] (17) And the work [or, the fruit] of RIGHTEOUSNESS [my emphasis] will be peace [Righteousness yields "peace" (Hebrew *shalom*); peace with God, peace in the heart; peace with one another; etc.], And the service of RIGHTEOUSNESS [my emphasis], quietness and confidence forever. (18) Then my people [God says] will live in a peaceful habitation, And in secure dwellings and in undisturbed resting places...." The main point I want to make here is that God pours out His righteous Spirit and His righteousness is manifested. During this present age His righteousness is manifested in the hearts and lives of Christians, as they walk by the Spirit (by grace through faith).

I'm turning to Isaiah 45:8, "Drip down, O heavens, from above, And LET THE CLOUDS POUR DOWN RIGHTEOUSNESS [my emphasis; God pours down His righteousness through new-covenant salvation.]; Let the earth open up and salvation bear fruit, And RIGHTEOUSNESS SPRING UP [my emphasis] with it, I, the LORD [Yahweh], have created it." We are part of God's new creation. Our righteousness is part of His creative work, but we have to appropriate these things by faith. God gets all the glory: His righteousness is imparted to us through the Sacrifice of His Son and by the Righteous, Holy Spirit.

Isaiah 46:12, 13. God is speaking, "Listen to Me, you stubborn-minded, Who are far from righteousness. (13) I BRING NEAR MY RIGHTEOUSNESS [my emphasis], it is not far off; and My salvation will not delay. And I will grant salvation in Zion, And My glory for Israel." God's righteousness and His salvation go together. A big part of what His salvation is all about is His solving the sin problem through the atoning death of the Lord Jesus Christ and making those who submit to His salvation righteous with His imputed and imparted righteousness. Nothing works right until we are made righteous. Sin always destroys divine order, starting with our all-important relationship with God.

Isaiah 56:1. "Thus says the LORD [Yahweh], 'Preserve justice and DO RIGHTEOUSNESS [my emphasis], For My salvation is about to come And MY RIGHTEOUSNESS [my emphasis] to be revealed [or, MANIFESTED]." Under the old covenant God's people were required to "do righteousness," but the sin problem had not been solved yet through the atoning death of the Lord Jesus Christ and by the life-giving, sanctifying work of the Holy Spirit that comes to believers through His death. The most "righteous" believers from Old Testament days will all confess that they needed to be saved through the Lord Jesus Christ. The most righteous sons of Israel submitted to the ministry of John the Baptist and then to the ministry of the Lord Jesus Christ when they called for repentance.

Isaiah 60:21. "Then ALL YOUR PEOPLE *WILL BE* RIGHTEOUS [my emphasis]; They will possess the land forever, The branch of My planting, THE WORK OF MY HANDS, THAT I MAY BE GLORIFIED [my emphasis]." We are saved and made righteous by the work of God's hands, and He must receive all the glory. "We are His workmanship, created in Christ Jesus for good works, which God prepared beforehand so that we would walk in them" (Eph. 2:10). But the Bible also makes it clear that we must repent and submit to God and His plan of salvation by faith, and we must walk by His Spirit by faith on a continuous basis, or we will not manifest (or fully manifest) His righteousness. We must work out our salvation day by day by faith (Phil. 2:12) by grace (Phil. 2:13). The fact that we must appropriate God's righteousness by faith does not detract from the fact that His righteousness comes 100 percent by His grace. In Romans 4:16, for example, the apostle Paul said, "For this reason, *it is* by faith, in order that *it may be* in accordance with grace." Faith appropriates what God makes available by grace. We don't earn/merit these things by faith.

"THEN ALL YOUR PEOPLE *WILL BE* RIGHTEOUS; They will possess the land forever, The branch of My planting, THE WORK OF MY HANDS, THAT I MAY BE GLORIFIED." To the extent we do not appropriate and walk in God's righteousness and every other aspect of our salvation, we rob Him of glory.

Isaiah 61:1-3. It is significant that Jesus quoted part of the words of Isaiah 61:1, 2 in Luke 4:18, 19 and said that this scripture was fulfilled in Him. "The Spirit of the Lord God is upon me [Me], Because the LORD [Yahweh] has anointed me [[Me. The word "Messiah" from the Hebrew means "Anointed One," and the word "Christ" from the Greek means "Anointed One." He, the God-man, was anointed by the Spirit of God like no ordinary man could be (see John 3:34, for example).]] To bring good news to the afflicted [The Lord Jesus Christ brought the good news of new-covenant salvation.] He has sent me [Me] to bind up the brokenhearted, To proclaim liberty [or, to proclaim release] to captives And freedom to prisoners [All of us were captive to spiritual death and in bondage to sin, but He came to proclaim release to the captives.]; (2) To proclaim the favorable year of the LORD [Yahweh] and the day of vengeance of our God [[Jesus' words in Luke 4:18, 19 stopped with the words "To proclaim the favorable year of the LORD." Most of the manifestation of the wrath of God is reserved for the end of this age.]]; To comfort all who mourn [[Mourning over things like the sinful state of God's people and the fact that His name is being blasphemed is a good thing. For one thing, people who are mourning over such things will be ready to submit to the Savior when He comes.]], (3) To grant those who mourn in Zion, Giving them a garland instead of ashes, The oil of gladness instead of mourning, The mantle of praise instead of a spirit of fainting. So they will be called OAKS OF RIGHTEOUSNESS [my emphasis], The planting of the LORD [Yahweh] that He may be glorified." Those who submit to the

Lord Jesus Christ become strong trees that are characterized by the righteousness of God. His righteousness is imparted to them through His saving work in Christ, and He is glorified. As I have mentioned, God gets 100 percent of the glory for our righteousness. Of course we can be righteous! This is the work of God! He makes us righteous through the atoning death of His Son and by His outpoured Spirit who comes to dwell within us, but we must appropriate and cooperate with God's saving grace by faith.

Isaiah 61:10, 11. "I will rejoice greatly in the LORD [Yahweh], My soul will exult in my God; For He has clothed me with garments of salvation, HE HAS WRAPPED ME WITH A ROBE OF RIGHTEOUSNESS [my emphasis], As a bridegroom decks himself with a garland, And as a bride adorns herself with her jewels [God imputes and imparts His righteousness to us through new-covenant salvation.]. (11) For as the earth brings forth its sprouts, And a garden causes the things sown in it to spring up, So the LORD GOD WILL CAUSE RIGHTEOUSNESS AND PRAISE TO SPRING UP BEFORE ALL THE NATIONS [my emphasis]." God's righteousness is manifested before the nations in the hearts and lives of those who submit to His new-covenant plan of salvation. They can see the "robe of righteousness" that God gives to those who submit to Him with repentance and faith. God will manifest His righteousness before all the nations in a fuller sense at the end of this age.

I won't read any more prophecies that speak of God's manifesting His righteousness in the hearts and lives of those who partake of new-covenant salvation, but I'll briefly comment on two other very important such prophecies that we have discussed already and then briefly discuss Isaiah 53:11. In Jeremiah 31:31-34, which is a prophecy dealing with new-covenant salvation (verse 32 even mentions the "new covenant"), God said that He was going to put His law within His people and write it on their hearts. In other words, He was going to transform their hearts and impart His righteousness to them. The prophecy also mentioned forgiving their sins and remembering them no more. Forgiveness is a very important part of new-covenant salvation, but I believe we should put about 90 percent of the emphasis on our actually becoming righteous with the righteousness of God.

We also discussed Ezekiel 36:25-27. There God prophesied, for one thing, that He would put His Spirit within us and cause us to walk in His statutes and that we would walk in His ordinances.

Isaiah chapter 53 is one of the most important passages in the Bible dealing with the atoning death of the Lord Jesus Christ and the glorious salvation that results from that Sacrifice. Isaiah 53:11 is a key verse in that chapter. It speaks of the RIGHTEOUS ONE (the Lord Jesus Christ) MAKING US RIGHTEOUS through His atoning death. Isaiah 53:11 is discussed in some detail on pages 26-28 of my book, *Holiness and Victory Over Sin: Full Salvation Through the Atoning Death of the Lord Jesus Christ*.

Now that we have considered quite a few passages in the Old Testament that prophesy of God's manifesting His righteousness in the hearts and lives of His people (believers), let's turn back to the first words of Romans 1:17. As I mentioned, I would translate the first part of the verse, **For by it [by the gospel] the righteousness of God is manifested.** The primary thing that the apostle meant was that God manifests His righteousness in the hearts and lives of Christians. He has dethroned spiritual death and sin and manifested His righteousness through new-covenant salvation. The apostle Paul elaborates on that all-important theme throughout much of the rest of the book of Romans, but Romans chapters 5-8 are of key importance. We have discussed, or will discuss, most of the verses of Romans chapters 5-8 in these articles.

Romans 3:21, 22 are an important cross-reference that speaks of God's righteousness being manifested in the lives of Christians. We'll study those verses later, but for now I'll quote the first part of Romans 3:21, "But now apart from the Law [the Mosaic Law, which was the foundation for the old covenant], THE RIGHTEOUSNESS OF GOD IS MANIFESTED [my emphasis]...." Also note Romans 1:18; it speaks of THE WRATH OF GOD BEING MANIFESTED from heaven against all ungodliness and unrighteousness of men who suppress the truth in unrighteousness. That's why all people need to be saved from bondage to sin and made righteous through the Lord Jesus Christ. The only way to avoid the wrath of God that is manifested now to some extent against all ungodliness and unrighteousness, and will be manifested in full measure at the end of this age, is to be transformed and become righteous through salvation in the Lord Jesus Christ. The wrath of God is manifested now (see Romans

1:18-32), even as the righteousness of God is manifested now. The righteousness of God is actually manifested in the hearts and lives of those who submit to God's new-covenant plan of salvation with repentance and faith. We don't just read about God's righteousness being revealed; it is actually manifested in the hearts and lives of Christians.

Back to Romans 1:17, **For by it** [by the gospel] **the righteousness of God is manifested from faith….** I would translated **by faith**. Normally the two Greek words used here (the Greek preposition *ek* and the noun for faith) are translated "by faith." I could give many examples, but I'll just give three. At the end of verse 17, the NASB translates these same two Greek words "by faith," and so do the NIV, KJV and the NKJV. Romans 5:1 is another example, and so is Rom. 9:30. I'll read Romans 9:30, "What shall we say then? That Gentiles, who did not pursue righteousness, ATTAINED RIGHTEOUSNESS, EVEN THE RIGHTEOUSNESS WHICH IS BY FAITH [my emphasis]." The only way we can receive God's imputed and imparted righteousness is "by faith" (or, we could say "through faith," or the equivalent). We appropriate God's saving grace by faith. The NIV, KJV, and the NKJV also translate "by faith" at Rom. 5:1, and the NIV also translates "by faith" at Rom. 9:30.

Back to Romans 1:17, **For by it** [by the gospel] **the righteousness of God is manifested by faith to faith….** The Greek preposition translated "to" is *eis*. The translation "to faith" is quite acceptable here, but we could also translate "unto faith." The righteousness of God comes "by faith" and it comes "to faith" or "unto faith." That is, it comes "to" or "unto those who have faith," faith in God and His Son and His gospel. The apostle emphasized the word *faith* here by using it twice. He strongly emphasized faith in his proclamation of the gospel (he received his gospel from the Lord Jesus Christ). He taught that we are saved by faith (a faith that appropriates God's grace); we are *not* saved by works. If we could earn salvation by our works, we wouldn't be saved by grace, and we could boast in ourselves, instead of giving all the glory to God.

I'll quote part of Romans 3:22 here because it is has so much in common with 1:17, "even *THE* RIGHTEOUSNESS OF GOD THROUGH FAITH IN JESUS CHRIST FOR [TO, UNTO] ALL THOSE WHO BELIEVE [my emphasis]…." Paul emphasized faith/believing here in 3:22 by using the words "faith" and "those who believe"; he used the word faith twice in Rom. 1:17. The Greek preposition that is translated "for" here is *eis*. This is the same preposition that was used with the word faith in Rom. 1:17, where it was translated "to faith." And as I mentioned, it could also have been translated "unto faith." Here in Rom. 3:22 I would translate "to all those who believe" or "unto all those who believe," instead of "for all those who believe."

In Romans 1:17 THE RIGHTEOUSNESS OF GOD comes BY FAITH, and it comes TO or UNTO the one who has FAITH. In Romans 3:22 THE RIGHTEOUSNESS OF GOD comes THROUGH FAITH (using a different Greek preposition), and it comes TO or UNTO ALL THOSE WHO BELIEVE. There is no substantial difference between the righteousness of God coming "by faith" or coming "through faith." And there is no substantial difference between the righteousness of God coming "to" or "unto those who have faith" and its coming "to" or "unto those who believe." Having faith in God and His Son and His gospel is the same thing as believing in God and His Son and His gospel.

Now back to Romans 1:17, **For by it the righteousness of God is manifested by faith to faith** [or, unto faith]; **as it is written, "But the righteous *man* shall live by faith."** The apostle quotes from Habakkuk 2:4 to back up what he has been saying in verse 17. However, I believe the alternative translation that the NASB gives in the margin is the correct translation, the one intended by Paul and the One who sent Him. I'll give that translation, **as it is written, "But HE WHO IS RIGHTEOUS BY FAITH** [my emphasis] **shall live."** In the first part of Rom. 1:17 Paul says that the righteousness of God is manifested by faith. Here at the end of the verse he quotes from Habakkuk 2:4, which says essentially the same thing with different words. It speaks of the one "who is righteous by faith." This quotation confirms that the way we become righteous with the very righteousness of God is BY FAITH. He imputes and imparts His righteousness to those who submit to the gospel by faith, and His righteousness is manifested in our hearts and lives. We cannot become righteous with the righteousness of God by trying harder to keep the Law, or any other way. The only way we can become righteous is by faith in God and His Son and His gospel (or we could say by believing in God and His Son and His gospel).

He who is righteous by faith SHALL LIVE. We LIVE in the sense that we are enabled to partake of the life of God now as born again Christians, and we will inherit the fullness of eternal life at the end of this age.

I'll read 1 John 3:7. This verse strongly confirms that our being made righteous by faith includes a lot more than our being forgiven and declared righteous. Many Christians have a hard time seeing beyond forgiveness and a declaration of righteousness in verses like Rom. 1:17. Our being made righteous very much includes our living in the righteousness of God by His grace. In other words, God actually imparts His righteousness to us, and we walk in His righteousness. "Little children, make sure no one deceives you [There were deceivers in John's day, and we have many deceivers in our day.]; the one who practices righteousness [or, THE ONE WHO IS DOING RIGHTEOUSNESS] is RIGHTEOUS, JUST AS HE [GOD] IS RIGHTEOUS [my emphasis]." If we are righteous as God is righteous, we will certainly be living with the victory over all sin, won't we? This is good news! What God calls us to do, He enables us to do. Verses like this were written to transform us, not to condemn us. We are able to be righteous as God is righteous because He imparts His righteousness to us, as He often prophesied He would do in the Old Testament. The First Epistle of John also makes it clear that Christians who have sinned can be restored through the Lord Jesus Christ and His atoning death. But it is totally unacceptable for Christians to just go ahead and sin with the understanding that they can be forgiven. That viewpoint seriously abuses God's grace.

I trust you can see the extreme importance of Rom. 1:16, 17. I'm going to read part of what I said in my book (*Holiness and Victory Over Sin*) under these verses. The gospel has the power to save everyone who believes. It has the power through the atoning death of the Lord Jesus Christ and His resurrection, and by the indwelling Holy Spirit, to dethrone sin, Satan, and spiritual death, and to make believers righteous. Having been saved from sin, believers will be saved from the wrath of God that will come against those living in sin (see, for example, Rom. 1:18-3:20; 5:9, 10; Eph. 2:3; 5:5-7; 1 Thess. 1:10).

... When the gospel is received in faith, the righteousness of God is manifested in the sense that believers are transformed by the saving power of God (see Rom. 1:16) and made righteous. The righteousness of God is dynamic; it overpowers sin and makes believers righteous. God puts His righteous, Holy Spirit within believers. ...

The righteousness of God can come to a person only one way – by faith (faith in God the Father; faith in the Lord Jesus Christ; faith in the gospel). It does not come by works of the Law, but by faith (see, for example, Rom. 3:20; 4:2; 9:32; 10:5; 11:6; Gal. 2:16; 3:2, 5; Phil. 3:9). By faith, Yes! By works of the Law, No! Righteousness must come from God. It cannot come from man in the flesh (man in spiritual death, man in bondage to sin). Man in the flesh cannot fully keep God's Law, so man in the flesh cannot be saved by the Law.

In my book I quoted part of what J. A. Zeisler said under Rom. 1:16, 17 in his commentary on Romans titled, *Paul's Letter to the Romans* (published by Trinity Press Int'l in 1989). I'll include two brief excerpts here. "It is crucial that [the power of God] should be mentioned in the transitional summary [referring to Rom. 1:16, 17], for a major part of the human problem, as Paul sees it, is that men and women are not free. It is not just that they need forgiveness, though they do, but even more that they are under alien power, especially that of sin.... To release them, they need a superior power, and a large part of the argument will be that they *can* be transferred from the power-sphere of sin and death to that of the divine Spirit, which brings true life as the people of God. See Rom. 1:18-3:9; 6:1-23; 8:1-11."

"Some have thought that God's righteousness becomes ours in the sense that a right standing/status is freely granted by God. No doubt this is so, but it is not just that. God's righteousness is how he acts, and when human beings are drawn into its power, they begin to act as they should, as his covenant people."

God bless you! His name be glorified! His will be done! His will be done in us! In Jesus' mighty name! Amen!

Holiness and Victory Over Sin #10

Holy Father, we humble our hearts before you. We want to rightly divide your Word, to understand it, to live it; for your glory and for our good. We pray in Jesus' mighty name! Amen!

Last time we discussed Rom. 1:16, 17 in some detail. In this article we will discuss many key verses from Romans chapter 3. We'll start with Romans 3:9. **What then? Are we better than they? Not at all; for we have already charged that both Jews and Greeks are all under sin.** Greeks means Gentiles here. Earlier in this epistle, the apostle Paul has *already charged that both Jews and Gentiles are all under sin.* All mankind, therefore needs to be saved through the Lord Jesus Christ.

Paul used the second half of Romans chapter 1 to demonstrate that the Gentiles were under sin, and he used chapter 2 and much of chapter 3 to demonstrate that the Jews were also under sin. The Jews had the Mosaic Law, but the Law did not solve the sin problem. The Law did not have the authority or power to dethrone spiritual death and sin, the spiritual death and sin that has reigned over mankind since the fall (see Romans chapter 5, for example). The apostle showed, in fact, that the Law intensified the sin problem (see Romans chapter 7, for example). God always planned to save all believers through the Lord Jesus Christ and His atoning death, including the believers from Old Testament days.

What then? Are we better than they? Not at all; for we have already charged that both Jews and Greeks are all under sin (Romans 3:9). We were under the guilt of sin and in bondage to sin. Like Paul said in Romans chapter 6, we were slaves of sin before we became born-again Christians. We were in spiritual death and under sin.

In Romans 3:10-18 Paul quoted many verses from the Old Testament to help confirm that all mankind is under sin. (He quoted mostly from the book of Psalms, but also from the book of Isaiah.) Then in Romans 3:19 he said, **Now we know that whatever the Law says** ["The Law" here refers to the entire Old Testament, as it does on occasion. As I mentioned, Paul's quotations here came from the books of Psalms and Isaiah.] **it speaks to those who were under the Law** [In other words, it speaks to the people of Israel.]**, so that every mouth may be closed and all the world** [all mankind] **may become accountable to God** [accountable to God because of their sin]**.**

Romans 3:20. **because by the works of the Law no flesh will be justified in His sight** [[The apostle Paul frequently made the point that nobody could be justified by God by the works of the Law, because man in the flesh (man in spiritual death; man without the indwelling Spirit of life and righteousness) cannot fully keep God's Law. The only way we can be justified in the full sense is through the Lord Jesus Christ and His atoning death.]] **for through the Law** *comes* **the knowledge of sin.** The Law accurately taught about sin, but it didn't have the authority or power to dethrone spiritual death and sin, and to make people righteous with the righteousness of God. As we have discussed, God imputes and imparts His righteousness to Christians through the atoning death of His Son and by giving His Righteous, Holy Spirit to dwell in them. We are saved by grace through faith.

Romans 3:21. **But now apart from the Law** [the Law which could not save us from spiritual death and bondage to sin and make us righteous with the righteousness of God] *THE* **RIGHTEOUSNESS OF GOD HAS BEEN MANIFESTED** [my emphasis] [[(This double bracket goes on for two paragraphs.) We discussed Rom. 1:17 in the last article. I'll read Romans 1:17 the way we discussed the verse, "For by it [by the gospel] *the* righteousness of God is manifested by faith [The righteousness of God is manifested in the hearts and lives of Christians. We must appropriate His righteousness by faith (faith in God the Father; faith in the Lord Jesus Christ; faith in the gospel of new-covenant salvation)] to faith [or "unto faith." That is, the righteousness of God is imputed and imparted to those who have faith]; as it is written, 'But he who is righteous by faith shall live.' " The apostle quoted from Habukkuk 2:4 to confirm the super-important point that the only way we can become righteous (with the very righteousness of God) is "by faith."

One of the primary points that the apostle made in Rom. 1:17 was that the righteousness of God is manifested in the hearts and lives of Christians. And we looked at quite a few passages from the Old Testament where God prophesied that He was going to manifest His righteousness in the hearts and lives of His people. For one thing, He prophesied that He was going to pour out His Spirit and cause His Righteous, Holy Spirit to dwell in His people and make them righteous. As we have discussed, however, we must walk by the Holy Spirit by faith on a continuous basis (which we are called and enabled to do) or the righteousness of God will not be fully manifested. Several prophecies showed that new-covenant salvation would come to pass through the atoning death of the Lamb of God. We briefly discussed Isa. 53:11 in the last article. That verse speaks of our being justified and made righteous through the atoning death of the Lord Jesus Christ. Isaiah chapter 53 is a key passage on His atoning death.]], **being witnessed by the Law and the Prophets.** The old covenant, even though it was from God and was good, could not dethrone spiritual death and sin and manifest the righteousness of God in the hearts and lives of believers; it was not given for that purpose. But the Old Testament did *bear witness* to the fact God was going to solve the sin problem and make believers righteous through new-covenant salvation. For one thing, the Old Testament contains a large number of passages that prophesied of that salvation.

Romans 3:22, 23. **even** *the* **righteousness of God through faith in Jesus Christ for all those who believe** [[Back in Rom. 1:17 the apostle spoke of the righteousness of God coming BY FAITH. Here in Rom. 3:22 he spoke of the righteousness of God coming THROUGH FAITH (using a different Greek preposition). There is no substantial difference between the righteousness of God coming by faith or coming through faith. Back in Rom. 1:17 Paul spoke of the righteousness of God coming "to" or "unto" those who have faith. The Greek preposition translated "to" or "unto" in 1:17 is *eis*; the same Greek preposition is used here in 3:22. I would translate "to [or, unto] all those who believe" here in 3:22, instead of "for all those who believe." So, in Rom. 1:17 Paul spoke of the righteousness of God coming "to [or unto] those who have faith," and here in 3:22 he spoke of the righteousness of God coming "to [or unto] all those who believe." There is no substantial difference between the righteousness of God coming to (or, unto) those who have faith and its coming to (or, unto) those who believe. The righteousness of God is imputed and imparted to those who submit to the gospel in faith/to those who believe the gospel.]]; **for there is no distinction; (23) for all have sinned and fall short of the glory of God.** There is no distinction among people in the sense that all are sinners and all need to be saved through submitting (in faith) to God and His Son and His gospel. God imputes and imparts His righteousness to us and manifests His righteousness in our hearts and lives through new-covenant salvation.

Romans 3:24. **being justified as a gift by His grace through the redemption which is in Christ Jesus.** Paul emphasized grace here by using the words *gift* and *grace*. God's gift is a manifestation of His grace. Paul repeatedly emphasized the point that our salvation comes 100 percent by grace through faith. It is not of works; it is totally unearned. We appropriate and cooperate with God's grace by faith. Faith is not a work; faith receives what God freely gives. Faith is nothing for us to boast about, any more than we can boast in ourselves for taking hold of a life preserver instead of drowning. God paid an infinite price in the Sacrifice of His Son to save us, and God (the triune God) must receive all of the glory for our salvation.

being justified as a gift by His grace. The words **being justified** here in 3:24 are being used in the very full sense we have discussed already (when we discussed Rom. 6:7). There is no way we can limit "being justified" here to being forgiven and having a legal declaration of righteousness. Being justified here includes God's overthrowing spiritual death and bondage to sin; His making believers alive (starting with the new birth); and His making believers righteous with His righteousness. His righteousness is imparted to us, and it is manifested in our hearts and lives as we walk by faith and by the Holy Spirit (which we are called and required to do). What the apostle said in Rom. 1:17 and Rom. 3:21, 22 about the righteousness of God being manifested in our hearts and lives is included in what the words "being justified" mean here in verse 24.

The Greek verb translated *justify* (in some form); the Greek noun translated "righteousness"; and the Greek adjective translated "righteous" are closely related. The Greek verb translated *justify* (*dikaioo*) and the Greek noun translated *righteousness* (*dikaiosune*) were both derived from the Greek adjective translated *righteous* (*dikaios*). If we are going to translate the participle of the Greek verb *dikaioo* "being justified" here in verse 24, which is widely accepted, then we must understand that being justified is being used in a very full sense. For more on this very important verb, see the chapter titled, "A Study on the Meaning of Justify/Justification as These Words Are Used in the New Testament" in my book *Holiness and Victory Over Sin*.

being justified as a gift by His grace through the redemption which is in Christ Jesus (Romans 3:24). These words **through the redemption which is in Christ Jesus** strongly confirm that **being justified** here means a whole lot more than being forgiven and having a legal declaration of righteousness. Redemption, which was common in the ancient world, dealt with purchasing slaves to set them free. We were spiritually dead slaves of sin, but God has redeemed us through new-covenant salvation in the Lord Jesus Christ. He has redeemed us out of the realm of spiritual death and bondage to sin through the atoning death of the Lord Jesus Christ.

102

Now we are born again children of God. We owe nothing to our former master of sin, but we owe everything to God, who has redeemed us at such a high cost to Himself. We are totally obligated, according to the terms of the new covenant, to be faithful to God and His Word by His grace, and to walk in His righteousness by His indwelling Righteous Spirit. This is good news! Very good news! What a salvation plan! What a Savior! I trust you can see that this redemption includes a lot more than being forgiven and having a legal declaration of righteousness. Being justified here includes our actually being made righteous with the imparted righteousness of God.

I'm going to turn to page 80 of my book and read most of what I said under the words **through the redemption which is in Christ Jesus** of Rom. 3:24. I trust you can see that it is quite important for us to understand what it means for us to be redeemed through the Lord Jesus Christ. I used the 1977 edition of the NASB in the book. I believe these words rather strongly confirm that (in Rom. 3:24) **being justified** includes the ideas of being set free from the authority and power of sin (and spiritual death) and being made righteous with the righteousness of God. Sin formerly reigned (see Rom. 5:21, for example), and we were slaves of sin (see, for example, Rom. 3:9-20; 6:6, 17-22; 8:2, 5-8; John 8:31-36); but now we have been redeemed through the all-important atoning death of the Lord Jesus Christ

The word **redemption** conveys the idea of buying a slave to set him free. We were slaves of sin, but we have been redeemed out of the kingdom of sin; we are no longer under the authority of sin (and spiritual death), and we are no longer to serve our old master of sin (by sinning). If we were forgiven but were still slaves of sin, we would not be redeemed. Can you imagine a former slave who had a terribly wicked master, but who has now been redeemed at a very high price (actually an infinite price), sneaking back to the old master's house to serve the old master of sin even one more time?

Let's consider several passages from the New Testament that deal with redemption in Christ Jesus, passages that emphasize God's making us righteous. I also listed several passages beyond the passages we will consider here. First I'll read what the apostle Paul said in 1 Corinthians 6:18-20, "Flee immorality. [Paul was dealing with the sin of immorality in

103

this context, but he consistently taught that we must flee from all sin.] Every *other* sin that a man commits is outside the body, but the immoral man sins against his own body. (19) Or do you not know that your body is a temple of the Holy Spirit who is in you, whom you have from God, and that you are not your own? [As Paul goes on to say in the next verse, God has bought us (including our bodies), and we must be faithful to Him (by His grace).] (20) For YOU HAVE BEEN BOUGHT WITH A PRICE [my emphasis; the infinite price of the Sacrifice of His Son]; therefore glorify God in your body." We glorify God by living for Him and being faithful to Him and His Word (by His grace through faith).

Galatians 4:4-7. The apostle Paul wrote this epistle to Gentile Christians. "But when the fullness of the time came; God sent forth His Son, born of a woman, born under the Law [The Lord Jesus Christ was born of the virgin Mary; He was born under the Mosaic Law in that He was a Jew. The Gentiles were not born under the Mosaic Law.], (5) in order that HE MIGHT REDEEM [my emphasis] those who were under the Law, that we might receive the adoption as sons. [The Lord Jesus Christ died for all mankind. All the people (both Jews and Gentiles) who submit to God's new-covenant plan of salvation are adopted into the family of God through union with the Lord Jesus Christ.] (6) And because you are sons [Paul writes to his Christian readers], God has sent forth the Spirit of His Son into our hearts, crying, 'Abba! Father!' [[The Spirit of God, who dwells in every true Christian from the time of our being born again, bears witness with our spirits that we have been adopted into the family of God, which enables us to cry out with sincerity and in truth "Abba! Father!" God has actually become our Father in this very special, glorious sense. "Abba" is an intimate Aramaic word for father.]] (7) Therefore you are no longer a slave [no longer a spiritually dead slave of sin], but a son; and if a son, then an heir through God." We will be glorified and inherit the fullness of eternal life at the end of this age. We will even reign with God.

Titus 2:11-14. (I'll read these verses from the NIV.) "For the grace that brings salvation has appeared to all men. (12) It teaches us to say 'No' to ungodliness and worldly passions, and to live self-controlled, upright and godly lives in this present age, (13) while we wait for the blessed hope— the glorious appearing of our great God and Savior, Jesus Christ [[I prefer a translation like the following for the second half of this verse: "the appearing of the glory of the great God and of our Savior, Jesus Christ." It is totally necessary for us to understand that the Lord Jesus Christ is fully deity with God the Father (and the Holy Spirit), but I believe the word God refers to God the Father here, as it typically does in the New Testament. For one thing, "the blessed hope" refers to our being caught up into the glory of God and glorified at the end of this age, when God the Father sends His Son back to the earth. In Colossians 1:27 Paul spoke of "Christ in you, the hope of glory." In Colossians 3:4 he said, "When Christ, who is our life, is revealed (or, manifested), then you also will be revealed (or, manifested) with Him in glory." And the apostle Peter spoke of our being partakers "of the glory that is to be revealed [or, manifested]" (see 1 Peter 5:1).]], (14) who gave himself for us TO REDEEM [my emphasis] us from all wickedness and to purify for himself a people that are his very own, eager to do what is good." We are REDEEMED out of the kingdom of wickedness and lawlessness and transferred to God's kingdom of righteousness and holiness by His powerful saving grace in Christ.

I'll read part of what I said under Titus 2:11-14 on pages 124, 125 of my book, *Holiness and Victory Over Sin*. First I'll read part of what I said regarding the Greek participle translated "instructing [us]" by the NASB and "teaching [us]" by the NIV. The Greek verb used here is *paideuo*. This verb is sometimes used for the training of a child. The *Amplified Bible* has, "It has trained us." The powerful saving grace of God in Christ instructs us/teaches us, but it does a lot more than that. It takes us by the hand, so to speak, and guides us, empowers us, enables us, and makes us righteous with the righteousness of God.

And I'll read part of what I said under the words, "to deny ungodliness and worldly desires and to live sensibly, righteously and godly in the present age" (using the wording of the NASB). It would be difficult to find a more clear statement of the fact that Christians are called and enabled to live righteous and godly lives throughout this present age. The same can be said for Titus 2:14. I'll read Titus 2:14 from the NASB, "who gave Himself for us TO REDEEM [my emphasis] us from every lawless deed [or, from all lawlessness] and to purify for Himself a people for His own possession, zealous for good deeds [or, good works]." We are saved by grace through faith, and we are enabled and required to live in God's righteousness, doing good works. Titus 2:13 speaks of the age to come. Christians are motivated to live righteous lives now (in part) by the fact that they know that the day of judgment is coming, and they want to be fully ready for that day. They want to be delivered from the wrath of God to come and to inherit the glory of God's eternal kingdom. They want to hear words like, "Well done, good and faithful servant."

Next we'll discuss 1 Peter 1:14-19, which is another very important passage that will (for one thing) help us understand what it means TO BE REDEEMED in Christ Jesus, with a strong emphasis on righteousness, holiness, and victory over sin. "As obedient children, do not be conformed to the former lusts *which* were *yours* in your ignorance [The apostle Peter was speaking of the former lusts of his Gentile readers in the years before they became born-again Christians.], (15) but LIKE THE HOLY ONE WHO CALLED YOU, BE HOLY YOURSELVES IN ALL *YOUR* BEHAVIOR [[my emphasis; To be holy means to be set apart for God from everything that is sinful and defiling. For us to be holy in all our behavior like the Holy One who called us certainly includes the victory over all sin, doesn't it? And Peter continues with this theme in the next verse.]]; (16) because it is written, 'YOU SHALL BE HOLY, FOR I AM HOLY.' [[I prefer the translation "Be holy," instead of "You shall be holy." This is a command, but what God commands us to do, He enables us to do. Peter made it quite clear here that Christians are called to be set apart from all sin and for God. This is a great blessing! This is a great privilege!]] (17) If you address as Father the One who impartially judges according to each man's work, conduct yourselves in fear during the time of your stay *upon earth* [[This is a strong warning that we must make it top priority to live for God in His righteousness and holiness. We must love God, and we must fear sinning against Him. The Old Testament and the New Testament both speak of our need to fear sinning against God. We do address God as our Father, and we have been informed (including here in this verse) that God is an impartial Judge. Since He will impartially judge each person according to their work, He will not show partiality to any, including Christians. (How we think and what we do shows who we are and what we love and what we believe in our hearts. What we do shows whether our faith is genuine, or not.) It is true, of course, that forgiveness is provided for Christians, but Christianity is about much more than forgiveness. If "Christians" are living in sin, they are not ready to stand before God.]], (18) knowing that you WERE NOT REDEEMED [my emphasis] with perishable things like silver or gold from you futile [and I might add, sinful] way of life inherited from your forefathers, (19) but with precious blood, as of a lamb unblemished and spotless, *the blood* of Christ." Notice that Peter speaks of our BEING REDEEMED by the atoning blood of Christ from a sinful way of living to living for God in His righteousness and holiness. Redemption includes a whole lot more than just being forgiven, as important as that is. The Lamb of God bore our sins with the guilt and the penalties (including the major penalties of spiritual death and bondage to sin), so that we could be redeemed out of the kingdom of spiritual death, sin, and lawlessness. We have been set free from slavery to sin. These verses (1 Peter 1:13-19) are discussed in some detail on pages 190-194 of my book, *Holiness and Victory Over Sin.*

Now we'll look at one last passage that speaks of our being redeemed out of the kingdom of sin and darkness and transferred to the kingdom of the Lord Jesus Christ, which is a kingdom of righteousness, holiness, life, and light. Let's look at Colossians 1:12-14. (We will discuss Col. 1:9-14 in some detail in a later article, and these verses are discussed on pages 146-151 of my book, *Holiness and Victory Over Sin,* so I'll be somewhat brief here.) "giving thanks to the Father, who has qualified us to share in the inheritance of the saints in light. [[It would be better to translate "in the light." The definite article is included with the word for light in the Greek. God's light includes His truth and His righteousness and holiness. God has qualified us, or made us fit, to dwell in His kingdom of light by delivering us from the kingdom of darkness and making us saints (holy people). Christians are saints in that they have been set apart by God and for God. They have been set apart from slavery to sin and from being part of the kingdom of sin and darkness. And they have been set apart for God; they have become slaves of righteousness, and they live in the kingdom of God, which is the kingdom of life, light, righteousness, and holiness.]] (13) For He delivered us from the domain [or, authority] of darkness [of the darkness], and transferred us to the kingdom of His beloved Son [Verse 14 expands on our being delivered from being slaves of sin in the kingdom of spiritual death, sin, and darkness], (14) in whom we have REDEMPTION [my emphasis; I would translate THE REDEMPTION. The definite article is included in the Greek. God's redemption is the redemption in that it is the theme of much Old Testament prophecy and is at the heart of new-covenant salvation. Verse 14 continues with the words, "the forgiveness of sins," but I can't live with the translation "forgiveness" for the Greek noun used here, *aphesis.* Redemption includes forgiveness, but it means a lot more than forgiveness. I would translate "the release from sins [with the guilt and penalties (including the major penalties of spiritual death and bondage to sin)]," or the equivalent. Before we became Christians we were under our sins (very much including the sin of Adam) with the guilt and the penalties (including the major penalties of spiritual death and bondage to sin). But God sent His Son to bear our sins (with the guilt and the penalties), and He redeemed us (through the atoning death of His Son) from the pitiful state of being spiritually dead and in bondage to sin. These things are discussed in some detail throughout my book, *Holiness and Victory Over Sin: Full Salvation Through the Atoning Death of the Lord Jesus Christ.* One of the chapters of the book is titled, "A Study on the Meaning of the Greek Noun *Aphesis.*" *Aphesis* is the Greek noun translated "forgiveness" (or the equivalent) in Col. 1:14 and quite a few other verses.

God bless you! His will be done! His will be done in us! In Jesus' name! Amen!

Holiness and Victory Over Sin #11

Holy Father, we humble our hearts before you. We confess that we are totally dependent on your grace. We want to rightly divide your Word; we want to know the balanced truth of what your Word teaches; we want to live in line with your Word. We pray in Jesus' name! Amen!

We have the great privilege to turn to ROMANS CHAPTER 5. This is a very important chapter, in a very important epistle.

Romans 5:1. **Therefore, having been justified by faith, we have peace with God through our Lord Jesus Christ.** This is another verse where the verb *justify* is being used in the very full sense we have discussed already. (It is also used in this very full sense in Rom. 5:9, and the noun "justification" is used in this very full sense in Rom. 5:16, 18.) We have been declared righteous; spiritual death and sin have been dethroned; and we have been born again and made righteous by the indwelling Righteous, Holy Spirit of God. We are justified by grace through faith in the Lord Jesus Christ and His all-important atoning death and resurrection.

In Romans 5:6-10 the apostle Paul speaks of what we were before we were justified by faith. In verse 6 he speaks of the time when "we were still helpless" and we were "ungodly." In verse 8 he speaks of the time when "we were yet sinners," and in verse 10 of the time when "we were yet enemies [of God]." **Having now been justified by faith** (Rom. 5:1), we are no longer "helpless" or "ungodly" or "enemies of God," and in the ideal case we would never ever sin against Him. We have been reconciled to God; we love Him; we want to do His will by His grace and for His glory. God's saving, sanctifying grace is more than sufficient, but we must appropriate that grace by faith on a continuous basis, which includes walking by the Holy Spirit on a continuous basis. Our faith must be based on what God's Word actually says.

I'll read Romans 5:1 again, **Therefore, having been justified by faith, we have peace with God through our Lord Jesus Christ.** If we were forgiven and declared righteous, but were still "ungodly" and "sinners" and "enemies" of God, we could not have peace with Him. We cannot have peace with God until we submit to Him and His plan of salvation from our hearts (by faith) and begin to live for Him by His sufficient, saving, sanctifying grace in Christ.

Let's look at Romans 8:6, 7. "For the mind [or, way of thinking] of the flesh is death, but the mind [or, way of thinking] of the Spirit [the Holy Spirit] is life and PEACE [my emphasis], (7) because the mind set on the flesh [or, the way of thinking of the flesh] is hostile toward God; for it does not subject itself to the law of God, for it is not even able *to do so*." We desperately needed a Savior! Before we became born-again Christians, we were, by definition, in the flesh, and we thought the sinful ways of the flesh, of the old man. We were not living for God in His truth and righteousness. We were living in sin; and much of our thinking was hostile toward God. We could not have PEACE with God while we were hostile toward Him, while we were thinking wrong in our hearts (which included our having wrong attitudes, wrong motives, and wrong priorities) and were living in sin. But now we are enabled to think right and live right through new-covenant salvation.

Back to Romans 5:1, **Therefore, having been justified by faith, we have peace with God through our Lord Jesus Christ.** Now the sin problem has been solved. We have been declared righteous; we have been set free from spiritual death and bondage to sin; we have been born again; and we have been made righteous with the imparted righteousness of God. We have been justified by grace through faith. God must receive all the glory for our salvation.

Romans 5:2. **through whom** [referring to the Lord Jesus Christ] **also we have obtained our introduction** [or, **we have obtained our access**] **by faith into this grace in which we stand** [[The Lord Jesus Christ has brought us into this realm of grace, the grace that provides everything we need to be saved and to live for God in this world, with the emphasis on our being enabled to live in the center of His will. Everything we need for this age has been provided through salvation in the Lord Jesus Christ. Paul continues and looks to the next age, when we will be glorified.]]**; and we exult** [or, **we boast**] **in the hope of the glory of God.** The word **hope** does not infer doubt, but it does refer to the future (the near future, I believe). **We exult** [or, **we boast**] **in the hope of the glory of God.** Quite often the New Testament speaks of this glory. In Colossians 1:5, for example, the apostle Paul speaks of "the hope laid up for you in heaven, of which you previously heard in the word of truth, the gospel." And in Colossians 1:27 he speaks of "Christ in you, the hope of glory."

Romans 5:3, 4. **And not only this** [not only do we exult (or boast) in the hope of the glory of God], **we also exult** [or, **boast**] **in our tribulations, knowing that tribulation brings about perseverance; (4) and perseverance, proven character; and proven character, hope.** Even the trials and tribulations work together for good, including our good (see Rom. 8:28). There is only one thing required of us. We must stay faithful to God and the new covenant by His grace through faith. We must keep walking by faith (faith in God and His Word) and by the Holy Spirit. We will then glorify God at all times, including during times of trials and tribulations, and we will come out of the difficult places better and stronger in faith and hope. For one thing, we will confirm that God's Word is true and His grace is sufficient.

Romans 5:5. **and hope does not disappoint** [[The idea here is that our hope of inheriting the glory of God at the end of this age will not be disappointed. Quite the contrary! As Paul continues, he confirms the idea that our hope will not be disappointed by speaking of the very special love that God has manifested toward every true Christian, by giving them His very special love gift of the Holy Spirit to dwell within them. First God sacrificed His Son to save us; then He gives us the Holy Spirit. What greater gifts could He possibly give us? The God who loves us like that (and has manifested that love to us as individuals) will not disappoint us regarding eternal glory. All we have to do is stay faithful by His grace.]],

because the love of God [the love of God for us as His adopted children] **has been poured out within our hearts** [I prefer the translation **into our hearts** of the NIV.] **because the love of God has been poured out into our hearts through the Holy Spirit who was given to us.** God has poured out of His heart into our hearts His love gift of the Holy Spirit to dwell within us. What a love gift! What a manifestation of love! The Greek verb that was translated "has been poured out" here was also used in Acts 2:33 of the pouring out of the Holy Spirit, starting on the Day of Pentecost. Those who have received the Holy Spirit must know that they have received the Holy Spirit. For one thing, the indwelling Spirit "testifies with our spirits that we are children [born-again children] of God" (see Romans 8:16). In Romans 8:9 the apostle makes it clear that the Holy Spirit dwells in every true Christian.

and hope does not disappoint, because the love of God has been poured out into our hearts through the Holy Spirit who has been given to us. And now that the Holy Spirit is dwelling within us, He testifies of the very special love the Father has for us, and He enables us to experience something of that love, Person to person. He also enables us to love the Father, to love our brothers and sisters in Christ, and to love the people of the world. Love is the first fruit of the Holy Spirit that Paul mentioned in Gal. 5:22, 23. The Holy Spirit produces that fruit in our hearts and lives as we walk by the Spirit on a continuous basis, which we are enabled and required to do. The God who has saved us and given us His Spirit will not disappoint us regarding our inheriting His eternal glory, but we must stay faithful by His grace, which includes all the work of the Spirit.

Romans 5:6. **For while we were still helpless, at the right time Christ died for the ungodly.** Before we became born-again Christians "we were still helpless" and "ungodly" (and "sinners" Rom. 5:8 and "enemies" Rom. 5:10) and we were in desperate need of the Savior. The Father sent His Son to die for us. As we have discussed, He (the Lamb of God) died for us, bearing our sins with the guilt and the penalties (including the major penalties of spiritual death and bondage to sin), so we could be partakers of His full salvation.

Romans 5:7, 8. **For one will hardly die for a righteous man; though perhaps for the good man someone would dare even to die. (8) But God demonstrates His own love toward us, in that while we were yet**

sinners, Christ died for us. Note the emphasis on God's love for us, as in verse 5. And note that the apostle speaks of the time "while we were yet sinners." Now we are justified (using this word in the very full sense we have discussed), and in the ideal case we would never sin again. That sounds good, doesn't it? Paul repeatedly makes this point throughout his writings, as do the other writers of the New Testament. I'll quote six typical verses. I'll use the NKJV for the first three verses. Romans 6:1, 2, "What shall we say then? Shall we continue in sin that grace may abound? Certainly not! How shall we who died to sin live any longer in it?" Romans 6:11, "Likewise you also, reckon yourselves to be dead indeed to sin, but alive to God in Christ Jesus our Lord." And Galatians 5:16 (I'll read this verse from the *Amplified Bible*), "But I say, walk *and* live habitually in the (Holy) Spirit—responsive to *and* controlled *and* guided by the Spirit; then you will certainly not gratify the cravings *and* desires of the flesh—of human nature without God." And lastly, I'll read 1 John 3:6, 7 from the NASB, "No one who abides in Him sins; no one who sins has seen Him or knows Him. (7) Little children, make sure no one deceives you; the one who practices righteousness [or, the one who is doing righteousness] is righteous, just as He [God] is righteous."

I'll read Romans 5:8 again; then we'll go on to Romans 5:9. **But God demonstrates His own love toward us, in that while we were yet sinners, Christ died for us. (9) Much more then, having now been justified in His blood, we shall be saved from the wrath *of God* through Him.** It is very important for us to see that the words **having now been justified in His blood** are used in a very full sense here, as they were in Romans 5:1. We are declared righteous, born again, and made righteous with the imparted righteousness of God. The atoning blood of the Lord Jesus Christ, backed up by the Holy Spirit, has the power to fully solve the sin problem and make us righteous with the very righteousness of God. We are no longer "helpless" and "ungodly" (see verse 6). We are no longer "sinners" (see verse 8). And we are no longer "enemies" of God (see verse 10). Now we have "peace" with God (see verse 1), and "we exult [or, we boast] in the hope of the glory of God" (see verse 2), which goes along with the fact that "we shall be saved from the wrath *of God*" and will be glorified at the end of this age (see verses 9, 11). If we are justified by His blood, we are ready to stand before God now and at the end of this age.

we shall be saved from the wrath *of God* through Him (Romans 5:9), through the Lord Jesus Christ and His saving work. His work includes restoring Christians who fall into sin when they sincerely repent (see 1 John 2:1, 2, for example).

Romans 5:10. **For if while we were enemies we were reconciled to God through the death of His Son** [[In verses 6 and 8 the apostle mentioned that Christ died for us. In verse 9 he mentioned that we are justified by His blood (His blood goes with His dying for us), and here in verse 10 he mentioned that we are reconciled through the death of Christ. Every true Christian understands that we are saved through the all-important atoning death of the Lord Jesus Christ.

As we have discussed, we were ungodly; we were sinners; and we were enemies of God before we became born-again Christians. We were thinking wrong in our hearts, and we were living in sin – we were rebels. But now we have been reconciled to God through the death of His Son. Our being reconciled to God includes His forgiving us, but it also very much includes our repenting and beginning to live for Him in His righteousness through the saving, sanctifying grace of God in Christ – by grace through faith. If we were still enemies of God, we would not be reconciled to God.]]**, much more, having been reconciled, we shall be saved by His life.** Now that the sin problem has been solved through the atoning death of Christ, and we have been justified (using the word justified in a very full sense), it will be easy for the resurrected, glorified Christ to save us from the wrath of God to come. (His wrath is coming against those who are committed to live in sin. On the wrath of God to come, see verse 9.) For one thing, He will glorify and rapture His people from the earth before God begins to pour out His wrath in the last days, and it is clear that we will begin to experience His glory on a very high level from that time on, instead of experiencing His wrath.

Romans 5:11. **And not only this** [that is, not only will we be saved from the wrath of God to come against sin]**, but we also** [or, **we even**] **exult** [or, **we even boast**] **in God through our Lord Jesus Christ, through whom we have now received the reconciliation.** We exult (or we boast) in God because we know that we will be glorified and begin to reign with Him in a never-ending reign. That is a lot more than just being saved from the wrath of God to come. Back in verse 2, Paul spoke of our exulting (or, boasting) in the hope of the glory of God. He means the same thing here. We exult (or, we boast) regarding the fact that we will inherit eternal glory at the end of this age, just as He promised.

Now we come to Romans 5:12-21, which are very important verses. First I'll briefly summarize what the apostle Paul says here. We, all mankind, were under Adam; he was the head of our race. And significantly, we were under the penalty for his sin, including spiritual death and bondage to sin. The old covenant could not solve this problem. It found us in spiritual death and in bondage to sin, and it left us in spiritual death and in bondage to sin. But now new-covenant salvation has come through the Lord Jesus Christ, and we (all true Christians) are under a new Head, the One called the last Adam in 1 Cor. 15:45. We are under Him, and we are united with Him, Him who is infinitely greater than Adam. The Lord Jesus Christ is deity with God the Father, a worthy Savior indeed. What a salvation plan! What a Savior! Amen!

In Christ, spiritual death and sin have been dethroned, and we are forgiven, born again, and made righteous and holy. That's Paul's emphasis here. In Christ the spiritual death, bondage to sin problem is solved. As we walk by faith and by the Holy Spirit (which we are enabled and required to do) the very righteousness of God is manifested in our hearts and lives. But God isn't near done yet. We will be glorified at the end of this age, and we will begin to reign with the Lord Jesus Christ in a never-ending reign. We will have an existence far above what Adam had before the fall. He was created with a physical body to live on the earth. We will have glorified bodies designed to live in God's heavenly kingdom. What a salvation plan! What a Savior! Amen!

Romans 5:12. **Therefore, just as through one man sin entered into the world, and death through sin** [[That "one man" was Adam. God had warned Adam that in the day he rebelled and ate of the forbidden fruit, he would die (see Gen. 2:17). Adam and Eve rebelled. They died spiritually that day, and the physical death process was initiated. (See Genesis chapter 3 for the details. I have a paper on Genesis chapters 1-3 on my internet site.) What a sad day, but before the foundation of the world, God had already planned to send His Son to save us from spiritual death and bondage to sin and to take us to heaven.]], **and so death spread to all men** [[Death spread to all men. All the descendants of Adam and Eve were born outside the garden of Eden into spiritual death, not having a life-flowing relationship with God. And so death spread to all men because of Adam's transgression, spiritual death and physical death. The fact that all mankind (except for born-again Christians) is under spiritual death and in bondage to sin is a dominant theme of the verses we are discussing. In verse 15, for example, the apostle says, "For if by the transgression of the one [Adam] the many died...." In verse 17 he says, "For if by the transgression of the one [Adam], death reigned through the one...." And in verse 21 he says, "as sin reigned in death."]], **because all sinned.** I can't live with this translation. I believe the apostle Paul (and the One who sent him) intended a translation like the following, **and so death spread to all men WITH THE RESULT THAT ALL SINNED**, or **ON THE BASIS OF WHICH ALL SINNED.** It is a dominant theme in the New Testament that all who are in spiritual death are in bondage to sin. Read Romans 8:1-8, for example, and the first words of Romans 5:21 say, "So that, as sin reigned in death." Where spiritual death reigns, sin reigns. Ever since the fall of Adam, spiritual death and sin have been reigning over all people to one degree, or another. I'll read Romans 5:12 again; then we'll go on to verse 13, **Therefore, just as through one man sin entered into the world, and death through sin, and so death spread to all men, with the result that** [or, **on the basis of which**] **all sinned.**

Romans 5:13. **for until the Law sin was in the world** [The Law here is the Mosaic Law, which God gave through Moses about 1400 BC.]**, but sin is not imputed when there is no law.** These words about sin's not being imputed when there is no law must be greatly qualified. The Old Testament makes it very clear that God took the sins of the people who lived in the days before the Mosaic Law very seriously, and He judged them because of those sins. For example, God destroyed all mankind except for Noah and his family at the time of the flood because of their sins. And God destroyed the people of Sodom and Gomorrah because of their sins. Both of those judgments took place in the years before the Mosaic Law was given. The important point that the apostle Paul is making here in verse 13 is that it was the sin of Adam that resulted in the death (both spiritual death and physical death) of the descendants of Adam. Adam's sin had very serious consequences for all his descendants.

Romans 5:14. **Nevertheless death reigned** [both spiritual death and physical death reigned] **from Adam until Moses, even over those who had not sinned in the likeness of the offense of Adam....** As I mentioned, Paul is making the important point that it was Adam's transgression that caused the death of his descendants. The apostle makes it clear here in verse 14 that they had sinned in the days before the Mosaic Law was given (and the Bible makes it clear that God held them accountable for those sins and judged them), but Paul is showing that DEATH CAME BECAUSE OF ADAM'S SIN. They sinned in the days before the Mosaic Law was given all right, but they did not sin **in the likeness of the offense [transgression] of Adam**.

Adam's transgression was much more serious than the sins of the people who sinned from Adam until Moses. Adam was the head of all mankind. He rebelled against God and transgressed a direct command where God had said, don't eat of the forbidden fruit, or you will die. And, significantly, when Adam rebelled against God, he was totally free. He was living in the garden, and he had a life-flowing relationship with God, unlike his descendants who were spiritually dead when they sinned. Now they weren't totally spiritually dead; they still had some freedom of the will, for one thing. That's why God could take their sins seriously. It is very clear that on judgment day God will judge people based on what they have done. They will answer for their sins, not for the sin of Adam.

Now I'll read all of Romans 5:14, **Nevertheless death reigned from Adam until Moses, even over those who had not sinned in the likeness of the offense of Adam, who is a type of Him who was to come.** At the end of verse 14, the apostle mentions that Adam is a type of Him who was to come. Paul didn't mind dwelling on the transgression of Adam with its very serious consequences for all mankind, because he had the good news of full salvation through the last Adam to share. As I mentioned, those who submit to God's new-covenant plan of salvation are saved from spiritual death and bondage to sin, and ultimately they are taken to a place much higher than what Adam had before the fall. We will be glorified and live in God's new Jerusalem that is permeated with His life, glory, righteousness, and holiness.

Romans 5:15. **But the free gift is not like the transgression** [[That is, the free gift of full salvation in the Lord Jesus Christ is not like the transgression of Adam in that the free gift is so much greater. For one thing, as the apostle is going to tell us in verse 16, the Lamb of God, the last Adam, died bearing the transgression of Adam with its guilt and penalties AND the sins of all mankind with the guilt and penalties. Also, as I have mentioned, the Lord Jesus Christ eventually takes all believers

116

(including the believers from Old Testament days) to a place much higher than what Adam had before the fall.]]. **For if by the transgression of the one [Adam] the many died, much more did the grace of God and the gift by the grace of the one Man, Jesus Christ, abound to the many.** The gift of full salvation abounds to all who submit to God and His Son and His gospel of new-covenant salvation. Christ died for all mankind, and all are invited to repent and submit (in faith) to God's new-covenant plan of salvation. Note the strong emphasis on God's grace here. Paul mentions the "free gift" then he speaks of "the grace of God and the gift by the grace," and in the next verse he speaks of "those who receive the abundance of grace and of the gift of righteousness." We are saved 100 percent by the grace of God in Christ, but (like Paul says in verse 17) we must receive God's grace. We receive and cooperate with His saving grace by faith.

Romans 5:16. **The gift is not like *that which came* through the one who sinned; for on the one hand the judgment *arose* from one *transgression* resulting in condemnation, but on the other hand the free gift *arose* from many transgressions resulting in justification.** Adam's one transgression led to the **condemnation** of all mankind. That condemnation included the penalties of spiritual death and bondage to sin. But that condemnation is overthrown for those who receive the free gift of God's **justification** that Paul mentioned here. The context shows that justification is being used here in the very full sense we have discussed already; it includes the declaration of righteousness; the overthrow of spiritual death and bondage to sin, the impartation of spiritual life (starting with the new birth), and the impartation of the righteousness of God. Notice, for example, that verse 17 mentions "the gift of righteousness" (which includes the imputed and imparted righteousness of God) and the fact that we now "reign in life," instead of our being reigned over in the realm of spiritual death. And in verse 18 Paul speaks of "the JUSTIFICATION OF LIFE." If we are justified, we have the life of God dwelling within us by the Holy Spirit, and the indwelling Righteous, Holy Spirit enables us to walk in the righteousness of God. Spiritual death and sin are under our feet. That sounds good, doesn't it?

Romans 5:17. **For if by the transgression of the one, death reigned through the one, much more those who receive the abundance of grace and of the gift of righteousness will reign in life through the**

One, Jesus Christ. As I mentioned, God's grace (His abundant, sufficient grace) dethrones sin (the sin that reigns wherever spiritual death reigns; see Rom. 5:21, for example), and His grace makes us righteous with the imputed and imparted righteousness of God. Now, instead of spiritual death and sin reigning over us, we reign in God's kingdom of life and righteousness, with spiritual death and sin under our feet. And in the very near future our victory over physical death will be manifested, and we will be glorified and begin to reign with the Lord Jesus Christ. Thanks be to God for such a salvation plan! Amen!

It's time to stop for now. God bless you!

Holiness and Victory Over Sin #12

Holy Father, we humble our hearts before you. We ask you to show us anywhere and everywhere that we are misunderstanding the gospel. We want to rightly divide your Word; we want to understand it; we want to live it; for your full glory and for our full good. We ask in Jesus' name with thanksgiving. Amen!

We discussed Rom. 5:1-17 in the last broadcast. Today we'll start with verse 18 and finish the chapter. What we say today builds on the last article.

Romans 5:18. **So then as through one transgression** [Adam's] **there resulted condemnation to all men** [We were all born under Adam and under the penalty for his sin. That penalty – that condemnation – included spiritual death and bondage to sin.]**, even so through one act of righteousness there resulted justification of life to all men.** There is widespread agreement that the **one act of righteousness** refers to the atoning death of the Lord Jesus Christ. He went to the cross bearing our sins with the guilt and the penalties to save us and to overthrow the devil and his kingdom. He bore our sins with the guilt and the penalties, very much including the sin of Adam with the penalties of spiritual death and bondage to sin, so we could be forgiven and get out from under those penalties. Forgiveness is provided because He bore our sins with the guilt. The new birth and victory over sin are provided because He bore our sins with the penalties of spiritual death and bondage to sin.

even so through one act of righteousness there resulted justification of life to all men. For one thing, the "justification of LIFE" overthrows the "condemnation" of spiritual DEATH and bondage to sin. Those who submit to God's new-covenant plan of salvation by faith receive the **justification of life.** They are justified by God, using the word *justified* in the very full sense we have discussed already; that is, we are declared righteous; spiritual death and bondage to sin are dethroned; we are born again; and we are made righteous by the imparted righteousness of God. We have the **justification of LIFE.** We are born again and have spiritual life; now the Spirit of LIFE dwells within us. We have righteousness and holiness; now the Righteous, Holy Spirit dwells within us, and He enables us to walk in the very righteousness and holiness of God.

Christ died for all, and salvation is offered to all, but many reject God's offer of salvation. We must submit to God's new-covenant plan of salvation with repentance and faith to be saved.

Romans 5:19. **For as through the one man's disobedience the many WERE MADE SINNERS** [my emphasis; As we have discussed, Adam's disobedience resulted in the spiritual death and bondage to sin of all his descendants – we **were made sinners.**]**, even so through the obedience of the One** [the Lord Jesus Christ, the last Adam] **the many WILL BE MADE RIGHTEOUS** [my emphasis]**.** The obedience of the Lord Jesus Christ certainly includes His atoning death here, but it need not be limited to that "one act of righteousness" (Romans 5:18). His whole life was one of obedience – He never sinned! **even so through the obedience of the One the many will be made righteous.** We are born again and made righteous with the imparted righteousness of God; the very Righteous, Holy Spirit dwells within us. He enables us to be righteous and holy as we walk by the Spirit on a continuous basis through faith, a faith that is based on God's Word.

Some Christians believe that the words **will be made righteous** here mean only that Christ's righteousness is imputed to us and that we are forgiven and have a right standing with God. I believe that viewpoint is a serious misunderstanding of the gospel, and that it significantly distorts the gospel. Adam's DISOBEDIENCE resulted in the DISOBEDIENCE of his descendants; we **were made sinners.** The last Adam's OBEDIENCE results in the OBEDIENCE and righteousness of those who become united with Him through new-covenant salvation. "And He Himself bore our sins [with the guilt and the penalties (including the major penalties of spiritual death and bondage to sin)] in His body on the cross, SO THAT WE MIGHT DIE TO SIN AND LIVE TO RIGHTEOUSNESS [my emphasis]; for by His wounds you were healed" (1 Peter 2:24).

Romans 5:20. **The Law** [the Mosaic Law] **came in so that the transgression would increase....** The Mosaic Law intensified the sin problem. For one thing, it was more serious to transgress God's commandments, after they had been given, than it was to sin against tradition or conscience. Also, the Law tended to arouse the desire for forbidden fruit. I'll read several cross-references that will help us understand what the apostle Paul meant about the Law increasing transgression: Romans 4:15, "for the Law brings about wrath, but where there is no law, there is no violation." Romans 5:13, "for until the Law sin was in the world, but sin is not imputed when there is no law." (We have already discussed this verse.) Romans 7:5, "For while we were in the flesh, the sinful passions, which were *aroused* by the Law [the Mosaic Law] were at work in the members of our body to bear fruit for death." Romans 7:8, 9, 11, "But sin, taking opportunity through the commandment, produced in me coveting of every kind; for apart from the Law [the Mosaic Law] sin was dead. (9) And I was once alive apart from the Law; but when the commandment came sin became alive and I died.... ... (11) for sin, taking opportunity through the commandment, deceived me and through it killed me." (We will discuss Romans chapter 7 verse-by-verse when we finish Romans chapter 5.) And I'll quote one last cross-reference that deals with the Mosaic Law's increasing transgression for man in the flesh (for man in spiritual death), 1 Corinthians 15:56, "The sting of death is sin, and the power of sin is the law."

I'll start to read Romans 5:20 again, **The Law came in so that the transgression would increase....** What good could come from transgression increasing? For one thing, God used the Law to help people see that they were sinners in desperate need of new-covenant salvation. Most people are very slow to see their sin, but God used the Law to help force sin out in the open, so that we could see our need for the Savior. See Romans 7:13 where Paul shows that through the Mosaic Law sin became "utterly sinful." As Paul shows throughout Romans chapter 7, man in the flesh, man in spiritual death, man who has been sold into bondage to sin, cannot be saved by the Mosaic Law. We must be saved by the Lord Jesus Christ, including the believers from Old Testament days.

Now I'll read all of Romans 5:20, **The Law came in so that the transgression would increase; but where sin increased, grace abounded all the more.** The saving grace of God in Christ abounded to fully solve the sin problem. Spiritual death and bondage to sin have been dethroned and God manifests His righteousness in the hearts and lives of Christians as they walk by the Holy Spirit on a continuous basis by faith (a faith that is based on God's Word). And, eventually, the saving grace of God in Christ will take us to a place much higher than what Adam had before the fall.

Romans 5:21. **so that, as sin reigned in death** [As we have seen, all of Adam's descendants were born into spiritual death and in bondage to sin – sin reigned in the realm of spiritual death.], **even so grace would reign through righteousness to eternal life** [or, unto eternal life; or, resulting in eternal life] **through Jesus Christ our Lord.** The saving grace of Christ reigns in the hearts and lives of Christians as we walk by faith, and spiritual death and sin are under our feet. Where the saving grace of Christ reigns, the righteousness of God is manifested in our hearts and lives. We can also say that the righteousness of God reigns instead of sin reigning. I'll read Romans 6:18, "and having been freed from sin, you became slaves of righteousness." And now that the sin problem has been solved and the righteousness of God is manifested and reigns in our hearts and lives, we are ready to stand before God, and we will inherit the fullness of eternal life at the end of this age. We are born again now, but when the Lord Jesus Christ returns, we will be glorified and inherit the fullness of eternal life. What a salvation plan! What a Savior! Amen!

I'll read one last verse that is an important cross-reference for Rom. 5:21, Romans 6:14, "For sin shall not be master over you, for you are not under law, but under grace." Now, instead of sin reigning in spiritual death, the saving grace of God in Christ reigns in our hearts and lives, and the righteousness of God is manifested in our hearts and lives. The Mosaic Law (or any other law) could not dethrone spiritual death and sin and make us righteous with the imparted righteousness of God. In fact, as we have seen, the Mosaic Law intensified the sin problem.

I'm going to read a paragraph from my book that I have under Romans 5:19, We need to take very seriously the effects of Adam's sin (the fall of man); however, we must also see that men still have a free will to some extent, and (in general) they are responsible before God for their actions, including their priorities, attitudes, motives, etc. All will be judged according to what they believe and what they do, according to their works (see, for example, Matt. 16:27; 25:1-46; Rom. 1:18-3:20; 14:11, 12; 1 Cor. 3:11-15; 2 Cor. 5:10; Rev. 20:12, 13; 22:11, 12). I doubt that Adam's sin will even be mentioned at *our* judgment. Each person is especially responsible to repent and submit to God and receive His offer of salvation in Christ Jesus (see, for example, John 3:16-21; 6:29; 14:6; Acts 4:12).

That concludes our verse-by-verse discussion of Romans chapter 5; now we'll go on to a verse-by-verse study of ROMANS CHAPTER 7, which is another very important chapter that deals extensively with the topic of righteousness, holiness, and victory over sin. First I'm going to turn to my paper titled, *The Interpretation of Romans Chapter 7 and Righteousness and Holiness: This Paper Deals Extensively with the Interpretation of Romans Chapter 7 by the Early (before AD 500) Christian Writers, and it Includes Many Excerpts from These Writers.* An abbreviated version of the paper is located on my internet site (Google to Karl Kemp Teaching). You could get a copy of the original version of the paper by contacting me.

I'm going to read most of the lengthy introduction of this paper. This paper builds on and supplements the verse-by-verse study of Romans chapter 7 on pages 104-116 of my book, *Holiness and Victory Over Sin.* It would be difficult to overstate the importance of rightly understanding Romans chapter 7.

Many evangelical Christians in our day (about half) understand Romans chapter 7 to teach that Christians cannot walk with the victory over sin during this present age. This widespread viewpoint has done great damage to the Body of Christ, obviously undercutting faith for victory over sin to one degree or another. But victory over sin can only come by grace THROUGH FAITH (a faith that must be based on God and His Word), through Christ's atoning death and resurrection, and in the power of the Holy Spirit.

At the outset of this paper, I want to make it clear that I know that there are many sincere, godly Christians who (from my point of view) misinterpret Romans chapter 7. It's not hard for some to misinterpret this passage when this has been the dominant view in certain segments of the Body of Christ for hundreds of years. Another factor that has lent itself to a misinterpretation of this passage is the low level of righteousness and holiness that has often existed in much of the church. I don't want to be perceived as attacking, or insulting, or showing disrespect for other Christians. I want to do everything I can do to promote true unity in the Body of Christ (but unity in the truth, especially the truth of the Christian basics; and unity in righteousness and holiness, not unity in sin), and I want this paper to be a blessing to the Body of Christ.

Some Christians, because they have so many other things right, and because they really are trying to make God and His will top priority, haven't been affected too much by their wrong interpretation of Rom. 7:14-25. Nevertheless, it stands true that the misinterpretation of this passage has done tremendous damage to the cause of righteousness and holiness in the Body of Christ. I believe it's time for many Christians to prayerfully reconsider their interpretation of Romans chapter 7. It's my prayer that this paper will help some toward that end.

The most common view of evangelical Christians in our day regarding righteousness and holiness is that the most we can hope for is to be progressively sanctified, thereby decreasing the amount of sin as time goes by, but never gaining the victory over sin as long as we live in this world. A major source for this inadequate viewpoint, which doesn't permit Christians to have faith for victory over sin, is the misinterpretation of Romans chapter 7. It's true that Christians must continue to grow throughout their lives in Christ, but the New Testament typically speaks of Christians being sanctified, abiding in a state of holiness, not of holiness being an elusive goal that is never reached in this life. I'm not talking about some way out absolute perfection; I'm talking about Christians, including Christians young in the faith, walking according to God's Word and by His Spirit in a reasonable way, and living for God as His born-again children in faithfulness, by His sufficient grace through faith.

Tremendous damage to the cause of righteousness and holiness in the Body of Christ has also come through the widespread misinterpretation of 1 John 1:8. Based on my studies, some eighty to ninety percent of

Christians (including evangelicals) understand 1 John 1:8 to teach that Christians cannot stop sinning in this life. More misinterpret 1 John 1:8 than Romans 7:14-25, but the misinterpretation of Romans chapter 7 is quite a bit more serious since it spells out the Christian's supposed bondage to sin in much more powerful terms. Galatians 5:17 is another verse that has often been misinterpreted, but it hasn't caused as much damage as the misinterpretations of Romans chapter 7 and 1 John 1:8. These verses are all discussed in my book, starting on page 194. We have already discussed Galatians 5:17 in these articles, and we will discuss 1 John 1:8 in some detail.

Many Christians who do not understand Romans chapter 7 to teach that Christians cannot quit sinning in this life have, nevertheless, been significantly influenced by the wrong interpretation of these verses, since it has been such a powerful force in lowering the Christian standard from any idea even close to walking in the righteousness and holiness of God. One manifestation of this fact is that whenever any Christians (like John Wesley or Charles Finney, for example) came on the scene teaching victory over sin in Christ, they were attacked with Rom. 7:14-25 and 1 John 1:8. A major, widespread capitulation to sin (to one degree or another) has taken place. The most widespread viewpoint, even among evangelicals, is that it is totally unrealistic, and unbiblical, to think of Christians not sinning. Based on what I have read of the writings of the ancient Christian church, we have lowered the standard for righteous living substantially below their standard. The quotations included in this paper from ancient Christian writers should suffice to demonstrate that point. The standard we must follow, of course, is the biblical standard; but we must understand what God's Word actually says.

One of the major manifestations of the fact that something is wrong with our present standard of righteousness and holiness is that we so seldom hear the words repent and repentance in the Body of Christ in our day. I'm speaking of repentance at the time of conversion, and of repentance for Christians. Coupled with this is the major problem of the out-of-balance teaching about God. We hear so much about His love, but we don't hear much about what the Bible says about His wrath. It's no wonder there is so little fear of God in so many Christians in our day, but the Bible, very much including the New Testament, makes it clear that it is necessary for us to have a proper fear of God. We should be afraid to sin against Him. ...

We don't need more condemnation in the Body of Christ, and thank God for forgiveness, but we do need more transformation to the righteousness and holiness of God. We must be open and honest before God to recognize and acknowledge our sin; we must be quick to repent; and we must make victory over all sin (by God's grace) a top priority item – God knows our hearts. Anything that God considers to be sin in our life is a serious matter; but on the other hand, we seriously confuse the issue when we call things sin that God doesn't consider to be sin (and this happens quite a bit).

We desperately need to make righteousness and holiness a top priority item, but we must understand that we receive and walk in God's righteousness and holiness by grace through faith (a faith based on God and His Word, His Word rightly divided), otherwise we'll just be striving in the flesh. We need all the grace that God has made available to us to defeat the world, the flesh, and the devil with his demons, including the grace that comes through other Christians. We don't need excuses for sin derived from misinterpretations of God's Word; that certainly will not work for good. It may make a person feel a little better about themselves for a while, but the heart/conscience of true Christians will never be satisfied while sin continues in us, or in the church – at least not if the Bible says what I think it says – and I'm sure that it does.

As a Christian young in the faith, I was often confronted with Romans chapter 7 by Christians sincerely trying to help me. I was frequently informed that I must be misunderstanding Romans chapter 6 and Romans chapter 8 (and other passages of Scripture) if I thought that the apostle Paul was actually saying that Christians are called to walk with the victory over all sin. They told me that Romans chapter 7 proves that it can't be so. I could not begin to count all the times I have been told that Romans chapter 7 proves that Christians cannot stop sinning throughout the last forty years. Many Christians believe it is deception and even heresy for Christians to believe they could ever stop sinning during this age. They are saying this, at least the primary reason sincere, Bible-believing Christians are saying this, because they believe it goes against the Bible (Romans chapter 7; 1 John 1:8; and Gal. 5:17, for example).

We often hear that all Christians sin daily in thought, in word, and in deed. But is this what the Bible really teaches? I don't think so! Back then (starting in 1964) I got motivated to (prayerfully) study the entire topic of righteousness, holiness, and victory over sin, very much including the interpretation of Romans chapter 7. I have been studying this topic more than any other ever since. What I have found is good news, very good news! What I am sharing in this paper is good news, very good news!

The key issue is whether the apostle Paul was speaking as a non-Christian or a Christian in Rom. 7:14-25. Was he speaking as a Christian when he said, for example, "For the good I wish, I do not do; but I practice the very evil that I do not wish" (Rom. 7:19)? It is significant, for one thing, that the dominant viewpoint of the early Christian writers up until the time the very influential Augustine changed his viewpoint (about AD 410), was that Paul was not speaking as a Christian in this passage. He was speaking for unregenerate mankind (those not born again). This was Augustine's earlier viewpoint, but in his later, anti-Pelagian years, he came to favor the viewpoint that Paul was speaking as a Christian in Rom. 7:14-25. Augustine had intense conflict with Pelagius in his later years.

It is very significant, however, that Augustine made a very substantial qualification to this interpretation. He said that if this passage deals with Christians, it speaks only of Christians having wrong thoughts and desires, which the Christians resist and fight against by the grace of God in Christ, not of Christians actually sinning. Even though the later viewpoint of Augustine was clearly wrong – Paul was not speaking as a Christian in this passage, and this qualification doesn't begin to fit what Paul said in this passage – if the Christians who believe this passage deals with Christians included this qualification, their interpretation would not hinder Christians from walking with the victory over sin.

Augustine mentioned that he was influenced by other Christian writers in coming to his new viewpoint. The three Christian writers that I am aware of who were early enough to have influenced Augustine all included the very substantial qualification that Augustine included. Methodius (about AD 260-311) probably was one of the writers who influenced Augustine; he was the earliest Christian writer that I am aware of who understood Rom. 7:14-25 to deal with Christians, and he clearly included the qualification. Not only did he include the qualification, but the excerpts from him in this paper also demonstrate that Methodius was strong on victory over sin for Christians. The only other two Christian writers who understood Rom. 7:14-25 to deal with Christians, who were early enough to have influenced Augustine that I am aware of, were Epiphanius (about AD 315-403) and Gregory of Nazianzus (about AD 329-390). They both included the qualification. Even though those brethren from long ago substantially qualified their interpretation that Rom. 7:14-25 was dealing with Christians, they (and especially Augustine, because of his great influence) opened a door that should not have been opened, and it was bound to happen that some would find it rather easy to drop the qualification, or greatly modify it. Many doors must be kept shut; you open them a little and eventually end up being shocked and overwhelmed with what comes into your tent/house/life.

There may be some Christians in our day who understand Rom. 7:14-25 to refer to Christians who include the important qualification that Augustine included, but I'm not aware of any. I'll repeat the qualification. These early Christian writers said that these verses speak of Christians having wrong thoughts and desires, which they resist and fight against by the grace of God in Christ, not of Christians actually sinning. I should mention that some Christians in our day believe it is sin for Christians to have wrong thoughts and desires. It's quite clear that these things are undesirable; they're part of the old man that hasn't been annihilated yet, and won't be annihilated until Jesus returns and we are glorified. But I believe the New Testament makes it clear that wrong thoughts and desires, when resisted and fought against by Christians in the power of the Holy Spirit, are not sin. They are part of the Christian's warfare, which we are supposed to win by God's sufficient grace. We win by not sinning. See Rom. 6:11-14; 8:4, 12-14; and Gal. 5:16, 17, for example. (We have already discussed these verses in these articles.) These verses speak of Christians not sinning as they, by the Holy Spirit, deny the old man the opportunity to manifest itself in sin. The wrong desires and thoughts of the old man may be there on occasion; that is the cause for the warfare spoken of in Gal. 5:17, for example; but that in itself doesn't constitute sin.

Some Christians believe that the Lord Jesus Christ taught that if a Christian has a lustful thought, he has already committed a serious sin, even the sin of adultery. I believe that is a serious misunderstanding of what the Lord said. We are about out of time, but let's take a quick look at what the Lord said in Matthew 5:27, 28. I'll read from the *New King James Version*, "You have heard that it was said to those of old, 'You shall not commit adultery.' But I say to you that whoever looks at a woman to lust for her has already committed adultery with her in his heart." Jesus was speaking here of a man who looks at a woman to lust for her, for the purpose of lusting for her. That is very different than a Christian having a lustful thought and turning his head rather than look at a woman with lust, very different indeed. I should also mention that Jesus spoke the words of Matt. 5:27, 28 in a context where He was making the important point that He had not come to lower the standard of righteousness that God had established under the old covenant, but rather to raise the standard through His saving work.

We'll come back to the interpretation of Romans chapter 7 in the next article. We thank you Holy Father for the truth. We want to know the full truth, the balanced truth of what your Word teaches.

Holiness and Victory Over Sin #13

Holy Father, we humble our hearts before you. We want to know the truth. We want to know the balanced truth of what your Word teaches. We want to understand it. We want to live it. In Jesus' mighty, holy name, Amen!

Last time when we stopped I was quoting from the lengthy Introduction of my paper titled *The Interpretation of Romans Chapter 7 and Righteousness and Holiness.* I'll quote a few more paragraphs from that Introduction. Another important point that we should discuss further is that it isn't a reasonable interpretation of Paul's words in Rom. 7:14-25 to say that he is speaking of a person only having wrong thoughts and desires. In Rom. 7:14b (the second half of the verse) the apostle Paul says, "But I am of flesh [to be of flesh/in the flesh means to be in spiritual death, without the Holy Spirit], sold [better yet, having been sold, referring back to the rebellion and fall of Adam (see Romans 5:12-21)], into [the abiding state of] bondage to sin." These words, and the following words, speak of an abiding state of bondage to sin, a state far more serious than a person's having an occasional wrong thought or desire.

In the verses that follow (in Rom. 7:15-25), Paul powerfully illustrates the fact that fallen man truly is in a state of slavery to sin by using for exhibit

A the predicament of a very sincere Jew, one who is totally convinced that the Mosaic Law is from God and true and that it must be obeyed from the heart (he may have even memorized the Law), but, nevertheless, his life frequently demonstrates that he truly is a slave of sin. Paul's primary point in these verses is to show that all mankind is so fallen that the Mosaic Law (even though it is from God and is good) isn't able to save fallen man from sin and death (it wasn't given by God for that purpose). All mankind, therefore, needs new-covenant salvation in Christ Jesus.

There are some Christians in our day who understand Rom. 7:14-25 to speak of a Christian(s), but who don't believe Paul is speaking of the normal Christian life in these verses. One such view is that Paul was speaking of an immature Christian, who hadn't yet learned to walk after the Spirit. This view is far from what Paul was dealing with in context, but it is a great improvement over any viewpoint that understands these verses to teach that Christians continue in bondage to sin, that they cannot stop sinning as long as they live, that they must necessarily fulfill their daily quota of sin.

I'm not making an attempt in this paper to equally present the different interpretations of Romans chapter 7. I'm putting most of the emphasis on what I'm sure is the correct interpretation, that Paul was not speaking of a Christian(s) in Rom. 7:14-25.

After the Introduction, this paper consists mostly of excerpts from others, but I'll make quite a few comments too; my comments are typically enclosed in brackets. I quoted the most extensively from Douglas Moo's recent commentary on Romans because I agree with him so much, and because he was so thorough. I also quote extensively from Arminius's dissertation on Romans chapter 7; I found this work to be very helpful. His dissertation was about two-hundred pages. Arminius lived from AD 1560 to 1609. The Arminians are named after him. I also quote extensively from John Chrysostom (AD 347-407). His ancient homilies (sermons) on Romans chapter 7 convince me that he understood this chapter very well. I also quote extensively from Augustine (under Arminius) and from Methodius. ...

I'm writing this Introduction last. May God's will be accomplished through this paper, and may His people be edified! A primary goal for this paper is to help bring about transformation in the Body of Christ, where it is needed. As I mentioned, we don't need more condemnation. Thank God for His mercy and grace toward us! But let's make it a top priority to do everything we can do to refrain from abusing His grace, for His full glory, and for our full good. His will be done! Amen!

I'll conclude this Introduction with the prayer the apostle Paul prayed for the newly founded church at Thessalonica, "Now may the God of peace Himself sanctify you entirely [in the *very* near future; that's what the apostle meant]; and may your spirit and soul and body [having been sanctified entirely] be preserved [or, be kept] complete [or, be kept sound], without blame at the coming of our Lord Jesus Christ." Amen!

Now I'm going to turn to pages 104-107 of my book, *Holiness and Victory Over Sin*, and read several paragraphs. Based on my studies and observations, I consider the viewpoint that Rom. 7:14-25 refer to a regenerate (born-again) Christian to be a serious mistake. I am totally convinced that the apostle Paul never intended that these verses be applied to Christians. This one misinterpretation tends to have enough power to override (or at least greatly dilute) the clear teaching of Romans chapter 6; Rom. 8:1-14; and the many other passages of the New Testament which teach that Christians can and should walk in victory over sin by grace through faith. This is good news, very good news!

If the view that Rom. 7:14-25 refer to a regenerate Christian(s) is in error, we need to face up to it. There won't be any rewards for defending and perpetuating doctrines or traditions that are wrong. Erroneous doctrines and traditions cause great damage to the Body of Christ. I'm not suggesting that there are many who are teaching views they know to be in error (though this does happen), but I am suggesting that many are very slow to consider the possibility of error in *their* doctrines or traditions. Victory over sin can only be realized by grace through faith, and we certainly cannot have a solid, Bible-based faith for victory over sin if we believe that the apostle Paul taught that we cannot have this victory. Victory over sin must be a very high priority item in the Christian faith according to the Scriptures.

Now we come to the heading, Romans chapter 7 and Romans 6:14. There is widespread agreement that Romans chapter 7 expands on Rom. 6:14. I'll read Rom. 6:14, "For sin shall not be master over you [or, have dominion over you], for you are not under law, but under grace." The Law [the Mosaic Law, or any other law] cannot save us from sin. The saving grace of God in Christ can save us from sin. In Rom. 6:14 the apostle Paul makes the important point that Christians have been set free from slavery to sin through the grace of God in Christ Jesus. He clearly infers that if we were still under the Mosaic Law, we would still be under the authority of sin. (Romans chapters 1-8 confirm this understanding.) In Romans chapter 7 the apostle shows that Christians, even Jewish Christians, are not under the Mosaic Law (see Romans 7:1-6). He also shows, at some length and in dramatic detail, that those under the Mosaic Law were definitely in bondage to sin along with the rest of mankind.

It was necessary for the apostle to show that the Mosaic Law (the old covenant) could not dethrone sin (the "sin which reigns in [spiritual] death," Romans 5:21) for at least two reasons. For one thing, many of the sons of Israel were clinging to the Law and not coming to the Lord Jesus Christ (the only One who could save them from sin). Also, the Judaizers were trying to bring the Mosaic Law into the Christian church in a manner that led to a very serious distortion of the gospel (see Gal. 1:6-10; 3:1-29; 5:1-12; and 6:12-16). The apostle had to show the weakness of the Law and the need for new covenant salvation in Christ Jesus. Fallen man (man in the flesh; man having been sold into bondage to sin, see Rom. 7:14, for example) cannot be saved by the Law

Does the apostle Paul give a comprehensive and balanced treatment of the Law in Romans chapter 7? Hardly. He could have written extensively on the blessings of the Law (see Rom. 3:1, 2; 7:12-14; and 9:4, 5), but that wasn't part of his commission. He knew that all people need the Lord Jesus Christ, and he had been sent to proclaim the gospel of new covenant salvation. Even though the apostle did not give a full and balanced treatment of the Law in Romans chapter 7, what he said was true.

Before we turn to a verse-by-verse study of Romans chapter 7, I want to include another excerpt from my paper titled, *The Interpretation of Romans Chapter 7 and Righteousness and Holiness*, starting on page 12. As this excerpt begins I'll be quoting from Douglas Moo's *Epistle to the Romans* (published by Eerdmans in 1996, pages 443-446). I start out quoting from him, but I make many comments in brackets. "The most important reasons for thinking the experience depicted in vv. 14-25 is that of an unregenerate person are the following [I believe the first five reasons of the six reasons Moo listed here are all very significant.]:

Reason #1. The strong connection of ego [that's the "I"] The strong connection of ego with 'the flesh' (vv. 14, 18, and 25) suggests that Paul is elaborating on the unregenerate condition mentioned in 7:5: 'being in the flesh.' [There's no doubt about it. The person in Rom. 7:14-25 is "in the flesh."]

Reason #2. Ego throughout this passage struggles 'on his/her own'…without the aid of the Holy Spirit. [Yes, I might add that the Holy Spirit is not mentioned at all in Rom. 7:14-25, but He is frequently mentioned in chapter 8.]

Reason #3. Ego is 'under the power of sin' (v. 14b); a state from which every believer is released (6:2, 6, 11, 18-22). [That's another very important reason.]

Reason #4. As the unsuccessful struggle of vv. 15-20 shows, ego is a 'prisoner of the law of sin' (v. 23). Yet Romans 8:2 proclaims that believers have been set free from this same 'law of sin (and death).' [That's another very important reason.]

Reason #5. While Paul makes clear that believers will struggle with sin (cf., e.g., Rom. 6:12-13; 13:12-14; Gal. 5:17 [[I might add that Paul didn't say in any of these verses that Christians will sin; a struggle with sin, yes; temptation, yes; we could sin, yes; but the apostle didn't say we will sin, and we won't sin if we walk by faith according to the terms of the new covenant, which includes walking by the Holy Spirit.]], what is depicted in 7:14-25 is not just a struggle with sin but a defeat by sin. This is a more negative view of the Christian life than can be accommodated within Paul's theology. [Very much so! I'll skip his reason 6 and continue to quote from Moo.] For those who find these arguments decisive, vv. 14-25 describe the struggle of the person outside Christ to do 'what is good,' a struggle that is doomed to failure because it is fought without the power of God that alone is able to break the power of sin. Deliverance from the situation comes with the converting, regenerating work of God in Christ, who transfers the believer from the realm of 'sin and death' to the realm of 'the Spirit of life' (v. 24b; 8:2). Within this general 'unregenerate' interpretation are various subdivisions. Some think that the text portrays

Paul's own experience under the law. Others think that Paul is describing Jews under the Law generally, or even all people confronted with 'the law of God.' There is further disagreement over the extent to which the description reflects the conscious experience of those 'under the law' and the extent to which Paul portrays the pre-Christian past from a Christian perspective." As I mentioned, I believe it is important to see that Rom. 7:14-25 incorporates Paul's Christian perspective. It does not, therefore, adequately reflect the pre-Christian experience of Paul (compare, for example, Phil. 3:4-6; Acts 23:1; 2 Tim. 1:3), or of the Jews in general. I'll quote Acts 23:1, "Paul, looking intently at the council [the Sanhedrin], said, 'Brethren, I have lived my life with a perfectly good conscience before God up to this day.' " For one thing, as Moo points out in the next excerpt in my paper (which I won't quote here), and as I mentioned in my discussion of Romans chapter 7 in my book, the apostle Paul wasn't aiming to give a balanced presentation of the Law, but to emphasize its weaknesses and our attendant need for new-covenant salvation in Christ. Douglas Moo agrees, by the way, that Paul incorporated something of his Christian understanding when he wrote Rom. 7:14-25.

I'm going to quote a few verses from the apostle Paul to show how different his life was as a Christian than the person described in Rom. 7:14-25. Paul had quite a testimony as a Christian. 1 Corinthians 11:1, "Be imitators of me, just as I also am of Christ." That's quite a testimony, isn't it? 1 Thessalonians 2:9-12, "For you recall, brethren, our labor and hardship, *how* working night and day so as not to be a burden to any of you, we proclaimed to you the gospel of God. (10) You are witnesses, and *so is* God, how devoutly and uprightly and blamelessly we behaved toward you believers; (11) just as you know how we *were* exhorting and encouraging and imploring each one of you as a father *would* his own children, (12) so that you would walk in a manner worthy of the God who calls you into His own kingdom and glory."

Let's start our verse-by-verse study with Romans 7:5. I'm turning to page 108 of my book, and I'll read the verse here. The *New American Standard Bible*, 1977 edition was used in the book. **For while we were in the flesh, the sinful passions, which were *aroused* by the Law** [referring to the Mosaic Law], **were at work in the members of our body to bear fruit for death.**

I'll comment on the words **while we were in the flesh.** Typically I'll be reading what I said in the book, but sometimes I modify what I said in the book for these articles. The NIV has, "when we were controlled by the sinful nature." In this context, **we** refers to Christians from a Jewish background; however, all Christians were "in the flesh" before being born again by the Spirit of God. But Gentiles were not under the Mosaic Law. Fallen man, by definition, is "in the flesh," devoid of the Spirit of God (see Rom. 8:1-16, for example).

Now we'll discuss the words **the sinful passions, which were *aroused* by the Law.** The Mosaic Law did not solve man's one basic problem, the sin problem; it intensified the sin problem. For example, when the Law tells man in the flesh that some things are forbidden, he is liable to say, "What have I been missing?" or, "Nobody is going to tell *me* what to do." See Romans 7:8, 11. I'll read those verses, Romans 7:8, "But sin, taking opportunity through the commandment, PRODUCED IN ME COVETING OF EVERY KIND [my emphasis], for apart from the Law sin *was* dead." Romans 7:11, "For sin, taking opportunity through the commandment [a commandment of the Mosaic Law], deceived me and through it killed me." The apostle was speaking of the commandment not to covet in both verses. We discussed (under Rom. 5:20) that the Law intensified the sin problem; for one thing, it was rebellion to transgress God's commandments, after He had given them through Moses.

Now we'll briefly discuss the words **to bear fruit for death** of Romans 7:5. See Rom. 6:21, 23. We were producing sinful fruit, and sinful fruit brings forth death, ultimately the second death of Revelation chapter 20.

Romans 7:6. **But now we have been released from the Law, having died to that by which we were bound, so that we serve in newness of the Spirit and not in oldness of the letter.** We'll briefly discuss the words **But now we have been released from the Law, having died to that by which we were bound.** In Rom. 7:1-4 the apostle Paul showed how these Christians from a Jewish background were released from the Law. They died to the Law when they were united with the Lord Jesus Christ and became Christians. But the really important thing is that they died to spiritual death and being in bondage to sin when they became Christians.

Now we'll discuss the words **so that we serve in newness of the Spirit and not in oldness of the letter.** The old covenant centered in **the letter** of the Mosaic Law. In Romans 2:29 the apostle also contrasts "the Spirit [the Holy Spirit]" with "the letter [of the Law]." 2 Corinthians 3:1-18 are another important cross-reference. 2 Corinthians 3:6 says, "who also made us adequate *as* servants of a new covenant, not of THE LETTER [the letter of the Mosaic Law], but of THE SPIRIT [the Holy Spirit]; for THE LETTER kills, but THE SPIRIT gives life." In 2 Corinthians 3:7 Paul calls the old covenant "the ministry of death, in LETTERS engraved on stones"; and in 2 Corinhians 3:9 he calls it "the ministry of condemnation," in contrast with "the ministry of THE SPIRIT" of 2 Corinthians 3:8. The Law brought "condemnation" and "death" in that it did not solve the sin problem, but rather intensified it.

In contrast with "the letter" of the Law, the new covenant is immersed in the Holy Spirit. Christians walk in "newness of life" by the Holy Spirit (see Rom. 6:4, for example); they have life by the "Spirit of life" (see Rom. 8:2; compare Rom. 8:10; 2 Cor. 3:6); and, significantly, they are sanctified and have the victory over sin by the Holy Spirit (see, for example, Rom. 2:29; 8:2-4, 13, 14; Gal. 5:5, 16; 2 Thess. 2:13; and Titus 3:5).

Romans 7:7. **What shall we say then? Is the Law sin? May it never be!** [Emphatically not! The Mosaic Law came from God, and it was good.] **On the contrary, I would not have come to know sin except through the Law; for I would not have known about coveting if the Law had not said, "YOU SHALL NOT COVET."** That's the tenth commandment (of the Ten Commandments) of the Mosaic Law.

Now let's discuss the pronoun "I" here. Paul is speaking for Israel, but in a fuller sense he is speaking for all mankind. I'm going to turn to page 9 of my paper on the Interpretation of Romans Chapter 7 and read part of a paragraph. This is quite important. These verses speak, for the most part, for those who were under the Mosaic Law (the people of Israel), but it seems that Paul intended his pronouns "I" (and "me") to have much application for all mankind, for all the descendants of fallen Adam. I believe it would be accurate to understand Romans 7:7-25 under a heading like "Fallen man confronted with the Mosaic Law. It cannot save us! We desperately need a Savior! He has come!" Gentiles can read this passage and see themselves if they would have only the Mosaic Law to save them. No matter how devoted to the Law we are, it cannot save us.

All Christians, whether from Jewish or Gentile backgrounds, must understand that the Mosaic Law (or any other law) is not able to save us from spiritual death and bondage to sin. The Law, in fact, as Paul shows in Romans chapter 7 and other places, intensifies rather than solves the sin problem.

Now back to page 109 of my book (*Holiness and Victory Over Sin*). We are discussing Rom. 7:7. We'll discuss the words, **Is the Law sin?** Emphatically, NO! (See Rom. 7:12-14, 16.) However, as we discussed under Rom. 7:5, 6, and as we will discuss further as we continue, the Law did intensify the sin problem. That's a very important point. The Law gave knowledge about sin, but it did not give the victory over sin (see Rom. 3:20, for example). Before the tenth commandment was given ("you shall not covet"), people could have done quite a bit of coveting without realizing it was sinful. After the Law was given, it became a transgression of God's Law to covet; and as Rom. 7:5, 6 show, the commandment aroused/produced coveting. Thank God for new covenant salvation in the Lord Jesus Christ!

Romans 7:8. This is a very important verse, and it goes with the following verses; they help explain one another. **But sin, taking opportunity through the commandment, produced in me coveting of every kind. For apart from the Law sin *is* dead.** The *New American Standard Bible* has the verb "is" in italics. We'll talk about that very important detail as we continue. Sin, not the Mosaic Law, was the basic problem, but sin used "the commandment" of the Law to help produce coveting. (See Rom. 7:5, 11. I'll read Romans 7:5 again, "For while we were in the flesh, the sinful passions, which were *aroused* by the Law, were at work in the members of our body to bear fruit [sinful fruit] for death.")

Now we'll discuss the words, **for apart from the Law sin *is* dead.** I believe the translation of the KJV (and the NKJV) conveys the intended meaning, **sin *was* dead.** The Greek behind these words does not include a verb corresponding to "is" or "was"; we must supply the verb in the English translation. I'm sure that the apostle Paul and the One who sent him intended the verb **was.** VERSES 8-13 ARE SET IN THE PAST TENSE. We will discuss the meaning of these words, **apart from the Law sin *was* dead** as we continue.

136

Now we come to a subheading, "When was sin dead?" Before the Mosaic Law was given, sin was relatively dead in the sense of that which Paul said in Rom. 4:15; 5:13, 14, 20; 7:5, 7-13; 1 Cor. 15:56 and Gal. 3:19. I'll read most of these verses. Romans 4:15, "for the Law brings about wrath, but where there is no law, there also is no violation." Romans 5:13, "for until the Law sin was in the world, but sin is not imputed when there is no law." I'll read the first half of Rom. 5:20, "The Law came in [The apostle is speaking of the Mosaic Law] so that the transgression would increase." I'll read Romans 7:9-11 and then 13, "I was once alive apart from the Law; but when the commandment came, sin became alive and I died; (10) and this commandment, which was to result in life, proved to result in death for me; (11) for sin, taking opportunity through the commandment, deceived me and through it killed me. ... (13) Therefore did that which is good [the Law] become *a cause of* death for me? May it never be! Rather it was sin, in order that it might be shown to be sin by effecting my death through that which was good [the Mosaic Law], so that through the commandment sin would become utterly sinful." And I'll read 1 Corinthians 15:56, "The sting of death is sin, and the power of sin is the law."

Sin was in the world before the Mosaic Law was given (see the book of Genesis, the book of Exodus up to the time the Mosaic Law was given; and Rom. 1:18-32; 5:12-14). However, the verses I quoted in the preceding paragraph show that sin was less alive before the Mosaic Law was given. We will discuss this important point further under Rom. 7:9-13. Before the Mosaic Law was given, "I" was more alive and sin was more dead. After the Law was given, sin was more alive, and I (speaking for those under the Law) was more dead.

God bless you!

Holiness and Victory Over Sin #14

Holy Father we humble our hearts before you. We admit that we are totally dependent on your grace to understand your word in our hearts and to live it. We pray in Jesus' mighty name. Amen!

Last time we went through Romans 7:8. We're ready for verse 9. I'm turning to page 110 of my book, *Holiness and Victory Over Sin*. I'll read Romans 7:9 from the book, which uses the *New American Standard Bible*, 1977 edition. **And I was once alive apart from the Law** [the Mosaic Law]**; but when the commandment came, sin became alive, and I died.** In verse 8 Paul had just said that sin was dead before the Mosaic Law was given. I'll read verse 8 and briefly comment on the verse. It's a very important verse. Romans 7:8, "But sin, taking opportunity through the commandment [Paul was speaking of the tenth commandment of the Mosaic Law that forbid coveting.], produced in me coveting of every kind; for apart from the Law sin *is* [*was*] dead."

The NASB has the verb "is" in italics. As we discussed in the last article, I would translate "sin *was* dead," with the KJV and NKJV. There is no verb in the Greek here; we must supply the verb in the English translation. I'm quite sure that the apostle Paul (and the One who sent Him) intended that we supply the verb *was*. VERSES 8-13 ARE SET IN THE PAST TENSE. "For apart from the Law sin *was* dead." This translation fits perfectly with verse 9 and the following verses. Sin was dead before the Mosaic Law was given (verse 8). Now verse 9 again, **And I was once alive apart from** [or, **without**] **the Law; but when the commandment came** [which was part of the Mosaic Law] **sin became alive, and I died.** Before the Law was given, Paul says, sin was dead. He means that sin was relatively dead – it was less alive. But when the Mosaic Law was given, **sin became alive, and I died.** We'll be discussing these things, aiming for the balanced truth of what God's Word teaches, as we continue.

It is obvious that sin was not totally dead before the Mosaic Law was given. We have already discussed the fact that there was a lot of sin, very serious sin, in the days before the Mosaic Law was given, and that God judged that sin, the flood and the destruction of Sodom and Gomorrah, for example. The Old Testament also shows that there was quite a bit of sin on the part of the people of Israel in the days before the Mosaic Law was given, and they experienced some judgment.

We come to the sub-heading, Who is the "I" and "me" of Romans 7:7-13? I have an endnote in the book here, I'll read part of the endnote, See, for example, J. A. Fitzmyer, *Jerome Biblical Commentary*, under Rom. 7:7-13. He says in part, "Ego [which is the Greek pronoun translated "I" in these verses] is depicted as existing before the Law (see Romans 7:7

and 9a), [existing] under the Law (see Romans 7:8-24), and freed from the Law in Christ (see Romans 7:25-8:29)...." [I listed two other commentators, F. Godet and H. A. W. Meyer, and then I listed Douglas Moo, *Romans 1-8*, published by Moody Press in 1991.] His heading for the section that covers Rom. 7:7-25 is "The History and Experience of Jews Under the Law," and his subheading for Rom. 7:7-12 is "The Coming of the Law." Commenting on the last words of Rom. 7:8, he says (in part): "in the years before Sinai [where the Mosaic Law was given], Paul asserts, sin was 'dead' to Israel. That sin was dead did not mean that it did not exist but that it was not as 'active' or 'powerful' before the Law as after...." Each of these four commentators summarizes the views on the identity of the "I" of Rom. 7:7-25. They all agree that Rom. 7:14-25 do not refer to a born-again Christian.

Now I'll turn back to page 110 under the heading Who is the "I" and "me" of Romans 7:7-13? The "I" of Rom. 7:7-13 (which builds on verses 1-6 and continues in verses 14-25) represents Israel, that segment of mankind (in the flesh) to whom the Mosaic Law was given. [[As we have discussed, Israel is in the spotlight here; they were the ones under the Mosaic Law; but in a fuller sense I believe the apostle Paul would have us see all mankind behind the pronouns "I" and "me."]] "I" pictures Israel before and after the giving of the Law to powerfully demonstrate that the Law intensified the sin problem. It could not solve the sin problem for fallen man, man in the flesh (see Rom. 8:3, for example). For the apostle to use the word "I" instead of a word like "Israel" (or, "those under the Law") was a less offensive way for him to make his point.

Gentile Christians would be very interested in this presentation because it would be understood that, if the Law and the old covenant had not been superseded by the new covenant, they too would have had to come to God through the old covenant and the Mosaic Law. Also, they had to deal with the Judaizers, who (for one thing) were trying to convince the Gentile Christians that they had to submit to the ceremonial laws of the old covenant.

Now we will discuss the words, **And I was once alive apart from** [or, **without**] **the Law** of Romans 7:9. When sin was more dead (verse 8), "I" was more alive. I have an endnote here, which I'm going to read (it covers two paragraphs), Spiritual death reigned before the Mosaic Law was given (see Rom. 5:12-21). This helps show that the words, "I was once

139

alive apart from [or, without] the Law" must be understood in a limited, relative sense. The terms spiritual life and spiritual death are often used in a limited, relative sense in the Bible. Spiritual death speaks of separation from God and His life, but God has never yet fully separated Himself from mankind and abandoned them to the fullness of spiritual death. The time will come, however, when spiritual death will be full and complete. Revelation 20:14, for example, mentions "the second death, the lake of fire."

In the sense of Rom. 7:8, 9, we can say that there was more spiritual life (and less spiritual death) before the Mosaic Law was given. However, those who are born again through the Lord Jesus Christ experience spiritual life on a much higher level (through the indwelling Spirit of God) than did Israel before the Mosaic Law was given. The fullness of eternal life is reserved for the future (see Rom. 6:22, 23; 8:13, for example). We have already been born-again, and when the Lord Jesus Christ returns we will be born into the fullness of eternal life and eternal glory.

Now I'm going to turn back to page 110, and we come to the heading, Chrysostom on Romans 7:9. Chrysostom, who was an important church Father, who lived from AD 347-407, commented on the words, "For I was alive without the Law once." He says, "When, pray, was that? Before Moses. See how he sets himself to show that it [the Law], both by the things it did, and the things it did not do, weighed down human nature. For when 'I was alive without the Law,' he means, I was not so much condemned."

And now we will briefly discuss the words **but when the commandment came** of Romans 7:9. The commandment, which prohibited coveting, came when the Mosaic Law was given.

Now we will discuss the words **sin became alive, and I died** of Romans 7:9. As sin became more alive through the commandment, "I" became more dead (less alive). In Romans 7:13 the apostle speaks of sin becoming "utterly sinful" through the commandment – it became more alive. In Rom. 7:10, 11, and 13 he speaks further of my being killed through the commandment. Being killed and dying go together.

Romans 7:10. **and this commandment, which was to result in life, proved to result in death for me.** The Mosaic Law (which included "this commandment," the commandment not to covet) "was to result in life" in the sense that it promised life for those who fulfilled it (see, for example, Lev. 18:5; 10:28; Rom. 10:5; and Gal. 3:12). "It proved to result in death" as Romans 7:5-13 show.

Romans 7:11. **for sin, taking opportunity through the commandment, deceived me, and through it killed me.** Note that the words **sin, taking opportunity through the commandment** were also used in verse 8. Sin used **the commandment** as a weapon, so to speak, to kill those under the Law. They were killed in the sense spelled out in Rom. 7:9-13.

I'll comment on the words **deceived me** of verse 11. See Gen. 3:1-6, 13, especially verses 5, 6, and 13. Genesis 3:13 mentioned that Eve *was deceived*. The apostle Paul mentioned that Eve *was deceived* in 2 Cor. 11:3 and 1 Tim. 2:14. Eve was deceived and she lusted after the forbidden fruit; then she rebelled against God's direct command. Apparently the idea here in Romans 7:11 is that sin **deceived me** by using **the commandment** of the Law to convince me that the things I am commanded not to covet must be very special and very good for me – I just can't be denied these things. We know that the devil was behind this deception for Eve and for those under the Law. We must not listen to the devil or give him any place in us.

Romans 7:12. **So then, the Law is holy, and the commandment is holy and righteous and good.** The Mosaic Law was from God and is **holy and righteous and good.**

Romans 7:13. **Therefore did that which is good** [the commandment] **become a cause of death for me? May it never be! Rather it was sin, in order that it might be shown to be sin by effecting my death through that which is good, that through the commandment sin might become utterly sinful.** Sin, not **that which is good**, caused my death. Sin caused my death.

This verse shows something of God's purpose in giving the Law. He used **the commandment** to help force sin out in the open **in order that it might be shown to be sin.** He caused sin to become **utterly sinful.** Those who had eyes to see could see the sin, and they could begin to humble their hearts in repentance; their hearts would be prepared to receive the only Savior from sin, the Lord Jesus Christ. In general, people are very slow to recognize and admit their sin.

Romans 7:14. **For we know that the Law is spiritual** [It came from God]**; but I am of flesh, sold into bondage to sin** [or, better yet, **having been sold into bondage to sin**]. As we have discussed in some detail, I don't believe that there is any possibility that the apostle Paul was speaking of a born-again Christian(s) here. For one thing, that view contradicts what Paul said throughout Romans chapters 1-6; Rom. 7:4-6; and what he will go on to say in Rom. 8:1-14, for example. We *were* of the flesh and under sin before we were born again. Now we are of the Holy Spirit. We were sold into spiritual death and bondage to sin when Adam rebelled, but we have been redeemed out of that pitiful state through new-covenant salvation.

We'll discuss the words **the Law is spiritual** of verse 14. The Law is **spiritual** in that it came from God. It is **spiritual** in contrast with fallen man who is **of [the] flesh.** There is a strong contrast in the New Testament between the Spirit (the Holy Spirit) and the flesh (see, for example, John 3:6; 6:63; Rom. 7:5, 6; 8:1-14; Gal. 3:3; 5:13-25; and 6:3). We have discussed this important point in some detail in previous articles.

Now we'll discuss the words **I am of flesh** of verse 14. If we take these words in the fullest sense, Paul is speaking for all mankind with his pronoun "I." All of Adam's descendants, very much including those who were living under the Mosaic Law, have been in the flesh (and in bondage to sin) since the time of the fall. The only way to get beyond being in the flesh (and in bondage to sin) is to be born again through the Lord Jesus Christ, and then to live and walk by the Holy Spirit on a continuous basis, which we are enabled and required to do. We will discuss the present tense **I am** of verse 14 as we continue.

We'll discuss the words **sold into bondage to sin** of verse 14. As I mentioned, I believe it would be better to translate **having been sold into bondage to sin.** Mankind was sold into bondage to sin by Adam, as Paul showed in some detail in Rom. 5:12-21. Also see Rom. 3:9, 19, 23; 5:6, 8, 10; 6:6, 7, 17-20, 22, and there are many other verses that could be listed.

It was not burdensome for Paul to emphasize the pitiful state of fallen mankind, including those under the Law, because he also had the answer (the only answer) to the sin problem. He had the good news of deliverance from sin, Satan, death (both spiritual death and physical death) through the Lord Jesus Christ. But mankind, including those living under the Mosaic Law, must see their need for deliverance (salvation) before they can see their need for the Lord Jesus Christ and His atoning death.

Now we come to a sub-heading, Adam Clarke on Romans 7:14. Adam Clarke worked with John Wesley; he died in 1832. I'll quote part of what he said under Rom. 7:14. "It is difficult to conceive how the opinion could have crept into the Church, or prevailed there, that 'the apostle speaks here of his *regenerate state* [his born-again state]; and that what was, in such a state, true of himself, must be true of all others in the same state.' This opinion has, most pitifully and most shamefully, not only lowered the standard of Christianity, but destroyed its influence and disgraced its character. It requires but little knowledge of the spirit of the gospel, and of the scope of this Epistle [Paul's epistle to the Romans], to see that the apostle is here either personating a Jew under the law and without the gospel or showing what his own state was when he was deeply convinced that by the deeds of the law no man could be justified, and had not as yet heard those blessed words: 'Brother Saul, the Lord…Jesus, that appeared unto thee in the way…hath sent me, that thou mightest receive thy sight, and be filled with the Holy Ghost,' Acts 9:17."

We come to the heading The Primary Message of Romans 7:7-25, Including a Discussion of the Change from the Past Tense to the Present Tense at Romans 7:14. In Rom. 7:7-25 the apostle Paul powerfully demonstrated the need for the sons of Israel and all men to go beyond the Mosaic Law to salvation in Christ Jesus. Fallen man (man in the flesh; man in spiritual death; man in bondage to sin) cannot (fully) keep the Law of God, and as we have discussed, the Law intensified the sin problem.

ROMANS 7:7-13 ARE SET IN THE PAST TENSE BECAUSE THESE VERSES CENTER IN THE PAST EVENT OF GIVING THE MOSAIC LAW, ABOUT 1,400 BC. In these verses the apostle shows a negative consequence of God's giving the Law: the sin problem was intensified. God's ultimate purpose in giving the Law, however, was positive, not negative.

NOW, STARTING AT ROMANS 7:14, THE APOSTLE SWITCHES TO THE PRESENT TENSE AND POWERFULLY ILLUSTRATES THE PRESENT TENSE REALITY OF THE PITIFUL STATE OF THOSE UNDER THE LAW. (This illustration is more effective in the present tense than it would have been in the past tense, and the Law was very much a present tense reality for the people of Israel at the time Paul wrote this epistle.) Also, this illustration is all the more effective because Paul chooses for his speaker (his "I," who represents those under the Law) an obviously sincere and devout son of Israel. These verses powerfully illustrate the truth of what was stated in Rom. 7:14: Man in the flesh truly is a slave of sin; he has been sold into bondage to sin and he cannot (fully) keep the Law of God, which is of a different order – it is spiritual. As we have discussed, it is important to see that these verses incorporate Paul's Christian perspective.

Again, the apostle could afford to speak of the pitiful state of fallen man in the most glaring terms because he also had the gospel answer for the sin problem. He has already given us this answer in Romans chapters 1-6 and in 7:4-6, and he powerfully continues with the new-covenant answer to the sin problem in Romans chapter 8.

Romans 7:15, 16. **For that which I am doing, I do not understand; for I am not practicing what I** *would* **like to** *do*, **but I am doing the very thing I hate. (16) But if I do the very thing I do not wish** *to do*, **I agree with the Law,** *confessing* **that it is good.** This sincere son of Israel (speaking for those under the Mosaic Law) knows that the Law is good, and there is something in him that wants to do the good that the Law requires. For one thing, he knows that sin has penalties even during this life and that the day of judgment is coming. However, he frequently ends up doing the very things he (in one sense) hates, namely sin. Why? Because he is in the flesh, truly a slave of sin. The apostle Paul is powerfully emphasizing that point here.

Romans 7:17. **So now, no longer am I the one doing it, but sin which indwells me.** Paul's intent here is to emphasize that this person truly is a slave of indwelling sin, not to try to excuse sin, or to say that the sinner is not responsible for his sin.

Romans 7:18-21. I'll make very little comment because Paul is repeating things he has already said for emphasis. **For I know that nothing good dwells in me, that is, in my flesh; for the wishing is present in me, but the doing of the good** *is* **not. (19) For the good that I wish I do not do; but I practice the very evil that I do not wish. (20) But if I am doing the very thing I do not wish, I am no longer the one doing it, but sin which dwells in me. (21) I find then the principle that evil is present in me, the one who wishes to do good.** It isn't good enough to WISH the good while living in servitude to sin. We need new-covenant salvation in the Lord Jesus Christ!

Now we come to a sub-heading, Do we have a free will? This is a very important question. To the extent that we are enslaved to sin and to the god of this world, we do not have a free will; but most people have a will that is free to some extent. (I should point out that mankind is responsible for getting into bondage to sin. This involves the sin of Adam, the sin of our forefathers, and our own sin.) No matter how great the bondage, God has a greater grace for those who will receive it by faith.

Romans 7:22. **For I joyfully concur with the law of God in the inner man.** The **inner man** here is essentially the equivalent of the "mind" of verses 23, 25. The **inner man** (as these words are used here) is not to be contrasted with the outer man (the physical body). If the sin problem was centered in the physical body, it would be very easy for God to solve the sin problem. He could just put to death all mankind and then take their righteous spirits to be with him forever. But this is not what the Bible teaches. The root of sin (sins like pride and unbelief) is of the heart (spirit, soul), not of the body. In Mark chapter 7, for example, Jesus taught that sin is of the heart.

The **inner man** here in verse 22 speaks of that something down in the heart of this sincere son of Israel (we could say *conscience*) that knows that the Law is from God and is good, and that knows that it is necessary for him to fulfill the requirements of the Law.

Romans 7:23. **but I see a different law in the members of my body, waging war against the law of my mind, and making me a prisoner of the law of sin which is in my members.**

145

the law of sin which is in my members. The Law of God in verse 22 is the Mosaic Law. The **law of sin** uses the same Greek word for "law," but the meaning is something like governing principle, or rule. This same Greek noun is used two times earlier in this verse with this meaning, and in verses 21, 25 and in Rom. 8:2.

the law [or, the governing principle, or, rule] of my mind. The **mind** in this verse and in Rom. 7:25 is essentially the equivalent of the "inner man" of verse 22. **The law [or, the governing principle, or rule] of my mind** is essentially the equivalent of my joyfully concurring with the law [Law] of God in the inner man of verse 22. The problem is that **the law [or, the governing principle, or rule] of sin which is in my members** typically overpowers **the law [or, the governing principle, or rule] of my mind**, thereby proving that the unregenerate person truly is a slave of sin; and proving that the Mosaic Law (and the old covenant established on that Law) cannot save us from sin; and proving that all mankind needs the Lord Jesus Christ, the only One who can save us from sin and spiritual death.

Romans 7:24. **Wretched man that I am! Who will set me free from the body of this death?** The words, **wretched man that I am!,** are certainly justified by the pitiful state described in Rom. 7:7-23.

Who will set me free from the body of this death? The apostle answers this question as he continues, and he has already answered it in Romans chapters 1-6 and in 7:4-6. Christians have been set free from "the law [or, governing principle, or rule] of sin which is in [the] members" (verse 23). They have been set free from being "in the flesh" (see Rom. 8:5-8, for example). As we learned in Romans 6:6, for example, "our old man was crucified with Christ that our body of sin might be done away with, that we should no longer be slaves to sin."

We have not been set free from the physical body. As we have discussed, the sin problem does not center in the physical body. The word "flesh" is often used of fallen man (spirit, soul, and body), man without (and in contrast with) the Spirit of God. **The body** here is not at all limited to the physical body. I have an endnote here. I'll read the second paragraph of this endnote. In the same sense that the flesh must be crucified (see Gal. 5:24) and the old man must be crucified (see Rom. 6:6; Gal. 2:20), we must be set free from "the body of this death" (Rom.

146

7:24). Colossians 2:11 speaks of the "removal of the body of the flesh by the circumcision of Christ," which is a circumcision of the heart by the Holy Spirit. Romans 2:29 speaks of the circumcision of the heart by the Holy Spirit. Colossians 2:13 says, "And when you were dead in your transgressions and the uncircumcision of your flesh, He [God the Father] made you alive together with Him [with Christ], having forgiven us all our transgressions." Also, the apostle Paul's putting to death the works of the BODY in Rom. 8:13 is the equivalent of his crucifying the FLESH with its passions and desires in Gal. 5:24.

Romans 7:25. **Thanks be to God through Jesus Christ our Lord! So then, on the one hand I myself with my mind am serving the law of God, but on the other, with my flesh the law of sin.** In response to the question at the end of verse 24, "Who will set me free from the body of this death," Paul says **Thanks be to God** [God the Father] **through Jesus Christ our Lord!** Compare 1 Corinthians 15:57, where the apostle says, "but thanks be to God, who gives us the victory through our Lord Jesus Christ."

Before going on to Romans chapter 8, where the apostle Paul discusses our victory over sin and death in glorious detail, he summarizes what he has been saying in Rom. 7:14-24 with the words **So then, on the one hand I myself with my mind am serving the law [Law] of God, but on the other, with my flesh the law of sin.** He is, therefore, still speaking from the point of view of the unregenerate man under the Law. The words **I myself with my mind am serving the law [Law] of God** build on verses 22, 23; the words **with my flesh** [I am serving] **the law of sin** build on verse 23 and much of Romans chapter 7.

God bless you!

Holiness and Victory Over Sin #15

Holy Father, we humble our hearts before you. We admit our total dependence on you. We want to understand your Word. We want to live in line with your Word. We come before you in the mighty name of Jesus. Amen!

I'm turning to page 194 of my book (*Holiness and Victory Over Sin*) and the heading, A Discussion of the Three Most Important Passages Often Used to Try to Prove that Christians Cannot Walk in Victory Over Sin During this Present Age. My studies indicate that the three most important such passages are Rom. 7:14-25 (we just completed a study of these verses); Gal. 5:17 (we have already thoroughly studied this verse in its context), and 1 John 1:8 (We come to 1 John 1:8 in this article, and we will thoroughly study this verse in its context.) Of these three, the first and third are the most often used (Rom. 7:14-25 and 1 John 1:8).

From my point of view, much damage has been done to the Body of Christ through a serious misunderstanding of these passages. I don't believe any of them suggests that Christians cannot walk in total victory over sin. In fact, each of these passages is set in a context that teaches victory over all sin. The New Testament consistently teaches that Christians can and should live without sin. This is the ideal, and we must aim at this target. Something is big time wrong if we are not trying to stop sinning and making it a top priority to live in the righteousness and holiness of God, by His grace, through faith. The call, and enablement, to walk in victory over all sin is a big part of what salvation in Christ is all about.

Salvation, including salvation from the authority and power of sin, comes by grace through faith. We cannot walk in victory over sin apart from faith for that victory, and since our faith is based on the Word of God – our faith must be based on the Word of God – we cannot have faith for victory over sin if we believe that some passages teach that such a victory is unattainable. All the many passages that clearly teach victory over sin (for example, Romans chapters 6, 8; Galatians chapter 5; and much of the First Epistle of John) must be substantially qualified by those who don't believe such a victory is possible. Victory over sin is often put off until after the resurrection.

It is very important for us to rightly divide the Word of God on this topic (and on every topic). There are powerful enemies arrayed against us that want to keep us in sin: the world, the flesh (the old man who wants to continue living in sin), and the devil and his hosts. We will never defeat the enemy on a consistent basis apart from the grace of God appropriated by faith.

I'm going to turn to page 200 of my book, *Holiness and Victory Over Sin: Full Salvation Through the Atoning Death of the Lord Jesus Christ*. We come to the heading, First John 1:5-2:6 and 2:28-3:12 with the Emphasis on the Meaning of 1 John 1:8. In order to understand this important epistle of the apostle John, and 1 John 1:8, we must understand that this epistle was written to refute a powerful heresy that had arisen in the Christian church. I have an endnote here, which I'll read: We need to go very slow and be very careful about calling any "Christian" a heretic. That is a serious charge. As we continue, it will be obvious that this movement involved a major deviation from the foundational truths of the gospel, a true heresy, a very serious heresy.

I'll read 1 John 1:8 from my book. I used the *New American Standard Bible*, 1977 edition, in my book. **If we say that we have no sin, we are deceiving ourselves and the truth is not in us.** We will be discussing this verse in some detail as we continue, but I'll briefly comment now. If we take this verse by itself, out of its context, it sounds like the apostle John is rebuking some Christians who thought they could walk with the total victory over sin. However, when we understand that the apostle wrote this epistle, every chapter of this epistle, to refute the Gnostic heretics, we can see that these words were aimed at the Gnostic heretics. They denied that sin is the problem, and they denied the atoning blood of Jesus Christ. They said that sin is not the problem, and the blood of Jesus is not the answer. They said, we don't have sin. That's not the problem, and we don't believe in the atoning death of Christ.

In 1 John 1:8, John was not rebuking some Christians who thought they could walk with the total victory over sin. He was rebuking the Gnostic heretics, who denied that they were sinners and denied the reality of the atoning blood of the Lord Jesus Christ. Throughout this epistle the apostle exhorts his Christian readers with the call and enablement to always walk with the victory over sin, over all sin.

Now I'm going to continue reading from page 200 of the book, but as I have mentioned, sometimes I modify what is written in the book for these articles. First John 2:18-26 help us understand this epistle. Let's look at verses 19 and 26. 1 John 2:19. **They went out from us, but they were not *really* of us; for if they had been of us, they would have remained with us; but *they went out*, in order that it might be shown that they all are not of us.** The heretics that John was speaking about here had

149

gone out from the true Christian church. 1 John 2:26. **These things I have written to you concerning those who are trying to deceive you.** The heretics were trying to persuade the others to follow them. The apostle John had to be concerned for the purity of the gospel and the welfare of the Christian church. He would also have desired to wake up, if possible, those who had already joined the heresy.

The following passages enable us to see something of the very serious errors associated with this heresy. I should point out that the Gnostic heretics didn't agree with one another on every detail.

1 John 2:22, 23. (These heretics denied that "Jesus is the Christ," and they denied "the Father and the Son." These are serious errors, aren't they?) **Who is the liar but the one who denies that Jesus is the Christ? This is the antichrist, the one who denies the Father and the Son. (23) Whoever denies the Son does not have the Father; the one who confesses the Son has the Father also.** The Gnostics had very wrong ideas about God. For one thing, they didn't believe in God the Father and God the Son. One Gnostic viewpoint was that the Old Testament God who created the physical world was an evil god, and an inferior god.

1 John 4:1-6. Rather than read what I said in my book here, I'll read the verses and discuss them in more detail.

1 John 4:1. **Beloved, do not believe every spirit, but test the spirits to see whether they are from God, because many false prophets have gone out into the world.** The **false prophets** were motivated by demon spirits, and they learned their false doctrines from spirits under the devil. **Do not believe every spirit, but test the spirits to see whether they are from God.** How do we test them? For one thing, we test them by what they teach. Do their doctrines line up with the gospel proclaimed by Christ's apostles, or are they proclaiming heretical doctrines? We can also test false prophets by how they live (see Matt. 7:15-23, for example).

1 John 4:2. **By this you know the Spirit of God: every spirit that confesses that Jesus Christ has come in the flesh is from God.** That may seem like an inappropriate test until we realize that the Gnostic heretics denied that Jesus Christ had come in the flesh. I'll read 2 John 1:7, "For many deceivers have gone out into the world, those who do not

acknowledge Jesus Christ *as* coming in the flesh. This is the deceiver and antichrist." For one thing, the Gnostics believed that physical matter is evil, and they denied that Jesus Christ had a physical body. They said he only *seemed* to have a physical body. Well, if He didn't have a physical body, then there could be no atoning death of the Lamb of God, but, as I mentioned, the Gnostic heretics didn't believe in the atoning death of the Lord Jesus Christ. Error upon error! I should point out that it was a widely held viewpoint in the ancient world that physical matter is evil.

1 John 4:3. **and every spirit that does not confess Jesus is not from God** [We must confess all that the Bible says about Jesus, including the fact that He came in the flesh.]**; this is the *spirit* of the antichrist, of which you have heard that it is coming and now it is already in the world.** The true Christian ministers (like the apostle John) taught that Jesus Christ had come in the flesh, but since the heretics denied it, this was an effective test to show that the Gnostic prophets were false prophets. What if you heard a minister say that Jesus Christ came in the flesh, but then he went on to teach other heresies? Of course that minister must be rejected.

1 John 4:4. **You are from God, little children, and have overcome them** [they have overcome the Gnostic heretics, and every other being aligned with the devil]**; because greater is He who is in you than he who is in the world.** The Spirit of God dwells in every true Christian (see Rom. 8:9, for example). The New Testament shows that Satan is the god of this world.

1 John 4:5. **They** [the Gnostic heretics] **are from the world; therefore they speak *as* from the world, and the world listens to them.** The heretics of each generation typically tell people what they want to hear. Heresies are designed by the devil to appeal to what people want to hear. In our day the devil pushes words like love and unity, but defining these words in a worldly way that doesn't leave room for the true gospel.

1 John 4:6. **We are from God** [The apostle John was speaking of himself and the other faithful ministers of God.]**, he who knows God listens to us; he who is not from God does not listen to us. By this we know the spirit of truth and the spirit of error.** How desperately we need the truth, the balanced truth, of what the Bible teaches. If we don't make the truth top priority, we probably won't find it. How precious is the truth!

There are all kinds of serious errors around today, including around Christianity. We must be very careful who we listen to! It could cost you your soul!

Next we come to 1 John 5:3-6. I'll read these verses and make a few comments; then I'll read what I said in the book. 1 John 5:3. **For this is the love of God, that we keep His commandments; and His commandments are not burdensome.** If we love God we will keep His commandments (see John 14:15, 21; and 15:10, for example). As we live in the righteousness and holiness of God, by His grace through faith, we will be keeping His commandments. This is a big part of what Christianity is all about. Living in the will of God by His grace is liberty, not bondage or burdensome.

1 John 5:4. **For whatever is born of God** [In context John is speaking of born-again Christians, they have been born again through the Lord Jesus Christ and by the indwelling Spirit of God.] **overcomes the world; and this is the victory that has overcome the world—our faith.** We overcome the world, the flesh (the old man), and the devil by grace through **our faith.** We are called (and enabled) to walk by the Holy Spirit on a continual basis by grace through faith (see Gal. 5:16, for example).

1 John 5:5. **Who is the one who overcomes the world, but he who believes that Jesus is the Son of God?** We believe in God the Father and God the Son. The Gnostic heretics denied that Jesus is the Son of God, for one thing (see 1 John 2:22, 23).

1 John 5:6. **This is the One who came by water and blood, Jesus Christ, not with water only, but with the water and with the blood. It is the Spirit** [the Holy Spirit] **who testifies, because the Spirit is the truth.** I'll read what I said in my book under 1 John 5:5, 6 (on page 201). 1 John 5:6 says, "This is the One who came by water and blood, Jesus Christ, not with the water only, but with the water and with the blood." The heretics acknowledged that Jesus came by "water" (referring to the water of baptism), but, significantly, they denied the reality of the all-important atoning blood of the Lord Jesus Christ. We have already seen that the heretics denied that Jesus Christ had come in the flesh, so it is not surprising that they denied His atoning blood. They denied that sin is the

problem and that they were sinners, and they denied their need for (and the reality of) the atoning blood of the Lord Jesus Christ.

The viewpoint of the Gnostic heretic Cerinthus, who lived in the days of the apostle John, was that Jesus was a man born of Joseph and Mary. How's that for a start? When Jesus was baptized in water, the Christ descended on Him, but the Christ left Him before the man Jesus died. From this heretical point of view, Jesus was not the Christ (see 1 John 2:22), and there was no atoning death for us. We will further discuss the all-important blood atonement and the Gnostic viewpoint when we come to 1 John 1:7-10.

It is widely agreed by the commentators that the apostle John was dealing with an early form(s) of the Gnostic heresy in this epistle. The problem is that most of these commentators do not incorporate this information when they interpret 1 John 1:8. I have pointed out some of the doctrinal deviations associated with this heresy. Throughout this epistle John also frequently alludes to the sinful (and unloving) lifestyle of these heretics (1 John 2:3-11; 3:3-24; 4:7, 8, 20, 21). It is not surprising that those who denied that they were sinners would be living in sin. Many of the Gnostics were noted for their sinful lifestyles. As I mentioned, the Gnostics did not believe in salvation from sin through the atoning blood of the Lord Jesus Christ. They believed in salvation through their own secret knowledge. (The word Gnostic comes from the Greek noun *gnosis*, which means "knowledge.") Their secret knowledge dealt with things like how this world was created by an evil god, and is enslaved by evil forces, and how to be saved through their secret knowledge.

Now we come to the heading 1 John 1:5-2:6.

1 John 1:5. **And this is the message we have heard from Him and announce to you that God is light, and in Him there is no darkness at all.** The light of God includes His truth, His righteousness, and His holiness.

1 John 1:6. **If we say that we have fellowship with Him and *yet* walk in darkness, we lie and do not practice the truth;** The heretics claimed they had fellowship with God. However, the fact that they were walking in the darkness (separate from the truth, righteousness, and holiness of

God) demonstrated that they did not really have fellowship with Him in the light.

<u>1 John 1:7.</u> **but if we walk in the light as He Himself is in the light, we have fellowship with one another, and the blood of Jesus His Son cleanses us from all sin.**

we have fellowship with one another. All those who have fellowship with God in the light have fellowship with one another in the light. The heretics were excluded. They belonged to the kingdom of this world, the kingdom of the darkness; they were walking in the darkness.

and THE BLOOD OF JESUS HIS SON CLEANSES US FROM ALL SIN [my emphasis]. This is the heart of the gospel. The heretics denied that Jesus is the Son of God (see 1 John 2:22-24; 3:23; 4:14, 15; 5:5, 9-13), and they denied that they were sinners and their need for the atoning blood of the Lamb of God (see, for example, 1 John 1:7-10; 4:1, 2; and 5:6). However, they did not keep the commandments of God (see 1 John 2:3-11; 3:3-23; 4:8, 20, 21, and 5:1-4). The heretics denied that sin is the problem, and they denied that the atoning blood of the Lord Jesus Christ is the answer. Talk about serious errors!

In sharp contrast with the heretics, all true Christians believe in the atoning blood of the Lamb of God. This precious blood of the Lamb of God [**cleansed**] us from all sin and enabled us to come into the light. This same blood continues to work in purifying (sanctifying) power and keeps us cleansed from all sin. It enables us to stay in the light; it enables us to live in an abiding state of righteousness and holiness. And *if* a Christian should sin, restoration is provided through the same atoning blood (see 1 John 2:1, 2). The Greek verb translated **cleanses** in this verse is in the present tense, which probably conveys the idea of continuous action.

Christians are CLEANSED from the guilt of sin, but in this epistle (and often in the New Testament) the emphasis is placed on the CLEANSING of our hearts and lives by the powerful (sanctifying) cleansing blood of the Lord Jesus Christ. We are CLEANSED in the sense that we are transformed/sanctified. The Greek verb *katharizo*, which is translated **cleanses** here, is frequently used of a transforming, sanctifying cleansing in the New Testament (see Acts 15:9; 2 Cor. 7:1; Eph. 5:26; Titus 2:14;

Heb. 9:14; James 4:8; and 1 John 1:9). THIS IS VERY IMPORTANT INFORMATION! We'll take the time to look at three of the seven verses I just listed:

In 2 Corinthians 7:1 the apostle Paul said, "Therefore, having these promises, beloved, LET US CLEANSE ourselves from all defilement of flesh and spirit, perfecting holiness in the fear of God." The words "having these promises" refer back to the promises mentioned at the end of chapter 6. The Greek verb behind the words "let us cleanse" is *katharizo*. The context shows that the apostle Paul wasn't just speaking of being forgiven and cleansed from the guilt of sin; he was speaking of cleansing our hearts and lives from everything unholy and sinful. By cleansing ourselves from all defilement of flesh and spirit, we perfect (or, complete) holiness, in the fear of God. The Bible (Old Testament and New Testament) makes it clear that God's people must have a healthy fear of being in sin and out of the will of God.

It must be understood, of course, that we cleanse our hearts and lives from everything sinful and unholy by the powerful grace of God in Christ, through His all-important atoning death, as we walk by faith and by the Holy Spirit on a continuous basis. This is good news! This is what we want, isn't it? We must appropriate these things by faith, in accordance with the gospel, but we must rightly divide God's Word and understand the gospel. God gets all the glory for our righteousness and holiness. His righteousness and holiness are imparted to us through new-covenant salvation in the shed blood of the Lamb of God. We have powerful enemies arrayed against us, and it isn't always easy or fun, but we must press on in faith and appropriate everything God has made available to us. What a great privilege to be called to be cleansed from everything sinful and unholy in our hearts and lives. *KATHARIZO*, what a significant verb!

Now I'll turn to Titus 2:14, another verse that uses *katharizo* of a sanctifying type cleansing from all sin. "[Christ Jesus] who gave Himself for us to redeem us from every lawless deed [or, to redeem us from all lawlessness; His powerful cleansing blood redeems us out of the kingdom of lawlessness, out of the kingdom of the darkness of this world.] who gave Himself for us to redeem us from all lawlessness, and TO PURIFY [*katharizo*; we could translate *purify*, or *cleanse*] for Himself a people for His own possession, zealous for good deeds [or, good works]." I believe it

155

is quite clear in this context that the apostle Paul was speaking of purifying the heart and life of believers from everything that is sinful and unholy and enabling them to live in the very righteousness and holiness of God, "zealous for good works."

We'll look at one last verse that uses *katharizo*, where the context shows that the verb is being used of a sanctifying type of cleansing, a cleansing that goes far beyond cleansing believers from the guilt of sin. I'll read James 4:8. "Draw near to God and He will draw near to you. CLEANSE [*katharizo*] [or, PURIFY] YOUR HANDS YOU SINNERS; and PURIFY YOUR HEARTS YOU DOUBLE-MINDED." It is quite clear in this context that James wasn't just exhorting his readers to ask God to forgive them. He was exhorting them to stop sinning (by the grace of God in Christ). A different Greek verb was used here for purifying the hearts, but purifying our hearts from double-mindedness (by the grace of God in Christ) is a big part of what new-covenant salvation is all about. The atoning blood of the Lamb of God is that powerful! Taking away the guilt of sin is very important, but that is about ten percent of the gospel. The atoning blood has the power to cleanse our hearts and lives from sin, by grace, through faith, in accordance with God's Word. This is the ideal. We must aim at this target.

I'll continue to read what I said under 1 John 1:7 on pages 202, 203. Throughout the studies contained in this book, I have been emphasizing that the blood of Jesus Christ (His atoning death) dethrones sin, Satan, and spiritual death – it gives Christians life and makes them righteous and holy – it enables them to live in an abiding state of righteousness and holiness. God gets all the glory for the victory that Christians experience. The other side of the coin is that God is denied glory to the extent that we do not walk in His righteousness and holiness, with the victory over all sin.

1 John 1:8. **If we say that we have no sin, we are deceiving ourselves and the truth is not in us.** I'll read what I said under the words **If we say that we have no sin.** The words **we have no sin** are exactly what we would expect the heretics to say in response to what John has just said at the end of verse 7. We know enough from this epistle (and it is confirmed by our knowledge of Gnosticism) to say that the heretics denied that they were sinners, and they denied their need for, and the reality of, the cleansing blood of the Lord Jesus Christ. They denied that they had

sinned (see verse 10), and they denied that they were living in sin, even though they were not keeping the commandments of God (see 1 John 2:3-6, for example).

Most Christians (I'm sorry to say) believe that here in 1 John 1:8 the apostle John was refuting the idea that Christians can walk in victory over sin. I'm quite sure, however, that this interpretation is wrong and that the apostle John would himself plead "guilty" to holding the viewpoint that Christians are called and enabled to walk with the victory over all sin, through the powerful cleansing blood of the Lord Jesus Christ, in the power of the Holy Spirit. In addition to the verses that we are considering in this study (1 John 1:5-2:6 and 2:28-3:12), also see 1 John 2:9-17; 3:13-24; 4:7-21; 5:1-5, 16-21; John 4:23, 24; 5:14, 24; 7:37-39; 8:31-36; 14:15-24; 15:10-17; 17:6-26; Rev. 2:1-3:22; 7:14; 12:11, 17; 14:4, 5; 19:7, 8; 21:8; and 22:11-15. The apostle John (under the inspiration of the Holy Spirit) also wrote the Gospel of John and the Book of Revelation. Many of the verses just listed state the victory over all sin in very strong, very clear, terms.

God bless you! May His name be glorified through His people (including us) to the maximum!

Holiness and Victory Over Sin #16

Holy Father, we humble our hearts before you; we want to rightly divide your Word; we want to understand it; we want to live in line with your Word by your sufficient grace. Thank you for full salvation in the Lord Jesus Christ. We pray in His mighty name. Amen!

Last time when we stopped we were discussing 1 John 1:8. This is a very important verse. Most Christians, something like 80-90 percent of Christians, believe this verse proves we can never stop sinning in this life. As I have mentioned, I believe they are making a serious mistake. The apostle John wrote 1 John 1:8 against the Gnostic heretics, not against Christians who thought they could have the victory over sin. The Gnostic heretics denied that sin was the problem, and they denied that the blood of Jesus is the answer. They denied they were sinners, and they denied the atoning blood of the Lord Jesus Christ. I'm very sure that John was dealing with the Gnostic heretics in 1 John 1:8.

I'm going to turn back to 1 John 1:5-7 and read these verses and make several comments for a brief review. **And this is the message we have heard from Him** [from the Lord Jesus Christ] **and announce to you, that God is light, and in Him there is no darkness at all.** [God's light includes His truth, His righteousness, and His holiness.] **(6) If we say that we have fellowship with Him and *yet* walk in the darkness, we lie and do not practice the truth** [These words were aimed at the Gnostic heretics. They claimed to have fellowship with God; they claimed that they had received the true gospel from God, but they were walking in the darkness; they didn't have God's truth, or His righteousness or holiness.]; **(7) but if we walk in the light as He Himself is in the light, we have fellowship with one another, and the blood of Jesus His Son cleanses us from all sin.** If we are walking in the light with God, we will have fellowship with one another, with the other Christians walking in the light, and that certainly excluded the Gnostic heretics, who were not walking in the light.

AND THE BLOOD OF JESUS HIS SON CLEANSES US FROM ALL SIN [my emphasis]. These words at the end of verse 7 are extremely important. Most Christians interpret these words to mean our past sins are washed away and now we have a clean slate with God. That much is true, and forgiveness is provided for Christians when they repent, but I'm totally sure that these words mean more than that. We discussed these words in some detail last time. The Greek verb translated **cleanses** here is *katharizo*. Last time we looked at three verses in the New Testament (but there are more than three verses) where this Greek verb is used of a transforming/sanctifying type cleansing or purifying. In other words, the blood of Jesus is so powerful that it can cleanse our hearts and lives so we stop sinning. That cleansing/purifying of our hearts and lives is a dominant theme of the New Testament. 1 Peter 2:24, for example, "He bore our sins in His body on the cross [He bore our sins with the guilt and the penalties, including the major penalties of spiritual death and bondage to sin], SO THAT WE MIGHT DIE TO SIN AND LIVE TO RIGHTEOUSNESS [my emphasis]...." Or, Romans chapter 6: The dominant theme of Romans chapter 6 is that we are called to walk in the righteousness and holiness of God through the atoning death of the Lord Jesus Christ. We have that great privilege. A walk in the righteousness and holiness of God is not automatic, but by grace through faith, we are enabled to walk in the righteousness and holiness of God. Or, Romans chapter 8: The same good news: because of the atoning death of Christ and through the Holy Spirit, we are set free from spiritual death and from being slaves of sin, and now we are called, enabled, and required to live in the righteousness and holiness of God. I'll read the glorious words at the end of 1 John 1:7 one more time, **and the blood of Jesus His Son cleanses us from all sin.**

1 John 1:8. **If we say that we have no sin** [[That's exactly what the Gnostic heretics would say in response to what the apostle John just said at the end of verse 7: "We don't need the blood of Christ; we don't believe in that. We are not sinners; we don't have sin; that isn't our problem."]], **we are deceiving ourselves, and the truth is not in us.**

Now I'm going to turn to page 203 of my book. This is where we stopped last time. We were ready to discuss the words, **we are deceiving ourselves and the truth is not in us.** These strong words were aimed at the heretics, not Christians who thought that they were living in victory over sin. The heretics were deceived and they were trying to deceive others (1 John 2:26; compare 1 John 3:7) I'll read 1 John 2:26, "These things I have written to you concerning those who are trying to deceive you." The Gnostic heretics were trying to get the true Christians to join them in their heresy. I'll also read 1 John 3:7, which is a very important reference, "Little children [John was speaking to all the true Christians.], let no one deceive you; the one who practices righteousness [or, the one who is doing righteousness] is righteous, just as He [God] is righteous." We'll discuss 1 John 3:7 later.

I'll continue to read what I said under the words **we are deceiving ourselves, and the truth is not in us** of 1 John 1:8. The truth was not in them (the Gnostic heretics); they were in the darkness, as the apostle says repeatedly in this epistle. To me it seems obvious that the apostle John intended these words of 1 John 1:8 to apply to the heretics. This epistle was written to refute this particular heresy, and every chapter deals to a significant extent with this heresy. There is widespread agreement in our day that the First Epistle of John deals with the Gnostic heresy, but the problem is that most Christians don't apply this information at 1 John 1:8.

We come to a sub-heading, <u>Commentators on 1 John 1:8</u>. It is common for those who write from a holiness/victory over sin perspective to agree that 1 John 1:8 does not teach that Christians cannot have the victory over sin. In addition to John Wesley and the two commentators I'll quote below (after 1 John 1:10), see, for example, Charles Finney in *Finney's Systematic Theology*, chapter 36.

<u>1 John 1:9.</u> **If we confess our sins, He is faithful and righteous to forgive us our sins and to cleanse us from all unrighteousness** [or, **from all wrongdoing**].

If we confess our sins. I believe these words, which build on 1 John 1:5-8, were meant to apply to the heretics. They have a general application, but I believe the apostle John was thinking of the heretics when he wrote these words. They were not confessing their sins; they were denying that they needed to be cleansed by the blood of Jesus Christ (see 1 John 1:6-8, 10; 3:7; and 5:6).

and to cleanse us from all unrighteousness [or, **all wrongdoing**]. **To cleanse** is a translation of *katharizo*, the verb used in 1:7. We discussed this very important verb in some detail under 1:7. **To cleanse** [or, **to purify**] **us from all unrighteousness** is to transform us/make us righteous. This cleansing goes far beyond the forgiveness of sins, which was mentioned earlier in 1:9. The Greek noun *adikia*, which is translated **unrighteousness** here, could just as well be translated "wrongdoing" or "wickedness." To be cleansed from all *adikia* is to be transformed/made righteous. God who is righteous (Greek *dikaios*) removes the unrighteousness (*adikia*) from the hearts and lives of those who submit to Him through the gospel and makes them righteous (*dikaios*).

On being righteous see, for example, 1 John 2:29 and 3:7. I'll read <u>1 John 3:7</u> again. It is a very important verse. "Little children, let no one deceive you; the one who practices righteousness (or, the one who is doing righteousness) is righteous, just as He [God] is righteous." The one who is doing righteousness is righteous. Christians are called to walk in the very righteousness of God, which certainly includes walking with the victory over all sin. Christians walk in the righteousness of God by grace through faith, in accordance with the terms of the new covenant. There is a strong emphasis in this epistle on the fact that true Christians live in righteousness and holiness (see 1 John 1:6, 7; 2:1, 3-11, 15-17, 28, 29; 3:1-24; 4:7-21; 5:1-5, 16-21).

1 John 1:10. **If we say that we have not sinned, we make Him a liar, and His word is not in us.** God is on record saying that all have sinned (see, for example Acts 4:12; 17:30, 31; Rom. 3:9-20, 23; 11:32; and Gal. 3:22). These heretics, however, denied that they had sinned. They clearly were not basing their opinion on the Scriptures. True Christians would not say we have not sinned. This verse helps confirm that 1 John 1:8 and 9 were also dealing with the heretics, not with true Christians. God is on record saying that all people are sinners and need to be saved from sin through the Lord Jesus Christ and His atoning blood; but as far as I know, He is not on record saying that Christians will necessarily continue to sin. That's a very important point!

Now we come to the heading, Several Quotations regarding 1 John 1:7-10. I'll quote part of what Adam Clarke said under 1 John 1:7, 8 and 9, *Adam Clarke's Commentary on the Bible*, abridged by Ralph Earle, published by Baker in 1967. Adam Clarke was an associate of John Wesley in the 1700s. Under 1 John 1:7 he says (in part); he is commenting on the words, "the blood of Jesus Christ." "The meritorious efficacy of His passion and death has purged our consciences from dead works, and *cleanseth us*, 'continues to cleanse us,' that is, to keep clean what it has made clean. And being cleansed from all sin is what every believer should look for, what he has a right to expect, and what he must have in this life in order to be prepared to meet his God. Christ is not a partial Savior; He saves to the uttermost, and He cleanses from all sin." Adam Clarke comes on pretty strong. I'll read a sentence that I have later on the page, "I should mention that in the days of Adam Clarke, who died in 1832, the controversy regarding holiness and victory over sin was quite heated."

Under 1 John 1:8 Adam Clarke says (in part); he is commenting on the words, "If we say that we have no sin." "This is tantamount [or, the equivalent] to verse 10: 'If we say that we have not sinned.' 'All have sinned and come short of the glory of God' [Rom. 3:23]; and therefore every man needs a Saviour, such as Christ is. It is very likely that the heretics, against whose evil doctrine the apostle writes, denied that they had any sin or needed any Saviour. [At least they denied they needed a Savior from sin.] Indeed the Gnostics even denied that Christ suffered [In

161

other words, they denied the atoning death of the Lord Jesus Christ.]." And he comments on the words, "we deceive ourselves." "By supposing that we have no guilt, no sinfulness, and consequently have no need of the blood of Christ as an atoning sacrifice."

Under 1 John 1:9, Adam Clarke says (in part); he is commenting on the words, "And to cleanse us from all unrighteousness," "Not only to forgive the sin, but to purify the heart. ... As all unrighteousness is sin, so he that is cleansed from all unrighteousness is cleansed from all sin. To attempt to evade this, and plead for the continuance of sin in the heart through life, is ungrateful, wicked, and even blasphemous [Like I said he comes on pretty strong]; for as he who says he has not sinned, verse 10, makes God a liar, who has declared the contrary through every part of His revelation; so he that says the blood of Christ either cannot or will not cleanse us from all sin in this life gives also the lie to his Maker, who has declared the contrary, and thus shows that the word, the doctrine of God, is not in him. Reader, it is the birthright of every child of God to be cleansed from all sin, to keep himself unspotted from the world, and so to live as nevermore to offend his Maker. All things are possible to him that believes, because all things are possible to the infinitely meritorious blood and energetic Spirit of the Lord Jesus."

I'll quote part of what Leo Cox said in a subsection titled "Failure to Be in the Light Brings Self-Deception" (he is discussing 1 John 1:6, 8, and 10); *Wesleyan Bible Commentary*, volume 6 of the 6 volume set, published by Hendrickson, it is a 1986 reprint. "Though his words may be misinterpreted, the writer is not contradicting himself in verses 7 and 8. He has claimed the cleansing of the blood for all sin (in verse 7). To state that claim is not the denial of sin; it is the acknowledgment of the sin, and of the full victory over it. Careful exegesis will avoid applying the condemnation of verse 8 to those who make humble claim of the promise in verse 7. When a Christian obtains the victory of full cleansing, and gives God the glory for this victory, he is not deceiving himself; he is honoring the blood of Christ that cleanseth from all sin. ... Again, it is erroneous to apply this statement [of 1 John 1:8] to those who claim God's victory over their sin by His grace. Christians do not deny the possibility of sinning, or the need for their 'Advocate with the Father' [referring to 1 John 2:1]. Christians do not claim that they have not sinned; they know that they have. However, they rely upon the grace of God that now keeps them from sinning and will keep them from sinning.

... Of course, Christians do not boast of sinlessness; they boast of Jesus Christ, and His victory for them and in them."

I'll also quote several sentences from what Leo Cox said under the subheading, "Confession Brings Forgiveness and Cleansing" (referring to 1 John 1:9). "One should never lay any limitation upon God's power to accomplish in His children the promise of full cleansing from sin through the blood of Christ. Any excuse for or allowance of the continuance of sin in the life of the believer is contrary to God's will for Christians and places a limitation upon the power of the cross of Jesus." I'll say Amen! to that.

1 John 2:1, 2. (I'm on page 206 of my book. First I'll read the verses. I used the *New American Standard Bible*, 1977 edition in my book.) **My little children, I am writing these things to you that you may not sin. And if anyone sins, we have an Advocate with the Father, Jesus Christ the righteous; (2) and He Himself is the propitiation for our sins; and not for ours only, but also for *those of* the whole world.**

I'll comment on the words **I am writing these things to you that you may not sin** of 1 John 2:1. These words are very important. As many have pointed out, the aorist tense of the Greek verb for sin here helps show that the apostle's meaning is THAT YOU MAY NOT COMMIT AN ACT OF SIN. That sounds good, doesn't it? That's what we want, isn't it? I'll read part of endnote 10 on pages 218, 219: Donald W. Burdick, *Letters of John the Apostle*, published by Moody press in 1985 says the following regarding the meaning of the words "that you may not sin." "Rather than to permit or encourage sin, John's purpose was to combat it. The Greek verb used here (from the verb *hamartano*, which means "I sin") is an ingressive aorist indicating that the apostle does not want his readers ever to commit even one act of sin. ... John is...aiming at the eradication of every act of sin." That's very important! In 1 John 2:1 the apostle John was exhorting his readers to never commit another act of sin. That's the ideal, and it is not some way out, unrealistic ideal.

Now I'll turn back to page 206 of my book (*Holiness and Victory Over Sin*). As many have pointed out, the aorist tense of the Greek verb for sin here helps show that the apostle's meaning is that you may not commit an act of sin. Verses like 1 John 2:3-6; 2:28-3:12; and 1:6, 7, and 9 help confirm this interpretation. These words in 1 John 2:1, by themselves,

163

should probably suffice to show that the apostle was not denying the possibility of full victory over sin in 1 John 1:8. That's a weighty point!

Now we'll discuss the words **And if anyone sins, we have an Advocate with the Father, Jesus Christ the righteous** of 1 John 2:1. I pointed out that the NIV has "But" in place of "And" here. As in the first part of this verse, the verb for sins is in the aorist tense. Here the apostle deals with the possibility (certainly not the necessity) of a Christian committing occasional acts of sin. The full restoration after any such act of sin comes through our Advocate, the Lord Jesus Christ, on the basis of His atoning death, when we repent.

Under 1 John 2:2 I said, the Lord Jesus Christ died for all men (see 1 Tim. 2:3-6, for example), but each person must appropriate the benefits of His atoning death through repentance and faith.

1 John 2:3-6. **And by this we know that we have come to know Him, if we keep His commandments. (4) The one who says, "I have come to know Him," and does not keep His commandments, is a liar, and the truth is not in him; (5) but whoever keeps His word** [which includes keeping His commandments], **in him the love of God has truly been perfected. By this we know that we are in Him: (6) the one who says he abides in Him ought to walk in the same manner as He walked.** Did you hear that? **The one who says he abides in Him** [in the Lord Jesus Christ] **ought to walk in the same manner as He walked.** We can all agree that the Lord Jesus Christ did not sin. These verses strongly confirm that Christians are called, enabled, required, and privileged to walk in the righteousness and holiness of God, with the total victory over sin. Talk about good news! These verses also further demonstrate that the heretics didn't really know God, no matter what they claimed for themselves.

1 John 2:3, 4. The apostle John makes it clear in these verses that true Christians do keep God's commandments. They walk in His righteousness (see, for example, 1 John 2:5, 6, 29; 3:3-12, 22-24; 5:2-4, 18, 19; John 14:15, 21; 15:10; Rom. 8:4; 2:26, 27). Surely John had the heretics in mind in verse 4, **The one who says, "I have come to know Him," and does not keep His commandments, is a liar, and the truth is not in him.** The heretics claimed to know God, but the fact that they

didn't keep His commandments demonstrated that they didn't really know Him.

1 John 2:5. **but whoever keeps His word, in him the love of God has truly been perfected. By this we know that we are in Him:**

whoever keeps His word. To keep God's word here in verse 5 is probably the equivalent of keeping His commandments in verses 3 and 4. (Compare the use of the words "word" and "commandments" in 1 John 2:7, 8 and in the Gospel of John 14:15, 21, 23, and 24.) The primary commandment is to walk in love (see, for example, 1 John 2:7-11; 3:10-12, 14-24; 4:7-21; 5:1-3; Matt. 22:34-40; John 13:34, 35; 15:12, 17; Rom. 13:8-10; Gal. 5:13-15; and James 2:8). Christians must love God, but they must also love the children of God. This epistle of John emphasizes both of these aspects of love.

in Him the love of God has truly been perfected. 1 John 4:12 helps us understand the meaning of these words, "if we love one another, God abides in us, and His love is perfected in us." (Also see 1 John 4:7, 17.) God's love is in Christians by His indwelling Spirit. The first fruit of the Holy Spirit listed by the apostle Paul in Gal. 5:22, 23 is love. To the extent Christians walk by God's Word and by His Spirit (which they are called to do on a continuous basis), they will manifest God's love; His love is perfected in them.

God's love has always been perfect, but it is not perfected in the Christian until the Christian walks in love on a continuous basis. A walk by the Holy Spirit is not automatic. Remember Gal. 5:16: Paul exhorts His born-again Christian readers to always walk by the Holy Spirit so they will not sin. When we become Christians we are enabled, and required, by covenant (the new covenant) to always walk by the Spirit through faith. The apostle John is not speaking of some unattainable level of love, but of a level that even a newly converted Christian can walk in, being enabled by God's grace and Spirit. This walk in love is a major part of the ideal state of righteousness and holiness that we are discussing in this chapter of my book (*Holiness and Victory Over Sin*).

1 John 2:6. **the one who says he abides in Him ought to walk in the same manner as He walked.** The apostle John undoubtedly wrote these words (at least in part) to help show that the heretics were not really

abiding in God, no matter what they claimed for themselves (see, for example, 1 John 1:6; 2:3-5; and 3:6). IT WOULD BE DIFFICULT TO IMAGINE A HIGHER CALL TO HOLINESS AND RIGHTEOUS LIVING THAN THE CALL EXPRESSED IN THIS VERSE! Every true Christian is called to abide in God and to walk in the same manner that Jesus Christ walked. (See, for example, 1 John 3:3-7; 4:17.) All true Christians will agree that Jesus walked above sin.

What a powerful statement of the fact that Christians are called and enabled to walk with total victory over sin. THIS ONE VERSE BY ITSELF SHOULD SUFFICE TO SHOW THAT THE APOSTLE JOHN WAS NOT SAYING IN 1 JOHN 1:8 THAT IF CHRISTIANS SAY THEY ARE WALKING WITH THE TOTAL VICTORY OVER SIN THEY ARE DECEIVING THEMSELVES! And, significantly, this epistle is filled with similar verses. For example, in 1:7 the apostle spoke of the blood of Jesus cleansing, or purifying, us from all sin. And as we discussed, the Greek verb used for cleansing/purifying in 1:7 is often used in the New Testament (as it is used in 1:7) of a sanctifying type of cleansing of the hearts and lives, which enables us to live in the righteousness and holiness of God. And the same verb is used the same way in 1:9, where John spoke of God's forgiving us AND cleansing (or purifying) us from all unrighteousness, or wrongdoing. In 2:1 the apostle said he was writing these things so his Christian readers would not commit an act of sin, that is, so that they would not sin at all. In chapter 2, verses 3 and 4 John emphasized the point that true Christians keep God's commandments. In 2:5 he spoke of true Christians keeping God's Word and of His love being perfected in them. In 2:29 he speaks of the fact that born-again Christians practice, or do righteousness, the very righteousness of God their Father. In 3:3 the apostle John speaks of our purifying ourselves just as God is pure. And in 3:7 he speaks of Christians practicing or doing righteousness, just as God is righteous. There are quite a few more similar verses in this epistle, but I'll just take time to read 1 John 3:8-12; I'll read these verses from the NIV, "He who does what is sinful is of the devil, because the devil has been sinning from the beginning. The reason the Son of God appeared was to destroy the devil's work. No one who is born of God will continue to sin, because God's seed remains in him; he cannot go on sinning, because he has been born of God. This is how we know who the children of God are and who the children of the devil are. Anyone who does not do what is right is not a child of God; nor is anyone who does not love his brother. This is the message you heard from the beginning: We should love one another. Do not be like Cain who belonged to the evil one and murdered his brother. And why did he murder him? Because his own actions were evil and his brother's were righteous."

God bless you! His name be glorified! His will be done in each one of us! In Jesus' mighty name! Amen!

Holiness and Victory Over Sin #17

Holy Father, we humble our hearts before you; we're making it top priority to understand your Word and to live it; we pray in Jesus' mighty name, Amen.

For a review I'm going to turn back to page 194 of my book. We come to the heading, <u>A Discussion of the Three Most Important Passages Often Used to Try to Prove that Christians Cannot Walk in Victory Over Sin During this Present Age.</u> My studies indicate that the three most important such passages are Rom. 7:14-25; Gal. 5:17; and 1 John 1:8. Of these three the first and third are the most often used, that is, Rom. 7:14-25 and 1 John 1:8. (We have already completed a study of Rom. 7:14-25, in its context, and Gal. 5:17, in its context, and we have started a study of 1 John 1:8, in its context.) From my point of view, much damage has been done to the Body of Christ through a serious misunderstanding of these passages. I don't believe any of them suggests that Christians cannot walk in total victory over sin. The New Testament consistently teaches that Christians can and should live above (without) sin. That's the ideal; we certainly must be aiming at the target. There's something seriously wrong if we are not trying to stop sinning and making it top priority to live in the righteousness and holiness of God, by grace through faith. The call (and enablement) to walk in victory over sin is a big part of what salvation in Christ is all about.

Salvation, including salvation from the authority and power of sin, comes by grace through faith. We cannot walk in victory over sin apart from faith for that victory, and since our faith is based on the Word of God – our faith must be based on the Word of God – we cannot have faith for victory over sin if we believe that some passages teach that such a victory is unattainable. All the many passages that clearly teach victory over sin (for example, Romans chapters 6 and 8; Galatians chapter 5, and the first epistle of John) cannot be taken at face value (they must be substantially qualified) by those who don't believe such a victory is possible. Victory over sin is often put off until after the resurrection.

It is very important for us to rightly divide the Word of God on this topic (and on every topic). There are powerful enemies arrayed against us that want to keep us in sin: the world, the flesh, and the devil and his hosts. We will never defeat the enemy on a consistent basis apart from the grace of God appropriated by faith.

In the last article we turned to page 200 of my book, *Holiness and Victory Over Sin,* under the heading, 1 John 1:2-6 and 2:28-3:12 with the Emphasis on the Meaning of 1 John 1:8. I'll read the first sentence I have here, "In order to understand this important epistle of the apostle John, and 1 John 1:8, we must understand that it was written to refute a powerful heresy that had arisen in the Christian church." We have discussed that heresy, the heresy of Gnosticism, quite a bit already.

1 John 1:8. **If we say that we have no sin, we are deceiving ourselves and the truth is not in us.** Many Christians think John wrote this verse to rebuke some Christians who thought they could walk with the victory over sin. I'm very sure that's a wrong interpretation of this verse. The apostle John wrote this verse (1 John 1:8) to refute the Gnostic heretics. This entire epistle was written to refute the Gnostic heretics. They denied that they were sinners, and they denied the atoning blood of the Lord Jesus Christ.

Last time we finished our study of 1 John 1:5-2:6; we are ready to begin a study of 1 John 2:28-3:12. I'll turn to page 208 and we come to the heading 1 John 2:28-3:12. These verses constitute one of the most clear and powerful statements in the New Testament which shows that Christians are enabled (and required) to walk in righteousness with the victory over all sin. If you hear this right, this is very good news. This passage is very important in its own right, and it also helps demonstrate that the apostle did not teach that Christians cannot have the victory over all sin in 1 John 1:8.

<u>1 John 2:28.</u> (I'm reading from my book, which uses the *New American Standard Bible*, 1977 edition.) **And now little children, abide in Him, so that when He appears, we may have confidence and not shrink away from Him in shame at His coming.** Isn't that an ugly thought? He comes, and we shrink away from Him in shame. We must make it top priority to always be ready for His coming.

abide in Him. Christians are exhorted to abide in God the Father and God the Son (see 1 John 1:3; 2:24). I'll read both of these verses, In <u>1 John 1:3</u> the apostle John said, "what we have seen and heard we proclaim to you also, that you also may have fellowship with us; and indeed our fellowship is with the Father, and with His Son Jesus Christ." What a Savior! What a salvation plan! We are invited to have fellowship with God the Father and God the Son. Now I'll read <u>1 John 2:24</u>, "As for you, let that abide in you which you heard from the beginning. [In other words, keep believing the true gospel, the gospel you received through the apostles; don't listen to heretics, including the Gnostic heretics; you must believe the truth.] If what you heard from the beginning abides in you, you also will abide in the Son and in the Father." Again, what a privilege to abide in, and to have fellowship with, God the Father and God the Son through new-covenant salvation. We abide in God by abiding in the truth, Spirit, life, light, righteousness, holiness, and love of God (see, for example, 1 John 1:6, 7; 2:6, 10, 24, 27; 3:6, 24; 4:12-19; 5:11-13).

so that when He appears, we may have confidence and not shrink away from Him in shame at His coming. The New Testament frequently speaks of the second coming of the Lord Jesus Christ. (The Greek noun translated **coming** here, and often, is *parousia*.) When He returns that's when the rapture will take place, for one thing. It is possible that we should also think of the coming (or presence) of God the Father here. As the margin of the NASB shows, "at His coming" could be translated "in His presence." God the Father is mentioned in 1 John 3:1 and at the end of 2:29, and His presence is frequently mentioned in conjunction with the return of the Lord Jesus Christ and the day of judgment (see, for example, Col. 1:22, 28; 1 Thess. 3:13; Jude 1:24; and Rev. 11:15-17).

Christians are frequently exhorted (in the New Testament) to make sure they are always fully ready for the return of the Lord Jesus Christ. We must abide in God, and as we have discussed, abiding in God includes abiding in the truth, the truth of the Word of God, and abiding in the righteousness and holiness of God. What a privilege; what a Savior; what a salvation plan! But we must stay faithful (by faith) to the new covenant by God's sufficient grace.

1 John 2:29. **If you know that He is righteous** [How many know that God is righteous, with no sin at all?]**, you know that everyone also who practices righteousness** [or, **everyone who is doing righteousness**] **is born of Him.** The Christian's righteousness comes from God, who gives us the new birth. He causes His Righteous, Holy Spirit of life to dwell in us through the atoning blood of the Lord Jesus Christ. God is righteous and His children (the ones who are born of Him) are enabled (and required) to be righteous. They are the ones who are practicing (or, who are doing) righteousness.

As we have discussed, God imputes and imparts His righteousness to Christians; He enables us to walk in His righteousness and holiness. This is a big part of what new-covenant salvation is all about. On practicing or doing righteousness, compare, for example, 1 John 1:6, 7, 9; 2:1-17; 3:3-24; 4:7-21; 5:1-4, 18, 19. I'll quote 1 John 3:7, 8a (We'll be coming to these verses as we continue with this study.) "Little children, let no one deceive you [there were many deceivers then, just like there are now]; the one who practices righteousness [or, the one who is doing righteousness] is righteous, just as He [God] is righteous. [How could you state the victory over sin that we are called to any more clearly or in stronger terms than that, to be righteous as God is righteous.] the one who practices sin [or, the one who is doing sin] is of the devil."

First John 2:29 strongly infers and 1 John 3:3-12 clearly state that those who are not practicing (or doing) righteousness (those who are living in sin) are not the children of God. The apostle John, in a style typical of the Scriptures, presents the black and white with very little recognition of the in-between gray area. We are not supposed to be living in the in-between gray area where so many Christians do live. It's very easy to live there; to be fleshly; to be worldly; to live in sin part of the time, but that's a dangerous place to live and a totally unsatisfying way to live. The good news is that God calls (and enables) Christians to live in the center of His will, in His righteousness and holiness. IF WE ARE RIGHTEOUS AS GOD IS RIGHTEOUS THAT CERTAINLY IS VICTORY OVER ALL SIN, IS IT NOT?

Before we go on to the next verses, let me remind you of 1 John 2:1, 2, "My little children, I am writing these things to you that you may not sin [that you may not commit an act of sin; that you may not sin at all]. And if anyone sins, we have an Advocate with the Father, Jesus Christ the righteous. And He Himself is the propitiation for our sins; and not for ours only, but also for *those* of the whole world." These verses make it very clear that born-again Christians should not be sinning at all (that's good news!), but they also make it clear that if Christians repent, they will be forgiven and restored through the atoning blood of the Lamb of God. Thank God for forgiveness. If we repent we certainly will be forgiven.

1 John 3:1, 2. **See how great a love the Father has bestowed upon us, that we should be called children of God; and *such* we are. For this reason, the world does not know us, because it did not know Him** [There are two kingdoms, the kingdom of God and the kingdom of this world. The devil is the god of this world system.]. **(2) Beloved, now we are children of God, and it has not appeared as yet** [or, **it has not been manifested as yet**] **what we shall be. We know that, when He appears, we shall be like Him, because we shall see Him just as He is.** Talk about a destiny! We shall be like Him! See under 1 John 2:28. When He appears, all who have loved His appearing (2 Tim. 4:8) will be resurrected/transformed into the glory of God's eternal kingdom. I'll read 2 Timothy 4: 7, 8; this is the apostle Paul right at the end of his life; he says, "I have fought the good fight, I have finished the course, I have kept the faith; in the future there is laid up for me the crown of righteousness, which the Lord, the righteous Judge, will award to me on that day; and not only to me, but also to all who have loved His appearing." If we love His appearing we will live in the light of that appearing. We will make it top priority to always be ready for His appearing, always living in His truth, His righteousness, and His holiness, by His sufficient grace.

We know that, when He appears, we shall be like Him, because we shall see Him just as He is (1 John 3:2). To be able to see Him just as He is will necessitate that we be glorified first. We will be born into the fullness of eternal life and glorified at the time of His return, and we will begin to reign with Him in a never-ending reign. What a salvation plan! What a Savior!

1 John 3:3. (This is a very weighty verse!) **And everyone who has this hope *fixed* on Him** [the hope that was just mentioned in 3:2; the hope of being glorified, of being like Him, of seeing Him as He is, of reigning with Him, etc.] **purifies Himself, just as He is pure.** Talk about a call to victory over all sin! Now we'll discuss these super-important words, **purifies himself, just as He** [God] **is pure.** I believe the apostle John is speaking (at least for the most part) of an ideal, once-for-all purification that is available at the beginning of the Christian life. That's the ideal; we stop sinning and begin to walk in the purity, righteousness, and holiness of God when we become Christians. What a glorious ideal! And God's grace is sufficient!

We walk in the purity, righteousness, and holiness of God by walking in accordance with His Word (by faith) and by walking in and after His Spirit (by faith). At conversion the Christian is born of God and begins to practice (or, to do) righteousness (see, for example, 1 John 2:29 and 3:6-12). The heretics that John was refuting when he wrote this epistle did not purify themselves; they did not walk in the truth or the righteousness of God. This proved that they were not children of God. Their "gospel" must be rejected.

The apostle tells us here that Christians are required to purify themselves (by the grace of God in Christ Jesus) and to be pure just as God is pure. HOW COULD YOU HAVE A MORE POWERFUL CALL TO RIGHTEOUSNESS AND HOLINESS, WITH THE VICTORY OVER ALL SIN? (See, for example, 2 Cor. 7:1; 1 John 1:5-7; 2:3-6, 29; 3:6-12, and I could have listed many more such references.) THIS VERSE, 1 JOHN 3:3, BY ITSELF, SHOULD SUFFICE TO DEMONSTRATE THAT THE APOSTLE JOHN WAS NOT DENYING THAT CHRISTIANS CAN WALK WITH THE TOTAL VICTORY OVER SIN IN THIS PRESENT LIFE IN 1 JOHN 1:8!

1 John 3:4. **Everyone who practices sin also practices lawlessness; and sin is lawlessness.** Apparently John made this somewhat obvious point (that sin is lawlessness) to underscore the fact that sin is a very serious matter. It is lawlessness; it is rebellion against God and His laws. The sin/lawlessness of the heretics proved that they did not really know God or love Him (see, for example, 1 John:1:5, 6; 2:3-6; and 3:6-12). This verse further emphasizes the fact that Christians should not have any sin. We are not rebels against God!

1 John 3:5. **And you know that He appeared in order to take away sins; and in Him there is no sin.** First we'll discuss the words **And you know that He appeared in order to take away sins.** The Lord Jesus Christ takes away the sins of those who submit to Him in faith. In this context the emphasis is on the fact that He takes away sins in the sense that He sanctifies His people and makes them righteous, which includes the fact that they stop sinning (see, for example, 1 John 2:29; 3:3, 4, 6-12; 1:5-7; 9; 2:1-6). The words, "He appeared in order to take away sins" are probably parallel in meaning with the words "The Son of God appeared for this purpose, that He might destroy [or, do away with] the works of the devil" of 1 John 3:8.

In one sense we can think of the sins of man being "the works of the devil." When people sin they are following the devil in his rebellion against God, and in a very real sense they yield to him and his kingdom and he works through them. This point of view makes it all the more obvious that Christians should not have any sins. Ultimately the Lord Jesus Christ will take away all sins from the earth so God's kingdom can be fully established. For those who continue in rebellion against God, this will necessitate removal by judgment (see, for example, Matt. 13:41, 42).

and in Him there is no sin. In Christ there never was any sin and never will be any sin, but it is also true that those who are in Him (those who abide in Him) are to be fully separate from all sin. In the next verse the apostle talks about our abiding in Christ. This is good news! God didn't have these things written to condemn us, but so that we might be sanctified by His sufficient grace through faith.

1 John 3:6. **No one who abides in Him** [in Christ] **sins; no one who sins has seen Him or knows Him.**

No one who abides in Him sins. These words build on verse 5. True Christians, by definition, abide in Christ. The heretics claimed they abided in God, but the apostle has informed us that they did not abide in Him. The ideal presented in this epistle (and throughout the New Testament) is that Christians are to walk in victory over all sin. I don't believe the apostle would have us dilute this ideal except to acknowledge the possibility (not the necessity) of an occasional act of sin. We discussed this point when we discussed 1 John 2:1, also see 1 John 5:16, 17.

The Greek verb *hamartano* that is translated **sins**" here in the first part of 3:6 is in the present tense. This Greek tense fits the idea that no one who abides in Christ can live in sin or be characterized by sin, and as we have discussed, the ideal presented in this epistle is that there should not be any sin at all. (A different Greek tense, the aorist tense, is used in 1 John 2:1, which we discussed when we discussed that verse.) The Greek verb translated **sins** here in the first half of 1 John 3:6 could be translated several different ways, including "keeps on sinning" with the NIV, "is a sinner" with the *New English Bible*, "lives in sin," "practices sin," "habitually sins," or "[deliberately and knowingly] habitually commits (practices) sin" with the *Amplified Bible*.

no one who sins. A Greek participle of *hamartano* in the present tense is used here. We could translate this participle several different ways, including "no one who continues to sin" with the NIV; "no one who lives in sin"; or, "no one who practices sin." The present tense of *hamartano* is also used in 1 John 3:8 ("the devil has sinned from the beginning") and in 1 John 3:9 ("and he cannot sin"; we'll discuss these words in some detail when we come to verse 9).

I'll skip the next paragraph. As I have mentioned, I frequently modify what is written in the book for these articles. The idea of practicing or continuing in sin (as in 1 John 3:4, 8, and 9, for example) is contrasted with the idea of practicing or continuing in righteousness. ... The ideal is for Christians to always continue in righteousness and never sin. This ideal is presented again and again throughout the first epistle of John (and throughout the New Testament).

no one who sins has seen Him or knows Him. These words were aimed (at least for the most part) at the Gnostic heretics (see, for example, 1 John 3:7; 1:6; and 2:3-6).

1 John 3:7. (As I have mentioned, this is a very important verse.) **Little children, let no one deceive you; the one who practices righteousness** [or, **the one who is doing righteousness**] **is righteous, just as He** [God] **is righteous.** 1 John 2:29 is an important cross-reference, "If you know that He [God] is righteous [and we do know that, don't we], you know that everyone also who practices righteousness [or, everyone who is doing righteousness] is born of Him." God imparts His

righteousness to His born-again children. The heretics (who were not practicing/doing righteousness) were trying to deceive John's readers (see 1 John 2:26 and 2 John 1:7). There are many deceivers in our day too; we must be very careful who we listen to; in the worst-case scenario, it could cost you your soul.

For the Christian to be righteous, just as God is righteous doesn't leave room for sin (see, for example, 1 John 1:5-7 and 9; 2:6; and 3:3). This is the Christian ideal, and it is very important for us to understand this ideal. This verse makes it very clear that John is not speaking of a mere positional, legal, imputed righteousness. He is speaking of Christians actually living in righteousness through the Lord Jesus Christ. Again, this is good news! We greatly distort the gospel if we put most of the emphasis on positional, legal, imputed righteousness, as it so often happens in our day. Furthermore, he is not speaking of a gradual growth out of sin into righteousness.

1 John 3:8. **the one who practices sin [or, the one who is doing sin] is of the devil; for the devil has sinned from the beginning. The Son of God appeared for this purpose, that He might destroy the works of the devil.** First we'll discuss the words, **the one who practices sin is of the devil; for the devil has sinned from the beginning.** The one who practices sin (or, the one who is doing sin) is following the devil in his rebellion against God, is part of the devil's kingdom, is motivated by the devil and demon spirits, and is a child of the devil (see, for example, 1 John 3:10, 12; Matt. 13:38; John 8:38, 41, 44; 12:31; 2 Cor. 4:4; Eph. 2:1-3; and 2 Tim. 2:26). According to the Scriptures, we cannot be neutral. If we are not faithful to God, we will be serving the devil to one degree or another.

As God enables His people to be righteous (see, for example, 1 John 2:29; 3:7), so the devil (and his demon spirits) work in the sons of disobedience (see Eph. 2:1-3, for example). This is not to say that those who are not submitted to God are totally controlled by the devil (most have considerable freedom), but his influence is very extensive.

for the devil has sinned from the beginning. The devil has been sinning since the time of his fall, which took place before the fall of man (see Genesis chapter 3, for example). In the context of 1 John chapter 3, it is probable that the words **from the beginning** refer back to the time when mankind joined Satan in his rebellion against God. In one sense (as we have discussed) the sins of man are the sins (or you could say, the works) of the devil. (See under 1 John 3:5, and see on the second half of 1 John 3:8). To say this is not at all to say that people are not responsible for their sins.

The Son of God appeared for this purpose, that He might destroy the works of the devil (1 John 3:8). As I mentioned under 1 John 3:5, we probably should equate these words with the words, "He appeared in order to take away sins" of 1 John 3:5. The Greek verb translated "destroy" here is *luo*. If we are going to equate the "sins" of 1 John 3:5 with **the works of the devil** of 1 John 3:8, then a translation like "do away with" would be preferable for *luo* here in verse 8. If we do not equate the "sins" of 1 John 3:5 with **the works of the devil**, the sins are at least included as part of **the works of the devil**. A major work of the Lord Jesus Christ throughout this present age is the removal of everything sinful from the hearts and lives of those who submit to Him and the gospel in faith. Ultimately (after His second coming), He will remove from God's kingdom the devil and all who continue to follow him, and all the devil's works.

We're almost done with this article. I'll read 1 John 2:29; 3:3, 4, 5-10, from the NIV: "If you know that he is righteous, you know that everyone who does what is right has been born of Him. ... (3) Everyone who has this hope in him purifies himself, just as he is pure. (4) Everyone who sins breaks the law; in fact, sin is lawlessness. (6) No one who lives in him keeps on sinning. No one who continues to sin has either seen him or known him. (7) Dear children, do not let anyone lead you astray. He who does what is right is righteous, just as he is righteous. (8) He who does what is sinful is of the devil, because the devil has been sinning from the beginning. The reason the Son of God appeared was to destroy the devil's work [or, works, the noun is plural in the Greek]. (9) No one who is born of God will continue to sin, because God's seed remains in him; he cannot go on sinning, because he has been born of God. (10) This is how we know who the children of God are and who the children of the devil are: Anyone who does not do what is right is not a child of God; nor is anyone who does not love his brother."

God bless you! His name be glorified; His will be done; His will be done in us! In Jesus' mighty name. Amen!

Holiness and Victory Over Sin #18

Holy Father, we humble our hearts before you. We want to rightly divide your Word. We want to understand it. We want to live it. We ask in Jesus' mighty, holy name. Amen!

When we stopped last time we were going through 1 John 2:28-3:12. Now we are ready to discuss 1 John 3:9. I'll read the verse from my book, *Holiness and Victory Over Sin: Full Salvation Through the Atoning Death of the Lord Jesus Christ*, which uses the *New American Standard Bible*, 1977 edition. **No one who is born of God practices sin, because His seed abides in him; and he cannot sin, because he is born of God.**

No one who is born of God practices sin. The fact that Christians do not practice sin is becoming a very familiar theme. Again, the ideal is victory over all sin. 1 John 3:10 (with 2:29) shows that born-again Christians "practice righteousness." "No one who is born of God practices sin" (or, "will continue to sin"), but those who are born of God "practice righteousness" (or, "do righteousness"; or, "will continue to do righteousness"). I'm on page 213 of my book (*Holiness and Victory Over Sin*). As I have mentioned, sometimes I modify what is written in the book for these articles.

because His seed abides in him. God's seed abides in every born-again Christian. We can speak of being born of the Word of God (see 1 Peter 1:23, for example), but here **His seed** probably refers to the indwelling Spirit of life, the Holy Spirit. As we walk by the Holy Spirit by faith, we walk in the righteousness and holiness of God.

and he cannot sin. The Greek more literally reads "<u>and he is not able to continue to sin</u>," or "<u>to live in sin</u>," or the equivalent. The Greek has the present tense infinitive of the verb *hamartano*, which is translated "to continue to sin," or the equivalent. (On the present tense of *hamartano*, see under 1 John 3:6. As we have discussed, the Greek present tense carries the idea of continuous action.) These words could be translated several other ways with essentially the same meaning, including, "he

177

cannot go on sinning" with the NIV; "he cannot practice sinning" with the *Amplified Bible*; and "he cannot be a sinner" with the *New English Bible.*

In 1 John 3:9 and throughout this epistle, the apostle John exhorts his readers with the need to continuously walk in the righteousness of God, with the victory over all sin. That's the ideal! But we know that John is not saying that it is impossible for a true Christian to commit an occasional act of sin. He has already made that point clear in 1 John 2:1. I'll read 1 John 2:1, "My little children, I am writing these things to you so that you may not sin [As we have discussed, the Greek verb *hamartano* is used in the aorist tense in 2:1. That tense carries the idea that you may not commit an act of sin, or the equivalent.] And [or, we could translate "But" with the NIV] But if anyone sins [Again the verb *hamartano* is in the aorist tense and carries the meaning, if anyone commits an act of sin, or the equivalent. John is dealing with the possibility (certainly not the necessity) of true Christians committing occasional acts of sin.], we have an advocate with the Father, Jesus Christ the righteous."

So, the apostle exhorts his readers to not sin at all in 1 John 2:1, but he acknowledges the possibility of occasional acts of sin. The New Testament confirms this point other places too. It's very clear that true Christians can sin, but the good news is that we are called (and enabled) to not sin at all. God's grace is sufficient for us to walk above sin. When we consider who Jesus is and what the Father has done for us in the sacrifice of His Son, it would be surprising, even shocking, if His grace wasn't sufficient to give us the total victory over sin. And especially when we consider the fact that God hates sin.

1 John 3:10. **By this the children of God and the children of the devil are obvious: anyone who does not practice righteousness** [or, **the one who is not doing righteousness**, or the equivalent] **is not of God, nor the one who does not love his brother.** In 1 John 3:8 the apostle says "the one who practices sin is of the devil." Here he says, "anyone who does not practice righteousness is not of God," and, therefore, is a child of the devil. 1 John 2:29-3:9, for example, show that the children of God do practice righteousness (they continue to do righteousness).

nor the one who does not love his brother. The apostle was speaking here of loving the brethren in Christ. "Loving the brethren" goes with keeping God's commandments and walking in His righteousness (see, for example, 1 John 1:7; 2:5-11; 3:14-24; 4:7-21; 5:1-3; John 13:34, 35; and 15:12, 17). In this matter also the heretics (the Gnostic heretics) proved that they were not the children of God; they did not love the brethren (see, for example, 1 John 1:5-7; 2:3-11, 19; 3:11, 12; and 4:20).

1 John 3:11. **For this is the message which you have heard from the beginning, that we should love one another.** The words **from the beginning** are also used in 1 John 2:7, "Beloved, I am not writing a new commandment to you, but an old commandment which you have had from the beginning; the old commandment is the word which you have heard." This message **that we should love one another** goes back to **the beginning** of Christianity. It was also included to some extent in the Old Testament.

1 John 3:12. **not as Cain, *who* was of the evil one** [the devil], **and slew his brother** [Abel]. **And for what reason did he slay him? Because his deeds were evil, and his brother's were righteous.** Verses 8 and 10 help explain what it means that Cain **was of the evil one.** He was a child of the devil, and he was doing a work of the devil when he killed his brother. The apostle Paul spoke of Satan working in the sons of disobedience in Eph. 2:2. This completes our study of 1 John 2:28-3:12.

I'll turn to page 214 of my book (*Holiness and Victory Over Sin*); we come to the heading, What Is Sin? It is very important for us to know the balanced truth of what the Bible teaches on this topic. We will not be able to fully discuss this important topic in this section, but a few comments are required. We frequently hear that the only way it would be possible for Christians to live in victory over sin would be to modify God's definition of sin. I don't agree with that assessment. The New Testament, which necessarily incorporates God's definition of sin, consistently speaks of victory over sin as the ideal standard for Christians.

Many examples are included in this book. Consider, for example, the words of the Lord Jesus Christ in the Sermon on the Mount (in Matthew chapters 5-7). I'll quote a few key verses from those chapters: Matthew 5:29, 30, "If your right eye makes you stumble [makes you sin], tear it out and throw it from you; for it is better for you to lose one of the parts of your body, than for your whole body to be thrown into hell. (30) If your right hand makes you stumble, cut it off and throw it from you; for it is better to lose one of the parts of your body, than for your whole body to go into hell." Matthew 5:48, "Therefore you are to be perfect, as your heavenly Father is perfect." Matthew 7:13, 14, 21-27, "Enter by the narrow gate; for the gate is wide, and the way is broad that leads to destruction, and many are those who enter by it. For the gate is small, and the way is narrow that leads to life, and few are those who find it. … (21) Not everyone who says to me, 'Lord, Lord,' will enter the kingdom of heaven; but he who does the will of my Father who is in heaven. Many will say to Me on that day, 'Lord, Lord, did we not prophesy in Your name, and in Your name cast out demons, and in Your name perform many miracles?' (23) And then I will declare to them, 'I never knew you; DEPART FROM ME, YOU WHO PRACTICE LAWLESSNESS [my emphasis].' Therefore everyone who hears these words of Mine and acts on them, may be compared to a wise man who built his house on the rock. And the rain fell, and the floods came, and the winds blew and slammed against that house; and *yet* it did not fall, for it had been founded on the rock. Everyone who hears these words of Mine and does not act on them, will be like a foolish man who built his house on the sand. The rain fell, and the floods came, and the winds blew and slammed against that house; and it fell—and great was its fall."

But didn't the apostle Paul say that he was the chief (or, the foremost) of sinners? He did, but he was speaking of his sinful pre-Christian state, when he was attacking the Lord Jesus Christ and the gospel and violently persecuting Christians. ((([This double parenthesis goes on for two paragraphs.] I'm going to turn back to endnote 12, where I discussed this topic. In 1 Timothy 1:12-16 the apostle Paul said, "I thank Christ Jesus our Lord, who has strengthened me, because He considered me faithful, putting me into service; (13) even though I WAS FORMERLY A BLASPHEMER AND A PERSECUTOR AND A VIOLENT AGGRESSOR [my emphasis]. And yet I was shown mercy, because I acted ignorantly in unbelief [back before he became a Christian]; (14) and the grace of our Lord was more than abundant, with the faith and love which are *found* in Christ Jesus. [The abundant grace of God in Christ was sufficient to transform Paul from being "the chief (or foremost) of sinners" to being the sanctified, faithful apostle to the Gentiles.] (15) It is a trustworthy statement, deserving full acceptance, that Christ Jesus came into the world to save sinners, among whom I am foremost *of all*. [The apostle Paul has already explained, back in verse 13, what he meant by calling himself the chief (or foremost) of sinners. He was attacking Jesus Christ and the gospel and violently persecuting Christians.] (16) And yet for this reason I found mercy, in order that in me as the foremost [of sinners], Jesus Christ might demonstrate His perfect patience, as an example for those who would believe in Him for eternal life." As I mentioned, the abundant grace of God in Christ was sufficient to transform Paul from being the "the [chief or] foremost of sinners" to being the sanctified, faithful apostle to the Gentiles.

Speaking of himself as a Christian, Paul spoke in very different terms (because of the sufficient sanctifying grace of God in Christ). He said, for example, "Be imitators of me, just as I also am of Christ" (1 Corinthians 11:1; compare 1 Cor. 4:16; Phil. 3:17). That sounds like the victory over all sin to me. I'll also quote 2 Corinthians 1:14, "For our proud confidence is this: the testimony of our conscience, that in holiness and godly sincerity, not in fleshy wisdom but in the grace of God, we have conducted ourselves in the world, and especially toward you." Also see 2 Cor. 1:12; 1 Thess. 2:1-12.))

I'm turning back to page 214. LET'S PUT THE EMPHASIS ON THE POWER OF THE ATONING BLOOD OF THE LAMB OF GOD TO TRANSFORM SINNERS INTO SAINTS, in accordance with the gospel of the new covenant. Let's not limit God's ability! The atoning blood of the Lord Jesus Christ is infinitely powerful, backed up by the infinite Spirit of God.

Everything short of absolute perfection should not be classified as sin, and the fact that we still have room for growth (and a need to grow) is not, in itself, sin. It will not work for good to call things sin when God doesn't. Christians can be tempted, and we can sin, and as all true Christians know, there is an intense warfare engaged against us by the world, the flesh, and the devil. It is important to know that being tempted, or having a wrong thought, or a wrong desire is not, in itself, sin. (([This double parenthesis goes on for two paragraphs.] I have an endnote here, which I'll read, 1 Corinthians 10:13 is an important verse that is relevant to this discussion. It says, "No temptation has overtaken you but such as is common to man; and God is faithful, who will not allow you to be tempted beyond what you are able, but with the temptation will provide the way of escape also, that you may be able to endure it [endure it without sinning that is]."

It is important to point out that Paul's primary message in 1 Cor. 10:1-22 was that the Christians at Corinth must flee immorality, idolatry, and rebellion. If they did not, they were sure to fall. We must, as far as it is possible, avoid all sources of temptation (see, for example, Rom. 13:11-14; 1 Tim. 6:9-11; 2 Tim. 2:22).))

(I'll turn back to page 214 and reread a sentence.) It is important to know that being tempted or having a wrong thought or a wrong desire is not, in itself, sin. (See Gal. 5:17, for example. We have already discussed Gal. 5:16-25 in previous articles, and this passage is discussed in some detail in the last chapter of my book (*Holiness and Victory Over Sin*). Even Jesus was, in one sense, tempted [see, for example, Heb. 2:18; 4:15; Luke 22:39-46]). The message of Gal. 5:16-25 and Rom. 8:12-14 is that Christians are enabled, by the indwelling Spirit of God, to keep the flesh (the old man) from manifesting itself in sin. There need not be an overt sinful act for sin to exist. In Gal. 5:19-21, for example, the apostle Paul lists "jealousy" and "envying" among "the deeds [works] of the flesh." Things like unbelief, pride, unforgiveness, jealousy, and envy are serious sins. There are also sins of omission (see, for example, James 4:17; 1 John 3:14-24). All sin is ultimately against God; it is a transgression of His laws (see 1 John 3:4).

Many Christians have often been too quick to label things as sin. One reason for this is that many Christians start with the assumption that we all sin often, and in many ways. With such an underlying assumption, it is no big deal to label one more thing as sin. Sin is a serious word. We should not use it loosely. But everything that God calls sin, we must be careful to call sin. And we must remain teachable before God and other Christians. It is all too easy to deceive ourselves and not see our sin. We must also be quick to repent and to ask for forgiveness before God and man. And we must make it top priority to walk in the righteousness and holiness of God by His sufficient grace.

Many say that our every thought, word, motive, attitude, and action is tainted by the flesh and is sinful. Significantly, however, the New Testament does not seem to share this point of view. The apostle Paul, for example, did not consider the active presence of the flesh (the old man) to be, in itself, sinful (see Gal. 5:16-25; Rom. 8:12-14; and 13:14). I don't believe God scrutinizes our every thought, word, motive, attitude, and action looking for the taint of sin. If anything, He is inclined toward generosity as He evaluates His blood-bought children. He is not a cold, impersonal computer in the sky. He is our loving heavenly Father.

Didn't the Lord Jesus Christ say that if a man has a lustful thought or desire he has sinned? No, that isn't quite what he said. He said, "everyone who looks at a woman to lust [for the purpose of lusting] for her has committed adultery with her already in his heart" (Matthew 5:28). The Lord was speaking of a man who willingly yields himself (his mind) for the purpose of lusting, not of a man who rejects and resists all such temptation.

Well, didn't the apostle Paul say that "whatever is not from faith [or, of faith] is sin" in Romans 14:23? (Romans chapter 14 is discussed verse-by-verse in my *A Paper on Faith*. That paper [and many other papers] is located on my internet site.) Some have taken these words out of context and understood them to say far more than what the apostle intended. (I'll give a few examples as we continue.) Misinterpretations like this cause considerable confusion in the Body of Christ and do a lot of damage.

In the context of Romans chapter 14, Paul is saying that if a Christian does something that is not in itself sinful, eating meat, for example, while doubting that it is OK with God, it is sin (see Rom. 14:13-15, 20-23). These words from Romans 14:23 ("whatever is not of faith is sin") should not be used to label as sinful every area of our lives in which we are not strong in faith. I'm sure the apostle desired that those who were "weak in faith" (see Rom. 14:1, 2) would become strong in faith. He did not, however, say that this particular weakness was sinful. Like I said, sin is a serious word. In Romans chapter 14 the apostle exhorts those strong in faith not to regard with contempt or to judge those weak in faith (see Rom. 14:1, 3, 10, 13). He also exhorts those weak in faith not to judge those strong in faith (see Rom. 14:3, 4, 10, 13). We have to be careful about judging others (see Matt. 7:1-5, for example).

I'm going to add to what I said on Romans chapter 14 in the book for this article. In Romans chapter 14 the apostle exhorted those strong in faith (that is, those who knew that it was OK for them to eat meat, for example), to fully accept those weak in faith (those who were not convinced in their hearts, for one reason, or another, that it was OK with God for them to eat meat, for example). Paul made it clear in Romans chapter 14 that those strong in faith should not put pressure on those weak in faith to go ahead and eat meat, for example, before they had faith in their hearts that it was OK before God for them to eat meat. The apostle said that if they ate meat before they had faith in their hearts that it was OK with God, it would be sin for them, even though eating meat is not sinful. And sin is a very serious matter.

Quite often I have heard Christians, very sincere Christians, take these words ("whatever is not of faith is sin") out of context and come up with ideas like Christians are sinning if they stay sick for a while, or if they go to a doctor, or if they take medicine because they should have faith to be healed, and the Bible says that whatever is not of faith is sin. Or, ideas like Christians are sinning if they are having financial problems, or if they are overweight, etc., etc., because they should have faith to get every problem solved quickly. It is very important for Christians to be strong in faith in every area, but ideas like those I just mentioned are far removed from what the apostle was saying in Rom. 14:23. Again, Paul was saying that it is sinful to eat meat, for example, when you doubt in your heart that it is OK with God. Sin is a serious matter, and it causes considerable confusion and damage when we call things sin that God doesn't call sin.

Several verses in 1 Corinthians are often taken out of context and used to label as sinful many areas that are far outside the scope of the apostle Paul's words. 1 Corinthians 3:16, 17 say, "Do you not know that you are a temple of God, and *that* the Spirit of God dwells in you? (17) If any man destroys the temple of God, God will destroy him for the temple of God is holy and that is what you are." And 1 Corinthians 6:19, 20 say, "Or do you not know that your body is a temple of the Holy Spirit who is in you, whom you have from God, and that you are not your own? (20) For you have been bought with a price, therefore glorify God in your body."

These verses have often been used to label as sinful such things as being overweight, working too much, not sleeping enough, not getting enough exercise, and not eating right. I'm not saying that God never considers such things to be sinful (and especially if He has been dealing with a Christian in one of these areas), but the apostle Paul wasn't dealing with such things in the verses just quoted. In 1 Cor. 3:16, 17 he was dealing with the serious sin of destroying segments of the Body of Christ though heresy, etc. (It should be noted that the "you," which is found four times in 1 Cor. 3:16, 17 is plural in the Greek. I'll read those verses again, "Do you [plural] not know that you [plural] are a temple of

God and *that* the Spirit of God dwells in you [plural]. If any man destroys the temple of God, God will destroy him, for the temple of God is holy, and that is what you [plural] are.") In 1 Cor. 6:15-20 Paul was dealing with the sin of gross immorality.

As I have mentioned, there are sins of omission, but we don't want to overuse (or, under use) this concept. Everyone can think of things they could have done differently. I could have gotten up earlier; I could have read the Bible more; I could have prayed more; I could have talked to that person; and so on. I'm not suggesting that such things are never sinful, but we need some restraint here. For one thing, the devil's hosts work to get Christians feeling condemned even when they haven't sinned. That completes our brief study regarding "What Is Sin?"

Holiness and Victory Over Sin #19

Holy Father, we humble our hearts before you. We admit our total dependence on you. We want to understand your Word. We want to live your Word. In Jesus' mighty, holy name. Amen!

I'm going to turn to page 141 of my book. A new chapter begins here, a very important chapter, A Study on the Meaning of the Greek Noun Aphesis. The Greek noun *aphesis*, which is used seventeen times in the New Testament, is translated "forgiveness" fifteen times by the NASB. The KJV translates it "forgiveness" or "remission" fifteen times. The only place where the NASB and the KJV translate *aphesis* other than "forgiveness" or "remission" is Luke 4:18, which uses this Greek noun two times. (We will discuss Luke 4:18 below.) The NIV has "forgiveness" or the verb "forgiven" in all the fifteen uses that exclude Luke 4:18. The BAGD Greek Lexicon lists each of these fifteen uses under "forgiveness" and equates forgiveness with the "cancellation of the guilt of sin."

Although "forgiveness" or the equivalent is widely accepted as the normal translation for *aphesis* in the New Testament, I don't believe this is an adequate translation in some verses. In my opinion, if forgiveness is understood in the typical sense of the cancellation of the guilt of sin, then this translation frequently says far less that what was intended by the Author [referring to God] and the author. I believe a translation like "release"; that is, "release [from sins with the guilt and penalties (including the major penalties of spiritual death and bondage to sin)]" is required in several verses. A translation like "release [from sins with the guilt and penalties (including the major penalties of spiritual death and bondage to sin)]" says much more than "forgiveness [of the guilt of sin]," though that is included. This suggested translation also includes the ideas of being set free from the kingdom of spiritual death and bondage to sin, and made alive spiritually and made righteous and holy.

In my opinion, there is far too little emphasis placed on the gospel truth of being made righteous and holy in the Christian church of our day. An understanding of this fuller sense of *aphesis* will serve as an important step in rectifying this very serious problem.

There is very much in common between *aphesis* (understood in this much fuller sense) and the idea of redemption. There is also very much in common with the idea of justification, when justification is used in the full sense that we have discussed in these articles and which is discussed in some detail in my book, *Holiness and Victory Over Sin*. When used in the full sense, justification includes being declared righteous, being set free from spiritual death and bondage to sin, being born again, and being made righteous and holy.

In this study we will first discuss Luke 4:18 (with Luke 4:16-21), where the context makes it very clear, and everyone seems to agree, that *aphesis* means much more than forgiveness. It means release, deliverance, liberty. At the end of the study of Luke 4:18, we will briefly discuss the meaning of *aphesis* as it is used in the Septuagint (the Greek Old Testament). That is quite important too.

We will then discuss five very important New Testament verses that use *aphesis*. (In this e-book, we will just look at two of these verses.) In each of these verses, *aphesis* has typically been translated forgiveness, or the equivalent. In my opinion, however, it is very important to see that *aphesis* means much more than forgiveness in each of these verses. Our understanding of the meaning of this Greek noun (as it is used in these verses) will significantly affect our understanding of the meaning of these very important verses. The two verses we will discuss in this article are Col.1:14 (with Col. 1:9-14) and Eph. 1:7.

Now we come to the heading, <u>Luke 4:18 and the Meaning of *Aphesis*</u>. First I'll read <u>Luke 4:16-21</u>, then we'll get into the details of Luke 4:18. **And He** [Jesus] **came to Nazareth, where He had been brought up; and as was His custom, He entered the synagogue on the Sabbath, and stood up to read. (17) And the book** [probably better, **the scroll**] **of the prophet Isaiah was handed to Him. And He opened the [scroll] and found the place where it was written, (18) "The Spirit of the Lord** [Yahweh] **is upon Me, Because He anointed Me to preach the gospel to the poor. He has sent Me to proclaim release** [Greek *aphesis*] **to the captives, And recovery of sight to the blind, To set free** [Greek *aphesis*] **those who are downtrodden, (19) To proclaim the favorable year of the Lord." (20) And He closed the [scroll], and gave it back to the attendant, and sat down; and the eyes of all in the synagogue were fixed upon Him. (21) And He began to say to them, "Today this Scripture has been fulfilled in your hearing."**

Now we'll get into the details of <u>Luke 4:18</u>. I'll read the verse again, **"The Spirit of the Lord** [Yahweh in the Hebrew] **is upon Me, Because He anointed Me to preach the gospel to the poor. He has sent Me to proclaim RELEASE** [my emphasis; Greek *aphesis*] **to the captives, and recovery of sight to the blind, To set free** [Greek *aphesis*] **those who are downtrodden...."** Note that *aphesis* is used twice in this verse. The quotation in Luke 4:18, 19 comes almost entirely from Isa. 61:1, 2. These verses in Isaiah prophesy regarding the anointed ministry of the Lord Jesus Christ, as these verses in Luke chapter 4 demonstrate. "The Christ" (from the Greek) and "the Messiah" (from the Hebrew) both mean "the Anointed One." Instead of "<u>release</u> to the captives," the KJV has "<u>deliverance</u> to the captives," and the NIV has "<u>freedom</u> for the prisoners." Instead of "to set free," the KJV has "to set at liberty," and the NIV has "to release." I prefer a more literal translation for these words in the last line of verse 18, "<u>to send out in the release</u>," or the equivalent. The *Amplified Bible* has (for the last words of Luke 4:18), "to send forth delivered those who are oppressed—who are downtrodden, bruised, crushed and broken down by calamity."

We were all "captives" in bondage to sin, Satan, and spiritual death; we were under our sins with the guilt and the penalties, back to Adam. But the Savior came to release the captives. He has released us (He has set us free) from bondage to sin, Satan, and spiritual death.

187

Isaiah chapter 53, for example, showed by what means the Servant of God would set the captives free. He bore our sins with the guilt and with the penalties (including the major penalties of spiritual death and bondage to sin). He set us free from sin, Satan, and spiritual death. He gives us spiritual life and makes us righteous and holy. Matthew 1:21 says, "And she will bear a son; and you shall call His name Jesus, for it is He who will save His people from their sins." He saves His people (all believers) from their sins with the guilt and with the penalties. He bore our sins with the guilt and with the penalties, including the major penalties of spiritual death and bondage to sin. The name *Jesus* means "The Lord [Yah, Yahweh] Saves."

The words **to proclaim release** [Greek *aphesis*] **to the captives,** which are quoted from Isa. 61:1, build on the old-covenant year of jubilee. The year of jubilee, which is spelled out in Lev. 25:8-55, was a year of release. Leviticus 25:10 says, "You shall thus consecrate the fiftieth year and proclaim a release [my emphasis] through the land to all its inhabitants. It shall be a jubilee for you, and each of you shall return to his own property, and each of you shall return to his family." The Hebrew verb for "proclaim" and the Hebrew noun for "release" that are used in Lev. 25:10 are also used in Isa. 61:1.

The last line of Luke 4:18 (which I would translate "to send out in *the* release") and Luke 4:19 ("to proclaim the favorable year of the Lord") also apparently build on the release of jubilee. In the Septuagint (the Greek Old Testament), *aphesis* is used some fifteen times in Lev. 25:8-55. [[I have an endnote here. I'll read part of this endnote. *Aphesis* is used twice in the Greek of Leviticus 25:10, "And ye shall sanctify the year, the fiftieth year, and ye shall proclaim a release [*aphesis*] upon the land to all that inhabit it; it shall be a year of release [*aphesis*], a jubilee for you; and each one shall depart to his possession, and ye shall go each to his family." In Lev. 25:28, 31, 33, 41, and 54, we read of persons or property going out in the release [*aphesis*]. In Lev. 25:13, 40, 50, 52, and 54, we read of "the year of *the* release [*aphesis*]." We will further discuss the meaning of *aphesis* as it is used in the Septuagint at the end of the study of Luke 4:18." Now I'll turn back to page 144 (of *Holiness and Victory Over Sin*).]]

One primary feature of the release of jubilee was that any Israelites who had sold themselves into bondage because of poverty were to be set free, if they had not been set free beforehand (Lev. 25:10, 39-43, 47-55). Another primary feature of the release of jubilee was that the Israelites were to return to any property they had temporarily lost; the property was released that the Israelites might return to that which had been given to them by God (Lev. 25:10. 13-17, 23-28, 31-33).

It is not hard to see how the release of jubilee prefigured the much greater RELEASE that was to be accomplished through the Lord Jesus Christ and new-covenant salvation. He has already RELEASED the captives from sin, Satan, and spiritual death, and He will ultimately overthrow every enemy, including physical death. "The creation itself also will be set free from its slavery to corruption into the freedom of the glory of the children of God" (Romans 8:21).

I should mention one more important feature regarding the release of jubilee. Leviticus 25:9 shows that it began on the Day of Atonement. The release of Christians has come through the Sacrifice of the Lord Jesus Christ, which was prefigured by the sacrifices of the Day of Atonement. Isaiah 61:1-3 build on Isaiah chapter 53, which is one of the most important chapters in the Bible dealing with the atoning death of the Lord Jesus Christ.

I'll briefly comment on the last two lines of Isa. 61:3 since these words are so relevant to the topic of holiness and victory over sin. The last two lines of Isaiah 61:3 say, "So they will be called oaks of righteousness, The planting of the LORD [Yahweh], that He may be glorified." There cannot be any substantial or permanent salvation for the people of God until they are set free from bondage to sin and made righteous. This release (deliverance) from sin and transformation to righteousness are the heart and foundation of new-covenant salvation in Christ Jesus. This is a whole lot more than the forgiveness of sins, as important as that is. God makes His people righteous; He makes them "oaks of righteousness," and He is glorified by our righteousness. He imputes and imparts His righteousness to us through the atoning death of Christ Jesus and by His outpoured Spirit. "For we are His workmanship, created in Christ Jesus for good works, which God prepared beforehand so that we would walk in them" (Ephesians 2:10).

We come to the subheading, Some concluding remarks on the meaning of aphesis as it is used in Luke 4:18. It is clear that aphesis is used in

Luke 4:18 with the sense of release or the equivalent. The forgiveness of guilt is included, but the salvation pictured in Luke 4:18 goes far beyond forgiveness. The captives are set free – released – from bondage to sin, Satan, and spiritual death, and they are born again and made righteous and holy.

We come to the heading, The Meaning of *Aphesis* as it Is Used in the Septuagint. The Septuagint is the Greek translation of the Hebrew Old Testament. It was widely used by the early Christian church and is frequently quoted in the New Testament. The Septuagint helped prepare many Greek words to communicate the Christian gospel, which spread across the Roman world in the Greek language.

Aphesis is used approximately forty-five times in the Septuagint, but I didn't find one clear example where it is used of forgiveness. It is used about twenty-five times of the release of jubilee. Some fifteen of those uses are found in Leviticus chapter 25. Approximately ten uses deal with the seventh-year release, which is different than the release of jubilee (see Deut. 15:1-18). Other uses are fountains of water and the torrents of water coming forth from the eyes of Jeremiah (in Lam. 3:48).

I am not suggesting that *aphesis* should never be translated forgiveness in the New Testament, but a translation like release (release from sins with the guilt and the penalties) is required in several verses.

Now we come to the heading, Colossians 1:9-14 with Special Emphasis on the Meaning of *Aphesis* as it Is Used in Colossians 1:14. First I'll read Colossians 1:9-11 and make a few comments. **For this reason also, since the day we heard *of it* we have not ceased to pray for you and to ask that you may be filled with the knowledge of His will in all spiritual wisdom and understanding, (10) so that you may walk in a manner worthy of the Lord, to please *Him* in all respects, bearing fruit in every good work and increasing in the knowledge of God; (11) strengthened with all power, according to His glorious might, for the attaining of all steadfastness and patience; joyously**

I'll read part of what I said under Col. 1:9-11. The apostle Paul was concerned that the Colossian Christians (and all Christians) be transformed/sanctified and **walk in a manner worthy of the Lord, to**

please *Him* in all respects (Col. 1:10). Christians must know the will of God (see verse 9) so they can cooperate with His grace, which includes His saving power (see verse 11). These verses show that Christians are enabled (and required) to live righteous, holy, fruitful, and steadfast lives (by the saving grace of God in Christ through faith). IN THE FOLLOWING VERSES, VERSES 12-14, THE APOSTLE PAUL GOES ON SPEAKING OF THE GLORY OF NEW-COVENANT SALVATION THAT REDEEMS SINNERS FROM THE KINGDOM OF SIN AND SPIRITUAL DEATH AND TRANSFERS THEM TO THE KINGDOM OF THE LORD JESUS CHRIST AND MAKES THEM RIGHTEOUS AND HOLY.

I'll read Colossians 1:12-14, then we'll get into the important details, **[joyously] giving thanks to the Father, who has qualified us to share in the inheritance of the saints in [the] light. (13) For He delivered us from the domain of [the] darkness, and transferred us to the kingdom of His beloved Son, (14) in whom we have [the] redemption, the forgiveness** [Greek *aphesis*] **of sins.**

Colossians 1:12, **[joyously] giving thanks to the Father, who has qualified us to share in the inheritance of the saints in [the] light.** First we'll discuss the words **who has qualified us**. We could also translate **who has made us fit**. The *Amplified Bible* has, "Who has qualified *and* made us fit." For one major thing, the Father has qualified us (or, made us fit) **to share in the inheritance of the saints in [the] light** by making us **saints** (holy people, set-apart-for God people).

God **has qualified us** [or, **made us fit**] **to share in the inheritance of the saints in [the] light** by delivering us from the kingdom of [the] darkness (with its spiritual death and bondage to sin), and transferring us to the kingdom of the Lord Jesus Christ, which is the kingdom of the light (with its truth and its righteousness and holiness). See verses 13, 14.

The word **saints** is a translation of the plural of the Greek adjective *hagios*, which is typically translated "holy" or "saint" in the New Testament. Christians are saints (holy people) in that they have been set apart (by God) for God. They have been set apart from the kingdom of the darkness, from spiritual death, and from sin. They have been transferred into the kingdom of the Lord Jesus Christ, which is the kingdom of the light, and they partake of the life of God (having been born again), and they become slaves of righteousness (having been redeemed

191

out of the kingdom of sin). Much of Col. 1:9-14 helps explain what it means to be "saints." Also see Col. 1:21-4:6 and 4:12, and see the last chapter of my book, *Holiness and Victory Over Sin*.

I'll read Colossians 1:12, 13 again, **[joyously] giving thanks to the Father, who has qualified us [or, made us fit] to share in the inheritance of the saints in [the] light. For He delivered us from the domain of [the] darkness, and transferred us to the kingdom of His beloved Son.** I would translate **in the light** and **of the darkness.** The definite article (the) is included in the Greek for both words. **The light** here at the end of verse 12 is contrasted with **the darkness** that is mentioned in verse 13. God is light and His kingdom is the kingdom of the light (see, for example, John 1:4-9; 8:12; 9:5; Acts 26:18; 1 Pet. 2:9; 1 John 1:5-7; Rev. 21:23; and 22:5). To be **in the light** includes being in the truth, life, righteousness, and holiness of God (cf. e.g., Matt. 5:14-16; John 3:19-21; 12:35, 36; 44-50; Acts 26:18; Rom. 13:12-14; 2 Cor. 6:14; Eph. 5:1-14; 1 Thess. 5:4-8; 1 John 1:5-9; 2:8-11).

I'll read Colossians 1:12 from the *Amplified Bible*, "Giving thanks to the Father, Who has qualified *and* made us fit to share the portion, which is the inheritance of the saints (God's holy people) in the light."

I'll read Colossians 1:13 again. **For He delivered us from the domain [the authority] of [the] darkness, and transferred us to the kingdom of His beloved Son [the Son of His love].** As I mentioned, **the darkness** of verse 13 is contrasted with **the light** of verse 12. Also, I would translate **the authority of the darkness** instead of **the domain of the darkness.** The *New American Standard Bible* points out in the margin that the more basic meaning of the Greek noun used here (*eksousia*) is "authority."

Formerly we were slaves of sin and the god of this world; we were under "the authority of the darkness." I'll quote what the apostle Paul said in Romans 13:12-14, "The night is almost gone, and the day is near. Therefore let us lay aside the deeds [or, the works] of [the] darkness and put on the armor of [the] light. Let us behave properly as in the day, not in carousing and drunkenness, not in sexual promiscuity and sensuality, not in strife and jealousy. But put on the Lord Jesus Christ, and make no provision for the flesh in regard to *its* lusts." And I'll quote what he said in Ephesians 5:8, 9, 11, 12, "for you were formerly darkness, but now you are light in the Lord; walk as children of Light (9) (for the fruit of the Light *consists* in all goodness and righteousness and truth).... (11) Do not participate in the unfruitful deeds [or, works] of [the] darkness, but instead *even* expose them; for it is disgraceful even to speak of the things which are done by them in secret."

God the Father has delivered us from the authority of the darkness, and transferred us to the kingdom of His beloved Son, or, better yet, "the kingdom of the Son of His love."

Acts 26:18 (which is discussed in detail later in this chapter) is an important cross-reference for Col. 1:12-14. I'll read Acts 26:18 (The Lord Jesus Christ was speaking to the apostle Paul), "to open their eyes so that they may turn from darkness to light and from the dominion [or, authority] of Satan to God, in order that they may receive forgiveness [Greek *aphesis*] of sins and an inheritance among those who have been sanctified by faith in Me."

The Greek noun translated "dominion" in Acts 26:18 is *eksousia*, the same noun translated "domain" in Col. 1:13. I prefer the translation "authority" in both verses. The dominion/domain/authority [kingdom] of the darkness is the equivalent of the dominion/domain/authority [kingdom] of Satan. The emphasis in Acts 26:18, as in Col. 1:9-14, is on the deliverance from the kingdom of sin, Satan, and darkness and the transformation to the righteousness, holiness, and light of the kingdom of the Lord Jesus Christ.

It is important to see that the emphasis of Col. 1:12, 13 goes far beyond the forgiveness of the guilt of sins, though that is included, and is very important. On being set free from the authority of sin, see, for example, John 8:31-36; Rom. 5:19-6:23; 8:1-14; 1 Cor. 6:9-11; Gal. 5:16-25; Eph. 4:17-6:20; Titus 2:11-3:11; and 1 Pet. 1:13-2:25. On being set free from the authority of Satan, see Matt. 28:18-20; John 16:11; Gal. 1:4; Eph. 1:20-2:10; 4:27; Col. 2:15; and Heb. 2:14-18. I'll quote two of the passages I listed here: Colossians 2:15, "When He [God the Father] had disarmed the rulers and authorities, He made a public display of them, having triumphed over them through Him [through the Lord Jesus Christ]." And Hebrews 2:14-18 (I'll read these verses from the NIV), "Since the children have flesh and blood, he too shared in their humanity so that by his death he might destroy him who holds the power of death—

that is, the devil—and free those who all their lives were held in slavery by their fear of death. For surely it is not angels he helps, but Abraham's descendants. For this reason he had to be made like his brothers in every way, in order that he might become a merciful and faithful high priest in service to God, and that he might make atonement for the sins of the people. Because he himself suffered when he was tempted, he is able to help those who are being tempted."

We're almost finished with this article. In closing I'll read one of the passages I listed on being set free from the authority of sin, John 8:31-36. "So Jesus was saying to those Jews who had believed Him, 'If you continue in My word, *then* you are truly disciples of mine; and you will know the truth, and the truth will make you free.' They answered Him, 'We are Abraham's descendants and have never yet been enslaved to anyone; how is it that You say, "You will become free"?' Jesus answered them, 'Truly, truly, I say to you, EVERYONE WHO COMMITS SIN IS THE SLAVE OF SIN [my emphasis]. The slave does not remain in the house forever; the son [I would translate Son, with the KJV.] does remain forever. SO IF THE SON [the Lord Jesus Christ] MAKES YOU FREE YOU WILL BE FREE INDEED [my emphasis].' " The Lord Jesus Christ sets us free from being slaves of sin. John chapter 8 is discussed verse-by-verse in my paper on John chapters 5-8 on my internet site.

We'll discuss Col. 1:14 in the next article. God bless you! May His name be glorified; His will be done; His will be done in us!

Holiness and Victory Over Sin #20

Holy Father, we humble our hearts before you. We're making it a top priority to understand your Word. We want to understand it. We want to live it. We want to be fully ready to stand before you. We pray in Jesus' mighty name. Amen!

Last time when we stopped we were on page 148 of my book, *Holiness and Victory Over Sin: Full Salvation Through the Atoning Death of the Lord Jesus Christ*. We are in the middle of a study of the Greek noun *aphesis*, which is a very important word. We were discussing Col. 1:9-14 at the end of the last article, which is a very important passage on the topic of holiness and victory over sin. We finished discussing verses 9-13 in the last article, and we are ready to discuss verse 14, a verse that uses *aphesis*.

Before I read Colossians 1:14, I'll read verses 9-13 with a few comments for review. What the apostle Paul said in verses 9-13 helps us understand what he went on to say in verse 14. These verses are strongly tied together in the Greek. Verses 9-14 are all part of the same sentence in the Greek. There is a very strong emphasis in these verses on our being delivered from the authority of the kingdom of the darkness and bondage to sin and of our being transferred to the kingdom of the Lord Jesus Christ, which is the kingdom of the light, and of our being made saints who walk in a manner worthy of the Lord to please Him in all respects by the authority and power of God.

For this reason also, since the day we heard *of it*, we have not ceased to pray for you and to ask that you may be filled with the knowledge of His will in all spiritual wisdom and understanding, so that you may walk in a manner worthy of the Lord, to please Him in all respects, bearing fruit in every good work and increasing in the knowledge of God; strengthened with all power, according to His glorious might, for the attaining of all steadfastness and patience; joyously giving thanks to the Father, who has qualified us [or, who has made us fit] to share in the inheritance of the saints in light [in the light], For He rescued [or delivered; the 1977 edition of the NASB has delivered and the 1995 edition has rescued] us from the domain [or from the authority] of darkness [of the darkness], and transferred us to the kingdom of His beloved Son [the Son of His love; Now I'll read verse 14], in whom [in Christ Jesus] we have redemption [we have the redemption], the forgiveness of sins [Greek *aphesis*].

The Greek noun *aphesis* is typically translated "forgiveness" or the equivalent in this verse, but as we have discussed and will further discuss in some detail, I don't believe this is an adequate way to translate *aphesis* in this verse and in several other verses. A translation like, **in whom we have the redemption, the release from sins [with the guilt and the penalties (including the major penalties of spiritual death and bondage to sin)]** is required. This other translation says so much more, and it agrees perfectly with what *the redemption* means and with what

195

the apostle Paul said in the preceding verses. The Lord Jesus Christ didn't just bear our sins with the guilt so we could be forgiven, as important as that is. He bore our sins with the guilt and with the penalties in His atoning death (very much including the penalties of spiritual death and bondage to sin), so He could forgive us and redeem us out of the kingdom of the darkness, with its spiritual death and bondage to sin. He bore our spiritual death, so we could be redeemed out of the kingdom of spiritual death and be born again. He bore our bondage to sin, so we could be redeemed out from under that evil taskmaster and be made righteous and holy with the imparted righteousness and holiness of God.

Now we'll get into the details of Colossians 1:14. I'll be reading from my book, which uses the *New American Standard Bible*, 1977 edition; sometimes I modify what is written in the book for these articles. We'll start with the words, **in whom we have redemption.** I would translate **the redemption.** The definite article is included in the Greek. God's redemption through Jesus Christ is **the redemption** in that it is the theme of much Old Testament prophecy and is at the center of new-covenant salvation. Also, the apostle does not first come to the idea of redemption at Col. 1:14; he has been speaking of the redemption, using different words, in the preceding verses, especially verse 13. On **the redemption** see under Romans 3:24 in chapter 6 of my book, *Holiness and Victory Over Sin*.

I'm going to turn back to page 80 (of *Holiness and Victory Over Sin*) and read part of what I said there in chapter 6. We're discussing the words through the redemption which is in Christ Jesus of Romans 3:24. I believe these words rather strongly confirm that in Romans 3:24 "being justified" includes the ideas of being set free from the authority and power of sin (and spiritual death) and being made righteous. Sin formerly reigned (see Rom. 5:21, for example), and we were slaves of sin (see, for example, Rom. 3:9-20; 6:6, 17-22; 8:2, 5-8; and John 8:31-36), but now we have been redeemed out of the kingdom of sin (and spiritual death) through the atoning death of the Lord Jesus Christ.

The word *redemption* conveys the idea of buying a slave to set him free. We were slaves of sin (according to the New Testament), but we have been redeemed out of the kingdom of sin; we are no longer under the authority and power of sin, and we are no longer to serve our old master of sin (by sinning). If we were forgiven but were still slaves of sin, we would not be redeemed. Let's briefly consider several passages that deal with the redemption in Christ Jesus, passages that emphasize the transformation to righteousness and holiness.

First we'll look at 1 Corinthians 6:18-20. "Flee immorality. Every *other* sin that a man commits is outside the body, but the immoral man sins against his own body. (19) Or do you not know that your body is a temple of the Holy Spirit who is in you, whom you have from God, and that you are not your own? (20) For you have been bought with a price; therefore glorify God in your body." We were bought with the price of Jesus' blood. His precious blood redeemed us out of the kingdom of sin, Satan, and spiritual death.

Now I'll read Titus 2:11-14 from the NIV, "For the grace of God that brings salvation has appeared to all men. (12) It teaches us [and, I might add, it enables us] to say 'No' to ungodliness and worldly passions and to live self-controlled, upright and godly lives in this present age, (13) while we wait for the blessed hope—the glorious appearing of our great God and Savior, Jesus Christ, (14) who gave himself for us TO REDEEM [my emphasis] us from all wickedness [or, lawlessness] and to purify for himself a people that are his very own, eager to do what is good." (I mentioned that Titus 2:11-14 are briefly discussed later in this chapter of my book, *Holiness and Victory Over Sin.*)

Now 1 Peter 1:14-19, which is another passage that speaks of *redemption* and puts a very strong emphasis on the need for Christians to be set apart from all sin for God. "As obedient children, do not be conformed to the former lusts which were *yours* in your ignorance [back before you became Christians], (15) but like the Holy One who called you, BE HOLY YOURSELVES ALSO IN ALL *YOUR* BEHAVIOR [my emphasis]; (16) because it is written, 'YOU SHALL BE HOLY, FOR I AM HOLY.' (17) And if you address as Father the One who impartially judges according to each man's work, conduct yourselves in fear during the time of your stay *upon* earth [We must be afraid to sin against God; that's a healthy fear and a necessary fear according to the Bible, both the Old and New Testaments.]; knowing that you were not REDEEMED [my emphasis] with perishable things like silver or gold from your futile [and I might add, sinful] way of life inherited from your forefathers, (19) but with precious blood, as of a lamb unblemished and spotless, *the blood* of Christ." Christians have been redeemed from their former futile, sinful way of life by the atoning blood of Christ. (First Peter 1:13-19 are discussed in the last chapter of this book, *Holiness and Victory Over Sin*.)

I'll turn back to page 148 and continue to quote what I said under Col. 1:14, Now we'll discuss the words "the forgiveness [*aphesis*] of sins" of Col. 1:14. As I have mentioned, I can't live with the translation "forgiveness" for *aphesis* here. I would translate **the release from sins [with the guilt and the penalties (including the major penalties of spiritual death and bondage to sin)]**, or the equivalent. With these words, which are in apposition with the words "we have [the] redemption," the apostle expands on what he means by "the redemption."

Formerly we were under our sins with the guilt and the penalties. (See chapters 1, 2, 3, 4 and 6 of my book.) To be under our sins with the penalties included being under the authority of sin, spiritual death, Satan, and the kingdom of the darkness. These enemies gained authority over us through our sins, especially Adam's one great transgression (see Rom. 5:12-21).

God sent His Son to bear our sins with the guilt and the penalties, and He delivered (rescued) us from the authority of the darkness (see Col. 1:13). The deliverance (rescue) of Col. 1:13 refers to the same basic gospel reality as do the expressions "the redemption" and "the release from [our] sins [with the guilt and the penalties (including the major penalties of spiritual death and bondage to sin)]" of verse 14. All these expressions include the forgiveness of the guilt of sin, but they also include much more. We were not just redeemed from the guilt to sin—we were redeemed out of the kingdom of sin. This means, among other things, that we are no longer required to (or supposed to) serve our former master of sin by sinning. This is very good news! This is what we want, isn't it?

Isaiah chapter 53 (which is discussed in this book, *Holiness and Victory Over Sin*) is a very important passage to show by what means we are released from our sins with the guilt and the penalties. That chapter deals with the all-important atoning death of the Lord Jesus Christ. The other passages that we are studying in this chapter of my book are all important illustrations of this concept of being released from sins with the guilt and the penalties (including the major penalties of spiritual death and bondage to sin). Since this concept is so important, and since it is not widely understood, let's consider several more illustrations:

First we'll look at Psalm 130:8. I'll read the verse, "And He will redeem Israel From all his iniquities." Iniquities is a translation of the plural of the Hebrew noun *awon*. I believe this Hebrew noun is used here (as it very often is) of the iniquities with the guilt and the penalties. (Chapter 2 of my book deals with the meaning of this Hebrew noun.) Israel needs to be redeemed from her iniquities with the guilt and with the penalties. Psalm 130:8, understood in its ultimate sense, prophesies of full salvation in the Lord Jesus Christ. The concept of being redeemed from iniquities with the guilt and the penalties in Psalm 130:8 is essentially the same thing as "the redemption, the release from sins [with the guilt and the penalties (including the major penalties of spiritual death and bondage to sin)]" of Col. 1:14.

Now we come to the subheading, "Several Commentators on Psalm 130:8." J. J. S. Perowne (*Commentary on the Psalms*, a 1989 reprint by Kregel), commenting on the words "[He will redeem Israel] from [all] his iniquities" says (in part), "The redemption includes the forgiveness of sin, the breaking of the power and dominion of sin, and the setting free from all the consequences of sin."

F. Delitzsch (Volume 5 of the Keil and Delitzsch commentaries on the Old Testament) says (in part), "...He, in the fullness of the might of His free grace, will redeem Israel from all its iniquities, by forgiving them and removing their unhappy inward and outward consequences. With this promise the poet comforts himself. He means complete and final redemption, above all, in the genuinely New Testament manner, spiritual redemption."

Now we'll take a quick look at Psalm 39:8, "Deliver me from all my transgressions; Make me not the reproach of the foolish." The word transgressions was translated from the plural of the Hebrew noun *pesha*. I believe the idea is "Deliver me from all my transgressions [with the guilt and with the penalties]," or just, "Deliver me from the penalties of my transgressions." The first chapter of my book deals with the meaning of the Hebrew noun *pesha*, and Psalm 39:8 is discussed in that chapter.

Now Matthew 1:21, another verse that will help us understand the concept of being saved from our sin [with the guilt and with the penalties]. "And she will bear a Son; and you shall call His name Jesus, for it is He who will save His people from their sins." That is, He will save His people from their sins [with the guilt and the penalties (including the major penalties of spiritual death and bondage to sin)]. Note the preposition "from" in Matt. 1:21 ("He will save His people from their sins [with the guilt and the penalties (including the major penalties of spiritual death and bondage to sin)]"), and note the preposition "from" in the next verse listed here, Rev. 1:5. I'll read Revelation 1:5, "To Him who loves us, and released us from our sins [released us from our sins with the guilt and with the penalties (including the major penalties of spiritual death and bondage to sin)] by His blood." I should mention that the preposition "from" was also used in Psalm 130:8 and Psalm 39:8, verses we just looked at.

Now 1 Peter 2:24, 25, "and He Himself bore our sins [He Himself bore our sins with the guilt and the penalties (including the major penalties of spiritual death and bondage to sin)] in His body on the cross, SO THAT WE MIGHT DIE TO SIN AND LIVE TO RIGHTEOUSNESS [my emphasis], for by His wounds you were healed. (25) For you were continually straying like sheep, but now you have returned to the Shepherd and Guardian of your souls." The Lord Jesus Christ, the Lamb of God, bore our sins with the penalties of spiritual death and bondage to sin so that we might be born again and live in the very righteousness and holiness of God, as His born-again children.

Now we come to the subheading, Two commentators on Colossians 1:14. Adam Clarke, who was an associate of John Wesley (in his commentary on the Bible abridged by Ralph Earle, published by Baker in 1967), commenting on the words "the forgiveness of sins," said, " 'The taking away of sins'; all the power, guilt, and infection of sin."

R. C. Lucas (The Message of Colossians and Philemon," published by Inter-Varsity Press in 1980) has an interesting discussion regarding the meaning of "the forgiveness of sins." I'll quote the major part of his primary paragraph on this topic, "The blessing of forgiveness has sometimes been devalued, as though it were no more than the wiping of the slate clean. But sin is always a power that holds people in thrall [in bondage], so, in Paul's teaching forgiveness must include the breaking of that power. It is inconceivable that God should forgive the past, and then send us back incapable of living a new life. PARDON WITHOUT DELIVERANCE WOULD BE A MOCKERY, AND IT IS NEVER SO CONTEMPLATED IN THE NEW TESTAMENT [my emphasis]. We ought not speak of 'mere forgiveness' as though this were but an initial blessing of the gospel. The gospel is precisely the offer of freedom because of the forgiveness of our sins. (E.g., Acts 13:38, 39.) That forgiveness flows from the cross where Christ not only cancelled our debt BUT ALSO DISARMED OUR ENEMY [my emphasis] (see Colossians 2:14, 15)."

I appreciate these words by R. C. Lucas, who is from England, but I'll make two brief comments. Most Christians don't use the word *forgiveness* in the full sense presented in this quotation, and I don't believe they ever will. Secondly, I believe a translation like "release from sins [with the guilt and the penalties (including the major penalties of spiritual death and bondage to sin)]" more accurately reflects the meaning intended for *aphesis* here in Col. 1:14, and in several other verses.

That completes our study of Col. 1:9-14, now we come to the heading Ephesians 1:7 and the Meaning of *Aphesis.* I'll read Ephesians 1:7, **In Him** [in Christ] **we have redemption through His blood, the forgiveness** [*aphesis*] **of our trespasses, according to the riches of His grace.**

In Him we have [the] redemption through His blood. As in Col. 1:14, I would translate **the redemption.** The definite article is included in the Greek in both verses. We discussed **the redemption** in some detail when we discussed Col. 1:14. The words **through His blood** speak of the all-important atoning death of the Lord Jesus Christ (see, for example, Rom. 3:24, 25; Titus 2:14; Heb. 9:12-15; 1 Pet. 1:18. 19; and 2:24, 25).

the forgiveness [Greek *aphesis*] **of our trespasses** of Eph. 1:7. As in Col. 1:14, these words are in apposition with the words "the redemption," and they expand on the meaning of "the redemption." And, as in Col. 1:14, I would translate **the release from our trespasses [with the guilt and the penalties (including the major penalties of spiritual death and bondage to sin)],** or the equivalent. "The trespasses [with the guilt and the penalties (including the major penalties of spiritual death and bondage to sin)]" here in Eph. 1:7 is the equivalent of "the sins [with the guilt and the penalties (including the major penalties of spiritual death and bondage to sin)]" in Col. 1:14.

The redemption through His blood, the release from our trespasses [with the guilt and the penalties (including the major penalties of spiritual death and bondage to sin)] includes our being set free from sin, Satan, and spiritual death. On our being set free from sin and being made righteous and holy, see Eph. 1:4; 2:1-10; 3:14-21; and 4:1-6:20. On our being set free from the authority of Satan, see Eph. 1:20-2:10; 4:8-10, 27; 5:8; and 6:10-18. (Although Satan has no legal authority over true Christians, we must still resist him. The warfare has not ceased, but we need not, and should not, be defeated.) On our being set free from spiritual death by the indwelling Spirit of life, see Eph. 1:13, 14; 2:5, 18; and 3:6.

Now we come to the subheading, <u>Several Commentators on Ephesians 1:7</u>. First I'll quote several sentences from Francis Foulkes, who is from New Zealand (*Epistle of Paul to the Ephesians*, published by Eerdmans in 1963). "His death means that *blood* has been shed as a sacrifice for sin; IT MAY ALSO BE DESCRIBED IN TERMS OF SIN'S DEFEAT AND SO RELEASE OF MAN FROM ITS BONDAGE [my emphasis]. The sacrifice is thus the means of redemption which is *the forgiveness of sins*. Sin involves the bondage of mind and will and members, but forgiveness is freedom, and *aphesis*, the word used here, MEANS LOOSING OF A PERSON FROM THAT WHICH BINDS HIM [my emphasis]." I very much appreciate what this commentator says here, but he is using the word *forgiveness* in a much fuller sense than most Christians do. Typically forgiveness is understood to mean the cancellation of the guilt of sin.

Next I'll quote several sentences from Henry Alford (*New Testament for English Readers*, volume 3; this reprint was published by Baker in 1983). Commenting on the words "the (or, our) Redemption," he says (in part), "[redemption] from that which brought us under God's wrath, the guilt AND POWER OF SIN [my emphasis], Matthew 1:21."

Later in his discussion of Eph. 1:7, Alford comments of the meaning of the words "the remission [or, forgiveness]…of our transgressions." He says, "explanation of the words, our Redemption: not to be limited, but extending to all riddance from the practice and consequences of our transgressions." Then he comments on the meaning of the words, "according to the riches of His grace," He says, "This alone would prevent the word 'remission' applying to merely the 'forgiveness' of sins. We have in this grace not only redemption from misery and wrath, not only forgiveness,—but we find in it the liberty, the glory, the inheritance of the children of God,—the crown of eternal life; compare 2 Corinthians 8:9." I'll read 2 Corinthians 8:9, "For you know the grace of our Lord Jesus Christ, that though He was rich, yet for our sake He became poor, so that you through His poverty might become rich."

The last commentator I listed here was John Wesley. I'll quote part of what he said under Eph. 1:7 in his *Explanatory Notes Upon the New Testament*. "...*we*—Who believe, have from the moment we believe, redemption from the guilt AND POWER OF SIN [my emphasis], *through his blood*—Through what he hath done and suffered for us."

That completes our study of Eph. 1:7 and the Greek noun *aphesis*. We'll go on to a study of EPHESIANS 1:3, 4. We won't finish this study today; we'll finish it in the next article. I'll be quoting from my paper that includes verse-by-verse studies of Ephesians chapters 1 and 4 that is on my internet site. I highly recommend that you take a look at that paper. For one thing, it has a lot to say about holiness and victory over sin.

I'll read Ephesians 1:3, 4. **Blessed *be* the God and Father of our Lord Jesus Christ, who has blessed us with every spiritual blessing in the heavenly *places* in Christ, (4) just as He chose us in Him before the foundation of the world, THAT WE WOULD BE HOLY AND BLAMELESS BEFORE HIM** [my emphasis]. The verse continues with the words, **In love**. We'll discuss those important words when we come to them.

Verse 3 starts with the word **Blessed.** I'll read what I said in a bracket regarding this word, The NIV has "Praise (be to)." God the Father is to be blessed/praised (with thanksgiving) for the blessings He has bestowed on us in Christ Jesus. This sentence, which continues through verse 14 in the Greek (what a glorious sentence!), puts a strong emphasis on praise to God for His gracious and glorious plan of salvation. In verse 6 the apostle Paul speaks of "the praise of the glory of His grace, which He freely bestowed on us in the Beloved [in Christ Jesus]," and in verses 12 and 14 he speaks of "the praise of His glory." In verse 7 he speaks of "the riches of His grace, which He lavished upon us." In verse 5 he speaks of "the kind intention [or, good pleasure] which He [God the Father] purposed in Him [or, probably better, "which He purposed in Himself"]."

I'll read verse 3 again, then comment further on the meaning of these words, **Blessed *be* the God and Father of our Lord Jesus Christ, who has blessed us with every spiritual blessing in the heavenly *places* in Christ.** The apostle goes on to speak of these spiritual blessings as he continues this long sentence. The primary blessings are spiritual, but the blessings are not limited to the spiritual dimension. Some of these blessings are available now, and some of them are reserved for the future (see Eph. 1:14, for example). Even now we have the victory "in the heavenly places" by virtue of our being "in Christ." On "the heavenly places," see Eph. 1:20; 2:6; 3:10; and 6:12. Note that the words "in Christ," or equivalent words (like "in Him" and "in the beloved") are repeatedly used in this long sentence (and in a large number of other passages in the New Testament), referring to the glorious union believers have with the Lord Jesus Christ (see verses 3, 4, 6, 7, 9, 11, and 13). Verse 5 shows that we are adopted as sons through Jesus Christ.

Now we come to Ephesians 1:4, **Just as He** [God the Father] **chose us in Him** [in Christ] **before the foundation of the world** [I have a lengthy discussion here, but I'm going to skip down to the next words for this article]**, THAT WE WOULD BE HOLY AND BLAMELESS BEFORE HIM** [my emphasis].... As I pointed out under verse 1, the Greek adjective translated "holy" here in verse 4 was translated "saints" in verse 1 (the adjective was plural in verse 1). Saints are holy (set apart) people. The call and enablement to be HOLY AND BLAMELESS is a major feature of the present spiritual blessings given to us in Christ Jesus. Our living in God's righteousness and holiness (by His grace) is the bottom line of Christianity (see, for example, Eph. 2:8-10; 3:14-6:17; Rom. 6:1-23; 8:1-14; 1 Pet. 1:13-25; 2:24; 4:1-6; Rev. 2:1-3:22; and 22:12-15).

Through the atoning death of the Lord Jesus Christ (see Eph. 1:7), and by the work of the Holy Spirit (see Eph. 1:13, 14, for example), Christians are enabled (by grace through faith) to live in a STATE OF HOLINESS AND BLAMELESSNESS—set apart by God for God, and living in the center of His will, with the victory over all sin. This is the ideal state that we can (and should) be living in as born-again Christians. Holiness is not optional for Christians (see Heb. 12:14, for example; I'll read Hebrews 12:14 from the NIV, "Make every effort to live in peace with all men and to be holy; WITHOUT HOLINESS NO ONE WILL SEE THE LORD [my emphasis].") We must make living in an abiding state of holiness a top priority. Christians aren't automatically holy. The only way we can live in an abiding state of holiness is by grace (which includes all the work of the Holy Spirit) through faith (a faith that is based on the good news spelled out in the New Testament).

In closing I'll read what I said in a parenthesis here. It's true, of course, that forgiveness is a foundational part of the Christian gospel. This truth is typically well understood by Christians, but there is a major problem when, as it so often happens, most of the emphasis is put on forgiveness and right standing. I believe we should put about ten percent of the emphasis on forgiveness and right standing and about ninety percent on being righteous and holy through the atoning death of the Lord Jesus Christ, in the power of the Holy Spirit, by grace through faith.

We'll come back to Eph. 1:4 in the next article. God bless you! His name be glorified! His will be done! His will be done in each one of us!

Holiness and Victory Over Sin #21

Holy Father, we humble our hearts before you. We want to know the balanced truth of what your Word teaches, and we want to live it. We pray in Jesus' mighty holy name. Amen!

Last time when we stopped we were looking at Ephesians 1:3, 4. I'll read those verses from the *New American Standard Bible*, 1995 edition. **Blessed be the God and Father of our Lord Jesus Christ, who has blessed us with every spiritual blessing in the heavenly *places* in Christ, (4) just as He chose us in Him before the foundation of the world, THAT WE WOULD BE HOLY AND BLAMELESS BEFORE HIM** [my emphasis]. **In love [in love].** Last time I was reading from my paper, *Verse-by-Verse Studies of Ephesians Chapters 1 and 4; and Romans 8:15-39.* That paper, which was published in July, 2000, is located on my internet site (Google to Karl Kemp Teaching).

I was reading what I said under the words, **that we would be holy and blameless before Him.** I'll read several sentences that I read at the end of the last article, then I'll continue to read what I said under these words of Eph. 1:4: Through the atoning death of the Lord Jesus (see Eph. 1:7) and by the work of the Holy Spirit (see Eph. 1:13, 14), Christians are enabled (by grace through faith) to live in a state of holiness and blamelessness – set apart (by God) for God, and living in the center of His will, with the victory over all sin. That sounds good, doesn't it?

It is true, of course, that forgiveness is a foundational part of the Christian gospel. That truth is typically well understood by Christians, but there is a major problem when, as it so often happens, most of the emphasis is put on forgiveness and right standing. In my opinion we should put about ten percent of the emphasis on forgiveness and about ninety percent on being righteous and holy through the atoning death of the Lord Jesus Christ in the power of the Holy Spirit. Holiness is the ideal state that we can, and should, be living in as born-again Christians. Holiness is not optional for Christians, and we must make holiness a top priority. See Heb. 12:14, for example. I'll read Hebrews 12:14 from the NKJV, "Pursue peace with all *men* and holiness, without which no one will see the Lord." Christians are not automatically holy; the only way we can live in an abiding state of holiness is by grace through faith (a faith that is based on the good news spelled out in the New Testament).

A major problem in the body of Christ is that many Christians (even the majority) don't believe we can actually live in a state of holiness. Living in a state of holiness means to be set apart for God and living for Him in righteousness, doing things His way, by His grace. It includes living with the victory over sin. The ideal, and it is not presented as an unrealistic ideal in the New Testament, is that we should not sin at all, by God's definition of sin. We must be aiming at that target. We certainly won't hit the target if we are not even aiming at it. But many Christians (even the majority) don't believe we can ever stop sinning in this life. And they even cite a few passages from the New Testament that supposedly prove that all Christians will necessarily continue to sin throughout their lives on the earth. (We have already discussed the three most important such passages in these articles: Romans chapter 7, 1 John 1:8, and Gal. 5:17.)

It is commonly said, for example, that we all sin daily in thought, in word, and in deed. Because of their understanding of what the Bible teaches, they (by their own admission) don't have faith for holiness and victory over sin. They don't think they are supposed to. Also, even if we know that the New Testament *does* call Christians to walk in holiness with the victory over all sin, the victory is very far from being easy or automatic – the world, the flesh, and the devil are engaged in intense warfare against us. For a study on the meaning of *holy, holiness*, I recommend the last chapter of my book, *Holiness and Victory Over Sin: Full Salvation Through the Atoning Death of the Lord Jesus Christ.* Included in that chapter are discussions of Eph. 5:27 and Col. 1:22, two other verses where the apostle Paul used the words holy and blameless.

I'm going to turn back to page 10 of this paper and quote from two commentators. First I'll quote part of what Klyne Snodgrass, a Southern Baptist scholar, said under Eph. 1:4-6. His book *Ephesians* was published by Zondervan in 1996. "Election always brings responsibility. God has chosen us to do something—namely, to live holy and blameless lives before Him (see Ephesians 1:4; compare Ephesians 5:27). ... Christians are to live in a holy and blameless manner before God (see Ephesians 1:4). This is not an oppressive weight, but as much privilege as it is responsibility. [Yes, I guess so! What a great privilege to be set free from spiritual death and bondage to sin to live in a holy and blameless manner before God!] We are called to live in keeping with God's intent for us." Amen!

Now I'll quote part of what D. Martyn Lloyd-Jones said under Eph. 1:4. I'm quoting from his book, *God's Ultimate Purpose, An Exposition of Ephesians Chapter 1*, published by Baker in 1978. "So we must always start with holiness, as the Scripture does, and therefore the preaching of holiness is an essential part of evangelism. I stress this matter because there are certain quite different ideas about evangelism, some indeed that say the exact opposite. They maintain that in evangelism the preacher does not deal with holiness. The one aim is 'to get people saved,' then later you can lead them on to holiness. But what is salvation? To be saved is to be rightly related to God, and that is holiness. The whole purpose of evangelism is primarily to tell men what sin has done to them, to tell them why they are what they are, namely, separated from God. It is to tell them what they need above everything else is not to be made to feel happy, but to be brought back into a right relationship with the God who is 'light and in him is no darkness at all.' But that means preaching holiness. To separate these two things, it seems to me, is to deny essential biblical teaching. We must start with holiness, and continue with it, because it is the end for which we are chosen and delivered." Amen!

I'll read Ephesians 1:4 again; then we'll discuss the last two words of this verse in some detail. **just as He** [God the Father] **chose us in Him** [in Christ Jesus] **before the foundation of the world, THAT WE WOULD BE HOLY AND BLAMELESS BEFORE HIM** [my emphasis]. **In love** [in love]. The NASB and the NIV, wrongly I believe, insert a period before the words "in love." In the first place, as I mentioned, verses 3-14 are all one sentence in the Greek. It is common for English translations to split this sentence up into several sentences. I don't necessarily object to this, but if we do add a period, we should add it after the words "in love," with no punctuation before the words "in love." My Greek New Testament and the NKJV have no punctuation before the words "in love" and a comma following. I prefer this translation. The *Amplified Bible* and the NRSV have no punctuation before "in love" and a period following. The KJV has no punctuation before "in love" and a colon following. I could live with either one of these translations. By inserting a period before the words "in love," the NASB and the NIV wrongly, from my point of view, eliminate the important relationship (intended by the apostle Paul) between our being "holy and blameless" and our (fully) abiding in an experiential love relationship with God.

We can speak of the love God had for us before we became Christians (see Eph. 2:4, 5, for example), but – and this is important – we aren't able to experience and abide in His love (at least not to any significant extent) while we are denying His existence and/or rebelling against Him, and before we come into a relationship with Him through the new covenant in the blood of Christ. For example, note what Paul said regarding the former (pre-Christian) status of the Christians from Gentile backgrounds in Eph. 2:1-3, 11-18; 4:17-19, 22; and 5:8-14. I'll read three of these verses, Ephesians 2:12 and 4:18, 19, "*remember* that you were at that time separate from Christ, excluded from the commonwealth of Israel, and strangers to the covenants of promise, having no hope and without God in the world." And Ephesians 4:18, 19, "being darkened in their understanding, excluded from the life of God because of the ignorance that is in them, because of the hardness of their heart; and they, having become callous, have given themselves over to sensuality for the practice of every kind of impurity with greediness."

We cannot be reconciled to God, have peace with Him (both mentioned in Eph. 2:16, 17, for example), and abide in His love without our attitudes, motives, and priorities being changed and our beginning to truly submit to Him to live for Him in His righteousness and holiness (by His grace in Christ). Our being reconciled to God, having peace with Him, and abiding in His love involve much more than just being forgiven, as important as that is. In John 15:10 Jesus said, "If you keep My commandments, you will abide in My love; just as I have kept My Father's commandments and abide in His love." He also said, "If you love Me, you will keep My commandments," and "He who has My commandments and keeps them is the one who loves Me, and he who loves Me will be loved by My Father, and I will love him and will disclose Myself to him" (John 14:15, 21).

On the important relationship between our being "holy and blameless" and our abiding in His love, see the discussion under Eph. 3:14-21, which is a very important cross-reference, in my *A Paper on Faith* (which is available on my internet site); see, for example, Exod. 20:1-6; Deut. 5:6-10; 7:6-16; 2 Chron. 6:14; Psalm 5:4-7; 11:4-7; 103:11; 145:20; 146:8, 9; Dan. 9:4; Hos. 9:15; Matt. 7:21-23; John 14:15-24; 15:9-14; 16:27; 1 Cor. 2:9; 16:22; James 4:8; Jude 1:21; Rev. 2:4, 5, 15, 16; and 3:1-6, 15-22. We can love only because God loved us first and we are now experiencing His love for us (see 1 John 4:7-21, for example). We are caught up into His love – we are caught up into the very love God the Father has for His Son, even as we are caught up into His life, His righteousness, and His holiness. (God Himself, the triune God, is the only source for these things and everything else that is good.)

A big part of what makes this work is the indwelling Holy Spirit, who is a very special, very personal love gift from God to those who become Christians (see Rom. 5:5, for example). He enables us to know about, and to directly experience, God's love for us (see, for example, Rom. 8:14-16, 26, 27; 1 Cor. 2:12, 13; 3:16; 6:19; 2 Cor. 1:22; 5:5, 13, 14; Eph. 1:13, 14; 2:18; 3:16-19; and 1 John 4:13), and who enables us to love (see Gal. 5:22, for example).

There's a lot of teaching around the body of Christ about God's unconditional love. I believe much of this teaching is simply wrong, and it can be dangerous. It goes far beyond the balanced teaching of the Bible to tell people that God will always continue to love them just the same no matter what they believe or what they do. This out-of-balance teaching is one reason there is so little fear of God and so little repentance and motivation for righteousness and holiness in so many Christians.

It's not that we can in ourselves be worthy of, or earn, God's love, we can't; but if we continue to reject and disdain His love and grace, we will ultimately be confronted with His wrath, not His love (see, for example, Rom. 2:4-10; Gal. 5:19-21; 6:7-9; Eph. 2:3 ["children of wrath" on the path that culminates in God's wrath in the day of His wrath]; 5:1-7; and Col. 3:5-11). The Old Testament verses that spoke of God's never-ending love for Israel, by the way, did not cover those individuals who willfully (and without repentance) forsook their covenant with God.

It is true, of course, that we must emphasize God's love, mercy, and forgiveness. For one thing, the devil and his hosts spend a lot of time attacking God's people, telling them that God doesn't love them, when He does; telling them that they have committed the unpardonable sin, when they haven't; telling them that they never can stop sinning, that God's grace isn't sufficient, etc. But it's not acceptable to put all the emphasis on God's love, mercy, and forgiveness. It won't work! We need the full gospel, which includes the balanced truth of what the Bible teaches. God knows our hearts. He knows if we are making Him and His Word top priority in our hearts. If we are not, we're going to have to change by His sufficient grace in Christ, through faith.

I have one last short paragraph here (in the paper on Ephesians chapters 1 and 4) where I mention an important section in this paper titled, "Further Discussion Aiming for a Balanced Biblical Understanding Regarding God's Love and the Love He Expects from His Born-Again Children." I believe that seven-page discussion is very important, but I won't include it in this e-book.

I'll turn back to page 45 in this paper (on Ephesians chapters 1 and 4), and we'll discuss EPHESIANS 4:17-32. These verses, and especially when coupled with Ephesians chapters 5 and 6, constitute one of the more significant passages in the New Testament exhorting Christians to walk in righteousness and holiness with the victory over all sin through salvation in the Lord Jesus Christ. This is good news, very good news!

So this I say, and affirm together with the Lord, that you walk no longer just as the Gentiles also walk [The non-Christian Gentiles were, of course, walking (living) in sin.], **in the futility** [or, "in the emptiness, vanity"] **of their mind** [[or, "of their way of thinking." Many Christians wrongly think that the words "mind" and "thinking" in the Bible are limited to something that man does with the head (the brain). That is a rather serious error. Our most important thinking takes place in the heart, inner man, spirit, soul, not in the head. For more on this important topic, see under Rom. 8:5-7 in my book, *Holiness and Victory Over Sin* (we discussed these verses in an earlier article), and see below under Eph. 4:18, 23. Ephesians 4:23 uses the same Greek noun for mind (or, way of thinking) used here in verse 17 (the Greek noun *nous*).]] **(18) being darkened in their understanding, excluded from the life of God because of the ignorance that is in them, because of the hardness of their heart** [[These last words, "because of the hardness of their heart," confirm that man is responsible for his sin. The sin problem centers in the heart of man (see Mark 7:20-23). From the heart, man must submit to God in faith; in the heart the priorities, attitudes, and motives are established. What we think about God, His Word, our priorities, attitudes, and motives constitute a big part of our important thinking.]] **(19), and they, having become callous** [Their consciences have become insensitive. The NIV has, "having lost all sensitivity."], **and they, having become callous, have given themselves over to sensuality for the practice of every kind of impurity with greediness** [or, "with insatiableness, covetousness." Colossians 1:21 speaks of the pre-Christian status of Paul's Gentile readers as being "alienated and hostile in <u>mind</u>, engaged in evil deeds."] **(20) But you did not learn Christ in this way** [[What they had learned about Christ and salvation through Him, and in union with Him, put the emphasis on the fact that God sent His Son to solve the sin problem through forgiveness, redemption from the kingdom of sin, and righteous and holy living by the indwelling Spirit of life, righteousness, and holiness.]], **(21) if indeed you have heard Him and have been taught in Him, just as truth is in Jesus** [See, for example, John 14:6; Eph. 1:13; and Col. 1:5. Significantly, Eph. 4:24 demonstrates that the *truth* includes righteousness and holiness.], **(22) that, in reference to your former manner of life, you lay aside the old self** [or, "put off the old self" or, "put off the old man."] [[(This double bracket goes on for three paragraphs.) Significantly, the aorist tense of the Greek infinitive used here fits the idea of LAYING ASIDE, OR PUTTING OFF THE OLD MAN ONCE-FOR-ALL AND COMPLETELY. I would translate the "old man" with the KJV and the NKJV. In Colossians 3:9, for example, the apostle Paul said, "SINCE YOU HAVE LAID ASIDE [or, PUT OFF] the old self [THE OLD MAN] WITH ITS EVIL PRACTICES [my emphasis]." In Romans 6:6 he spoke of our OLD MAN HAVING BEEN CRUCIFIED WITH CHRIST; and in Galatians 5:24 he said that "those who belong to Christ HAVE CRUCIFIED THE FLESH [THE OLD MAN] WITH ITS PASSIONS AND DESIRES [my emphasis]." Having crucified the flesh in Gal. 5:24 means the same thing as the crucifixion of the old man in Rom. 6:6. Here in Eph. 4:22 the apostle exhorts his Christians readers to once-for-all and completely put off anything that remains of sin. By God's definition the old man is to be crucified when we become Christians. The old man has not been annihilated though, and we still have the all-too-real potential to let the old man (the flesh) manifest itself in sin as long as we live in this world.

Many verses in the New Testament show that it is not uncommon for Christians to still have sinful things, things that are part of the old man, that need to be put off. The New Testament (and the experience of all Christians) makes it very clear that the old man is not automatically put to death. The old man will continue to live and manifest itself in sin to the extent Christians do not walk by the Holy Spirit by faith on a continuous basis (see Gal. 5:16, 17, for example). Christians cannot have faith to walk above sin unless they know for sure that this is what God has called them to. This widespread lack of knowledge and faith is a big part of the problem in our day.

Ephesians 4:25, which uses the same Greek verb as 4:22, is an important cross-reference. In 4:25 the apostle exhorts his readers to put off falsehood (lying) and to speak the truth. Putting off falsehood is part of what it means to put off the old man. It should be obvious that Paul means TO PUT OFF FALSEHOOD ONCE- FOR-ALL AND COMPLETELY, and the aorist tense of the Greek participle used in verse 25 fits that viewpoint. Also, as the apostle continues with verses 25-31 he mentions some of the other sinful things that are to be put off once-for-all and completely. Compare Col. 3:8; Heb. 12:1; James 1:21; and 1 Pet. 2:1.]], **which is being corrupted** [[I prefer the translation of the KJV, **which is corrupt**, instead of "which is being corrupted." I'm not denying the fact that, in some ways, the world is becoming more corrupt all the time, but I don't believe Paul incorporated that idea here.]] **in accordance with the lusts of deceit** [[There is a strong contrast in these verses between the *truth* of God and the *lies, deceit, deception* of the devil and the world. The KJV and the NKJV have "according to the deceitful lusts"; the NIV has "by its deceitful desires." Note that the words *truth* and *lies, deceit, deception* all relate to the mind, way of thinking. The mind, way of thinking of those who walk by the Holy Spirit always lines up with the truth, which as Eph. 4:24 shows, includes righteousness and holiness. When people lust after wrong (sinful) things it is because they have been deceived and led astray by sin and Satan (this started with Eve in the garden); they have been deceived and led away from God and His truth, righteousness, and holiness. This doesn't mean, of course, that people have an excuse for their sin. Hebrews 3:13 exhorts Christians "to encourage one another day after day…so that none of you will be hardened by the deceitfulness of sin."]], **(23) and that you be renewed in the spirit of your mind….** This verse is extremely important, but (in my opinion) typically not well translated, or well understood. I refer the reader to what I said above under verses 17, 18, including the references to my book. We'll discuss this verse, with cross-references, to the end of this article.

I'll quote an endnote from pages 138, 139 of my book (*Holiness and Victory Over Sin*), I would translate Eph. 4:23 as follows, "AND BE RENEWED BY THE SPIRIT [the Holy Spirit] IN YOUR MIND [or, "IN YOUR WAY OF THINKING"]." This verse explains, in large part, *how* Christians are to once-for-all and completely be transformed from their former sinful state (see Eph. 4:17-19, 22). Significantly, in Ephesians 4:17 the apostle says, "This I say, therefore, and affirm together with the Lord, that you walk no longer just as the Gentiles also walk in the futility [or, "emptiness, vanity"] of their mind [or, "of their way of thinking"]." The Greek noun *nous*, which is translated "mind" by the NASB in Eph. 4:17, is also used here in Eph. 4:23. The Holy Spirit enables Christians to be renewed in their minds, in the way they think (see under Rom. 8:5-7 on pages 118, 119 in my book, *Holiness and Victory Over Sin*).

The Holy Spirit enables Christians to have right priorities, right attitudes, and right motives and to think (and live) in line with the righteousness and holiness of the truth of God. This is all part of having a renewed mind. (The mind/way of thinking is not at all limited to the head. Our most important thinking takes place in the heart/spirit/inner man.) For Christians to be renewed in their minds/in the way they think, they must submit in faith to God and the Word of God, where they learn the truth of

God, especially the truth of the gospel of new-covenant salvation (see Eph. 4:20, 21), and they must walk by the Spirit of God on a continuous basis. It takes the Word of God plus the Spirit of God for us to have a renewed mind. And we have to think right in our hearts before we can live right.

Romans 12:2 says, "And do not be conformed to this world, but be transformed by the renewing of your mind...." The Greek noun that was translated "renewing" here is *anakaínosis*. The Greek noun that was translated "mind" here is *nous*, the same Greek noun used in Eph. 4:17, 23. It would be better to translate "the renewal of your mind [or, "the renewal of your way of thinking"]" in Rom. 12:2 with the BAGD Greek Lexicon than "the renewing of the mind." The translation "renewal" fits better with the ideal once-for-all renewal pictured in Eph. 4:17-32; Rom. 8:1-14; Rom. 12:1, 2; and in many other passages. Romans 12:1-8 are discussed in some detail in my *A Paper on Faith* that is available on my internet site.

I believe Eph. 4:23 and Rom. 12:2 both speak (at least for the most part) of an ideal once-for-all renewal rather than a lifelong process. Note the once-for-all nature of the exhortations of Eph. 4:17-6:20 and Rom. 12:1, 2. This is not to deny that there should be a lifelong process of growth, but the old man and sin is to be put off once-for-all and completely. Like I mentioned above, the apostle Paul wasn't exhorting his readers to gradually put off lying in Eph. 4:25. ANYTHING THAT IS SINFUL IS TO BE PUT OFF NOW WITH A HIGH PRIORITY, BY GRACE THROUGH FAITH. Christians should continue to grow throughout their lives in Christ (as the apostle Paul said, we are being transformed from glory to glory [2 Cor. 3:18]), but in the ideal case, there will not be a continual growing out of sin because we will be living in an abiding state of righteousness and holiness, with the victory over all sin. That sounds good, doesn't it?

It's time to stop. We will finish the discussion of Eph. 4:23 and go on to Eph. 4: 24-32 in the next article.

God bless you. May His good will be done in us! His grace is sufficient! In Jesus' mighty name! Amen!

Holiness and Victory Over Sin #22

Father, we humble our hearts before you. We want to rightly divide your Word. We want to live in line with your Word. In Jesus' mighty name! Amen!

When we stopped last time, we were discussing Ephesians 4:17-32. We'll start where we stopped last time. I was reading what I said on these verses in my paper that includes verse-by-verse studies of Ephesians chapters 1 and 4. That paper is on my internet site. First I'll read Ephesians 4:17-23 from the *New American Standard Bible*, 1995 edition with a few comments; then I'll read the last paragraph that I have under Eph. 4:23 in the paper; that's where we stopped last time.

So this I say, and affirm together with the Lord, that you walk no longer just as the Gentiles also walk, in the futility [or, "in the emptiness"] **of their mind** [or, "of their way of thinking." Paul was especially concerned about the thinking we do in our hearts, in our inner man. If we think wrong in our hearts, we will live wrong.]**, (18) being darkened in their understanding, excluded from the life of God because of the ignorance that is in them, because of the hardness of their heart; (19) and they, having become callous, have given themselves over to sensuality for the practice of every kind of impurity with greediness. (20) But you did not learn Christ in this way, (21) if indeed you have heard Him and have been taught in Him, just as truth is in Jesus, (22) that, in reference to your former manner of life** [your former *sinful* manner of life]**, you lay aside the old self** [or, "put off the old self" or, "PUT OFF THE OLD MAN." As we have discussed, the apostle is exhorting his Christian readers to ONCE-FOR-ALL AND COMPLETELY PUT OFF ANYTHING AND EVERYTHING THAT IS SINFUL.]**, which is being corrupted** [or, better, **which is corrupt** with the KJV] **in accordance with the lusts of deceit** [Deceit and deception are the opposite of the truth, and as verse 24 shows, the truth includes righteousness and holiness.] **(23) and that you be renewed in the spirit of your mind** [[This verse is extremely important but, in my opinion, typically not well translated or well understood. I (in agreement with others) would translate, "and BE RENEWED BY THE SPIRIT (the Holy Spirit) IN YOUR MIND" (or, "IN YOUR WAY OF THINKING"). This verse explains, in large part, *how* we can begin to think right in our hearts and to live in the righteousness and holiness of the

215

truth. Our way of thinking is renewed when we submit to God and His Word and walk by the Spirit of God (by faith), and the righteousness and holiness of God are manifested in our hearts and lives. We discussed these super-important things in some detail in the last article (and in earlier articles). Now I'll read the last paragraph that I have under Eph. 4:23 in my paper on Ephesians chapters 1 and 4:

As Christians we should be living in the righteousness and holiness of God, with the victory over all sin (that is the ideal); and we should be growing (growing in knowledge and wisdom, growing more like the Lord Jesus Christ, growing in the fruit of the Spirit, etc.) This is good news! If we rightly respond to God's Word (with humble faith), it will bring transformation. And if we should slip into sin, God, who knows our hearts, knows if we are making Him and His Word top priority. I'm sure He finds it rather easy to forgive and to sanctify those who are quick to repent and who making Him, His Word, and His righteousness top priority.]], **(24) and put on the new self** [[I prefer, "PUT ON THE NEW MAN." We can't stop with putting off the old man; we must also put on the new man. When we discussed verse 22, I mentioned that the aorist tense of the Greek verb used there fits the idea of putting off the old man once-for-all and completely. The aorist tense of the Greek verb used here in verse 24 fits the idea of PUTTING ON THE NEW MAN ONCE-FOR-ALL AND COMPLETELY. I listed some verses here. One of the verses I listed is Colossians 3:10, which is another verse where the apostle Paul spoke of putting on the righteous and holy new man. I also listed Romans 13:14, which I'll read, "But put on the Lord Jesus Christ, and make no provision for the flesh in regard to *its* lusts."]], **which in *the likeness of* God** [[(This double bracket goes on for five paragraphs.) The NASB has the words "the likeness of" in italics. I could live with this translation, but the Greek more literally reads **in accordance with God**, which I prefer. Instead of being in accordance with sin and the lies/deceit/deception of the devil, the new man in Christ is **in accordance with God.** These words probably include the ideas that the new man has been created by God (see Eph. 2:10, for example) and that it is in accordance with the will of God and His truth, which (as the words that follow in verse 24 demonstrate) includes His righteousness and holiness.

When we think of Christians being **in accordance with God**, we think of Gen. 1:26; 5:1; and 9:6. Genesis 1:26 speaks of man's being created in the image of God, but it must be understood that's God's new creation in

Christ takes man to a much higher place than what Adam had before the fall (see 1 Cor. 15:44-57, for example). I had a footnote here, which I'll read, Most of the glory of what it means to be a son of God in union with Jesus Christ, who is the unique Son of God, is reserved for the (near) future ("Christ in you the hope of glory"), but we have already entered into the preliminary phase of that glory, including the imputation and impartation of the righteousness and holiness of God.

When Christians are thinking right and living right through new-covenant salvation, they are living **in accordance with God** – they certainly are not sinning.

Ephesians 4:22-24, and especially verse 24, demonstrate *how* the apostle can exhort Christians to "be imitators of God, as beloved children" in Ephesians 5:1. That's quite a challenge, isn't it? And it certainly includes the victory over all sin. Along this same line, compare, for example Matt. 5:48; 1 Cor. 11:1; 1 John 2:5, 6; and 3:1-10. I'll read some of these verses. In Matthew 5:48 Jesus said (I am using capital letters for emphasis), "THEREFORE, YOU ARE TO BE PERFECT, AS YOUR HEAVENLY FATHER IS PERFECT." In 1 Corinthians 11:1, the apostle Paul said, "BE IMITATORS OF ME, JUST AS I ALSO AM OF CHRIST." And I'll read what the apostle John said in 1 John 2:6, "THE ONE WHO SAYS HE ABIDES IN HIM [IN CHRIST] OUGHT HIMSELF TO WALK IN THE SAME MANNER AS HE WALKED." I'll also read what he said in 1 John 3:3 and then 3:6, 7, "And EVERYONE WHO HAS THIS HOPE FIXED ON HIM PURIFIES HIMSELF, JUST AS HE IS PURE." And, "NO ONE WHO ABIDES IN HIM SINS; NO ONE WHO SINS HAS SEEN HIM OR KNOWS HIM. Little children, MAKE SURE NO ONE DECEIVES YOU; THE ONE WHO PRACTICES RIGHTEOUSNESS [or, "THE ONE WHO IS DOING RIGHTEOUSNESS"] IS RIGHTEOUS, JUST AS HE IS RIGHTEOUS."

"THEREFORE BE IMITATORS OF GOD, AS BELOVED CHILDREN" (Eph. 5:1) undoubtedly builds on the last verse of chapter 4, and the preceding verses. I'll read the last verse of chapter 4, "Be kind to one another, tender-hearted, forgiving each other, just as God in Christ also has forgiven you." When Christians do the things spoken in that verse, and the preceding verses, they are imitating God (by His saving, enabling, sanctifying grace). (Now we continue with Eph. 4:24.)]] **has been created in righteousness and holiness of the truth.** [[IT IS

IMPORTANT TO KNOW THAT THE TRUTH OF GOD INCLUDES HIS RIGHTEOUSNESS AND HOLINESS. When people use the word TRUTH in our day, they typically don't include righteousness and holiness, but God's truth puts an emphasis on His righteousness and holiness. When we submit to the truth of the gospel, which is backed up by the mighty Holy Spirit of God, we become righteous and holy new creations, for His glory.]] **(25) Therefore, laying aside** [or, **putting off**] **falsehood** [As I mentioned, putting off falsehood, is just part of putting off the old man once-for-all and completely.] **speak truth each one of you with his neighbor, for we are members of one another.** [Speaking the truth is the opposite of speaking falsehood (lying), and the fact that we are members of one another in the Body of Christ makes it all the more imperative for us to speak the truth to one another.] **(26) be angry, and yet do not sin** [See Psalm 4:4]**; do not let the sun go down on your anger** [[Most agree that Paul was not exhorting his readers to be angry here, but cautioning them to make sure that anger doesn't lead to sin. As James 1:19 cautions, we must be "slow to anger." It is possible for Christians to be angry without sinning (see Mark 3:5, for example), but anger can be sinful, and it can lead to great sin. That's why the apostle cautions believers to quickly deal with the cause of the anger and to not let the sun go down on their anger. Sometimes we can get issues resolved quickly, before the sun goes down. On those occasions where the issues cannot be resolved quickly, or be resolved at all (for one thing, we cannot act for the other person or persons who may be involved), we can take our concern to God (we can cast our care upon Him) and leave it there. He will take care of the details; they will be in good hands; and we can stay in peace and rest. What a privilege! See Rom. 12:17-21; 1 Pet. 5:7, for example.]] **(27) and do not give the devil an opportunity** [[more literally, "DO NOT GIVE THE DEVIL A PLACE." Compare John 14:30; James 4:7. We don't have to, and we must not, give the devil any place in us. We would give him a place in us, for example, by allowing anger to continue to abide in our hearts. We would give the devil a place in us if we allow things that aren't true (very much including false doctrine), or any sin, to have a place in us (including stealing, see verse 28; or speaking unwholesome words, see verse 29).]] **(28) He who steals must steal no longer; but rather he must labor, performing with his own hands what is good, so that he will have something to share with one who has need. (29) Let no unwholesome word proceed from your mouth, but only such *a word* as is good for edification according to the need *of the moment,* so that it will give grace to**

218

those who hear. (30) Do not grieve the Holy Spirit of God [[I'll read Isaiah 63:10, "And they [God's people] rebelled And grieved His Holy Spirit; Therefore He turned Himself to become their enemy, He fought against them." All sin, including accepting false doctrine, grieves the Holy Spirit. We must make God and His truth, righteousness, and holiness top priority, and if we should slip into false doctrine or any other sin, we must be quick to repent.]], **by whom** [the Holy Spirit] **you were sealed for the day of redemption.** [[We were sealed with the promised Holy Spirit when we submitted to God and His gospel in faith and became born-again Christians through the Holy Spirit of life who began to dwell in us (see Eph. 1:13; Rom. 8:9, for example). We have already been REDEEMED out of the kingdom of sin and spiritual death, but we are still waiting for the DAY OF REDEMPTION, when we will be glorified. The day of redemption will begin when the Lord Jesus Christ returns. At that time all true Christians will be caught up into the fullness of eternal life and will begin to reign with Him.]] **(31) Let all bitterness and wrath and anger and clamor and slander be put away from you, along with all malice** [This is part of the putting off of the old man that the apostle spoke of in verse 22.] **(32) Be kind to one another, tender-hearted, forgiving each other, just as God in Christ also has forgiven you.** This is part of the putting on of the new man that the apostle spoke of in verse 24. The Bible strongly warns Christians that they must forgive if they expect to be forgiven and to maintain their forgiven status before God (see, for example, Matt. 6:12, 14, 15; 18:21-35). Also, Christians must be quick to ask for forgiveness before God and before any people they have wronged. And there are many situations where more than asking forgiveness is required, things like repenting and making things right as far as it is possible.

That completes our study of Eph. 4:17-32, but I'll make a brief comment regarding Ephesians chapters 5, 6 and read 5:1 again before we go on to the next study. Ephesians chapters 5, 6 continue with the strong exhortation for Christians to walk in the manner they are called (and enabled) to walk, in the truth, righteousness, and holiness of God. In Ephesians 5:1 the apostle Paul said, "Therefore be imitators of God, as beloved children." He certainly exhorted his readers to walk with the victory over all sin.

Now we'll turn to a very important, but somewhat brief, discussion of the first three chapters of my book, *Holiness and Victory Over Sin.* The information contained in these chapters will help us understand the all-important atoning death of the Lord Jesus Christ. The primary emphasis is on the fact that He dethroned spiritual death and sin in His atoning death and enables us to be born again and to live in the very righteousness and holiness of God.

For a start I'll read a few paragraphs from the Introduction of the book, starting on page 1. Chapters 1, 2, and 3 of this book have much in common. Chapter 1 is titled, A Study on the Meaning of the Hebrew Noun "Pesha." Chapter 2 is titled, A Study on the Meaning of the Hebrew Noun "Awon." And chapter 3 is titled, A Study on the Meaning of the Hebrew Noun "Chet." These three Hebrew nouns are similar in meaning. The NASB and KJV typically translate *pesha* as "transgression," *awon* as "iniquity," and *chet* as "sin." A prime goal for these three chapters is to show that these Hebrew nouns include within their range of meaning the ideas of sin (iniquity, transgression), guilt of sin, AND PENALTY FOR SIN.

It is quite significant, but it is not widely known, that these Hebrew nouns (unlike the English nouns) include within their range of meaning the idea of penalty for sin. (Sin always has penalties and consequences.) An understanding of the fuller meaning of these Hebrew nouns will enable us to better translate and better understand many very important passages of Scripture. For one thing, this insight will enable us to better understand sacrificial offerings. Since our salvation is founded on the all-important atoning sacrifice of the Lord Jesus Christ, it is very important for us to understand these offerings.

In chapter 2 (of this book) we will discuss Lev. 16:20-22. They are key verses in the chapter that deals with the very important sacrifices of the Day of Atonement. This was the one day of the year that the high priest entered the holy of holies with sacrificial blood. The verses we will discuss speak of the offering of the second goat of the sin offering (sometimes called the "scapegoat"). It is important to understand that when the high priest placed all the *awon* (plural) of the sons of Israel on the second goat, he was placing on it all their iniquities with the guilt and with the penalties. The sacrificial goat was then driven to a land cut off, a land cut off from the life and blessings of God. The goat took the place of, and bore the penalty for, those who had sinned. If the goat had not taken their place, those who had sinned would have been driven from the camp of God. The sacrificial offerings (speaking of the sacrificial offerings in general) bore the sins of the sons of Israel with the guilt and with the penalties (including the death penalty).

The passage that we will discuss the most extensively in chapters 1, 2, and 3 is Isaiah chapter 53. This is probably the most important chapter in the Bible that deals with the atoning death of the Lord Jesus Christ. (Well over half of the combined content of chapters 1, 2, and 3 deals with verses from Isaiah chapter 53.) All three Hebrew nouns (*pesha, awon,* and *chet*) are used in this chapter of Isaiah.

As we will discuss, there were very definite limits to what could be accomplished through the old-covenant sacrifices. They did not have the authority or power to dethrone sin, spiritual death, or Satan and the demons. The one sacrifice of the Lord Jesus Christ, however, had no such limitations. Isaiah chapter 53 shows that full salvation – including the new birth and the victory over sin – is provided through His atoning death. He bore our *pesha, awon,* and *chet* so we could have full salvation, including ultimate glory in God's new Jerusalem.

Every aspect of our salvation comes to us through the atoning death of the Lord Jesus Christ. Mankind was under spiritual death, which came as a penalty for sin (Adam's sin); but now we (all true Christians) have been born again and are indwelled by the Spirit of LIFE (the Holy Spirit). Closely connected with spiritual death, mankind was in bondage to sin, but now we have been set free and are enslaved to God and His righteousness. Jesus Christ, the Lamb of God, bore the guilt of our sin, so we could be forgiven. HE BORE THE PENALTY OF SPIRITUAL DEATH, SO WE COULD GET OUT FROM UNDER THAT PENALTY AND BE BORN AGAIN. AND HE BORE OUR BONDAGE TO SIN, SO WE COULD BE MADE RIGHTEOUS AND HOLY WITH THE VERY IMPARTED RIGHTEOUSNESS AND HOLINESS OF GOD. Many key aspects of our salvation are reserved for the future (like resurrection and glorification); these things will also come to us through the atoning death of the Lord Jesus Christ.

Now I'm going to reread a sentence from the Introduction of the book; then we'll turn to chapter 2 of the book, A prime goal for these studies is to show that these Hebrew nouns include within their range of meaning the ideas of sin (transgression, iniquity), guilt of sin, AND PENALTY FOR SIN.

I'm turning to chapter 2, which is titled, <u>A Study on the Meaning of the Hebrew Noun "Awon."</u> Awon is used some 230 times in the Hebrew Old Testament. Some spell it *avon.*

The NASB translates *awon* as follows: iniquity(ies) (189), guilt (21), guilty (1), PUNISHMENT (12), PUNISHMENT FOR INIQUITY (6), blame (1).

The KJV has: iniquity(ies) (218), mischief (1), PUNISHMENT(S) (6), PUNISHMENT OF INIQUITY (4), sin (1), fault (2).

The NIV has: sin(s) (109), iniquity(ies) (22), guilt (35), CONSEQUENCES OF SIN (3), PUNISHED (2), PUNISHMENT (9), PUNISHMENT FOR SINS (1), and they translated this Hebrew noun quite a few other ways too.

I believe the NASB, KJV, and the NIV are typically correct in those places where they translate *awon* as "punishment," "punishment for iniquity," or the equivalent. In my opinion, however, there are many more verses where this emphasis should be recognized. The BDB Hebrew Lexicon (under *awon*) lists SIXTY-FOUR verses under the sub-heading "consequences of, or punishment for, iniquity." (The KJV has "punishment(s)" or "punishment of iniquity" ten times; the NASB has "punishment" or "punishment for iniquity" eighteen times; and the NIV is similar.) I agree with the BDB Hebrew Lexicon on at least most of these sixty-four listings, and I would add several more to their list, including Isa. 53:5 and Dan. 9:16.

Now we come to the heading <u>Quotations from the Article on *Awon* in the Theological Wordbook of the Old Testament</u> (which was published by Moody Press in 1980). "Moreover, as the above references indicate, it [*awon*] denotes both the deed and its consequences, the misdeed and its punishment. Both notions are present, but sometimes the focus is on the deed ('sin'), and at other times on the outcome of the misdeed ('punishment'), and sometimes on the situation between the deed and its consequence ('guilt')."

I'll quote one more paragraph from this important article. "The remarkable ambivalence between the meanings 'sin as an act' and 'penalty' shows that in the thought of the OT [Old Testament] sin and its penalty are not radically separate notions as we tend to think of them. Rather in the OT the action of man and what happens to him are presupposed to be directly related as one process within the basic divine order." For one thing, God wanted His people to understand that He hates sin and sin has penalties/consequences.

Now we'll discuss Genesis 4:13, one of the many verses in the Hebrew Old Testament that uses *awon*. For a start, I'll read Genesis 4:8-13 from the *New American Standard Bible*, 1995 edition. ... **And it came about when they were in the field, that Cain rose up against Abel his brother and killed him. (9) Then the LORD** [Yahweh] **said to Cain, "Where is Abel your brother?" And he said, "I do not know. Am I my brother's keeper?" (10) He** [Yahweh] **said, "What have you done? The voice of your brother's blood is crying to Me from the ground. (11) Now you are cursed from the ground, which has opened its mouth to receive your brother's blood from your hand. (12) When you cultivate the ground, it will no longer yield its strength to you; you will be a vagrant and a wanderer on the earth." (13) Cain said to the LORD** [Yahweh], **"My punishment** [my *awon*] **is too great to bear!"**

The NASB, KJV, NKJV, NIV, and the BDB Hebrew Lexicon all translate *awon* as "punishment" here in Gen. 4:13. The context makes is clear that Cain was complaining about his *punishment*. Genesis 4:2-10 spell out the iniquity of Cain that led to this "punishment," and verses 11, 12, and 14 spell out something of the "punishment" (penalty) that Cain was to bear.

"To bear" is a translation of the Hebrew verb *nasa*. This Hebrew verb is frequently used with *awon* in the Old Testament. (This verb is also used with the Hebrew noun *chet* in the Old Testament.) We often hear of persons bearing their *awon* or *chet*, with the emphasis on the fact that they are bearing the punishment/penalty/chastisement for their iniquity/sin. Several places we read of a sacrificial offering (especially the Lamb of God) bearing the *awon* or *chet* in place of those who sinned. Cain was bearing his *awon*; he was bearing his iniquity with the guilt and with the punishment/penalty, but the context puts the emphasis on his bearing the punishment/penalty for his iniquity.

The Lord Jesus Christ, the Lamb of God, didn't just bear our sin with the guilt so we could be forgiven, as important as that is. I think essentially all evangelical Christians understand that the Lord bore our sin with the guilt so we could be forgiven, but that's only a rather small part of what He did for us (and earned for us) in His all-important atoning death. He bore our sins with the guilt AND WITH THE PENALTIES (ON THE CROSS), including the major penalties of spiritual death and bondage to sin, not to mention hell. He bore the penalty of spiritual death that originated with the rebellion and fall of Adam and Eve, so we could get out from under that penalty and be born again. AND HE BORE OUR BONDAGE TO SIN, SO WE COULD GET OUT FROM UNDER THAT EVIL TASKMASTER AND LIVE IN THE VERY RIGHTEOUSNESS AND HOLINESS OF GOD THROUGH NEW COVENANT SALVATION IN UNION WITH THE LORD JESUS CHRIST. I'll read 1 Peter 2:24, one of a very large number of verses in the New Testament that shows that we are set free from bondage to sin and enabled to live in the righteousness of God through the atoning death of the Lord Jesus Christ, **and He Himself bore our sin in His body on the cross** [HE BORE OUR SIN with the guilt AND WITH THE PENALTIES (INCLUDING THE MAJOR PENALTIES OF SPIRITUAL DEATH AND BONDAGE TO SIN)], **SO THAT WE MIGHT DIE TO SIN AND LIVE TO RIGHTEOUSNESS** [my emphasis]; **for by His wounds you were healed.** And verse 25 goes on to say, **For you were continually straying like sheep, but now you have returned to the Shepherd and Guardian of your souls.**

The new birth and holiness and victory over sin have been provided and are available to us now. At the end of this age we will be glorified and begin to reign with the Lord Jesus Christ in God's new Jerusalem. Those glorious things will also come to us through the all-important atoning death of the Lord Jesus Christ. Of course our salvation is also dependent on His subsequent resurrection, ascension, etc.

It's time to stop. We'll come back to the study of these three Hebrew nouns in the next article. God bless you!

Holiness and Victory Over Sin #23

Holy Father, we humble our hearts before you. We want to know you. We want to please you. We thank you for full salvation through the atoning death of the Lord Jesus Christ. We pray in His mighty, holy name! Amen!

Last time when we stopped we were in the middle of a study of the first three chapters of my book, *Holiness and Victory Over Sin: Full Salvation Through the Atoning Death of the Lord Jesus Christ*. (The book is available on my website and at amazon.com.) I'm going to reread three paragraphs from the Introduction to the book. Chapters 1, 2, and 3 have much in common. Chapter 1 is titled A Study on the Meaning of the Hebrew Noun "Pesha"; chapter 2 is titled A Study on the Meaning of the Hebrew Noun "Awon"; and chapter 3 is titled A Study on the Meaning of the Hebrew Noun "Chet." These three Hebrew nouns are similar in meaning. The NASB and KJV typically translate *pesha* as "transgression," *awon* as "iniquity"; and *chet* as "sin." A prime goal for these three studies is to show that these Hebrew nouns include within their range of meaning the ideas of sin (transgression, iniquity), guilt of sin, AND PENALTY FOR SIN.

It is quite significant, but it is not widely known, that these Hebrew nouns (unlike the English nouns) include within their range of meaning the idea of penalty for sin. (Sin always has penalties/consequences). An understanding of the fuller meaning of these Hebrew nouns will enable us to better translate and better understand many passages of Scripture. For one thing, this insight will enable us to better understand sacrificial offerings. Since our salvation is founded on the atoning sacrifice of the Lord Jesus Christ, it is very important for us to understand these offerings.

In Chapter 2 we will discuss Lev. 16:20-22. (We'll turn to those verses when we finish this paragraph.) They are key verses in the chapter that deals with the very important sacrifices of the Day of Atonement. This was the one day of the year that the high priest entered the holy of holies with sacrificial blood. The verses we will discuss speak of the offering of the second goat of the sin offering (sometimes called the "scapegoat"). It is important to understand that when the high priest placed all the *awon* of the people of Israel on the second goat, he was placing on it all their iniquities with the guilt AND WITH THE PENALTIES. This sacrificial goat was then driven to a land cut off (a land cut off from the life and blessings of God). The goat took the place of, and bore the penalty for, those who had sinned. If the goat had not taken their place, those who had sinned would have been driven from the camp of God. The sacrificial offerings (speaking of the sacrificial offerings in general) bore the sins of the people of Israel with the guilt and with the penalties (including the death penalty).

Now I'll turn back to page 15 of my book (*Holiness and Victory Over Sin*) and we'll discuss Leviticus 16:20-22 in some detail. First I'll read verse 20, **When he** [Aaron the high priest] **finishes atoning for the holy place, and the tent of meeting and the altar, he shall offer the live goat. The holy place** speaks of the holy of holies; **the tent of meeting** speaks of the outer compartment. (See Lev. 16:15-17.) **The altar** refers to the sacrificial altar. **The live goat** is the second goat of the sin offering (see Lev. 16:5, 7-10, 15-19). It is important to see that both of these goats were required to complete this one, very special sin offering. I'll comment briefly on the first goat of this sin offering as we continue.

I'll read Leviticus 16:21, **Then Aaron shall lay both of his hands on the live goat, and confess over it all the iniquities** [plural of *awon*] **of the sons of Israel, and all their transgressions** [plural of *pesha*] **in regard to all their sins; and he shall lay them on the head of the goat and send *it* away into the wilderness by the hand of a man who *stands* in readiness.** Aaron transferred **all the iniquities…and…transgressions** of the people of Israel with the guilt AND WITH THE PENALTIES to the second goat of the sin offering. Note, **and he shall lay them on the head of the goat.** After this transfer, the sacrificial goat bore the *awon* (plural) and the *pesha* (plural) of the people of Israel (see verse 22). These *awon* and *pesha* that were put on the second goat of the sin offering were not different than the *awon* and *pesha* that were borne by the first goat of the sin offering, whose blood was taken into the holy of holies (see Lev. 16:15-19). The sacrifice of both goats was required to complete this one, very special sin offering of the Day of Atonement.

Although Leviticus chapter 16 doesn't mention this detail, Aaron undoubtedly also put his hands on the head of the first goat of the sin offering. That would have been standard procedure (see, for example, Lev. 1:4; 3:2, 13; 4:4, 15, 24; 8:14, 18). And undoubtedly there was a confession of sin over the first goat of the sin offering, as there was over the second goat. I'll quote part of what C. F. Keil says here (Keil and Delitzsch, *Commentary on the Old Testament*, Vol. 1). "As both goats were intended for a sin offering, the sins of the nation were confessed upon both, and placed upon the heads of both by the laying on of hands; though it is of the living goat only that this is expressly recorded, being omitted in the case of the other, because the rule laid down in chapter 4:4ff. was followed. By both (by both goats) Israel was delivered from all sins and transgressions."

I believe we must qualify the idea that all the *awon and pesha* were taken away on the Day of Atonement. The fully willful and defiant sins were not removed (see, for example, Num. 15:27-36; Heb. 9:7). Numbers 15:30, 31 say, "But the person who does *anything* defiantly, whether he is native or an alien, that one is blaspheming the LORD [Yahweh]; and that person shall be cut off from among his people. (31) Because he has despised the word of the LORD [Yahweh] and has broken His commandment; that person shall be completely cut off; his guilt [His *awon*, very much including the penalty for his iniquity] *shall be* on him." To be "cut off" meant to be put to death, as Num. 15:30-36 show (see, for example, Exod. 31:14, 15; Lev. 20:1-5). "His *awon* [his iniquity with the guilt AND WITH THE PENALTY] shall be on him."

Now I'll read Leviticus 16:22, but I don't fully agree with this translation. **And the goat shall bear** [Hebrew verb *nasa*] **on itself all their iniquities** [plural of *awon*] **to a solitary land; and he shall release the goat in the wilderness.** It is not adequate to just think of the second goat bearing "all [the] iniquities" of the people of Israel. This goat was bearing "all their iniquities" with the guilt AND WITH THE PENALTIES, and in this context, the emphasis is placed on the fact that the goat was bearing the penalty for the iniquities of the people of Israel. The BDB Hebrew Lexicon (under *awon*) lists this verse (Lev. 16:22) under the sub-heading, "consequences of, or punishment for, iniquity." This goat was taken from the camp of God (the place of His life and blessings) "to a solitary land [to a land cut off]" instead of (in place of) those who had sinned. It is also true that the first goat of the sin offering was put to death bearing the penalty for the iniquities of the people of Israel. I have an endnote, which I'll read, In the light of verse 21, we can rightly say that this goat was bearing all their iniquities with the guilt and with the penalties and all their transgressions with the guilt and with the penalties.

Instead of "to a solitary land," I would translate **to a land cut off**. The *Amplified Bible* has, "to a land cut off (a land of forgetfulness and

227

separation, not inhabited)!" C. F. Keil (the commentator mentioned above) speaks of the "land cut off." The Hebrew noun I would translate "cut off" is *gezerah*. The BDB Hebrew Lexicon (under *gezerah*) says, "*unto a land of separation*, of the goat for Azazel...." We'll discuss the name *Azazel* as we continue. (The verb *gazar*, from which *gezerah* was derived, is used in Isaiah 53:8: "He [the Lamb of God] was cut off out of [or, from] the land of the living.") If the iniquities of the people of Israel (with the guilt and with the penalties) had not been transferred to the goats of the sin offering, the people of Israel would have been driven from the camp of God **to a land cut off** (a land cut off from the life and blessings of God), bearing their *awon*.

Out in the **land cut off**, Azazel was "god" (Satan is called "the god of this world" in 2 Cor. 4:4). A note in the margin of the NASB at Lev. 16:8, 10, and 26 mentions that the Hebrew noun translated "scapegoat" means "*goat of removal*, or else a name, *Azazel*." I'll read Leviticus 16:8, "Aaron shall cast lots for the two goats, one lot for the LORD [Yahweh] and the other lot for the scapegoat." I agree with the common view that Azazel speaks of Satan or an evil being subordinate to him. There was, of course, no idea of sending a sacrifice to Azazel, but this sacrifice of the second goat of the sin offering powerfully demonstrated to the people of Israel that if it were not for the sacrifices of the Day of Atonement, they would have lost the protective care of their covenant relationship with God and would have been driven out to a land cut off where Azazel was god.

Now we come to the heading, <u>All the Old Covenant Sacrifices, and Especially Those on the Day of Atonement and Passover, Pointed to the One Sacrifice of the Lord Jesus Christ</u>.

The old covenant sacrifices were effective to a point, but they could not dethrone sin and death (see Heb. 7:11-10:18, for example). I have already mentioned that the old covenant sacrifices could not even atone for the willful and defiant sins of the people of Israel. They certainly could not remove the curse of death (either spiritual death or physical death) that had been part of the existence of man since the fall. Death (both spiritual death and physical death) came as a PENALTY FOR SIN, the sin of Adam (see Gen. 2:17; 3:3, 17-24; and Rom. 5:12-21).

The Sacrifice of the Lamb of God had no such limitations. He, by His one Sacrifice, has once-for-all dethroned sin, Satan, and death for all believers. He bore all our sins, iniquities, and transgressions with all the guilt and with all the penalties. He bore our death (a penalty for sin). Now we are born again and have spiritual life; when He returns all the believers who will have died before that time will be resurrected, and all believers will be born into the fullness of eternal life. It is only through His atoning death that anyone can enter new Jerusalem (see, for example, Rev. 21:27; 20:15; and 7:14 with 22:14).

Sin has been dethroned through the atoning death of the Lord Jesus Christ; we are not under the authority of sin (see, for example, Rom. 6:1-23; 8:1-14; 1 Pet. 1:14-19; 2:24, 25). Satan has also been dethroned through the atoning death of the Lord Jesus Christ; he has no authority over believers (see, for example, Matt. 28:18-20; Eph. 1:19-2:10; 4:27; Col. 2:15; Heb. 2:14-18; and Rev. 12:11). The final judgment of Satan will come to pass (at the right time; see Rev. 20:10) because of the atoning death of the Lord Jesus Christ (see John 12:31-33; 16:11).

Now we come to a study of Isaiah 53:4-6. I'll read Isaiah 53:4, **Surely our griefs [or, sicknesses] He Himself bore, and our sorrows [or, pains] He carried; Yet we ourselves esteemed Him stricken, Smitten of God, and afflicted.**

Surely our griefs [or, sicknesses] He Himself bore. The Hebrew noun translated **griefs** is *choli*. The NASB has "or *sickness*" in the margin. (The noun is plural in the Hebrew.) The NIV translates "infirmities." There is no doubt that the basic meaning of *choli* is sickness, and I would translate "sicknesses" here in Isaiah 53:4. I have an endnote on the meaning of *choli*, which I'll read, The BDB Hebrew Lexicon gives "sickness" as the basic meaning of *choli*. Out of the twenty-four uses of *choli* in the Old Testament, the KJV translates it as "sickness(es)" nineteen times, "is sick" one time, and "grief(s)" four times. The NASB translates *choli* as follows: affliction (1); disease (2); illness (3); sick (1) sickness(es) (15); and grief(s) (2). The only places where the NASB translates *choli* as grief(s) is in Isaiah 53:3, 4. Also see the comments regarding Matt. 8:14-17 under Isaiah 53:4.

I have another endnote dealing with the meaning of *choli*, which I'll read, I believe "sicknesses" would be a far better translation than "griefs" in Isa. 53:4. "Sickness" is a more comprehensive term, which (when used in its fullest sense as it is here) embraces "grief" and a whole lot more. *Choli* includes physical sickness and mental and emotional sickness, including grief. This Hebrew noun is also used in a figurative sense in the Old Testament, as the two following paragraphs will demonstrate.

Choli is used in Isa. 1:5, which speaks of the condition of the nation of Judah after it had been chastened by God; more severe chastening, however, was yet to come. Isaiah 1:5, "Where will you be stricken again, *As* you continue in *your* rebellion? The whole head is sick [*choli*], And the whole heart is faint.' (Isaiah 1:5 should be read with Isa. 1:4-9.)

Jeremiah 10:19 says, "Woe is me, because of my injury! My wound is incurable. But I said, 'Truly this is a sickness [*choli*], and I must bear it.' " These words speak of the condition of Judah in the days of the Babylonian invasions and exiles. (Read with Jer. 10:17-22.) Hosea 5:13 also uses *choli* in a figurative sense.

I believe we should understand *choli* in the fullest possible sense in Isa. 53:4, including spiritual sickness.

I'll turn back to our discussion of the words, **Surely our griefs [sicknesses] He Himself bore** of Isaiah 53:4. We come to the sub-heading, But how did the Lamb of God bear our sicknesses? He bore our sicknesses when (as Isaiah 53:11 says) He bore our *awon*, that is, when He bore our iniquities with the guilt AND WITH THE PENALTIES. He bore our sicknesses when (as Isaiah 53:12 says) He bore our *chet*, that is, when He bore our sin with the guilt AND WITH THE PENALTIES. To appreciate the two previous sentences, we must understand that under the old covenant, which is the framework within which Isaiah chapter 53 was written, sickness (including physical sickness) was typically considered to be a punishment, penalty, chastisement for sin. (See chapter 4 of my book *Holiness and Victory Over Sin*, which deals with this topic.) We will further discuss the meaning of these words as we continue with this study of Isa. 53:4-6.

Now we'll discuss the next words of Isaiah 53:4, **And our sorrows [or, pains] He carried.** The margin of the NASB has "or, *pains*" in place of "sorrows." The BDB Hebrew Lexicon gives "pain" as the basic meaning of this Hebrew noun (*makob*). The range of meaning of *makob* covers physical pain, mental pain, etc. In this context I would translate "pains" and take this word in the fullest possible sense. ... As with bear *choli* in the first line of Isa. 53:4, so here, the Lamb of God carried our pains when He bore our *awon, pesha,* and *chet.* Our "pains" were part of the punishment/penalty/chastisement that He bore in our place.

Now we'll discuss the last words of Isaiah 53:4, **Yet we ourselves esteemed Him stricken, Smitten of God, and afflicted.** The Lamb of God was "stricken, smitten of God, and afflicted" when He bore the penalty for our sins in His atoning death. The *Amplified Bible* is helpful on Isaiah 53:4, "Surely He has borne our griefs – sickness, weakness, and distress – and carried our sorrows *and* pain [of punishment]. Yet we *ignorantly* considered Him stricken, smitten and afflicted by God [as if with leprosy] [Matt. 8:17]."

Matthew 8:14-17 are an important cross-reference for Isa. 53:4; I'll read those verses, "And when Jesus had come to Peter's home, He saw his mother-in-law lying sick in bed with a fever. (15) And He touched her hand, and the fever left her; and she got up and waited on Him. (16) And when evening had come, they brought to Him many who were demon-possessed; and He cast out the spirits with a word, and healed all who were ill (17) in order that what was spoken through Isaiah the prophet might be fulfilled, saying, 'He Himself took our infirmities, and carried away our diseases.' " Matthew 8:17 loosely quotes from Isa. 53:4. These verses in Matthew help demonstrate that *choli* means much more than "grief," and they help show that spiritual and physical healing are included in the atonement. (See below under the words "we are healed" of Isa. 53:5. and see chapter 5 of this book (*Holiness and Victory Over Sin*), which is titled, A Study to Show that Healing and Health Are Included in the New Covenant Atonement. Matthew 8:14-17 are discussed in that chapter.

Now we'll discuss Isaiah 53:5. **But He was pierced through for our transgressions** [plural of *pesha*], **He was crushed for our iniquities** [plural of *awon*]; **The chastening for our well being** [for our *shalom*] *fell upon Him, And by His scourging we are healed.*

He was crushed for our iniquities [plural of *awon*]. (It is convenient to discuss the second line of verse 5 before the first line.) I believe the following translation better reflects the intended meaning, **He was crushed** [crushed unto death] **by our iniquities with the guilt and with the penalties**, or just, **He was crushed** [crushed unto death] **by the penalties for our iniquities.**

By is a reasonable way to translate the Hebrew preposition used here. (See endnote 8 in the book.) Just about everything said in chapters 1, 2, 3, and 4 of this book (*Holiness and Victory Over Sin*) supports the suggested translation for this second line of Isa. 53:5. The Lamb of God bore our *awon* [plural] (see Isa. 53:11). **He was crushed** [crushed unto death] by them. The wages of sin is death. The Hebrew verb translated "He was crushed" here is also used in Isa. 53:10.

I favor the longer suggested translation for this second line of Isa. 53:5, **He was crushed by our iniquities with the guilt and with the penalties.** We want to make sure that we don't lose sight of the fact that the Lamb of God was bearing (and taking away) our iniquities with the guilt and with the penalties. He was not just bearing (and taking away) the penalties.

Now we'll discuss the first line of Isa. 53:5, **He was pierced through for our transgressions** [plural of *pesha*]. I believe a translation like the following better communicates the intended meaning, **He was pierced through** [pierced through unto death] **by our transgressions with the guilt and with the penalties**, or just, **He was pierced through** [pierced through unto death] **by the penalties for our transgressions.** Chapter 1 of this book (*Holiness and Victory Over Sin*) deals with the meaning of the Hebrew noun *pesha*.

The Lamb of God **was pierced through** and killed when He bore our transgressions with the guilt and with the penalties, including the death penalty. Although a different Hebrew verb for "pierce" is used in Psalm 22:16 and Zech. 12:10, those verses are important cross-references. Psalm 22 prophesies of the atoning death of the Lord Jesus Christ. I'll read Psalm 22:16, "For dogs have surrounded me; A band of evildoers has encompassed me; They pierced my hands and my feet." And Zechariah 12:10 prophesies of the conversion of the end-time remnant of Israel, "I will pour out on the house of David and on the inhabitants of

Jerusalem, the Spirit of grace and of supplication, so that they will look on Me whom they have pierced; and they will mourn for Him, as one mourns for an only son, and they will weep bitterly over Him like the bitter weeping over a firstborn."

We come to the sub-heading, Commentators on Isaiah 53:4, 5. I recommend the commentary by F. Delitzsch on these verses (Vol. 7 of the Keil and Delitzsch *Commentary on the Old Testament*) and the commentary by E. J. Young (Vol. 3 of the *Book of Isaiah*, 1981 reprint by Eerdmans). I'll quote part of what E. J. Young said on the first two lines of Isa. 53:5, "[When we say that the Lamb of God bore our *awon* and our *pesha*] we are saying that he bore the punishment that was due to us because of those sins, and that is to say that he was our substitute. His punishment was vicarious. ["Vicarious" means that He took our place.] Because we had transgressed, he was pierced to death; and being pierced and crushed to death was the punishment that he bore in our stead." Dr. Young has a footnote; I'll read part of that footnote, "At the same time, if we merely assert that the servant bore the punishment of our sins, we have not done justice to the scriptural teaching. We must insist that in their fullness he bore our sins. ...."

Now we'll discuss the words **The chastening for our well-being** [Hebrew *shalom*] *fell* **upon Him** of Isaiah 53:5. These words fit the familiar pattern of Isaiah chapter 53. The Lamb of God took our place; He took **the chastening** – the penalty – for our sins. Through Him and His all-important atoning death, believers receive "well being"/peace/*shalom*. I believe we should understand *shalom* in the fullest possible sense. I have an endnote here, which I'll read, The BDB Hebrew Lexicon has seven sub-headings under *shalom*. I'll list the first six sub-headings to show the breadth of the meaning of this word: "(1) *completeness* in number; (2) *safety, soundness* in body...*is safe, secure*; (3) *welfare, health, prosperity*; (4) *peace, quiet, tranquility, contentment*; (5) *peace, friendship*: (a) human relations (b) *peace* with God; and (6) *peace* from war." That completes the endnote; now I'll continue reading what I said under the words **The chastening for our well-being** [*shalom*] *fell* **upon Him.** During this age believers are enabled to have peace with God, peace with self, and to a significant extent peace with others, especially with other believers. We have been born again and set free from slavery to sin. (See under Isa. 53:11.) We can begin to receive the benefits provided through the atoning death of the Lord Jesus Christ, including healing for the whole man (spirit, soul, and body), but some key aspects of our salvation, including most of the glory, are reserved for the future. <u>What about physical healing, for example?</u> We will not eradicate all physical sickness from the Body of Christ during this present age, but I am very sure that God has provided much more healing than we have been appropriating (see chapter 5 of this book). He is glorified when we are healed and enter into other benefits of our salvation.

It is important to see that all the *shalom* of this age and of the eternal age to come has been given to believers through the atoning death of the Lamb of God. What a salvation plan! What a Savior! The Lamb of God didn't just bear our sins with the guilt so we could be forgiven, as significant as that is. He bore our sins with the guilt AND WITH THE PENALTIES, INCLUDING THE MAJOR PENALTIES OF SPIRITUAL DEATH AND BONDAGE TO SIN, NOT TO MENTION HELL. (I am not saying that Jesus died spiritually; He never sinned or ceased being God the Son – He was the perfect Lamb of God. See my paper *Did Jesus Die Spiritually?* on my internet site.) Through Him we are born again and made righteous and holy with the very righteousness and holiness of God. In His atoning death, the Lord Jesus earned a *very* full salvation for us, which includes our being glorified and beginning to reign with Him in a never ending reign. Glory be to God the Father, God the Son, and God the Holy Spirit!

It's time to stop. We'll come back to our study of Isa. 53:4-6 in the next article. God bless you!

Holiness and Victory Over Sin #24

Holy Father, we humble our hearts before you. We thank you for salvation! We thank you for your Word! We want to understand your Word! We want to live your Word! In Jesus' mighty, holy name! Amen!

Last time when we stopped we were in the middle of an important study of <u>Isaiah 53:4-6</u>. I'm going to turn to page 22 of my book, *Holiness and Victory Over Sin,*" and we're ready to discuss the last words of <u>Isaiah 53:5</u>, **and by His scourging we are healed.** The Hebrew noun translated **scourging** is *chaburah*. This Hebrew noun is singular here in verse 5.

The BDB Hebrew Lexicon gives "stripe/blow" as the basic meaning of *chaburah*, and referring to its use in this verse says, "of blows inflicted on suffering servant of Yahweh." In a parenthesis they point out that this is a "singular collective" noun. The NIV translates *chaburah* as "wounds" here. The KJV and NKJV translate "stripes."

I don't believe we should limit *chaburah* to the literal scourging (or stripes) that Jesus bore. Rather the "wound" (the mortal wound) includes everything that He bore for us that killed Him, very much including the beatings, scourging, and especially His crucifixion. **By His wound** [His mortal wound) **we are healed.** The healing that God has provided for us came through the atoning death of the Lord Jesus Christ in its entirety, not just through His scourging.

I believe the words **we are healed** should be understood in the fullest possible sense. Physical healing and mental and emotional healing are included (see chapter 5 of this book, which is titled A Study to Show that Healing and Health are Included in the New Covenant Atonement). Physical healing and mental and emotional healing are included, but much more important is the spiritual healing – we are healed from spiritual death and bondage to sin and demon spirits. On this spiritual healing, see under Isa. 53:11 below. Also, most of the content of these articles deals with this spiritual healing that ultimately takes us to heaven.

First Peter 2:24, which quotes these words from Isa. 53:5 is an important cross-reference. Also, 1 Pet. 2:25 apparently builds on Isa. 53:6. I'll read 1 Peter 2:24, 25. "And He Himself bore our sins [He bore our sins with the guilt and with the penalties, INCLUDING THE MAJOR PENALTIES OF SPIRITUAL DEATH AND BONDAGE TO SIN] in His body on the cross, THAT WE MIGHT DIE TO SIN AND LIVE TO RIGHTEOUSNESS; FOR BY HIS WOUNDS YOU WERE HEALED [my emphasis]. (25) For you were continually straying like sheep, but now you have returned to the Shepherd and Guardian of your souls."

As the margin of the NASB shows, the literal translation is "wound" (singular), not "wounds." The Greek of 1 Pet. 2:24 uses the singular collective noun for "wound," as does the Hebrew of Isa. 53:5.

The apostle Peter emphasized the much more important spiritual healing that we receive in Christ in these verses. We return to God, die to sin, and live to righteousness through the atoning death of the Lord Jesus Christ. As we have discussed, the Lamb of God didn't just bear our sins with the guilt, so we could be forgiven; He bore our sins with the guilt and with the penalties (including the major penalties of spiritual death and bondage to sin), so we could be born again and live in the very righteousness and holiness of God.

Sin, Satan, and death (both spiritual death and physical death) have been dethroned through the atoning death of the Lord Jesus Christ, but we will not see the full manifestation of the "healing" wrought at Mount Calvary until we see the new heaven and new earth with its new Jerusalem of Revelation chapters 21, 22. I'll quote Revelation 21:27, "and nothing unclean, and no one who practices abomination and lying, shall ever come into it [into new Jerusalem], but only those whose names are written in the Lamb's book of life." The title "Lamb" (used in Rev. 21:27) points to the all-important atoning death of the Lord Jesus Christ.

Now we come to Isaiah 53:6. I'll read the verse, **All of us like sheep have gone astray, Each of us has turned to his own way; But the LORD** [Yahweh] **has caused the iniquity** [the *awon*] **of us all to fall on Him.** First we'll discuss the words **All of us like sheep have gone astray, Each of us has turned to his own way.** (See 1 Pet. 2:25.) These words picture mankind in rebellion against God – doing their own thing – and in desperate need of the Savior and Shepherd. They are (in a preliminary sense) bearing the penalty for their sin, but the greater penalty (the much greater penalty) is yet to come, starting with the day of judgment.

Now we'll discuss the words **But the LORD** [Yahweh] **has caused the iniquity** [the *awon*] **of us all to fall on Him.** In the last article I showed that it is very important to understand that the Hebrew noun *awon* includes within its range of meaning the ideas of iniquity, guilt of iniquity, AND PENALTY FOR INIQUITY. There is no substantial difference between our *awon* falling upon the Lamb of God here in verse 6, the Lamb being crushed by our *awon* in verse 5, the Lamb bearing our *awon* in verse 11, or the Lamb bearing our *chet* in verse 12. He bore our iniquities, our sins, and our transgressions with the guilt and with the penalties in His atoning death. I am not satisfied with the translation "iniquity" for *awon* here in verse 6. Something like the following is

236

required, **But the LORD [Yahweh] has caused the iniquity of us all [with the guilt and with the penalties] to fall on Him.**

We come to the subheading, <u>Commentators on Isaiah 53:6</u>. F. Delitzsch (Vol. 7 of the Keil and Delitzsch *Commentary on the Old Testament*) says (in part), "But *awon* is used to denote not only the transgression itself, but also the guilt incurred thereby, and the punishment to which it gives rise. All the great multitude of sins, and mass of guilt, and weight of punishment, came upon the Servant of Jehovah [Yahweh] according to the appointment of the God of salvation, who is gracious in holiness."

E. J. Young (Vol. 3 of the *Book of Isaiah*) says (in part), "The guilt that belonged to us God caused to strike him, i.e. he as our substitute bore the punishment that the guilt of our sins required."

D. A. Kidner, (*New Bible Commentary: Revised*, published by Eerdmans in 1970) says (in part), "[Isaiah 53:6] is perhaps the most penetrating of all descriptions of sin and atonement, uncovering the fecklessness which is second nature to us, and the self-will which isolates us from God and man alike; but also the divine initiative which transferred our punishment to the one substitute. The metaphor whereby *iniquity is laid on him* is clarified by, for example, Genesis 4:13; Leviticus 5:1, 17 (where one pays one's own penalty) and by, for example, Leviticus 10:17; 16:22 (where the liability falls on another)." Either we are bearing our sins with the guilt and with the penalties, or we submit (by faith) to the very full salvation that was purchased for us when the Lamb of God bore our sins with the guilt and with the penalties. Praise God for such a salvation plan!

Now we have the privilege to discuss <u>Isa. 53:11</u>. I'll turn to page 26 of my book and read the verse, **As a result of the anguish of His soul, He will see *it* and be satisfied; By His knowledge [or, By the knowledge of Him] the Righteous One, My Servant, will justify [or, will make righteous] the many, As He will bear their iniquities** [plural of *awon*].

This is another verse that the BDB Hebrew Lexicon (under *awon*) lists under the subheading, "consequences of, or punishment for, iniquity." Commenting specifically on Isa. 53:11, the BDB Hebrew Lexicon says (in part), "*the consequences of their iniquities he shall bear,* compare…Lamentations 5:7…." The KJV and the NIV both translate the plural of *awon* as "iniquities" here in Isa. 53:11, as does the NASB. I would translate **He will bear their iniquities with the guilt and with the penalties, including the major penalties of spiritual death and bondage to sin**, or the equivalent. Through His all-important atoning death, the Lord Jesus Christ earned the right to overthrow spiritual death and sin and to make believers righteous with the very righteousness of God, and to ultimately take us to eternal glory.

We'll discuss the first words of Isaiah. 53:11, **As a result of the anguish of His soul.** The Lamb of God underwent this "anguish of His soul" when He took upon Himself all our iniquities with the guilt and with the penalties in His atoning death. The physical pain that the Lamb of God bore for us in His atoning death was only a small part of what He bore for us when He took our place. For one thing, our sins separated Him from God the Father, and He cried out, "My God, My God, why hast thou forsaken Me."

Now we'll discuss the next words of verse 11, **He will see *it* and be satisfied.** What will He see? Isaiah 53:10 says that "He will see *His* offspring." Verses 10 and 11 use the same Hebrew verb for "He will see," and I believe the use of this verb in verse 11 builds on its use in verse 10. "He will see *His* offspring." "His offspring" embraces all the people who will be born into the fullness of eternal life through His atoning death. "His offspring" is the equivalent of "(the) many" of Isa. 53:11, 12. ... He will see His offspring and be satisfied. "...And the good pleasure of the LORD [Yahweh] will prosper in His hand" (Isa. 53:10).

The Lord Jesus Christ knew that it was the Father's will for Him to die in our place; He knew that He was earning the right to save all believers; and He knew that the devil and those who follow him would be judged and removed from God's kingdom forever through His all-important death.

Now we'll discuss the words **By His knowledge [or, by the knowledge of Him] the Righteous One, My Servant, will justify [or, will make righteous] the many** of Isaiah 53:11. I agree with the many who understand the words, "by His knowledge" in the sense "by the knowledge of Him" (as in the margin of the NIV). The Hebrew can be translated either way. People are saved by knowing the Lord Jesus Christ, in accordance with the gospel, by faith and by the Holy Spirit.

The words **the Righteous One, My Servant** here in Isa. 53 11 refer to the Lord Jesus Christ, the very special Servant of God the Father. He always was, and always will be, righteous in every way, and He earned the right to make us righteous.

Now we'll discuss the words, **the many** of verse 11. The same Hebrew adjective (*rabbim*) that is translated "the many" in verse 11 is used twice in verse 12. (Isaiah 53:12 is discussed in chapter 3 of this book, *Holiness and Victory Over Sin*.) **The many** embraces all believers (all the elect). They are the "offspring" of the Lord Jesus Christ spoken of in Isa. 53:10.

Now we'll discuss the words **will justify** [or, **will make righteous**] **the many.** The Hebrew verb that is translated "will justify" or, "will make righteous" here is one of the most important words (it is probably the most important word) used in Isaiah chapter 53 to speak of the benefits that come to believers through the atoning death of the Lord Jesus Christ. But what does "justify" mean? As I mentioned we could also translate "will make righteous."

Many Christians understand "justify" here to mean only that we are forgiven the guilt of our sin and are declared righteous by God. To be forgiven and declared righteous is an important part of what "the Righteous One" earned for the many, but if we stop here, we stop far short of what this Hebrew verb means in Isa. 53:11. THE LORD JESUS CHRIST DIDN'T JUST BEAR THE GUILT OF OUR SIN IN SOME ISOLATED LEGAL SENSE SO WE COULD BE FORGIVEN AND DECLARED RIGHTEOUS – HE BORE OUR SIN WITH THE GUILT AND THE PENALTIES, INCLUDING THE MAJOR PENALTIES OF SPIRITUAL DEATH AND BONDAGE TO SIN, SO WE COULD HAVE FULL SALVATION. For one thing, as we have discussed in some detail, when God declares us righteous when we submit (by faith) to His new-covenant plan of salvation, He is, at the same time, declaring the overthrow of sin and spiritual death, which reigned over us before we became born-again Christians. Sin, spiritual death, and the demons have lost the authority they had over us.

A MAJOR FEATURE OF NEW-COVENANT SALVATION IS OUR BEING SET FREE FROM THE AUTHORITY AND POWER OF SIN THROUGH THE ALL-IMPORTANT ATONING DEATH OF THE LORD JESUS CHRIST! The New Testament repeatedly declares that Christians are transformed and made righteous through His atoning death. (See, for example, Rom. 6:1-14; 7:4-6; 8:1-17; 2 Cor. 5:14-21; Gal. 1:4; 2:19-21; 3:13, 14; 5:16-25; 6:14, 15; Eph. 5:25-32; Col. 1:21-23; 2:10-15; 3:1-11; Titus 2:11-14; 3:1-8; Heb. 9:11-10:31; 13:12; 1 Pet. 1:13-2:25; 3:13-4:6; 1 John 1:7, 9; 2:28-3:12; Rev. 1:5; 7:14; and 12:11.) The Greek verb *dikaioo*, which is normally translated "justify" in some form in the New Testament, is frequently used in a very full sense that includes the ideas of being forgiven and declared righteous; being set free from sin, spiritual death, and Satan; and being made righteous with the imparted righteousness of God.

See chapter 6 of this book (*Holiness and Victory Over Sin*), which is titled, A Study on the Meaning of Justify/Justification as These Words Are Used in the New Testament, and we have already discussed this super-important topic quite a bit in these articles. If the Hebrew verb in Isa. 53:11 is to be translated "will justify," then "justify" must be understood in a very full sense. It is important to understand that God doesn't offer forgiveness and a right legal standing in isolation from the transformation to righteousness and holiness that is manifested when Christians (having been set free from spiritual death and bondage to sin) begin to walk by the Holy Spirit by faith, in accordance with the terms spelled out in the gospel of new-covenant salvation.

I believe it would be better to translate the Hebrew verb **will make righteous** instead of "will justify." In the Hebrew text this verb stands next to the adjective *tsaddiq*, which is translated **the Righteous One.** (The Hebrew adjective and verb are closely related, both having the same root.) **The Righteous One**, the Lord Jesus Christ, makes His people like Himself. Through His atoning death, His resurrection, and His subsequent ministry as our Great High Priest, HE MAKES US RIGHTEOUS! His ministry includes giving the Righteous, Holy Spirit to dwell in us believers. He enables us to walk in the righteousness of God, with the victory over all sin. Victory over all sin is the ideal to which we are called. But as we have discussed in some detail, we must walk by faith (faith in God, His Son, and in His Word) and by the Holy Spirit on a continuous basis (which we are called and enabled to do), or the total victory over sin will not be manifested in our hearts and lives. We must aim at the target of walking with the victory over all sin by God's grace. After we are glorified, we will be conformed to the image of the Lord Jesus Christ (see Rom. 8:29).

I'll read the *Amplified Bible* on Isa. 53:11. I'll emphasize the translation of the Hebrew verb we are discussing and the full sense in which the *Amplified Bible* translates *awon* by using all capital letters for these words. "He shall see *the fruit* of the travail of His soul and be satisfied; by His knowledge of Himself [which He possesses and imparts to others] SHALL My [uncompromisingly] righteous One, My Servant, JUSTIFY AND MAKE many RIGHTEOUS – UPRIGHT AND IN RIGHT STANDING WITH GOD; for He shall bear their INIQUITIES AND their GUILT [WITH THE CONSEQUENCES, says the LORD (YAHWEH)]."

I'll also quote a few sentences from Ross Price as he comments on Isa. 53:11. (This quotation is taken from Vol. 4 of the *Beacon Bible Commentary*, published in 1966.) "Thus by His wise submission to His Father's will He imparts to many His own righteousness. ... 'Justify many' means 'make the masses righteous.' ... It is through Him that they attain that new quality of life on a higher plane."

That completes our study of Isa. 53:11 and our somewhat brief study of the Hebrew nouns, *pesha, awon,* and *chet.* I trust you can see that it is very important for us to understand the breadth of meaning of these Hebrew nouns.

Now I'm going to turn to page 156 of my book, and we come to the heading, Hebrews 10:8-18 with Special Emphasis on the Meaning of *Aphesis* as it Is Used in Hebrews 10:18." Hebrews chapters 8-10 contain some of the most important teaching in the Bible that deals with the atoning death of the Lord Jesus Christ and the resultant full salvation for believers. This teaching puts a strong emphasis on the fact that sin has been overthrown through the atoning death of the Lord Jesus Christ and Christians are called (and enabled) to walk in the righteousness and holiness of God. Hebrews 10:18 is a key summarizing verse. If we misunderstand the meaning of *aphesis*, as it is used in this verse, which from my point of view is commonly done, it tends to significantly distort the powerful sanctifying message of Hebrews chapters 8-10.

First I'll read Hebrews 10:8, 9, **After saying above, "sacrifices and offerings and whole burnt offerings and *sacrifices* for sin thou hast not desired, nor hast thou taken pleasure *in them*" (which are offered according to the Law** [referring to the Mosaic Law, which was the foundation for the old covenant]), **(9) then He said, "Behold I have come to do thy will." He takes away the first in order to establish the second.** That is, "He takes away the first [covenant, the old covenant] in order to establish the second [covenant, the new covenant in the blood of Christ]." That's a dominant theme in the Epistle to the Hebrews.

Now we come to Hebrews 10:10, which is a very important verse. I'll read the verse, **By this will** [referring to the "will" of God just spoken of in verse 9] **WE HAVE BEEN SANCTIFIED THROUGH THE OFFERING OF THE BODY OF JESUS CHRIST ONCE FOR ALL** [my capitalization for emphasis]. See Heb. 2:11; 9:13, 14; 10:14, 29; and 13:12. As we have seen again and again throughout these studies, full salvation, which includes being forgiven, being set free from spiritual death and bondage to sin, and being born again and made righteous and holy comes to us through the all-important atoning death of the Lord Jesus Christ.

Now we come to the subheading A Discussion on the Meaning of the Words, "We Have Been Sanctified" of Hebrews 10:10. I can be somewhat brief here since this important topic is discussed in the last chapter of my book, *Holiness and Victory Over Sin*. (We'll turn to that chapter when we finish this study of Hebrews 10:8-18.) THESE WORDS, **WE HAVE BEEN SANCTIFIED,** SPEAK OF THE SANCTIFIED STATE IN WHICH CHRISTIANS ARE CALLED (AND ARE ENABLED) TO DWELL. To say the same thing using different words, WE HAVE BEEN MADE HOLY; WE ARE SAINTS; WE HAVE BEEN SET APART FROM SIN BY GOD FOR GOD; WE LIVE IN AN ABIDING STATE OF HOLINESS WITH THE VICTORY OVER ALL SIN. The NIV translates, "we have been made holy." The New Testament frequently uses the words, sanctify, holiness; holy; and saint in the ideal sense I have briefly summarized in this paragraph.

Christians are called to live in an abiding state of holiness, but Christians are not automatically sanctified, and sanctified Christians do not automatically maintain a state of holiness. ((I have an endnote here, which I'll read, See, for example, Heb. 2:18; 3:16-19; 4:1-16; 5:11-14; 6:1-12; 10:19-39; 12:1-29; 13:1-25. Hebrews 12:5-13 speak of God's chastening/disciplining of His children (as required) that they may share His holiness (see Heb. 12:10); that they may be righteous (see Heb. 12:11). The Bible makes it clear that God's people do not always respond with repentance when they experience His chastening/disciplining.

Hebrews 12:14 (NIV) says, "Make every effort to live in peace with all men and to be holy; without holiness no one will see the Lord." To be holy (to live in an abiding state of holiness) must be a top priority for Christians.

It should be pointed out that the holiness of Christians comes from God by grace through faith, based on the atoning death of the Lord Jesus Christ, and by the power of the indwelling Holy Spirit. We certainly don't want to say that chastening/disciplining is the basis for our holiness, but it can help motivate us to repent, etc. That completes the endnote.))

I'll turn back to page 158. We must walk by faith (based on what the New Testament teaches), and we must walk by the Holy Spirit on a continuous basis; otherwise, we will not live in an abiding state of holiness. The world, the flesh, and the devil are waging warfare against us, sometimes intense warfare.

The ideal presented in the New Testament is for Christians to be sanctified from the time of conversion. Then throughout the Christian life there will be growth as we are changed from glory to glory (see 2 Cor. 3:18). This need for growth is not sin, and in general, the New Testament does not use the verb "sanctify" (or the closely related words) to speak of this growth. In the ideal case we will live in a state of holiness and we will be growing.

Now we'll go on to Hebrews 10:11-13. I'll read the verses, **And every priest stands daily ministering and offering time after time the same sacrifices, which can never take away sins; (12) but He, having offered one sacrifice for sins for all time, sat down at the right hand of God, (13) waiting from that time onward until His enemies be made a footstool for His feet.**

I'll read what I said regarding verses 11, 12. The old covenant sacrifices were effective to a point, but they could **never take away sins.** (Also see Hebrews 10:4.) For one thing, they could not atone for (and take away) the willful and defiant sins of the people of Israel. Hebrews 9:7, for example, speaks of the high priest making atonement "for the sins of the people committed in ignorance" on the Day of Atonement. And, significantly, the old covenant sacrifices could not take away the transgression of Adam with the penalty of spiritual death. And as the apostle Paul showed in Romans chapter 5, for example, bondage to sin came when spiritual death came. The old-covenant sacrifices could not take away spiritual death and bondage to sin, so they certainly could not solve the sin problem and sanctify God's people. They could **never take away sins** from God's people. The writer of Hebrews makes the point in 10:3, 4 that the fact that the sacrifices of the Day of Atonement (and all the other sacrifices) needed to be repeated year after year demonstrated that those sacrifices could not solve the sin problem and sanctify the hearts and lives of God's people.

By contrast, the **one sacrifice for sins** of the Lord Jesus Christ does have the authority and power to take away sin(s) and sanctify the hearts and lives of God's people. Hebrews 9:26, for example, says, "He has been manifested to put away sin by the sacrifice of Himself." He took away our past sins with the guilt and with the penalties back to Adam through His atoning death; He dethroned spiritual death and sin; and, significantly, HE TOOK AWAY SIN(S) IN THE SENSE THAT HE GAVE US SPIRITUAL LIFE AND ENABLES US TO LIVE IN THE VERY RIGHTEOUSNESS AND HOLINESS OF GOD. In the ideal case there won't be any more sinning after we become Christians. That sounds good doesn't it? WE MUST AIM AT THAT TARGET! And it is very clear that we will not be sinning after we are glorified through the atoning death of the Lord Jesus Christ. Unlike the old covenant priests, our Great High Priest was able to sit down because (in one very real sense) His work was finished (He sat down at the right hand of God the Father [see verse 12]). He is waiting for the Father's time for Him to return and subdue His enemies in His end-time judgment of the world. He will make them a footstool for His feet.

Next time we'll start with Hebrews 10:14, a very important verse. I'll read the verse, "FOR BY ONE OFFERING HE HAS PERFECTED FOR ALL TIME THOSE WHO ARE SANCTIFIED [my emphasis]." God bless you!

Holiness and Victory Over Sin #25

Holy Father, we humble our hearts before you. We want to rightly divide your Word. We want to understand your Word. We want to live your Word. We want to glorify you. In Jesus' mighty name! Amen!

Last time when we stopped, we were in the middle of a study of Hebrews 10:8-18. Now we're ready for Hebrews 10:14, a very important verse. For a start I'll read Hebrews 10:10, 14 from the NASB, 1977 edition, which was used in my book, *Holiness and Victory Over Sin: Full Salvation Through the Atoning Death of the Lord Jesus Christ.* (The book is available at my website and at amazon.com.) **By this will** [the will of God, which was spoken of in verses 7, 9] **we have been sanctified through the offering of the body of Jesus Christ once for all.** [**We have been sanctified** is a perfect tense in the Greek, which communicates the idea that we have been sanctified and we now live in an abiding state of holiness.] **(14) For by one offering He has perfected for all time those who are sanctified.**

I'll read what I said in my book under the words **For by one offering He has perfected** (but as I have mentioned, sometimes I modify what is written in the book for these articles). The old covenant sacrifices could not perfect the worshippers, because, as we have seen, they could not dethrone sin, impart spiritual life, or sanctify the hearts and lives of the believers (see Heb. 7:11, 19; 9:9; and 10:1). I'll read Hebrews 10:1, "For the Law [the Mosaic Law, which was the foundation for the old covenant], since it has *only* a shadow of the good things to come [referring to new-covenant salvation, which is based on the sacrificial death of the Lord Jesus Christ] *and* not the very form of things, can never, by the same sacrifices which they offer continually year by year, make perfect those who draw near."

By one offering [Hebrews 10:14], however, the Lord Jesus Christ has dethroned sin, imparted spiritual life, sanctified believers, and removed the veil at the entrance to the holy of holies, thereby opening the way into the presence of God. **For by one offering He has perfected for all time those who are sanctified.** The PERFECTION of believers includes having spiritual life and being sanctified, and it includes having access to God (see, for example, Heb. 7:19, 25; 10:19-22; and Eph. 2:18-22). On the words **He has perfected,** see Heb. 11:39, 40. I have an endnote that discusses these verses. I'll read the endnote, Since these verses (Heb. 11:39, 40) are quite important, and since their meaning is not especially obvious, it will be helpful to discuss them.

First I'll read Hebrews 11:39, 40, "And all these [the believers from Old Testament days, who are spoken of throughout Hebrews chapter 11], having gained approval through their faith, did not receive what was promised, (40) because God had provided something better for us [for *us* new covenant believers], so that apart from us they should not BE MADE PERFECT [my emphasis]." The believers who lived in the days of the Old Testament could "not receive what was promised" until it became available through the atoning death of the Lord Jesus Christ and new-covenant salvation. "What was promised" includes the being "made perfect" spoken of in Heb. 11:40 (and in Heb. 10:14 and other verses). Hebrews 11:40 says that "apart from us they could not be made perfect." They had to wait for the Lord Jesus Christ to overthrow spiritual death and sin by His atoning death and to open the way into the presence of God. Now that this salvation has become available, these believers HAVE BEEN MADE PERFECT along with us, the new covenant believers.

Although this PERFECTION has been provided for new covenant believers, many Christians have not been walking in the fullness of this perfection. For one thing, THIS PERFECTION INCLUDES BEING SANCTIFIED AND LIVING IN AN ABIDING STATE OF HOLINESS. True Christians can sin, but to the extent we sin, we are not living in a state of holiness, or walking in the perfection spoken of here. But as long as we are living in the center of God's will, by His saving grace, by faith, it can be said that we have been perfected, even though it is understood that we still have the potential to walk in the flesh and to sin; even though it is understood that we still have a need to grow in the things of God; and even though it is understood that we have not been glorified yet.

Let's briefly discuss what it meant for those Old Testament believers to be perfected. Hebrews 12:23 speaks of those believers with the words, "the spirits of righteous men made perfect," and it shows that they are now in heaven. They are called "spirits" because they died physically and have not yet received their resurrection bodies. They are called "righteous" because they were believers and were accepted by God; and as Hebrews chapter 11 and many other passages show, those believers lived (relatively) righteous lives (by grace) through faith (see Heb. 11:4, 7, 33; and Gen. 6:9, for example). I'll read part of Genesis 6:9, "Noah was a righteous man, blameless in his time; Noah walked with God."

Although those believers lived relatively righteous lives, they are saved by grace through the atoning death of the Lord Jesus Christ. Before He had dethroned sin and death (both spiritual death and physical death) and made them perfect, those believers were in spiritual death, like all the descendants of Adam. At death they went to Sheol/Hades (the abode of the dead), but not in the sense that it was a place of punishment for them (see, for example, Gen. 37:35; Psalm 16:10; Isa. 38:10; Luke 16:22-31; 23:43; and Acts 2:27-32). (*Sheol* is a Hebrew word; *Hades* is a Greek word.) The name *Paradise* was sometimes used for the believer's compartment in Sheol/Hades. (These things are discussed in more detail in my verse-by-verse discussion of Ephesians chapter 4 on my internet site: Google to Karl Kemp Teaching.) Now that the sin problem has been solved and spiritual death has been overthrown through the atoning death of the Lord Jesus Christ, those believers have been taken to heaven. This is a big part of what it meant for the Old Testament believers to be "made perfect."

Those believers are still waiting for their resurrection bodies (with the exception of the select group mentioned in Matt. 27:52, 53), even as new covenant believers are waiting. The glory reserved for us in the future, including reigning with the Lord Jesus Christ, will come to us (all believers) through His all-important atoning death. (I recommend the commentary by F. F. Bruce on Heb. 11:39, 40 (*Epistle to the Hebrews*, published by Eerdmans in 1964) and the commentary by F. Delitzsch (*Epistle to the Hebrews*, a 1978 reprint by Klock and Klock). That completes the endnote, now I'll turn back to where we were on page 159.

I'll read Hebrews 10:14 again, **For by one offering He has perfected for all time those who are sanctified.** I'll read what I said under the words **for all time.** This **one offering** solved the sin problem for all believers, including the believers from Old Testament days (see Heb. 11:39, 40). Every person who enters God's new Jerusalem will enter because of this one offering (see Rev. 21:27, for example). And if a Christian should slip into sin, restoration is provided when they repent through this same **one offering** (see 1 John 2:1, 2, for example).

I'll comment briefly on the words **those who are sanctified** of Heb. 10:14, **Those who are sanctified** are the one who **have been sanctified through the offering of the body of Jesus Christ once for all** of Heb.

10:10. They have been set apart by God for God, set apart from everything unholy and sinful.

Now we come to the subheading, A Discussion of Hebrews 8:6-13 and 9:13, 14. These passages are very important, and they will help us understand Heb. 10:8-18. I'll read Hebrews 8:6-13 from the NIV, **But the ministry Jesus has received is as superior to theirs** [the old covenant high priests] **as the covenant of which he is mediator is superior to the old one, and it is founded on better promises. (7) For if there had been nothing wrong with that first *covenant,* no place would have been sought for another. (8) But God found fault with the people and said: "The time is coming, declares the Lord, when I will make a new covenant with the house of Israel and with the house of Judah.** ["The Lord" is Yahweh in the Hebrew throughout this passage. We Gentiles can be very thankful for the fact that God has invited us to be saved through the new covenant too.] **(9) It will not be like the covenant I made with their forefathers when I took them by the hand to lead them out of Egypt, because they did not remain faithful to my covenant, and I turned away from them, declares the Lord. (10)** [This is a very important verse. It speaks of God's sanctifying His people by an inner transformation.] **This is the covenant I will make with the house of Israel after that time, declares the Lord. I will put my laws within their minds and write them on their hearts. I will be their God, and they will be my people. (11) No longer will a man teach his neighbor, or a man his brother, saying, 'Know the Lord.' Because they will all know me, from the least of them to the greatest. (12) For I will forgive their wickedness and will remember their sins no more." (13) By calling this covenant "new," he has made the first one obsolete; and what is obsolete and aging will soon disappear.** The very important quotation contained in verses 8-12 is from Jeremiah 31:31-34, a very important prophecy.

I'll read what I said under Hebrews 8:9, This verse shows why a new and better covenant was needed. The people of Israel were sinners (like the rest of the offspring of Adam), and they rather consistently broke the old covenant – "they did not remain faithful to [God's] covenant."

I'll read Hebrews 8:10 again, then comment on this super-important verse. **This is the covenant I will make with the house of Israel after**

that time, declares the Lord. I will put my laws in their minds and write them on their hearts. I will be their God, and they will be my people. This verse is extremely important to help us understand the nature of the new-covenant salvation that became available through the all-important atoning death of the Lord Jesus Christ. At Mt. Sinai God had given the people of Israel His laws, but in general, they did not take His laws into their hearts and live by them (see Heb. 8:9). By the new covenant, however, God dethroned the sin and spiritual death that was reigning in the hearts of His people; by His indwelling, life-giving, sanctifying Spirit, He puts His laws "within their minds" and "on their hearts." (The renewal of the mind by the Word of God and the Spirit of God is discussed under Rom. 8:5-7 in chapter 6 of this book, *Holiness and Victory Over Sin.*) These words through Jeremiah were an effective way for God to say that He would make His people (true Israel) righteous and holy. CHRISTIANS (as they walk by faith and by the Holy Spirit) FULFILL THE REQUIREMENT OF GOD'S LAW IN THEIR DAILY LIVES (see Rom. 8:4, for example).

Under Hebrews 8:11 I said, God's people know Him on an experiential level through His indwelling Spirit (see, for example, John 17:3; Rom. 8:14-16; and 1 John 2:3, 4, 12-14). And under Hebrews 8:12 I said, This verse speaks of the all-important forgiveness of sins that has been provided through the atoning death of the Lord Jesus Christ.

Now we come to the subheading Hebrews 9:13, 14. These verses are very important, but I'll skip them for this article. Now we come to Hebrews 10:15-18. (We have already discussed Heb. 10:8-14.) I'll read these verses from the NASB, 1977 edition, but I don't fully agree with this translation. We'll get into the details as we continue. **And the Holy Spirit also bears witness to us; for after saying, (16) "This is the covenant that I will make with them after those days, says the Lord: I will put my laws upon their heart, and upon their mind I will write them."** *He then says,* **"and their sins and their lawless deeds I will remember no more." (18) Now where there is forgiveness** [Greek *aphesis*] **of these things, there is no longer** *any* **offering for sin.**

Hebrews 10:15 says, **the Holy Spirit also bears witness to us.** The writer of Hebrews means that the Holy Spirit bears witness to the truthfulness of what has been said in the preceding verses about the sin problem (which was not solved by the old covenant) being solved now through new-covenant salvation. The idea is that the Holy Spirit bears witness in that He was the One who spoke through Jeremiah the prophet, who is loosely quoted in the two verses that follow, verses 16, 17.

Hebrews 10:16, 17. This loose quotation from Jer. 31:31-34, which was quoted in fuller form in Heb. 8:8-12 (verses that I quoted above), confirms that the sin problem has been fully solved by the new covenant. In Heb. 10:16, 17 the writer just loosely quotes that part of Jer. 31:31-34 that directly deals with salvation from sin. Especially relevant is his loose quotation with the words, **I will put My laws upon their heart, and on their mind I will write them** in verse 16. This "quotation" effectively shows that a major feature of new-covenant salvation is the inner transformation (sanctification) of believers. New-covenant believers are set free from the authority and power of sin and enabled to live in the righteousness and holiness of God. He puts His righteous laws upon the hearts and minds of Christians, and as we walk by the Holy Spirit (by faith, in accordance with the gospel), we fulfill the requirement of God's moral Law (see Rom. 8:4; 2:26, 27; and Ezek. 36:26, 27). That part of Jer. 31:31-34 that is quoted in Heb. 10:17 speaks of complete forgiveness as God remembers our sins and lawless deeds no more.

At the end of verse 16, the NASB has the words **He then says** in italics. The KJV has nothing to correspond with these added words, and my United Bible Societies' *Greek New Testament* (fourth revised edition) does not include these words. The manuscript evidence for these added words is extremely weak. I believe it is very important that we do not include these added words. If we add these words, we set the stage to misunderstand verse 18, which is a very important summarizing verse. The super-important words **I will put my laws upon their heart, and upon their mind I will write them** of verse 16 are wrongly isolated from verse 18 by these added words.

It is true that we expect some words like "He then says" because verse 15 ends with the words "for after saying," and we expect the counterpart for these words. However, if we were to add words like "He then says," we should add them in the middle of verse 16, just before the words, "I will put my laws upon their heart." That way the added words would not lead to a misinterpretation of verse 18. As quite a few commentators have pointed out, apparently the writer of Hebrews used the words that were translated "says the Lord" in verse 16 to serve as the counterpart for the words at the end of verse 15.

Now we come to Hebrews 10:18. I'll read the verse again, but I'm not satisfied with this translation, **Now where there is forgiveness** [Greek *aphesis*] **of these things, there is no longer** *any* **offering for sin.** Rightly understood, this verse well summarizes the fact that the sin problem has been fully solved in the One Sacrifice of the Lord Jesus Christ, very much including the inner transformation (sanctification) spoken of with the words, "I will put my laws upon their heart, and upon their mind I will write them." I believe it is clear that "forgiveness" is not an adequate translation for *aphesis* here in verse 18, at least not if we think of forgiveness in the widely accepted narrow sense of the forgiveness of the guilt of sin. In earlier articles we rather thoroughly discussed the fact that *aphesis* is sometimes used in a much fuller sense in the New Testament.

I believe an expanded translation like the following conveys the intended meaning: **Now where there is RELEASE from these things** [that is, release from being under our sins with the guilt and the penalties (back to Adam)—WITH THE EMPHASIS ON OUR BEING RELEASED FROM THE PENALTIES OF SPIRITUAL DEATH AND BONDAGE TO SIN]— **there is no longer** *any* **offering for sin.** Since His one Sacrifice fully solved the sin problem, there is no longer a need for further sacrificial offerings.

Actually, if all we had was the forgiveness of the guilt of sin, we would still need a Savior to set us free from bondage to sin, spiritual death, and Satan. We would still be spiritually dead sinners in rebellion against God and His laws. However, since the One Sacrifice was fully effective and met every need, as the writer of Hebrews says again and again, there is no need for any further sacrifice. Also, if a Christian should slip into sin, forgiveness and restoration are provided through the One Sacrifice (see 1 John 2:1, 2, for example). That concludes our study of Heb. 10:8-18, very important verses. (In 2015 I wrote a paper on Hebrews chapters 8-10; it is available on my internet site. Google to Karl Kemp Teaching.)

Now I'll turn to the last chapter of my book; the chapter is titled Holiness and Victory Over Sin Through the Lord Jesus Christ and His Atoning

<u>Death</u>. This chapter originated with the study of the meaning of the words "we have been sanctified" of Hebrews 10:10.

The Greek verb behind the words "we have been sanctified" is *hagiazo*. This Greek verb, which is used twenty-eight times in the New Testament, is normally translated "sanctify" (in some form) by the NASB and the KJV. The NIV translates it "sanctify" (in some form) thirteen times. The NIV also translates *hagiazo* as consecrated, hallowed, made holy, make(s) holy, makes sacred, and set apart.

Hagiazo was derived from the adjective *hagios*, which is used over two hundred times in the New Testament and is normally translated Holy/holy or saint(s) by the NASB, KJV, and the NIV. The Greek noun *hagiasmos*, which was derived from the verb *hagiazo*, is used ten times in the New Testament and is normally translated holiness or sanctification by the NASB and KJV. The NIV has holiness four times. It also has be sanctified, holy, holy life, and sanctifying. The Greek noun *hagiosune*, which was derived from the adjective *hagios*, is used three times in the New Testament and is translated holiness by the NASB and KJV. The NIV has holiness two times and holy one time.

It is beyond the scope of this study to discuss the range of meaning of hagiazo, hagios, hagiasmos, and hagiosune. This study will be limited to one very important, but not well understood, New Testament use of these words. These Greek words are frequently used to communicate the idea that Christians are actually to be SET APART from sin and to live for God in an abiding state of holiness (basically) from the time of conversion. This is the ideal, and the New Testament does not present it as an unrealistic or unattainable ideal.

I have observed over the years that many Christians do not have an adequate understanding of the meaning of words like holiness, holy, saint, and sanctify. There are at least two ways in which these words are often misunderstood:

   1. Some reduce holiness to the mere positional or ceremonial. From this point of view, Christians are automatically holy, even if they are living in sin. I'm not saying that these words are never used in a positional, ceremonial sense, but this is not the typical New Testament use of these words.

2. Others agree that holiness means that Christians are actually set apart from sin for God, but they deny that Christians can be holy now, during this present life. According to this widespread viewpoint, the best a Christian can hope for (have faith for) is to be in a process (a sanctifying process) in which the amount of sin is decreasing as the years go by. I agree that Christians must be growing (see 2 Cor. 3:18, which speaks of our being transformed from glory to glory), but the New Testament doesn't normally use the words sanctify, holiness, etc. to speak of this growth. And, significantly, THE NEW TESTAMENT MAKES IT VERY CLEAR THAT CHRISTIANS ARE ACTUALLY TO BE SET APART FROM SIN – TO BE DEAD TO SIN AND TO BE SET APART FOR GOD. In the ideal case, we will be living in a state of holiness, and we will be growing. This is good news!

Our faith must be based on what the Bible actually says. If we believe that the Bible says that we cannot have the victory over sin now, we certainly will not have the victory over sin. The world, the flesh, and the devil are very real opponents, and we cannot walk in victory over them apart from the sufficient grace of God in Christ, which is appropriated by faith. I'm not talking about the power of positive thinking; I'm talking about trusting God and being sanctified by His saving power and for His glory. It is necessary for us to understand the Word of God, but we will never understand it (to a satisfactory extent) if we wrongly define key words like sanctify and holiness.

In the following study the verses listed under hagiazo, hagiasmos, hagiosune, and hagios were chosen because the context, and sometimes the form of the verb (for example, "we have been sanctified") helps demonstrate that these Greek words fit the ideal pattern we are discussing in this chapter: that we are actually supposed to be set apart from sin and to live in an abiding state of holiness now. I have not included every verse that fits this pattern, but I believe the verses I have listed are more than sufficient to demonstrate that this pattern is widespread in the New Testament.

Several verses I have listed do not quite fit the ideal pattern, but they help demonstrate this pattern. These verses deal with situations in which some Christians were not adequately set apart from sin. Four such verses are 1 Thess. 5:23; 2 Tim. 2:21 (both verses are listed under the verb hagiazo) and 2 Cor. 7:1; 1 Thess. 3:13 (both verses are listed under the noun hagiosune). In each of these verses the apostle Paul was concerned that this inadequate situation be soon rectified and these Christians become sanctified. ...

We come to the heading Some Verses that Use Hagiazo and Fit the Ideal Pattern. I listed Acts 26:18 (discussed in chapter 7 of this book, *Holiness and Victory Over Sin*); 1 Cor. 1:2 (discussed below); 1 Cor. 6:11; Eph. 5:26 (both discussed below); 1 Thess. 5:23 (discussed below); 2 Tim. 2:21 (discussed below); and Heb. 10:10, 14, 29 and 13:12 (Hebrews 10:10, 14 are discussed in chapter 7 of this book, and we have discussed these verses in this article and the last article.)

I'll reread Hebrews 10:10, 14; then I'll read Hebrews 10:29 in its context with Hebrews 10:26-31. Hebrews 10:10, **By this will** [the will of God] **WE HAVE BEEN SANCTIFIED through the offering of the body of Jesus Christ once for all.** The verb **we have been sanctified** is perfect tense in the Greek. Hebrews 10:14, **For by one offering He has perfected** [using the perfect tense in the Greek] **for all time THOSE WHO ARE SANCTIFIED.** "Those who are sanctified" in verse 14 are the ones who "have been sanctified" of verse 10.

Hebrews 10:26-31. **For if we go on sinning willfully after receiving the knowledge of the truth, there no longer remains a sacrifice for sins, (27) but a terrifying expectation of judgment and the fury of a fire which will consume the adversaries. (28) Anyone who has set aside the Law of Moses dies without mercy on** *the testimony of* **two or three witnesses. (29) How much severer punishment do you think he will deserve who has trampled under foot the Son of God, and has regarded as unclean the blood of the covenant** [the new covenant] **BY WHICH HE WAS SANCTIFIED** [my emphasis]**, and has insulted the Spirit of grace** [the Holy Spirit, through whom Christians are born again and sanctified]**? (30) For we know Him who said, "vengeance is mine, I will repay." And again, "the Lord will judge His people." (31) It is a terrifying thing to fall into the hands of the living God.**

The writer of Hebrews very strongly exhorted and warned his Christian readers here (and other places in this epistle) of the awesome seriousness of turning their backs on the new covenant that had sanctified them. He was dealing with the super-serious sin of apostasy in context, but his words don't leave room for any rebellion (sin) against God and His covenant.

We must take this warning against falling away from the faith very seriously (see my paper *Once Saved, Always Saved?*), but the Bible also speaks quite a bit about Christians who have fallen away from the faith to one degree or another repenting and turning back to God. Quite often the devil has convinced backsliden Christians that they have gone too far and there is no possibility that God will forgive and restore them. God is merciful toward the repentant. I strongly encourage every Christian who has fallen away from the faith to one degree or another, to turn back to God.

We'll continue with this important study in the next article. God bless you!

Holiness and Victory Over Sin #26

Holy Father, we humble our hearts before you. We want to understand holiness. We want to live holiness, by your grace, and for your glory. In Jesus' mighty, holy name! Amen!

I'll turn back to where we stopped last time, on page 172 of my book (*Holiness and Victory Over Sin*). We come to the heading, <u>Some Verses that use the Greek Verb *Hagiazo* and Fit the Ideal Pattern</u>. The Greek verb *hagiazo*, which is used twenty-eight times in the New Testament, is normally translated sanctify (in some form) by the NASB and the KJV. The NIV translated it sanctify (in some form) thirteen times. It also translated hagiazo as consecrated, hallowed, made holy, make(s) holy, makes sacred, set apart, and holy. Hagiazo was derived from the adjective *hagios*, which is used over two hundred times in the New Testament, and is normally translated Holy/holy or saints.

In the ideal pattern born-again Christians are set apart by God and for God; we are set apart from everything unholy and sinful, and we are set apart for God and His truth, His righteousness, and His holiness. In the ideal case we would be sanctified and live in an abiding state of holiness basically from the time we become Christians. God has paid an infinite price in the sacrifice of His Son to save and sanctify believers, and He has given the Holy Spirit (the infinite Spirit), to dwell in our hearts, thereby imparting His life, His righteousness and His holiness.

We certainly should not tell prospective converts, or those young in the faith, that God expects those young in the faith to continue to sin. We don't need excuses for sin. We must teach them in a thorough and balanced way what God has provided for them and what He requires of them. And we must do everything we can to help them, rather than being quick to condemn them if they should miss it. We cannot walk in the righteousness and holiness of God by the Holy Spirit, by faith, if we don't know, and understand, the gospel. We certainly should know, and understand, the basics of the gospel *before* we commit ourselves to God to become Christians.

In this study we will look at several passages from the New Testament where the context, and sometimes the form of the verb (for example, "we have been sanctified"), demonstrate that the ideal pattern we have been discussing is widespread in the New Testament. The first passage we will look at is 1 Corinthians 1:1, 2. First I'll read the verses from my book. I used the NASB, 1977 edition, in the book. **Paul, called *as* an apostle of Jesus Christ by the will of God, and Sosthenes our brother, (2) to the church of God which is at Corinth, to those who have been sanctified [Greek verb *hagiazo*] in Christ Jesus, saints by calling [or, called to be saints], with all who in every place call upon the name of our Lord Jesus Christ, their *Lord* and ours.**

To those who have been sanctified is a translation of the Greek perfect participle of the verb *hagiazo*. **Saints** is a translation of the plural of the Greek adjective *hagios*. Many believe that *hagiazo* and *hagios* are used in 1 Cor. 1:2 in a ceremonial, positional sense. I believe this understanding misses the intent of the apostle. It is true that this epistle shows that there was quite a bit of sin in the church at Corinth. Paul knew the state of the church at Corinth when he wrote this epistle, and at the outset of the epistle he reminds his readers that Christians (all Christians, including the Christians at Corinth, if they really are Christians) are required, by God's definition, to be set apart from sin – they are required to be sanctified, to be saints. If the lives of some of the Christians at Corinth don't match God's definition, they will have to change, and with a high priority – they must submit to the sanctifying grace of God in Christ

Jesus. (See, for example, 1 Cor. 5:1-6:20; 10:1-22; 11:17-34; 2 Cor. 5:20-6:2; 6:14-7:1; and 12:20-13:11.)

Christians are called (and enabled) to live in a state of set apartness. This holy state is acquired and maintained in union with the Lord Jesus Christ. We are literally united with Him as born-again Christians, through the indwelling Spirit of God. We partake of the benefits of His atoning death (and of His resurrection life).

Now we'll discuss the words **saints** [plural of *hagios*] **by calling** of 1 Cor. 1:2. The KJV has **called *to be* saints.** The NIV has **called to be holy.** Christians are **called** [Greek *kletos*] **to be saints** [**holy people**], even as Paul was "called [Greek *kletos*] to be an apostle" (the KJV and the NIV both translate "called *to be* an apostle" in 1 Corinthians 1:1). Both calls came from God, and He provided the enabling grace.

The Corinthian Christians were **called to be saints.** They were "called to be saints" **with all who in every place call upon the name of our Lord Jesus Christ, their *Lord* and ours.** In other words, the Corinthian Christians were called to be saints (called to be sanctified; called to live in an abiding state of holiness) along with every true Christian. God didn't have a different call for the Christians at Corinth. The issue was whether the Christians at Corinth were answering God's call and submitting to His Lordship and His sanctifying grace. It is obvious that some at Corinth were (to a significant extent) walking in the flesh (which is a very dangerous thing to do), and some undoubtedly were not real Christians. See 1 Cor. 3:1-3, for example. In 2 Corinthians 13:5 the apostle said, "Test yourselves to see if you are in the faith; examine yourselves! Or do you not recognize this about yourselves, that Jesus Christ is in you— unless indeed you fail the test."

The next verses we will discuss, 1 Cor. 6:8-11, help confirm the interpretation just given for 1 Cor. 1:2.

I'll read 1 Corinthians 6:8-11, **On the contrary, you yourselves wrong** [Greek verb *adikeo*] **and defraud, and that *your* brethren. (9) Or do you not know that the unrighteous** [plural of the Greek adjective *adikos*] **shall not inherit the kingdom of God? Do not be deceived; neither fornicators, nor idolaters, nor adulterers, nor effeminate, nor**

homosexuals, (10) nor thieves, nor *the* covetous, nor drunkards, nor revilers, nor swindlers, shall inherit the kingdom of God. (11) And such were some of you; but you were washed, but you were sanctified [Greek verb *hagiazo*], **but you were justified in the name of the Lord Jesus Christ, and in the Spirit of our God.**

Many commentators point out the important connection between **the unrighteous** (plural of *adikos*) of verse 9 and the verb **you** [yourselves] **wrong** (Greek verb *adikeo*) of verse 8. The Greek verb *adikeo* and the Greek adjective *adikos* are closely related; the verb was derived from the adjective. I'll read 1 Cor. 6:8 and the first part of verse 9 again, **On the contrary, you yourselves wrong** [*adikeo*] **and defraud, and that your brethren. Or do you not know that the unrighteous** [*adikos*] **shall not inherit the kingdom of God.** There's a powerful warning there! Such warnings are common throughout the New Testament.

The message of 1 Cor. 6:8-10 was that some of the Christians at Corinth were going to have to repent – their sin was incompatible with Christianity; they were not on the path that leads to an inheritance in God's eternal kingdom (see Gal. 5:19-21; Eph. 5:3-8; and Col. 3:5-11, for example). The apostle said they must "not be deceived." Their eternal destiny was at stake (see Gal. 6:7-9, for example).

Now we'll discuss the words **but you were sanctified** of verse 11. I believe the apostle wrote these words to remind the Corinthian Christians that holiness is a big part of what it means to be a Christian (see 1 Cor. 1:2). In any area where some of the Christians at Corinth were not sanctified, they would have to quickly change (by the grace of God in Christ) and become sanctified. The apostle knew, when he wrote these words, that some at Corinth were not adequately sanctified (see 1 Cor. 6:1-8, especially verse 8; 1 Cor. 6:15-20; 5:1-13; 10:1-22; 11:17-34; 2 Cor. 6:14-7:1; and 12:20-13:11).

We have been sanctified (and washed and justified) **in the name of the Lord Jesus Christ, and in the Spirit of our God** (1 Cor. 6:11). The sanctifying Spirit dwells in every born-again Christian. On the meaning of "you were justified," see chapter 6 of this book (*Holiness and Victory Over Sin*). The verb *justified* is undoubtedly used here in the very full sense we have discussed in these articles that includes being declared righteous; being set free from spiritual death and bondage to sin, being born again, and being made righteous and holy with the imparted righteousness and holiness of God. Praise God for such a salvation!

Now we come to the next passage under the heading, Some Verses that Use *Hagiazo* and Fit the Ideal Pattern. We'll discuss Ephesians 5:22-33, another very important passage. First I'll read the verses, **Wives, *be subject* to your own husbands, as to the Lord. (23) For the husband is the head of the wife, as Christ also is the head of the church, He Himself *being* the Savior of the body. (24) But as the church is subject to Christ, so also the wives *ought to be* to their husbands in everything. (25) Husbands, love your wives, just as Christ also loved the church and gave Himself up for her; (26) that He might sanctify her** [Greek verb *hagiazo*], **having cleansed her by the washing of water with the word, (27) that He might present to Himself the church in all her glory** [or, **glorious**], **having no spot or wrinkle or any such thing; but that she should be holy** [Greek adjective *hagios*] **and blameless. (28) So husbands ought also to love their own wives as their own bodies. He who loves his own wife loves himself; (29) for no one ever hated his own flesh, but nourishes and cherishes it, just as Christ also *does* the church, (30) because we are members of His body. (31) FOR THIS CAUSE A MAN SHALL LEAVE HIS FATHER AND MOTHER, AND SHALL CLEAVE TO HIS WIFE; AND THE TWO SHALL BECOME ONE FLESH. (32) This mystery is great; but I am speaking with reference to Christ and the church. (33) Nevertheless let each individual among you also love his own wife even as himself; and *let* the wife *see to it* that she respect her husband.**

I'll briefly comment on Ephesians 5:25. First I'll read the verse again, **Husbands, love your wives, just as Christ also loved the church and gave Himself up for her.** These words speak of the all-important atoning death of the Lord Jesus Christ.

Ephesians 5:26. **that He might sanctify** [*haziazo*] **her, having cleansed her by the washing of water with the word.**

First we'll discuss the words **that He might sanctify her.** As often, we see that the holiness of Christians results from the atoning death of the Lord Jesus Christ (see, for example, Rom. 3:21-25; 4:25-5:10; 5:17-21; 6:1-14; 7:4-6; 8:1-14; 2 Cor. 5:14-21; Gal. 1:4; 2:19-21; 5:24; Eph. 1:7;

2:1-10; Col. 1:21-23; 2:11-15; 3:1-11; Titus 2:11-14; Heb. 9:11-10:39; 13:12; 1 Pet. 1:13-25; 2:24, 25; 1 John 1:7, 9; 2:1, 2). Some understand **sanctify** here in a ceremonial, positional sense; others understand it to speak of a lifelong sanctifying process (where the amount of sin decreases as the years go by). I believe that the apostle Paul (and the One who sent him) intended the words **that He might sanctify her** in the ideal sense that we have been discussing: that Christians are actually to be set apart from sin and to live in an abiding state of holiness. This is good news!

Now we'll discuss the words **having cleansed her by the washing of water with the word** of Eph. 5:26. **Having cleansed** is a translation of the Greek aorist participle of the verb *katharizo*. We have discussed this important Greek verb quite a bit already in earlier articles. It is significant that this Greek verb is frequently used in the New Testament of a moral, transforming, sanctifying cleansing of the heart and life, including here in Eph. 5:26. (See Acts 15:9; 2 Cor. 7:1; Titus 2:14; Heb. 9:14; James 4:8; and 1 John 1:7, 9.)

This is so important I'll take the time to read two of these verses. In 2 Corinthians 7:1 the apostle Paul said, "Therefore, having these promises, beloved, let us cleanse ourselves from all defilement of flesh and spirit, perfecting holiness in the fear of God." "Let us cleanse [*katharizo*] ourselves [by the saving grace of God in Christ] from all defilement of flesh and spirit, perfecting holiness in the fear of God." And I'll read what the apostle Paul said in Titus 2:14, "[Christ Jesus], who gave Himself for us [in His atoning death] to redeem us from every lawless deed [or, "to redeem us from all lawlessness"] and to purify [*katharizo*; to purify, or "to cleanse"] for Himself a people for His own possession, zealous for good deeds [or, good works]."

There is very much overlap between the meaning of *katharizo* ("cleanse" or "purify") and *hagiazo* ("sanctify"). Apparently the idea here in Eph. 5:26 is that the "sanctifying" is accomplished by the "cleansing." I would translate **cleansing** here with the NIV (or, **purifying**) instead of **having cleansed.**

I agree with the widely accepted view that **the washing of water** refers to water baptism here (Eph. 5:26). (I have an endnote, which I'll read, The Greek noun translated **washing** here is *loutron*. The only other place this

260

Greek noun is used in the New Testament is Titus 3:5. See the discussion of Titus 3:5 in chapter 6 of this book, *Holiness and Victory Over Sin*.) It is obvious that water baptism in itself cannot cleanse a heart and life from sin, but the occasion of water baptism is the most appropriate (biblical) occasion for the believer to complete the transaction of dying with Christ to the old man and to sin (see, for example, Rom. 6:3, 4; Col. 2:11-13; and 1 Pet. 3:18-4:6. The life-giving, sanctifying Spirit, the Holy Spirit, is essential to the cleansing of the heart and life. (See under Titus 3:5 in chapter 6 of this book.)

The apostle spoke of being cleansed **by the washing of water with the word** here in Eph. 5:26. I believe the words **with the word** speak of "the word" of the gospel. The blood of Christ cleanses/sanctifies, being backed up by the Holy Spirit of power, but apart from our active faith in "the word" of the gospel, the cleansing/sanctifying does not take place. We must hear the gospel (which centers in the Lord Jesus Christ and His atoning, saving, sanctifying work); we must understand the gospel (at least we must understand the basics of the gospel); and we must submit (on a continuous basis) to the gospel from our hearts in faith. Furthermore, we must submit (in faith) to God the Father who gave us the gospel and to the Lord Jesus Christ. Apart from "the word" of the gospel, our faith in that word, and the work of the Holy Spirit, water baptism has no content or reality. It becomes another dead ritual. There is also a *confession* of the word (see Rom. 10:8-10, for example).

We must appropriate God's sanctifying grace on a continuous basis by faith. This very much includes walking by the Holy Spirit by faith on a continuous basis. The apostle Paul said, "walk by the Spirit [the Holy Spirit], and you [most certainly] will not carry out the desire [the sinful desire] of the flesh [the old man]" (Gal. 5:16).

Now we come to Ephesians 5:27, another very important verse. I'll read the verse again, **that He might present to Himself the church in her glory** [or, **glorious**], **having no spot or wrinkle or any such thing, but that she would be holy and blameless.** Many understand this verse to speak of that which will come to pass at the end of this age, after the church is glorified. There is no doubt that the church will be **holy and blameless** at that time, but I am quite sure that verse 27 speaks of that which is supposed to be true of the church throughout this age. The evidence for this viewpoint is very strong.

In Eph. 5:22-33 the apostle uses the *present* relationship between Christ and the church to illustrate how the husband and wife should be related. This illustration would be ineffective if the church had not already become united with the Lord Jesus Christ. In verses 29-33 Paul emphasizes the fact that the two – Christ and the church – HAVE BECOME ONE. The Lord Jesus Christ is "the head of the church" at the present time, even as "the husband is the head of the wife" (see Eph. 5:23). The New Testament emphasizes the fact that true Christians are literally united with the Lord Jesus Christ now through His atoning death in our place, which we have appropriated by faith, and by the indwelling Holy Spirit.

The Lord Jesus Christ has completed His atoning work and the church is enabled, and required, to be faithful, which includes our being **holy and blameless** throughout this present age. In Eph. 1:4 the apostle has already informed us that we are enabled, and required, to be **holy and blameless** now, and we will further discuss this important point as we continue.

Now we'll discuss the words **that He might present to Himself the church** of Eph. 5:27. In the sense that the verb **present** is used here, the presentation has already taken place. The Greek verb (*paristemi*) that is translated **He might present** here is also used in Rom. 6:13, 19; and 12:1 of Christians once-for-all presenting themselves, or their bodies, to God. The New Testament also speaks of a future presentation of the church (see, for example, 2 Cor. 4:14; 11:2; Col. 1:22, 28), but it would be rather strained to include that future presentation here. Quite a few commentators agree that the presentation of Eph. 5:27 takes place during this present age (and I list quite a few commentators in an endnote in the book).

Now we'll discuss the words **in all her glory** of Eph. 5:27. A note in the margin of the NASB says, "literally, glorious." These words are a translation of the Greek adjective *endoksos*, which I would translate **glorious**, or the equivalent. The KJV and NKJV have "glorious." The church (including every true Christian) should be "glorious" throughout this age in that it has been sanctified, cleansed, made "holy and blameless," etc. The Greek adjective *endoksos* is used in Luke 7:25 of the "glorious/splendid" clothing of the rich. The only other uses of this adjective in the New Testament are Luke 13:17 ("the entire multitude was rejoicing over all the glorious things [*endoksos*] being done by Him") and 1 Cor. 4:10 ("you are distinguished [*endoskos*], but we are without honor"). None of these verses, including Eph. 5:27, uses *endoksos* of the glory of the age to come, but this is not to say that this adjective cannot be used of the future glory. The words that follow here in Eph. 5:27 expand on what the apostle means by **glorious**.

Now we'll discuss the glorious words **having no spot or wrinkle or any such thing, but that she should be holy and blameless** of Eph. 5:27. The New Testament teaches that the Christian church (including each individual Christian) should be **holy and blameless** now, throughout this present age. See Eph. 1:4; 1:7 (these verses are discussed in chapter 7 of this book, *Holiness and Victory Over Sin*, and we have discussed these verses in earlier articles of this e-book); and see Eph. 2:1-10; 3:14-21; 4:1-6; 4:17-6:20.

Ephesians 1:4 NKJV says, "just as He [God the Father] chose us in Him [in Christ] before the foundation of the world, THAT WE SHOULD BE HOLY AND WITHOUT BLAME BEFORE HIM [my emphasis] in love." I'll also read Philippians 2:15, "that you may prove yourselves to be BLAMELESS AND INNOCENT, CHILDREN OF GOD ABOVE REPROACH [my emphasis] in the midst of a crooked and perverse generation, among whom you appear as lights in the world." And I listed some other verses here.

It is true, of course, that verses like Eph. 4:13, 14 show that some Christians in the apostle Paul's day were not adequately set apart, but we ought not infer from this that they shouldn't have been, or couldn't have been. The Christian ideal is frequently mentioned in the epistle to the Ephesians, and throughout the New Testament, including the words of Ephesians 5:24, "as the church is subject to Christ."

Now we come to Ephesians 5:28. I'll read the verse again, **So husbands ought also to love their own wives as their own bodies. He who loves his own wife loves himself.** As the following verses show, the husband **who loves his own wife loves himself** in that the two have become one.

I'll read Ephesians 5:29-33 again and briefly comment on these verses, **For no one ever hated his own flesh, but nourishes and cherishes it,** just as Christ also *does* the church, (30) because we are members of His body. (31) [Now the apostle quotes from Gen. 2:24 about the husband and wife becoming one flesh, applying these words to the glorious union between the Lord Jesus Christ and true Christians.] **FOR THIS CAUSE A MAN SHALL LEAVE HIS FATHER AND MOTHER AND SHALL CLEAVE TO HIS WIFE; AND THE TWO SHALL BECOME ONE FLESH. (32) This mystery is great** [this mystery of the two becoming one], **but I am speaking with reference to Christ and the church. (33) Nevertheless let each individual among you also love his own wife even as himself; and** *let* **the wife** *see to it* **that she respect her husband.**

The Lord Jesus Christ **nourishes and cherishes** the church (verse 29) as an extension of Himself; **we are members of His body** (verse 30); in a very real sense **the two have become one** (verses 31, 32). In the sense that the apostle Paul is speaking here, the two – Christ and His people – have already become one. We must – we have the privilege – of being faithful to Him now! We don't want to commit spiritual adultery! The fact that the apostle speaks of our having already been presented to Christ in a glorious union, where the two have become one, does not deny the fact that Paul can also speak of our being presented to Christ at the end of this age. We are using figurative language when we speak of the glorious union the church has with the Lord Jesus Christ, and figurative language can be quite flexible. This is figurative language, but it deals with very real, glorious, spiritual realities.

Now we come to the subheading, 2 Corinthians 11:2 is an important cross-reference for Ephesians 5:27. Let's look at 2 Corinthians 11:2-4; I'll read the verses. The apostle Paul said, **For I am jealous for you with a godly jealousy; for I betrothed you to one husband, that to Christ I might present you** *as* **a pure virgin. (3) But I am afraid, lest as the serpent deceived Eve by his craftiness, your minds should be led astray from the simplicity and purity** *of devotion* **to Christ. (4) For if one comes and preaches another Jesus whom we have not preached, or you receive a different spirit which you have not received, or a different gospel which you have not accepted, you bear** *this* **beautifully.**

Using the figurative language of 2 Cor. 11:2, the Christians at Corinth (and all true Christians) have been **betrothed** to Christ. The Greek verb translated **betrothed** is *harmozo*. It is significant that the basic meaning of this verb is "to join." The betrothal of which the apostle spoke (unlike the typical engagements of our day) was conclusive and binding. Unfaithfulness after betrothal was regarded as adultery. (See Deut. 22:23, 24; James 4:4. The Bible frequently speaks of the spiritual adultery of God's people.) There is no doubt that the apostle considered every true Christian to be already joined to the Lord Jesus Christ (see, for example, Rom. 6:1-11; 7:4; Gal. 2:20; Eph. 5:22-32; and 1 Cor. 6:15-20).

The apostle's point of view in 2 Cor. 11:2-4 was that the church started out *as a pure virgin.* There was a **simplicity and purity** *of devotion* **to Christ.** The church has been betrothed to one husband, and it must stay faithful to Him. Faithfulness/purity includes pure doctrine and holy living. The church must stay pure for the day of the final presentation. Although the verb present is used in a different sense in 2 Cor. 11:2 than in Eph. 5:27, both passages (2 Cor. 11:2-4 and Eph. 5:24-27) emphasize the need for all Christians to be **holy and blameless** throughout this age.

We'll come back to this important study in the next article. God bless you!

Holiness and Victory Over Sin #27

Holy Father, we humble our hearts before you. We want to understand your Word. We want to live your Word. In Jesus' mighty name! Amen!

When we stopped last time we were discussing the last chapter of my book. The chapter is titled, Holiness and Victory Over Sin Through the Lord Jesus Christ and His Atoning Death. I'll read part of the introductory comments of this chapter for a review. The Greek verb *hagiazo*, which was derived from the adjective *hagios*, is normally translated "sanctify" (in some form) by the NASB and the KJV. The Greek adjective *hagios* is normally translated "Holy/holy" or "saints" by the NASB and the KJV. The Greek noun *hagiasmos*, which was derived from the verb *hagiazo*, is normally translated "holiness" or "sanctification" by the NASB and the KJV. And the Greek noun *hagiosune*, which was derived from the adjective *hagios*, is translated "holiness" by the NASB and the KJV.

This study will be limited to one very important – but not well understood – New Testament use of these super-important Greek words. These words are frequently used to communicate the idea that we are actually to be set apart from sin and to live for God in an abiding state of holiness (basically) from the time we become born-again Christians. This is the ideal (it sounds good doesn't it?); and the New Testament does not present it as an unrealistic or unattainable ideal.

In the following study the verses listed under *hagiazo, hagiasmos, hagiosune,* and *hagios* were chosen because the context (and sometimes the form of the verb; for example, "you were sanctified") helps demonstrate that these Greek words are used in the ideal sense we are considering in this chapter. I have not included all such verses, but the verses I have listed are more than sufficient to demonstrate that this ideal pattern is widespread in the New Testament.

Several verses I have listed do not quite fit the ideal pattern, but they help demonstrate that this pattern does exist. These verses deal with situations in which some Christians were not adequately set apart from sin. In each of these verses, the apostle Paul was concerned that this inadequate situation be soon rectified and these Christians become sanctified. I mentioned four such verses here. Two of the verses (1 Thess. 5:23; 2 Tim. 2:21) are listed under the Greek verb *hagiazo.* We will discuss these verses next:

When we stopped last time we had two more verses to discuss under the heading, Some Verses that Use *Hagiazo* and Fit the Ideal Pattern. Now we come to 1 Thessalonians 5:23, a very important verse. I'll read the verse, **Now may the God of peace Himself sanctify** [Greek verb *hagiazo*] **you entirely; and may your spirit and soul and body be preserved** [or, **be kept**] **complete, without blame at the coming of our Lord Jesus Christ.**

A little background information will help us understand this verse. The Christian church at Thessalonica had been recently founded by the apostle Paul "amid much opposition" (1 Thess. 2:2). He even found it necessary to leave Thessalonica before he wanted to on the occasion of his first visit there (see Acts 17:1-16; 1 Thess. 1:6; 2:14-18; and 3:1-13). In Paul's First Epistle to the Thessalonians, he mentioned some of his concerns regarding the state of the newly founded church at Thessalonica (see 1 Thess. 3:10-13; 4:1-12; 5:12-15, 19-22).

With this background information, 1 Thess. 5:23 is easy to understand. The apostle prayed that God would **SANCTIFY...ENTIRELY** those recently converted Christians, who had known "much opposition," and then KEEP THEM IN THAT STATE OF HOLINESS, so that they would be **WITHOUT BLAME at the coming of [the] Lord Jesus Christ.** He prayed that God would do what was necessary to bring about the full sanctification of the church at Thessalonica. He was asking for a transformation to an abiding state of holiness in the very near future, as soon as possible.

For God to send the apostle Paul to Thessalonica was one way He could substantially meet the need of this church. See the discussion of 1 Thess. 3:10-13 later in this chapter. (We will discuss these verses later in this article.) The Thessalonian Christians themselves also had a major part to play in their sanctification (see, for example, 1 Thess. 4:1-12; 5:12-22; Rom. 6:1-23, especially verse 19; Rom. 8:12-14; 2 Cor. 7:1; and 2 Tim. 2:21). God does not sanctify people, or keep them sanctified, apart from their cooperation by faith.

The apostle wanted the Thessalonian Christians (and all Christians) to live their entire Christian lives IN A STATE OF HOLINESS, WITHOUT BLAME before God. Living in this state, they would always be ready for the **coming of [the] Lord Jesus Christ**, and they would be **without blame** on the day of judgment. Sounds good, doesn't it? I'll read Philippians 2:14, 15, "Do all things without grumbling or disputing, so that you will prove yourselves to be BLAMELESS AND INNOCENT, CHILDREN OF GOD ABOVE REPROACH in the midst of a crooked and perverse generation, AMONG WHOM YOU APPEAR AS LIGHTS IN THE WORLD [my emphasis]."

Now we'll discuss 2 Timothy 2:21, another very important verse. I'll read the verse, **Therefore, if a man cleanses himself from these *things*, he will be a vessel for honor, sanctified** [Greek verb *hagiazo*], **useful to the Master, prepared for every good work. Sanctified** is a perfect participle in the Greek, which fits the idea of Christians entering an abiding state of holiness. The apostle says that if these Christians will cleanse themselves from all that is sinful and defiling, including false

267

doctrine (see 2 Tim. 2:14-18), they will be sanctified. Of course it is to be understood that these Christians would *cleanse themselves* by the grace of God in Christ. It seems that Paul was speaking about those in the ministry in these verses, but what he says is applicable to all Christians. Sin will always interfere with our ability to serve God.

2 Corinthians 7:1 is a very important cross-reference for 2 Timothy 2:21. I'll read 2 Corinthians 7:1, **Therefore, having these promises, beloved, let us cleanse ourselves from all defilement of flesh and spirit, perfecting [or, completing] holiness in the fear of God.** We'll discuss 2 Cor. 7:1 later in this article.

Now we come to the next major heading, Some Verses that Use *Hagiasmos* and Fit the Ideal Pattern. The Greek noun *hagiasmos*, which was derived from the verb *hagiazo*, is used ten times in the New Testament. The NASB translates it "sanctification" eight times; "sanctifying work" one time; and "sanctity" one time. The KJV has "holiness" five times and "sanctification" five times. The NIV has "holiness" four times. It also has "be sanctified," "holy," "holy life," and "sanctifying." I typically prefer the translation holiness for this noun. Christians are called (and enabled) to live in an abiding state of holiness. The verses we will discuss here under *hagiasmos* are Rom. 6:19, 22; 1 Thess. 4:3, 4, and 7; and 2 Thess. 2:13.

We come to Romans 6:19, 22. I'll be brief here because these verses are discussed in chapter 6 of this book (*Holiness and Victory Over Sin*), and we have already discussed Romans chapter 6 verse-by-verse in these articles. I'll read the last part of Romans 6:19, **so now present yourselves as slaves to righteousness, resulting in sanctification.** I would translate **resulting in holiness.** The KJV, NKJV, and the NIV all have holiness instead of sanctification here; **so now present yourselves as slaves to righteousness resulting in holiness, resulting in *an abiding state of* holiness.**

Romans 6:22, **But now having been freed from sin and enslaved to God, you derive your benefit [or, you have your fruit], resulting in sanctification [or, better yet, resulting in holiness, resulting in *an abiding state of* holiness].** The KJV, NKJV, and the NIV all have holiness here instead of sanctification.], **and the outcome eternal life.** We're going to inherit eternal life in its fullness at the end of this age.

Now we come to 1 Thessalonians 4:1-8, another very important passage that will help us understand holiness. The Greek noun *hagiasmos* is used three times in this passage. **Finally then, brethren, we request and exhort you in the Lord Jesus, that, as you received from us** *instruction* **as to how you ought to walk and please God** *just as you actually do walk*, **that you may excel still more. (2) For you know what commandments we gave you by** *the authority of* **the Lord Jesus. (3) For this is the will of God, your sanctification** [Greek noun *hagiasmos*; I would translate **your holiness**]; *that is*, **that you abstain from sexual immorality; (4) that each of you know how to possess his own vessel** [his own body] **in sanctification** [Greek noun *hagiasmos*; I would translate **in holiness**] **and honor, (5) not in lustful passion, like the Gentiles who do not know God; (6)** *and* **that no man transgress and defraud his brother in the matter** [How would a "Christian" defraud his brother in the matter? By getting involved with his wife, or his daughter, for example.] **because the Lord is** *the* **avenger in all these things, just as we also told you before and solemnly warned** *you*. **(7) For God has not called us for the purpose of impurity, but in sanctification** [*hagiasmos*; I would translate **in holiness**.] **(8) Consequently, he who rejects** *this* **is not rejecting man but the God who gives His Holy Spirit to you.**

These verses make it quite clear that holiness excludes all sexual immorality. Paul's area of concern when he wrote these verses was sexual immorality, undoubtedly because he had learned from Timothy that this sin still existed to some extent in the newly founded church at Thessalonica (see 1 Thess. 3:1-6), but all other sin is also incompatible with holiness. The context makes it clear that the apostle was not thinking of a process of gradual withdrawal from this sin (or, any other sin). In verse 6 he spoke of God's being **the avenger in all these things.** And verse 8 confirms that Paul considered this to be a very serious matter, **Consequently, he who rejects** *this* **is not rejecting man but the God who gives His Holy Spirit to you.** God sets us apart for Himself by sealing us with the Holy Spirit, and the Holy Spirit enables us to live in a state of holiness, as we walk by the Spirit, by faith, on a continuous basis.

The next verse listed under *hagiasmos* is 2 Thessalonians 2:13. This verse is discussed in some detail in my book. Here I'll just read this verse with a few brief comments. **But we should always give thanks to God for you, brethren beloved by the Lord, because God has chosen you from the beginning for salvation through sanctification** [Greek noun *hagiasmos*] **by the Spirit** [or, better, **for salvation in** *an abiding state of* **holiness** *produced by the Holy* **Spirit**] **and faith in the truth.** If we submit to the truth of the gospel and walk by the Holy Spirit on a continuous basis by **faith in the truth**, which we are called (and enabled) to do, we will live in an abiding state of holiness. That sounds good, doesn't it?

Now we come to the next major heading, Some Verses that Use *Hagiosune* and Fit the Ideal Pattern, the pattern that Christians are actually supposed to be set apart from sin and to live for God in an abiding state of holiness, by His sufficient grace, through faith. The Greek noun *hagiosune*, which was derived from the Greek adjective *hagios*, is only used three times in the New Testament. It was translated "holiness" by the NASB and the KJV; the NIV has "holiness" two times and "holy" one time. Two of these verses are quite important for this study, 2 Cor. 7:1 and 1 Thess. 3:13. We'll discuss both of these verses in this article.

First I'll read 2 Corinthians 6:14-7:1; then we'll discuss 2 Corinthians 7:1, another verse that will help us understand holiness. **Do not be bound together with unbelievers; for what partnership have righteousness and lawlessness** [**Righteousness** is the opposite of **lawlessness.**]**, or what fellowship has light with darkness?** [God's light includes His truth, His righteousness, and His holiness.] **(15) Or what harmony has Christ with Belial, or what has a believer in common with an unbeliever? (16) Or what agreement has the temple of God with idols? For we are the temple of the living God; just as God said, "I will dwell in them and walk among them; and I will be their God, and they shall be my people. (17) Therefore come out from their midst and be separate," says the Lord, "and do not touch what is unclean; and I will welcome you. (18) And I will be a father to you, And you shall be sons and daughters to Me," says the Lord Almighty. (7:1) Therefore, having these promises, beloved, let us cleanse ourselves from all defilement of flesh and spirit, perfecting holiness** [Greek

270

noun *hagiosune*; **perfecting holiness** or, **completing holiness**] in the fear of God.

The words, **having these promises** refer back to the promises quoted from the Old Testament in 2 Cor. 6:14-18. There is a very strong emphasis in these verses on the need for Christians to be set apart once-for-all from all forms of sin, darkness, uncleanness, etc. For one thing, the apostle Paul was concerned about the sinful acceptance of false apostles by some at Corinth (see 2 Cor. 11:4, 12-15).

Now we'll discuss the words **let us cleanse ourselves from all defilement of flesh and spirit** of 2 Cor. 7:1. The Greek verb *katharizo*, which is translated **let us cleanse** here, is frequently used of a moral, sanctifying cleansing (or, purifying) in the New Testament, as it is here (see Acts 15:9; Eph. 5:26; Titus 2:14; Heb. 9:14; James 4:8; and 1 John 1:7, 9). Most of these references speak of God as the One who does the cleansing, but it is always understood that these things don't just happen automatically – we must cooperate with the cleansing/sanctifying grace of God through faith.

This verse makes it clear that true Christians can be defiled in the **spirit** (inner man, heart). Our spirits are not just automatically made clean or kept clean. The apostle Paul knew that there was some sin in the church at Corinth, and he wanted to see this unacceptable condition rectified at once. He was not thinking of a gradual, lifelong cleansing (or, purifying) process.

Now we'll discuss the words, **perfecting holiness** [Greek noun *hagiosune*] **in the fear of God.** As the Corinthian Christians cleansed (or, purified) themselves **from all defilement of flesh and spirit**, they would be **perfecting** [or, **completing**] **holiness.** They would be removing those things that were incompatible with holiness. The BAGD Greek Lexicon (under *hagiosune*) says, "*to perfect holiness* [equals] become perfectly holy (2 Corinthians 7:1)." The Bible (both the Old and New Testaments) teaches that Christians should fear sinning against God, and that they should fear having unresolved sin in their lives that needs to be dealt with through repentance. If we are in sin, we need to run to Him, not run from Him; run to Him and be forgiven by His grace, and be sanctified by His grace.

I'll read the *Amplified Bible* on 2 Cor. 7:1, "Therefore, since these [great] promises are ours, beloved, let us cleanse ourselves from everything that contaminates *and* defiles body and spirit, and bring [our] consecration to completeness in the (reverential) fear of God."

Now we'll discuss 1 Thessalonians 3:13, another important verse on holiness. I'll read 1 Thessalonians 3:6-13, **But now that Timothy has come to us from you, and has brought us good news of your faith and love, and that you always think kindly of us, longing to see us just as we also long to see you, (7) for this reason, brethren, in all our distress and affliction we were comforted about you through your faith; (8) for now we *really* live, if you stand firm in the Lord. (9) For what thanks can we render to God for you in return for all the joy with which we rejoice before our God on your account, (10) as we night and day keep praying most earnestly that we may see your face, and may complete what is lacking in your faith? (11) Now may our God and Father Himself and Jesus our Lord direct our way to you; (12) and may the Lord cause you to increase and abound in love for one another, and for all people, just as we also *do for you*; (13) so that He may establish your hearts without blame in holiness [Greek noun *hagiosune*] before our God and Father at the coming of our Lord Jesus with all His saints.**

We have already discussed 1 Thess. 4:1-8; 5:23 in this article. Both of those passages help us understand these present verses. Given the background, which we have briefly discussed already, with the church at Thessalonica having been started "amid much opposition" (1 Thess. 2:2), which even included the apostle Paul's finding it necessary to leave Thessalonica before he wanted to, it was not surprising that there was something still lacking in the faith of the newly converted Christians at Thessalonica. I'll read 1 Thessalonians 3:10 again, **as we night and day keep praying most earnestly that we may see your face, and may complete what is lacking in your faith.** The apostle Paul knew the state of the church when he wrote this epistle because he had sent Timothy to Thessalonica to "find out about their faith" and to "strengthen and encourage them as to [their] faith]," and Timothy had just returned to Paul after visiting Thessalonica (see 1 Thess. 3:1-6).

Paul knew that his apostolic ministry could go a long way toward meeting the need of the Christians at Thessalonica, so he prayed that God would direct his way to them (1 Thess 3:10, 11). In verse 12 he prayed for an increase in love on the part of those Christians. It was not that they were totally deficient in love, but there was room for improvement (see 1 Thess. 1:3; 3:6; and 4:9, 10).

I'll read 1 Thessalonians 3:13 again; then we'll get into the details, **so that He may establish your hearts without blame in holiness** [*hagiosune*] **before our God and Father at the coming of our Lord Jesus with all His saints** [plural of *hagios*].

What the apostle says here is essentially the equivalent of what he prayed for in 1 Thessalonians 5:23. I'll read that verse again, "Now may the God of peace Himself sanctify you entirely; and may your spirit and soul and body be preserved [or, "be kept"] complete, without blame at the coming of our Lord Jesus Christ." In 1 Thess. 5:23 Paul prayed that the Christians at Thessalonica would be sanctified entirely in the very near future, as soon as possible, and then be kept in that state without blame at the coming [Greek *parousia*] of the Lord Jesus Christ. Here in 3:13 the apostle requests that God establish their hearts without blame in holiness at the coming [*parousia*] of the Lord Jesus Christ. As in 5:23 Paul wanted to see them established **without blame in holiness** in the very near future, as soon as possible, and then for them to continue to abide in that state. That way they would always be fully ready to stand before God, whenever the Lord Jesus Christ would come. That sounds good, doesn't it?

Many verses speak of the fact that we must get ready and stay ready to stand before God at the end of this age. (See Rom. 14:10-12; 2 Cor. 5:10; Col. 1:21-23, 28; and Jude 24, for example). And many verses speak of the coming of the Lord Jesus Christ at the end of this age. (See Matt. 24:3, 27, 37, 39; 1 Thess. 1:10; 2:19; 4:15; 5:23; 2 Thess. 1:10; 2:1; 1 Cor. 15:23; and Phil. 3:20, 21, for example.)

Paul concluded 1 Thess. 3:13 with the words **with all His saints.** The apostle's meaning was not that the Lord Jesus Christ will come **with all His saints**, though it is true that He will bring the departed saints with Him when He comes (see 1 Thess. 4:13-18, for example). For one thing, many of **His saints** will still be living on the earth at the time of His return.

273

Rather, the apostle was concerned that the hearts and lives of the Thessalonian Christians be established **without blame in holiness** and then kept in that state so that they will be fully ready to stand before God **without blame in holiness** along **with all** [the other] **saints.**

Now we come to the next major heading, Some Verses that Use *Hagios* and Fit the Ideal Pattern. The Greek adjective *hagios*, which is used more than two hundred times in the New Testament, is normally translated "Holy/holy" or "saints." I listed the following verses under this heading: Rom. 1:7; 12:1; 1 Cor. 1:2 (we discussed this verse in the last article); Eph. 1:4; 5:3, 27 (we discussed Eph 5:27 in the last article); Col. 1:12, 22; 1 Thess. 3:13 (which we just discussed); 2 Tim. 1:9; 1 Pet. 1:15, 16; and 2 Pet. 3:11.

The first verse we will look at is Romans 1:7. I'll quote the verse from the KJV, **To all that be in Rome, beloved of God, called *to be* saints** [plural of *hagios*]: **Grace to you and peace from God our Father, and the Lord Jesus Christ.** The NKJV and the NIV also have **called *to be*** [or, **to be**] **saints.** The NASB has "called *as* saints." Christians are called to be saints, holy people, set apart for God and His righteousness people. As we have been discussing, God calls (and enables) us to be saints. In the ideal case, we will walk in accordance with God's Word and walk by the Holy Spirit on a continuous basis by faith, and live in an abiding state of holiness. That sounds good, doesn't it?

In 1 Corinthians 1:2, which we discussed in the last article, the apostle Paul also used the words **called *to be* saints.** As we discussed, we were **called *to be* saints**, even as Paul was "called to be an apostle." God's grace enables us to be saints, even as His grace enabled Paul to be a faithful apostle. The words, "called *to be* an apostle" were used in 1 Cor. 1:1. I'll read 1 Corinthians 1:1, 2 from the NKJV, **Paul, called *to be* an apostle of Jesus Christ through the will of God, and Sosthenes *our* brother, (2) to the church of God which is at Corinth, to those who are sanctified in Christ Jesus, called *to be* saints, with all who in every place call on the name of Jesus Christ our Lord, both theirs and ours.**

Romans 12:1. I'll read this verse and part of the next verse from the NIV, **Therefore, I urge you, brothers, in view of God's mercy, to offer your** bodies as living sacrifices, holy [Greek *hagios*] and pleasing to God—this is your spiritual act of worship. (2) Do not conform any longer to the pattern of this world, but be transformed by the renewing [better, by the renewal] of your mind.**

The apostle was calling for a once-for-all presentation of ourselves, including our bodies, to God and for the accompanying once-for-all renewal of our minds (of the way we think, especially of the way we think in our hearts), including our attitudes, motives, and priorities. As he said, "DO NOT CONFORM ANY LONGER TO THE PATTERN OF THIS WORLD, but be transformed by the renewal of your mind [renewal of the way you think]." Paul was not calling for a gradual withdrawal from the sinful "pattern of this world." We must think right in our hearts to live right for God.

The apostle goes on in verse 3 to give an important illustration of what he means by having a renewed mind. I'll read the first part of verse 3 from the NASB, **For through the grace given to me** [the enabling grace of God for him to fulfill his ministry] **I say to everyone among you not to think more highly of himself than he ought to think….** One of the primary manifestations of walking in the flesh is the tendency to think more highly of ourselves than we ought to think. Pride (with unbelief) is at the root of sin. Romans 12:1-8 are discussed in my *A Paper on Faith* that is located on my internet site (karlkempteachingministries.com).

On the renewal of our minds by the Spirit of God, see under Rom. 8:5-8 in chapter 6 of this book (*Holiness and Victory Over Sin*). We have discussed these verses and this topic in earlier articles of this e-book. Of course the Word of God also plays a key role in the renewal of our minds. We should continue to grow throughout our lives in Christ (in knowledge, wisdom, etc.), but in the ideal case we will not be gradually leaving sin behind – we will be living in an abiding state of righteousness and holiness. That sounds good, doesn't it?

We'll come back to this important topic in the next article. God bless you!

Holiness and Victory Over Sin #28

Holy Father, we humble our hearts before you. We want to understand the new covenant. We want to live the new covenant, by your grace and for your glory. In Jesus' mighty holy name! Amen!

When we stopped last time, we were on page 186 of my book (*Holiness and Victory Over Sin*), under the heading, Some Verses that Use *Hagios* and Fit the Ideal Pattern. The Greek adjective *hagios* is used more than two hundred times in the New Testament; it is normally translated "Holy/holy" or "saints." A saint is a holy person, a person *set apart* for God. The "ideal pattern" refers to Christians actually being set apart from all sin and everything defiling, and living for God in an abiding state of holiness, by His grace, through faith, in accordance with the terms of the new covenant. This is good news, very good news! This is what we want, isn't it?

We come to Ephesians 5:3-8. I'll read verse 3. (I used the *New American Standard Bible*, 1977 edition, in my book.) **But do not let immorality or any impurity or greed even be named among you, as is proper among saints** [plural of *hagios*]. **Immorality or any impurity or greed must never be named** as existing **among** the **saints.** The NIV's translation is effective, "But among you there must not be even a hint of sexual immorality, or of any kind of impurity, or of greed, because these are improper for God's holy people." BEING HOLY/BEING A SAINT, INCLUDES BEING SET APART FROM IMMORALITY, IMPURITY, GREED, AND EVERYTHING ELSE THAT IS SINFUL AND DEFILING! Ephesians 5:4-8 (and the verses that follow) continue with the same emphasis on the need for Christians to live in an abiding state of holiness.

I'll read Ephesians 5:4, 5. **and *there must be no* filthiness and silly talk, or coarse jesting, which are not fitting** [which are not fitting for saints]**, but rather giving of thanks. (5) For this you know with certainty, that no immoral or impure person or covetous man, who is an idolater, has an inheritance in the kingdom of Christ and God.**

It's important to see that the **immoral [person]** of verse 5 refers back to the word **immorality** of verse 3; that the **impure person** of verse 5 refers back to the word **impurity** of verse 3; and that the **covetous man** of verse 5 refers back to the word **greed** of verse 3. In verse 5 Paul said, **covetous man, who is an idolater.** In other words, the covetous man makes an idol of the things he covets.

I'll read Ephesians 5:5 again, **For this you know with certainty, that no immoral or impure person or covetous man, who is an idolater, has an inheritance in the kingdom of Christ and God.** If we don't have **an inheritance in the kingdom of Christ and God** the Father, we are not headed for heaven. This makes holiness very important, doesn't it?

I'll read Ephesians 5:6 and make a few comments, **Let no one deceive you with empty words** [There were deceivers in Paul's day, and there are many deceivers in our day.]**, for because of these things** [What things? The sinful things the apostle has been talking about] **the wrath of God comes upon the sons of disobedience.** The way to avoid **the wrath of God** is to live as sons of obedience (through the sanctifying grace of God in Christ) instead of living as **sons of disobedience.** We must make truth, obedience, holiness and righteousness top priorities.

I'll read Ephesians 5:6-8. **Let no one deceive you with empty words, for because of these things** [these sinful things] **the wrath of God comes upon the sons of disobedience. (7) Therefore do not be partakers with them** [The **sons of disobedience** will partake of **the wrath of God.** We certainly don't want to be **partakers with them** of **the wrath of God.**]**; (8) for you were formerly darkness** [Darkness goes with sin, Satan, and his kingdom of darkness.]**, but now you are light in the Lord; walk as children of light.** God's **light** includes His truth, His righteousness, and His holiness. In the ideal case Christians will walk as children of light in an abiding state of holiness, by His sufficient grace, through faith. WE MUST AIM AT THAT TARGET!

Holiness is not an optional matter for Christians (see Rom. 2:1-16; 1 Cor. 6:9-11; Gal. 5:19-21; and Col. 3:5-11, for example). Holiness is a big part of what new-covenant salvation is all about. I'll quote Hebrews 12:14 from the NKJV, "Pursue peace with all *men,* AND HOLINESS, WITHOUT WHICH NO ONE WILL SEE THE LORD [my emphasis]." This is good news; God enables us to do what He calls us to do. Also, the New Testament makes it clear that God forgives Christians when they sincerely repent.

Now we come to Colossians 1:21-23. I'll read the verses, **And although you were formerly alienated and hostile in mind, *engaged* in evil** deeds, **(22) yet He has now reconciled you in His fleshly body through death, in order to present you before Him holy** [Greek *hagios*] **and blameless and beyond reproach—(23) if indeed you continue in the faith firmly established and steadfast, and not moved away from the hope of the gospel that you have heard, which was proclaimed in all creation under heaven, and of which I, Paul, was made a minister.**

The study of Col. 1:9-14 in chapter 7 of this book (*Holiness and Victory Over Sin*) should be read as an introduction for this study of Col. 1:21-23. (We discussed Col. 1:9-14 in an earlier article in this e-book.) Also, most of the content of chapters 6-8 of my book (*Holiness and Victory Over Sin*) is relevant to this study of Col. 1:21-23.

Now I'll read Colossians 1:21 again, and we'll discuss the verse, **And although you were formerly alienated and hostile in mind, *engaged* in evil deeds.** They **were formerly alienated** from God (see Eph. 2:12; 4:18; both verses use the same Greek verb as Col. 1:21 for "alienated/excluded"). Colossians 1:21 speaks of the former sinful lifestyle of the Colossian Christians, their lifestyle before they became born-again Christians (see, for example, Col. 1:3, 14; 2:11, 13; 3:5-9; Eph. 2:1-3; 4:17-5:14). They had been **hostile in mind** (see Rom. 8:5-8; 12:2; and Eph. 4:17, 18); they had been **hostile in mind, *engaged* in evil deeds.** If we think wrong in our hearts, we will live wrong.

I'll read Colossians 1:22 again, **yet He has now reconciled you in His fleshly body through death, in order to present you before Him holy** [Greek *hagios*] **and blameless and beyond reproach.** I believe the word **He** in **He has now reconciled** speaks of God the Father. See verses 19, 20, for example. God the Father has reconciled us to Himself **in** [or, **by**] **the body of** [Christ's] **flesh through death**; that is, He has reconciled us to Himself by Christ's atoning death. The NIV has, **But now he has reconciled you by Christ's physical body through death.**

I'll read the first part of Romans 5:10, "For if while we were enemies, we were reconciled to God through the death of His Son." As we discussed under Rom. 5:10 in chapter 6 of this book (*Holiness and Victory Over Sin*), and in an earlier article in this e-book, being reconciled to God necessarily includes the transformation (to the righteousness and holiness of God) of those who were formerly "ungodly" (Rom. 5:6);

formerly "sinners" (Rom. 5:8); and formerly "enemies [of God]" (Rom. 5:10). This glorious transformation is frequently spoken of in the New Testament (including Col. 1:9-14; 2:10-15; and 3:1-4:1).

The Christians at Colossae were no longer **alienated and hostile in mind,** *engaged* **in evil deeds** (Col. 1:21). They had been renewed in mind and were now engaged in righteous deeds. The old man had been buried (see Col. 2:11, 12), and they had "laid aside the old [man] with its evil practices" (Col. 3:9). They had been made alive together with Christ (see Col. 2:12, 13), and they had "put on the new [man], which is renewed in knowledge after the image of him that created him" (Col. 3:10 KJV). Colossians 2:5-7 say, "For though I am absent in the flesh, yet I am with you in spirit, rejoicing to see your *good* order and the steadfastness of your faith in Christ. (6) As you have therefore received Christ Jesus the Lord, so walk in Him, (7) rooted [or, "having been rooted"; this is a perfect participle in the Greek] and built up in Him and established in the faith, as you have been taught, abounding in it with thanksgiving" (NKJV). Colossians 4:12 says, "Epaphras, who is one of your number, a bondslave of Jesus Christ, sends you his greetings, always laboring earnestly for you in his prayers, that you may stand perfect and fully assured in all the will of God."

I'll read Colossians 1:21, 22 again (incorporating the translation of the NIV for the first part of verse 22), **And although you were formerly alienated and hostile in mind,** *engaged* **in evil deeds, (22) yet He** [God the Father] **has now reconciled you by Christ's physical body through death** [through Christ's atoning death] **to present you before Him** [Himself] **holy** [Greek *hagios*] **and blameless and beyond reproach.** The apostle wrote from the viewpoint that the Colossian Christians were already **holy and blameless and beyond reproach**, and in verse 23 he went on to say that they had been **firmly established**; and were **steadfast** in the faith. Other statements by Paul in this epistle show that he was being somewhat generous here. (See Col. 1:9-11, 28, 29; 2:1-4, 16-23; 3:1-4:1; and 4:13). He knew, for one thing, that some false teachings had been accepted by some at Colossae.

Now we'll discuss the words **in order to present you before Him** [Himself] **holy and blameless and beyond reproach** of Colossians 1:22. I would translate **before Himself** instead of **before Him.** The *New English Bible* has, **so that he may present you before himself.** All

Christians will be presented before God the Father at the end of this age (see, for example, Rom. 14:10-12; Col. 1:28; 2 Cor. 4:14; 1 Thess. 3:13; and Jude 1:24). I'll read Colossians 1:28, which is one of the verses I just listed, "We proclaim Him [Christ], admonishing every man and teaching every man with all wisdom, so that we may present every man complete [or "perfect"] in Christ."

Now we'll discuss the words **holy** [Greek *hagios*] **and blameless.** The apostle Paul also used these words together in Eph. 1:4; 5:27. He used the words "holy and blameless" in Eph. 1:4; 5:27 in the ideal sense that Christians are called, enabled, and required to be holy and blameless. We have already discussed Eph. 5:27 in some detail under the Greek verb *hagiazo*. Paul's viewpoint here in Col. 1:22 is essentially the same as in Eph. 1:4; 5:27.

Paul wrote Col. 1:22 from the viewpoint that his readers at Colossae were **holy and blameless and beyond reproach**, but in the next verse he emphasized the need for his readers to maintain that state (by the grace of God in Christ) until Christ returns (or until the end of their lives on the earth). Then they will be presented before God the Father **holy and blameless and beyond reproach** (see 1 Thess. 3:13; 5:23; and Jude 1:24, for example).

The Greek noun *amomos* translated "blameless" in Col. 1:22; Eph. 1:4; 5:27 is also used in Jude 1:24; Phil. 2:15; Heb. 9:14; 1 Pet. 1:19; and Rev. 14:5. I'll read Philippians 2:14-16, "Do all things without grumbling or disputing; so that you will prove yourselves to be blameless and innocent, children of God above reproach [*amomos*] in the midst of a crooked and perverse generation, among whom you shine as lights in the world, holding fast the word of life, so that in the day of Christ I will have reason to glory because I did not run in vain nor toil in vain."

Now I'll read Colossians 1:23 again, and we'll discuss this verse, **if indeed you continue in the faith firmly established** [or, "having been firmly established"; this is a perfect participle in the Greek] **and steadfast, and not moved away from the hope of the gospel that you have heard, which was proclaimed in all creation under heaven, and of which I, Paul, was made a minister.**

First we'll discuss the words, **if indeed you continue in the faith firmly established and steadfast. The faith** is the Christian faith (see, for example, Acts 6:7, 14:22; 2 Cor. 13:5; Gal. 1:23; 3:23; 1 Tim. 1:2; 3:9, 13; 4:1, 6; 5:8; 6:10, 21; 2 Tim. 3:8; and Titus 3:15). To **continue in the faith** includes continuing in the truth of the gospel (correct doctrine) and continuing in the righteous and holy lifestyle required by the gospel. As I mentioned, the apostle wrote from the somewhat generous viewpoint that the Christians at Colossae were already **holy and blameless and beyond reproach** and **firmly established and steadfast.** This epistle makes it clear that some of the Christians at Colossae needed to make some changes. That isn't too surprising, it is?

The Greek verb translated **you continue** is *epimeno*. This same verb was used in Romans 11:22, "but to you [The apostle Paul was speaking to Gentile Christians.] God's kindness, if you continue [*epimeno*] in His kindness; otherwise you also will be cut off." It was also used in Acts 13:43, "were urging them to continue [*epimeno*] in the grace of God." A similar verb (*emmeno*) was used in Acts 14:22; Gal. 3:10; and Heb. 8:9. Each of these verses helps us understand the meaning of the words **continue in the faith** here in Col. 1:23. I'll quote Acts 14:21, 22, "And after they [Paul and Barnabus] had preached the gospel to that city and had made many disciples, they returned to Lystra and to Iconium and to Antioch, (22) strengthening the souls of the disciples, encouraging [or, exhorting] them to continue [*emmeno*] in the faith, and *saying,* 'Through many tribulations we must enter the kingdom of God.' " 1 Timothy 6:10 speaks of some who "have wandered away from the faith," and 1 Timothy 6:21 speaks of some who have "gone astray from the faith."

Now we'll discuss the words **and not moved away from the hope of the gospel that you have heard, which was proclaimed in all creation under heaven, and of which I, Paul, was made a minister** of Col. 1:23. **The hope of the gospel** speaks of the glory that all true Christians will begin to share at the time of the return of the Lord Jesus Christ (see, for example, Col. 1:5, 27; 3:4; Rom. 5:2; and 8:17-25). One of the verses I just listed was Colossians 1:5, "because of the hope laid up for you in heaven, of which you previously heard in the word of truth, the gospel." To **continue in the faith firmly established and steadfast** (of Col. 1:23) is to **not [be] moved away from the hope of the gospel** (of Col. 1:23). Those who do *not* continue in the faith until the end forfeit **the hope of the gospel** (Col. 1:23).

Now we come to 1 Peter 1:13-19, still under the major heading Some Verses that Use _Hagios_ and Fit the Ideal Pattern. I'll read the verses. **Therefore, gird your minds for action, keep sober _in spirit_, fix your hope completely on the grace to be brought to you at the revelation of Jesus Christ. (14) As obedient children, do not be conformed to the former lusts _which were yours_ in your ignorance, (15) but LIKE THE HOLY ONE** [Greek _hagios_] **WHO CALLED YOU, BE HOLY** [Greek _hagios_] **YOURSELVES ALSO IN ALL _YOUR_ BEHAVIOR** [my emphasis]; **(16) because it is written, "YOU SHALL BE HOLY** [or, **"BE HOLY"**; Greek _hagios_], **FOR I AM HOLY** [Greek _hagios_]**." (17) And if you address as Father the One who impartially judges according to each man's work, conduct yourselves in fear during the time of your stay _upon earth_; (18) knowing that you were not redeemed with perishable things like silver or gold from your futile way of life** [and I might add, "from your sinful way of life"] **inherited from your forefathers, (19) but with precious blood, as of a lamb unblemished and spotless, _the blood_ of Christ.**

I'll read 1 Peter 1:13 again and comment briefly on this verse, **Therefore, gird your minds for action, keep sober _in spirit_, fix your hope completely on the grace to be brought to you at the revelation of Jesus Christ.** As Christians live in the light of the return of the Lord Jesus Christ and the glory this will mean for them (see 1 Pet. 1:3-7; 4:13; 5:1, 4, 6, 10; Rom. 5:2; Col. 1:5, 22, 23, 27; and Titus 3:7, for example), they will be strongly motivated to live for God in His righteousness and holiness.

I'll read 1 Peter 1:14 again and comment on this verse, **As obedient children** [or, **children of obedience**], **do not be conformed to the former lusts _which were yours_ in your ignorance.** Christians must be **children of obedience.** These Christians from a Gentile background must not be conformed any longer to their former sinful lifestyle (see 1 Pet. 1:18; 4:2-4, for example). They have put off the old man and have become born-again new creations in Christ Jesus (see 1 Pet. 1:22, 23; 2:1, 2, 24, 25; Rom. 6:1-23; 2 Cor. 5:14-17; Eph. 4:17-5:4; Col. 2:10-15; and 3:1-11, for example). I'll read the first part of Romans 12:2, which uses the same Greek verb for "conform," "And do not be conformed to this world, but be transformed by the renewing [or, better, "renewal"] of your mind."

Now I'll read 1 Peter 1:15, 16 again and comment on these verses, **but LIKE THE HOLY ONE** [Greek *hagios*] **WHO CALLED YOU, BE HOLY** [Greek *hagios*] **YOURSELVES ALSO IN ALL YOUR BEHAVIOR** [my emphasis]; **(16) because it is written, "YOU SHALL BE HOLY** [or, **BE HOLY**; Greek *hagios*], **FOR I AM HOLY** [Greek *hagios*]."** Instead of **YOU SHALL BE HOLY**, I prefer the NIV's "Be holy." This is a command, but what God commands us to do, He enables us to do (by His grace).

It would be difficult to imagine a stronger statement of the fact that Christians are called to be (and enabled to be) set apart from all sin than the exhortation contained in these two verses. (See Matt. 5:48; 1 John 2:6, 29; 3:3-12; and 4:17, for example.) It is clear that Peter was speaking of Christians actually being set apart from all sin and living for God in an abiding state of holiness. He said, "but LIKE THE HOLY ONE WHO CALLED YOU, BE HOLY YOURSELVES IN ALL YOUR BEHAVIOR."

Now I'll read 1 Peter 1:17 again and comment on this verse. **And if you address as Father the One who impartially judges according to each man's work, conduct yourselves in fear during the time of your stay upon earth.** Christians do address God as Father; we are His born-again children. In 1 Pet. 1:3, 23 Peter spoke of our being "born again"; and in 1:14 he spoke of our being "children of obedience." Knowing that God will judge us according to our "work" should provide very strong motivation for us to live in His righteousness and holiness. Our righteousness and holiness (our righteous works) are produced by the saving, sanctifying grace of God in Christ, through faith. (See Eph. 2:8-10; Gal. 5:5, 16-18, 22-25; and Titus 2:14, for example.)

Since God will impartially judge each person according to their work, He will not show partiality to any, including Christians. Our "work," what we do, shows what is in our hearts. Faith without works is dead; it isn't saving faith. It is true, of course, that forgiveness is provided for Christians when they repent, but Christianity is about much more than forgiveness. If "Christians" are characterized by sin, they will be condemned (see Matt. 3:1-12; 7:13-27; 16:24-27; John 5:28, 29; Rom. 2:1-16; 6:21-23; 1 Cor. 6:9-11; 2 Cor. 5:10; Gal. 5:19-21; 6:7-9; Eph. 5:5-7; Col. 3:5-7; Rev. 21;7, 8; and 22:10-15, for example).

I'll read Revelation 22:12-15, which is one of the passages I just listed. I'll read these verses from the NIV. The Lord Jesus Christ is speaking here. "Behold, I am coming soon! My reward [My recompense] *is* with Me, and I will give to everyone according to what he has done. (13) I am the Alpha and the Omega, the First and the Last, the Beginning and the End. (14) Blessed are those who wash their robes, that they may have the right to the tree of life and may go through the gates into the city [the city of God's new Jerusalem]. (15) Outside are the dogs, those who practice magic arts, the sexually immoral, the murderers, the idolaters and everyone who loves and practices falsehood." "Those who wash their robes" are the ones who cleanse themselves and become sanctified through the sanctifying blood of the Lord Jesus Christ, which is backed up by the all-powerful Holy Spirit (see Rev. 7:14; 19:8, for example).

In John 5:28, 29 Jesus spoke of the coming hour of judgment "in which all who are in the tombs will hear His voice, and will come forth; those who did the good *deeds* [or, *works*] to a resurrection of life, those who committed the evil *deeds* [or, *works*] to a resurrection of judgment [condemnation]."

I'll read 1 Peter 1:17 again, **If you address as Father the One who impartially judges according to each man's** [The 1995 edition of the NASB has "one's."] **work, conduct yourselves in fear during the time of your stay *upon*** [The 1995 edition of the NASB has "*on*."] ***earth.*** Those who know that they will face the judgment of God must "conduct themselves in [reverent] fear [before Him]," living in His righteousness and holiness, always staying fully ready for the day of judgment. Such things as correct doctrine (though necessary), godly parents, or the externals of religion will not prepare us to stand before God any more than they sufficed for the children of Israel (see Matt. 3:7-10; John 8:31-47; and Rom. 2:1-29, for example).

"Christians" could be rejected on the day of judgment (see Matt. 7:13-27, for example). It is also true that a Christian could make it to heaven but lose rewards because of living by the flesh in certain areas (see 1 Cor. 3:5-15, for example). It is a serious matter for Christians to be unfaithful to God, and we must have a reverent fear regarding this matter. We will all have to answer to Him (see Rom. 14:10-12, for example). The Bible shows that we must have a healthy fear of all sin (see Matt. 10:28; Luke

1:50; 12:5; Acts 9:31; 2 Cor. 7:1; Phil. 2:12; Heb. 4:1; and 1 Pet. 2:17, for example).

Now I'll read 1 Peter 1:18, 19 again, and we'll discuss these verses, **knowing that you were not redeemed with perishable things like silver or gold from your futile way of life inherited from your forefathers, (19) but with precious blood, as of a lamb unblemished and spotless, *the blood* of Christ.** Christians have been redeemed from their former futile [sinful] way of life by the **precious blood [of Christ]** (see 1 Pet. 2:24, 25; 3:18; and 4:1-6, for example; and see under Rom. 3:24 in chapter 6 of this book, *Holiness and Victory Over Sin*). I'll read 1 Peter 2:24, "and He Himself bore our sins [He bore our sins with the guilt and with the penalties, including the major penalties of spiritual death and bondage to sin] in his body on the cross, so that WE MIGHT DIE TO SIN AND LIVE TO RIGHTEOUSNESS [my emphasis]...."

As we have discussed in some detail, the Lamb of God bore our sins with the guilt and with the penalties (including the major penalties of spiritual death and bondage to sin), so we could be forgiven, be redeemed out of the kingdom of sin, be born again, and be made righteous and holy with the imparted righteousness and holiness of God. God paid an infinite price in the sacrifice of His Son to save and sanctify us. When we learn who Jesus is and what He has done for us in His atoning death, and the fact that God hates sin, it is inconceivable that the blood of Christ does not have the power to set us free from all sin, as we appropriate that power through faith.

We're almost finished with this article and with this e-book. I'll read a few key verses on the topic of holiness and victory over sin. I'll read Galatians 5:16, 24, **But I say, walk by the Spirit** [the Holy Spirit], **and you** [most certainly] **will not carry out the desire** [the sinful desire] **of the flesh** [of the old man]. ... **(24) Now those who belong to Christ Jesus have crucified the flesh with its passions and desires.** And I'll read Romans 6:1, 2, and 11 from the NKJV, **What shall we say then? Shall we continue to sin that grace may abound? (2) Certainly not! How shall we who died to sin live any longer in it? ... (11) Likewise you also, reckon yourselves to be dead indeed to sin, but alive to God in Christ Jesus our Lord.** And lastly, I'll read Romans 8:3, 4, **For what the Law** [the Mosaic Law] **could not do, weak as it was through the flesh, God *did*, sending His own Son in the likeness of sinful flesh and *as*** *an offering* for sin, He condemned sin in the flesh, (4) so that the requirement [the righteous requirement] of the Law might be fulfilled in us, who do not walk according to the flesh, but according to the Spirit [the Holy Spirit].

This is the last article on the topic of righteousness, holiness, and victory over sin. We haven't covered everything in this e-book (in these twenty-eight articles), but we have rather thoroughly discussed this super-important topic. What we have found is good news, very good news. I trust that many of you will get my paperback book, *Holiness and Victory Over Sin: Full Salvation Through the Atoning Death of the Lord Jesus Christ.* The paperback book contains a large amount of information that is not included in the e-book.

The topic of righteousness, holiness, and victory over sin is also discussed in some detail in many of my papers that are located on my internet site. The book and CDs of the radio broadcasts are available on my internet site (Google to Karl Kemp Teaching), and the book is available at amazon.com. I'll list quite a few of my papers that are located on my internet site; many of them deal with issues of foundational importance for Christianity: *A Paper on Faith; Once Saved, Always Saved? The Christian, the Law, and Legalism; Did Jesus Die Spiritually? Logos and Rhema; Spirit and Soul; Who Do We Worship?; Who Do We Pray To?; The Name Yahweh and God the Father and God the Son; More on the Trinity; Genesis Chapters 1-3; John 1:1-18 and Colossians 1:15-3:17; John 1:19-4:54; John Chapters 5-8; John Chapters 10-12; John Chapters 13-17; John Chapters 18-20; Interpretation of Romans Chapter 7 and Righteousness and Holiness; Romans Chapters 9-11; Some Comments on "Destined to Reign" by Joseph Prince; Shall We Write Off Kenneth E. Hagin? Dave Hunt? How About E. W. Kenyon?; Some Comments on "Four Blood Moons": by John Hagee; Some Powerful (Rather Shocking) Statements in 1 John: Christians Being Pure and Righteous just as the Son of God is Pure and Righteous, Etc.*

God bless you! May His will be fully accomplished in us and through us! In Jesus name!

Made in the USA
Columbia, SC
01 September 2018